UNDERSTANDING ETHNIC CONFLICT

Understanding Ethnic Conflict

THE INTERNATIONAL DIMENSION

RAJAT GANGULY
Tulane University

and

RAY TARAS
Tulane University

An imprint of Addison Wesley Longman, Inc.

New York • Reading, Massachusetts • Menlo Park, California • Harlow, England
Don Mills, Ontario • Sydney • Mexico City • Madrid • Amsterdam

Editor-in-Chief: Pam Gordon
Acquisitions Editor: Peter Glovin
Marketing Manager: Suzanne Daghlian
Project Coordination and Text Design: Electronic Publishing Services Inc., NYC
Cover Designer: Chris Hiebert
Art Studio: Electronic Publishing Services Inc., NYC
Full Service Production Manager: Christine Pearson
Manufacturing Manager: Hilda Koparanian
Electronic Page Makeup: Electronic Publishing Services Inc., NYC
Printer and Binder: Maple-Vail Book Manufacturing Group
Cover Printer: Phoenix Color Corp.

Library of Congress Cataloging-in-Publication Data

Ganguly, Rajat.
　　Understanding ethnic conflict : the international dimension / Rajat Ganguly and
　Ray Taras.
　　　p.　cm.
　　Includes bibliographical references and index.
　　ISBN 0-673-99808-8
　　　1. Ethnic relations—Political aspects.　2. Ethnic relations—
International cooperation.　3. World politics.　4. Nationalism.
5. Conflict management—Political aspects.　6. Conflict management—
International cooperation.　I. Taras, Ray.　II. Title.
　GN496.G36　1998
　　305.8—dc21　　　　　　　　　　　　　　　　　　97-19843
　　　　　　　　　　　　　　　　　　　　　　　　　　CIP

ISBN 0-673-99808-8

12345678910—MA—00999897

ABOUT THE AUTHORS

Rajat Ganguly received his education at universities in India and the United States. He obtained his doctorate at Tulane University and has taught political science at Tulane University, the University of West Florida, and the University of Southern Mississippi.

Ray Taras has served on the faculty of universities in England, Canada, and the United States. He has taught at the universities of Kentucky, Michigan, and Vermont and has been professor of political science at Tulane University and National Fellow at the Hoover Institute, Stanford University.

CONTENTS

Preface: Nationalism at the Turn of the New Millennium   xi

Acknowledgments   xv

**PART I   ETHNIC CONFLICT AND INTERNATIONAL POLITICS:
                A CONCEPTUAL FRAMEWORK   1**

Chapter 1: ETHNIC CONFLICT ON THE WORLD STAGE   3
    Ethnic Conflict Resurgent in a Post-Bipolar World   3
    The Formation and Persistence of Ethnic Identity   6
    Definitions   9
    The Political Mobilization of Ethnic Groups   12
    Indirect Theories of Ethnic Political Mobilization and Conflict   14
        Negative Theories of Integration   14
        Negative Theories of Cohesion   15
        Indirect Theories of Disintegration   18
    Direct Theories of Ethnic Political Mobilization and Conflict   19
        The Primordialist Approach   19
        The Internal Colonialism Approach   21
        The Communalist Approach   22
    Ethnic Political Mobilization: Linking Causes and Objectives   23
    Ethnic Conflict and International Relations   31

Chapter 2: ETHNIC CONFLICT AND INTERNATIONAL NORMS   41
    Introduction   41
    International Norms Affecting Ethnonationalism   42
        The Doctrine of Sovereignty   42
        Self-Determination and Ethnosecessionist Movements   48
    The General Case for Secession: Obsolescence of the State   53
    Moral Grounds That Justify Secession   57
    Conclusion   64

Chapter 3: ETHNIC CONFLICT AS AN INTERNATIONAL
                PROBLEM   68
    Introduction   68
    The Internationalization of Ethnic Conflict   68
        Diplomatic Activity of Ethnosecessionists and States Confronted
        with Ethnic Conflict   69
        Partisan Intervention in Ethnic Conflicts   74

Ethnic Conflict and International Terrorism   81
Ethnic Conflict and Refugee Flows   82
The Ethnicization of International Politics   83
  Globalization, Interdependence, and Ethnic Conflicts   83
  International Conflict and Its Ethnic Fallout   84
  Ethnic Conflict as a Consequence of Empire and State Collapse   86
  The End of Bipolar Superpower Rivalry and Its Effect
  on Ethnic Conflicts   88
  The Link Between Arms Trading, Drug Trafficking,
  and Ethnic Conflict   90
Conclusion   91

Chapter 4:   RESOLVING ETHNIC CONFLICTS THROUGH
INTERNATIONAL THIRD-PARTY ACTION   96
Why Resolving Ethnic Conflicts Is Important   96
Ethnic Conflict Resolution by International Third Parties   97
  Peacekeeping   97
  Peacemaking   98
  Peacebuilding   101
Ethnic Conflict Resolution by the United Nations   101
  The United Nations as a Peacekeeper   103
  The United Nations as a Peacemaker   107
  The United Nations as a Peacebuilder   110
States as Third Parties in Ethnic Conflict Resolution   114
  Major Powers in Ethnic Conflict Resolution   114
  Ethnic Conflict Resolution by Third-World Regional Powers   116
Regional Organizations as Third Parties in Ethnic
Conflict Resolution   118
International Nongovernmental Organizations as Third Parties
in Ethnic Conflict Resolution   120
Conclusion   122

PART II   CASE STUDIES   127

Chapter 5:   NATIONALISM AND THE COLLAPSE OF AN EMPIRE:
THE SOVIET UNION, RUSSIA, AND CHECHNYA   129
The Breakdown of Empires   129
Why Did Ethnic Conflict Occur?   131
  Soviet Imperialism and Great Russian Nationalism   131
  Democratization as a Source of Ethnic Conflict   134
  The Conflict of Identities   135
  Nationalist Mobilization in Post-Soviet Russia   137
  The Core Ideas of Russian Nationalism   139
  Russian Nationalists Resurgent   140

Russia's New Minorities   143
Russia and Chechnya   144
Chechen Ethnosecessionism   147
International Reaction   149
Noninternationalization of the Chechen Conflict   151
Third-Party Mediation in Chechnya   154
Conclusion   156

Chapter 6: CONSTITUTIONAL SEPARATIST MOVEMENTS:
CANADA AND QUEBEC NATIONALISM   160
Introduction   160
Why Has Ethnic Conflict Occurred? Sources of
Quebec Nationalism   161
    British Colonization   161
    Confederation   163
    Economic Stagnation   164
    Conscription Crises   165
    Disputed Borders   166
    The Quiet Revolution   167
    Quebec's Exclusion from the Canadian Constitution   169
    The Failure to Bring Quebec Back In   170
    The Growth of the Sovereignty Movement   171
Why Peaceful Secession Is Rare   174
International Reaction   176
Can a Constitutionally Based Dispute Be Internationalized?   178
What Can External Parties Do About the Conflict in Canada?   180

Chapter 7: PROTRACTED ETHNIC WARS: THE
TAMIL-SINHALESE CONFLICT IN SRI LANKA   184
Introduction   184
The Precedent of Bangladesh's Secession   185
    Genesis of the Bangladesh Crisis   185
    Internationalization of the Bengali Secessionist Movement   186
    The Road to War   187
Why Did Ethnic Conflict Occur in Sri Lanka?   188
    The Issue of Original Inhabitancy and Traditional Homeland   189
    Cultural and Religious Issues   191
    The Issue of Language   193
    Economic Issues   195
    The Political Fallout   195
    The Drift Toward Tamil Militancy   197
    The Escalation of Ethnic Violence in the 1980s   199
International Reaction Toward Sri Lanka's Ethnic War   199
International Covert Involvement in Sri Lanka   200
Other International Aspects of Sri Lanka's Ethnic Conflict   201

Resolution Attempt: International Third-Party Action in Sri Lanka   202
The Parthasarathy Initiative and the All-Party Conference   203
The Thimpu Talks   204
The December 19 Proposals   205
The Indo-Sri Lankan Accord   205
Tamil-Sinhalese Reactions to the Indo-Sri Lankan Accord   207
Implementation of the Indo-Sri Lankan Accord   208
Why Did India's Resolution Attempt Fail in Sri Lanka?   211
Changing International Perception of Sri Lanka's Ethnic War:
Withdrawal of the IPKF and Its Aftermath   213
Conclusion   215

Chapter 8: WEAK STATES AND ETHNIC CONFLICT: SECESSIONISM
AND STATE COLLAPSE IN AFRICA   225
Introduction   225
Weak States   226
Secessionism in the Congo   227
Secessionism in Nigeria   228
Secessionism in Ethiopia   231
Sources of Conflict: The Colonial Legacy   231
Pan-Africanism and Pan-Ethiopianism   233
Military Repression   234
Ethiopia's Collapse, Eritrea's Independence   235
International Reaction to Eritrean Indepence   237
Internationalization   237
External Mediation   240
Weak States, Politicized Identities in Central Africa   241

Chapter 9: THE U.S. RESPONSE TO NATIONALISM   247
Studying Post-Bipolar Policy Making   247
The U.S. Experience as a Foreign Policy Influence   248
Cultural Diversity   248
Cultural Features   251
Toward a U.S. Grand Strategy on Ethnic Conflict   253
The United States and the Third Reordering   254
The United States and Internationalization of Conflicts   256
Ethnic Conflict and U.S. Foreign Policy Makers   258
Foreign Policy Analysts on Contemporary Ethnic Conflict   261
The Anti-Interventionists   261
Qualified Interventionists   262
Clinton and the Principle of Self-Determination   265
Bosnia as a Case Study of U.S. Intervention   268
Conclusion   275

Selected Bibliography   *281*
Index   *289*

Preface

NATIONALISM AT THE TURN OF A NEW MILLENNIUM

Nationalism, ethnicity, and religion are among the most powerful political forces in the world today. They define the fault lines of contemporary civilizations. Samuel Huntington has argued that the clash of civilizations will mark international politics in the future.[1] Civilizations are founded on nationalism, ethnicity, and religion. Huntington's view about a coming clash of civilizations was representative of the disappointment found among many scholars that the winding down of the cold war had failed to assure global peace and stability.

At the turn of a new millennium it is unclear what kind of world order will be established to manage the community of nations. To be sure, a global wave of democratization occurring in the last quarter of the twentieth century was reassuring. By 1995, more than 60 percent (117 of 191) of the world's independent countries were formally democratic. When combined with the growth of free market economies in many of the world's countries, it appeared that a universal political and economic civilization was in the process of being constructed. It came as a great surprise, then, that a parochial, inward-looking political force—nationalism—emerged as the dominant ideology in many countries of the world.

Nationalism has been, arguably, the nineteenth and twentieth centuries' most powerful political idea. It has been the concept around which the modern state system was created and remains intact today. The idea of nationalism was instrumental in transforming the basis of rulers' legitimacy from a dynastic principle to one grounded in a nation's self-determination. This notion emerged in Europe in the late eighteenth century, spread to Latin America early in the nineteenth century, and then served as the ideological underpinnings of anticolonial movements throughout the twentieth century.

Nationalism's negative effects have invariably overshadowed its constructive contribution. Implementing the principle of self-determination confronts the logistical problems of holding a fair plebiscite, formulating the agenda (questions to be asked in the plebiscite), controlling migration into and out of the state, and guaranteeing state security.[2] Adjudicating the legitimacy of claims and counterclaims of various groups for self-determination has emerged as a major challenge for international society. And what are these groups that claim the right to enjoy "national" self-determination? There are many practical difficulties associated with defining a *collective self*, or *national identity*. How the criteria defining a nation are arrived at—on the basis of a common culture, language, race, religion, shared historical experience, living on "historic" lands—has been a constant source of friction.

Even in the rare cases that national self-determination has been accorded by the international community, the principle has proved ineffective in protecting minorities' rights. The nationalist idea created the problem of minorities by identifying a dominant nation in the state (usually through citizenship and official language laws) and subordinate groups (those not having linguistic rights equal to the dominant one). The nationalist idea was also instrumental in worsening the plight of minorities once the modern state-system was in place. Because they were sovereign, states demanded undivided loyalty from their citizens. In consequence, this consideration not only often precluded states from granting rights to minorities within their borders, but it also induced states to increase the assimilationist pressure on their minorities. In some cases the reaction of minorities was to organize secessionist movements. In turn, this quickly led to the outbreak of civil wars in various countries in the world.

Some of the worst crimes against humanity have been committed in the name of nationalism. In this century the horrors of Nazism and fascism—both extreme, exclusionary ideologies—remain imprinted on human memory. Although the world promised itself "never again," the rise of extreme nationalism in various parts of the globe a half-century after Nazism's defeat raises concerns about the ability of political structures to contain various forms of racism and discrimination.

It has never been more important to study nationalism and ethnic conflict. The number of books published in recent years on nationalism (see the Bibliography at the end of this volume) is an indication of the subject's significance for specialists and students alike. There has been far more analysis of the domestic factors that cause ethnic conflict than of the international aspects of such conflict, so our study seeks to redress the balance. We ask four fundamental questions about nationalism and ethnic conflict and we furnish some answers to them: (1) Why does ethnic conflict occur? (2) How does the international system (meaning both the community of states, its international organizations, and individual countries) react to ethnic conflict? (3) Why do some ethnic conflicts become internationalized and others do not? (4) What can be done to resolve such conflicts—should external parties intervene or not?

The book is organized in the following way. Part I provides the conceptual tools for understanding nationalism and ethnic conflict. Part II applies these tools and presents case studies of recent ethnic conflicts. Chapter 1 examines what ethnic conflict is, what its sources are, and how it differs from other types of conflict. It inquires into the reasons why this type of conflict has reemerged as a worldwide political phenomenon in the 1990s. Chapter 2 considers the connection between ethnic conflict and international relations. It describes the normative context framing ethnic conflict, that is, how the international community invokes doctrines of sovereignty and nonintervention in the internal affairs of states to withhold recognition of secessionist claims. But in this chapter we also evaluate the moral grounds that can legitimate a group's right to separate from an existing state and form a separate one. Chapter 3 looks at the many factors that can lead to internationalization of ethnic conflict. These range from support for ethnic kin in other states to financing military operations through drug trafficking. Here we are concerned with highlighting the processes of conflict transformation. Chapter 4 studies how ethnic conflicts can be resolved by international third-party action. It weighs the causes and consequences of external intervention in ethnic disputes, whether carried out by individual states or by international organizations. We address the crucial question about whether outside intervention helps or hinders resolution of ethnic conflict.

Case studies make up Part II of the book. Each case explains why an ethnic conflict has occurred, how the international system has reacted, why the conflict has or has not been internationalized, and reasons for intervention or nonintervention by external parties. Cases have been chosen to reflect particular combinations of ethnosecessionist demands and outside intervention. We include two cases where separation has not occurred (the Quebec sovereigntist movement and the Tamil Eelam movement) and two where it has or may result (Eritrea and, disputably, Chechnya). Of these four cases, two had third-party military intervention (the USSR in Ethiopia, India in Sri Lanka) and two did not (Quebec and Chechnya). We clearly cannot generalize on such a small number of cases, but they do permit us to illuminate the relationship between ethnic conflicts and international responses to them.

The cases in this book were also selected for their contemporary importance, the different lessons that can be learned from each of them, and their representation of different parts of the globe (Europe, North America, Asia, and Africa). We recognize that other cases of internationalized ethnic conflict could be chosen. We do indeed examine the case of former Yugoslavia, in particular, Bosnia, in Chapter 9, but primarily in terms of the U.S. foreign policy response. We also identify the causes of violence in Rwanda and Burundi in Chapter 8. Important cases that we do not study include Kurdistan, Kashmir, and breakaway regions of former Soviet republics (Abkhazia in Georgia, Nagorno-Karabakh in Azerbaijan, and Trans-Dniester in Moldova). Many liberal democracies have felt centrifugal tendencies in the 1990s, such as the United Kingdom, Spain, and Italy; these deserve separate treatment, too. We hope that our cases will stimulate interest so that readers will wish to learn more about other similar situations emerging in the contemporary world.

Chapter 5 focuses on the Russian-Chechen conflict and explains why, despite the lack of international support, Chechnya made a gallant challenge to become independent from the Russian Federation. The theme that we address is how the dismantling of an empire—the former Soviet Union—can precipitate a wave of nationalist assertion and ethnic conflict, often gnawing away at the power of the hegemonic nation. Chapter 6 assesses the constitutional crisis in Canada posed by the Quebec sovereignty movement. It raises the more general question of whether legal methods of secession, as through a referendum, may threaten Western liberal democratic states with breakup. Chapter 7 deals with the Tamil–Sinhalese conflict in Sri Linka. The theme that we address here is that protracted ethnic conflicts like that in Sri Lanka are deep rooted, offer many opportunities for internationalization, and are difficult to resolve through third-party action. Thus while there was no third-party intervention in our first two cases, intervention did occur for a time in Sri Lanka, and we analyze in what way conflict transformation occurred as a result of such intervention by India. Chapter 8 examines a rare case of successful secession in the developing world, that of Eritrea from Ethiopia. Here, too, third parties were crucial to the outcome: the withdrawal of Soviet support for the central Ethiopian government together with U.S. diplomatic activity on behalf of Eritrean rebels were enough for a protracted ethnic conflict to end with the victory of the breakaway group.

Finally, Chapter 9 considers the U.S. response to ethnic conflict worldwide. Because of its potential to act as the world's sole superpower, the U.S. is regularly required to make foreign policy decisions as to whether to intervene in faraway ethnic conflicts. American interests are frequently involved in regional nationalist conflicts in indirect, but nonetheless important, ways. In concluding this book, we argue that more than just regional power balances or standards of morality are at stake in distance ethnic conflicts. The U.S. may be affected firsthand by distant disputes that, at first blush, seem to involve only ancient, localized hatreds.

By examining ethnic conflict occurring in different conditions, the chapters in Part II reveal how contemporary nationalist movements take dissimilar forms, elicit differentiated responses from the international community, and may, to a greater or lesser degree, be impervious to conflict resolution efforts by third parties.

We recognize that nationalism is neither the sole explanation for most of what happens in politics, nor is its mobilizing potential constant over time and space. In fact, we are drawn to the conclusion that only certain types of nationalism are likely to endure for a long time to come. In international politics, it is power, security, and prosperity more than nationalist ideology that determine what is in a state's "national interest." Even the term national interest is a misnomer because we are usually talking about "interests of state" (called more precisely in French raisons d'état). A state's objectives generally take precedence over the interests of a particular nation within it. And 80 percent of the world's countries in the world are multinational, made up of several nations.

To be sure, a nationalist ideology may identify what amount of power, security, and prosperity befits a nation. Should not a great nation, nationalists would say, be a great power? The moment that two ethnic groups within one state or two states in proximity to each other define their interests in this way—literally as their national interest—ethnic conflict is in the making. We hope that the focus of *Understanding Ethnic Conflict: The International Dimension* on the interstices of nationalism, ethnic conflict, and international politics provides an innovative perspective on the study of these otherwise familiar subjects.

Notes

[1]Samuel Huntington, "The Clash of Civilizations." *Foreign Affairs*, 72, 3, Summer 1993, pp. 22–49.

[2]James Mayall, *Nationalism and International Society*. (Cambridge: Cambridge University Press, 1990), pp. 50–57.

ACKNOWLEDGMENTS

In our effort to examine nationalism and international politics in as comprehensive and comparative a way as possible, we have incurred debts that, though we cannot repay, we would very much like to acknowledge.

Critical comments on various sections of the book have been made by Philip Blair (Council of Europe), François Grin (University of Geneva), Guy Lachapelle (Concordia University, Montreal), and William Safran (University of Colorado). By inviting authors to present papers based on individual chapters at conferences and seminars, the following individuals assured us of constructive criticism at a pivotal stage of the project: Michael Branch (University of London), Ronald Marquardt (University of Southern Mississippi), Bo Peterson (Uppsala University), Tom Rice (University of Vermont), Mikko Salo (University of Joensuu, Finland), Kate See (Michigan State University), and Brian Turner (Randolph Macon College, Virginia).

We would also like to thank the fourteen reviewers, a list as long as it is distinguished, who offered critiques of the project: Professor David Carment, The Norman Patterson School of International Affairs, Carleton University; Professor Sharyl N. Cross, Department of Political Science, San Jose State University; Professor Larry Elowitz, Department of Political Science, Georgia College & State University; Professor V. P. Gagnon, Peace Studies Program, Cornell University; Professor Sumit Ganguly, Woodrow Wilson International Center; Professor Gregory Gleason, Department of Political Science, University of New Mexico; Professor Chaim D. Kaufmann, Department of Political Science, Lehigh University; Professor Steve J. Mazurana, Department of Political Science, University of Northern Colorado; Professor Getachew Metaferia, Department of Political Science and International Studies, Morgan State University; Professor Andrew A. Michta, International Studies, Rhodes College; Professor Alexander J. Motyl, The Harriman Institute, Columbia University; Professor Stephen Saideman, Department of Political Science, Texas Tech University; Professor Gabriel Topor, Department of Political Science, Columbia University; Professor M. Crawford Young, Department of Political Science, University of Wisconsin

We learned from all of them. In addition, we would like to express our gratitude to Professor Gabriel Almond (Stanford University), who painstakingly provided us with a model of lucid argumentation for several of the chapters. The authors also wish to acknowledge the general intellectual advice offered by Professor Robert Robins (Tulane University), and Professor Jerold Waltman (University of Souther Mississippi).

We are grateful to Peter Glovin, acquisitions editor at Longman, for doing the seemingly impossible: getting four final readers to evaluate the book within a month.

Finally, if the authors were usually cheerful while researching, writing, reresearching, and rewriting this book, it is thanks primarily to their (usually) good-humored spouses, Malgosia and Mishtu.

PART I

Ethnic Conflict and International Politics: A Conceptual Framework

chapter 1

Ethnic Conflict on the World Stage

ETHNIC CONFLICT RESURGENT IN A POST–BIPOLAR WORLD

At the turn of the twenty-first century, it is unclear what kind of world order may be established to manage the community of nations. In the 1990s countervailing tendencies that instilled both hope and fear about world order appeared in international politics. Just before this remarkable decade began, the destruction of the Berlin Wall in November 1989 symbolized the beginning of a new era in international politics. Indeed, William Keylor has written that he was "entirely confident in characterizing the second half of the 1980s and the first half of the 1990s as the most important transitional period in the history of international relations in this century."[1]

Although there was some disillusion in the 1990s that global peace had failed to materialize, in many important ways political optimism has been justified. A number of regional conflicts with cold war overtones that previously "had been thought intractable were becoming amenable to some form of settlement."[2] These included the Middle East peace process, accords to end civil wars in Angola and Mozambique, peace settlements in Central American states, and the winding down of hostilities in former Yugoslavia. The collapse of communism in the Soviet Union and Eastern Europe also led to a renewed emphasis on democracy and the democratic way of life. The reduction in international tensions as a result of the termination of the cold war ushered in an era of great-power cooperation. These developments were a start in forging a more peaceful, stable, and benign international system.

The end of superpower rivalry, which in its time had engendered many proxy wars, Soviet-backed "popular" revolutions, U.S.-inspired military coups, and a frightening arms race, led many—including then U.S. President George Bush—to believe that a new international order based on peace and democracy was at hand. But by the mid–1990s, the idealism reminiscent of post–World War I days and of the vision of another U.S. president, Woodrow Wilson, had begun to vanish. The cold war had not been the war to end all wars either.

The emergence of various impediments—old as well as new—in the movement toward a more peaceful and democratic world order drew considerable attention. The reduction in international tension was not uniformly spread around the world—the number of interstate wars was significantly reduced, but the wars seemed to be replaced by a proliferation of low-intensity regional conflicts. There were festering wars in former Soviet space from Chechnya to Tajikistan. Tensions between India and Pakistan over Kashmir's status increased, while violence escalated in and around Israel even as peace talks were being held. Seemingly intractable political problems plagued Somalia, Rwanda, and Bosnia-Hercegovina.

The transition to democracy also did not look to be a smooth process. Mass poverty in most parts of the globe, disunity and fragmentation of the center in many developing states and former Soviet lands, and fundamentalist ideology in much of the Islamic world looked set to frustrate or reverse democratic reforms. Scholars long suspected that carrying out political change is contingent upon ensuring economic development. For one, Dennis Austin maintained that poverty is the most serious impediment for greater democratization, particularly in the developing world, because it acts as a "basic structural restraint" on political reforms. Compounded by a lack of internal cohesion, governing elites in weak states would become "fearful of the consequences of democratic concessions" because "fragmented societies will use democracy not only to demand reform but to justify disunity." The Western device of defusing strong political opposition by calling for elections does not work "where the holding of elections raises the political temperature to a pitch of violence and where conflict between majorities and minorities is fixed by the immutability of number." This was demonstrated in Algeria where democratic elections caused political polarization and a cycle of violence. Democratic gains were also jeopardized by autocratic leadership, a problem made worse, as Austin observed, by "the predilection of certain peoples to support, even revere, these leaders."[3]

In short, instability in former Soviet space; the growing strength of right-wing nationalism in Russia; economic problems associated with German reunification; recession in parts of Western Europe; monetary and trade disputes between the European Union, the United States, and Japan; and the friction between the United States and China over human rights, copyright laws, and arms exports could all undermine the effectiveness of international cooperation among the major powers in reducing tensions and promoting peace and stability around the world.

Although they recognize general trends and structural problems as sources for fin-de-siècle political conflicts,[4] most observers agree that the most serious challenge to a new international order has come from the outbreak of ethnic conflicts both within and between states in various parts of the world. Although the phenomenon of conflict based on ethnic identity and solidarity is not new—clashes between communities organized along ethnic and cultural lines have occurred since the dawn of human civilization—the distinguishing feature of "the current era is not the existence of competitive ethnic solidarities but their global political salience."[5] Thus Ryan was right when he noted that from the initial moments of the formation of the postbipolar world, various manifestations of ethnic conflict were perceptible in the first, second, and third worlds.[6] In the first world—the democratic West—the politicization of ethnicity mainly took the form of "ethnic revival" and increased political assertiveness among various national minority ethnic groups such as the Basques and Catalans in Spain; the Bretons and the Corsicans in France; the Walloons and the Flemish in Belgium; the Scots, Welsh, and Irish in the United Kingdom; African Americans in the United States; and French-speaking Quebecers in Canada. Moreover, partially in response to rising anti-immigrant sentiments, immigrant communities in France, Germany, England, and to a lesser extent the United States organized to better protect and promote their political, economic, and sociocultural rights. The reemergence of radical right-wing nationalism on the streets of Germany, at the ballot box in France, in Jewish settlements in Israeli-held territories indicated the more exclusionary character nationalism took among sections of ethnic majorities.

Rapid transformation and liberalization of Eastern Europe spurred the growth of a number of ethnic trouble spots in this region, such as between Romania and Hungary regarding the status of the Hungarian minority in Transylvania, and between Czechs and their Gypsy, or Romany, population. In the former Yugoslavia, ethnic violence between Serbs, Croats, and Muslims reached an intensity unknown in Europe since World War II. Also, in the former Soviet Union, the breakup of central authority went hand in hand with nationalist mobilization on the part of titular and nontitular nationalities. The culmination of this process's first phase was the dissolution of the Soviet empire and the transformation of the fifteen Soviet republics into independent, sovereign states. But as evidenced by the ongoing brutal war that began in 1994 between Russia and one of its independence-minded provinces, Chechnya, the outcome of a second round of nationalist assertion is unclear. What is clear though is the potential for new types of ethnic conflict within and between the Soviet successor states because of the proliferation of diaspora populations and secessionist/irredentist claims that followed the breakup of the Soviet Union.[7] So it is not a surprise that ethnic conflicts exploded in the Russian Federation and also in the other new states such as Georgia (between majority Georgians and breakaway Abkhazians), Armenia and Azerbaijan (over the territory of Nagorno-Karabakh), Moldova (between Trans-Dniester Russians and the majority Romanian-speaking population), and Ukraine (over Crimea, involving a three-cornered struggle among Ukrainians, Russians, and Crimean Tatars).

Finally, in many states of the developing world, the post–bipolar era has witnessed an intensification of ethnic identities and conflicts. In these states, the politicization of ethnic communities and the outbreak of ethnic violence can be viewed as a legacy of colonialism that created artificial boundaries—and even states—by ignoring cultural divisions and popular aspirations. In their postcolonial political history, many of these states had to confront ethnonationalist mobilization whenever minorities—and occasionally even majorities—felt unjustly treated and regarded the new dominant cultural groups as neocolonialists. Very few of these ethnic clashes—in the Congo,

Nigeria, Sudan, Lebanon, Afghanistan, Bangladesh, India, Pakistan, Sri Lanka, or Myanmar—have been resolved satisfactorily.[8]

The resurgence of ethnic and secessionist conflicts in many parts of the world at the beginning of the early 1990s was closely associated with the end of the cold war between East and West. The ideological conflict between liberalism and Marxism and the strategic confrontation between rival military blocs became obsolete as the Soviet empire disintegrated. Realist theorists of the international system, such as Kenneth Waltz, contend that the scope for alliance building and for more autonomous foreign policy on the part of states increased in the more fluid, even anarchic environment of a non–bipolar system. Had realist theorists also examined ethnic nationalism and secessionism, they might have added that the number of claims for separatism and statehood also increased when two contending camps lost interest in reining in their respective allies.

To be sure, ethnic conflicts have been an enduring feature of the post–World War II international landscape. We can agree with ethnic conflict specialists Ted Gurr and Barbara Harff that "The 'explosion' of ethnopolitical conflicts since the end of the Cold War is, in fact, a continuation of a trend that began as early as the 1960s."[9] Analyzing 233 groups included in their minorities-at-risk study, they found that the worldwide magnitude of ethnic rebellion—not merely protest—increased approximately fourfold from the initial period 1950–1955 to the last quinquennial of the cold war, 1985–1989.

If only because the end of U.S.–Soviet rivalry has done nothing to wind down such conflict, we need to take a fresh look at ethnonationalist and secessionist movements—the two are conceptually distinct—and why they have persisted and multiplied. As well, the possibility that nationalism may be the ultimate winner in the aftermath of the ideological confrontation between liberalism and Marxism and that ethnonationalist movements may prove more strategically destabilizing than the East–West conflict is further reason to give attention to such forms of conflict.

THE FORMATION AND PERSISTENCE OF ETHNIC IDENTITY

Ethnic identity has been defined by Esman as "the set of meanings that individuals impute to their membership in an ethnic community, including those attributes that bind them to that collectivity and that distinguish it from others in their relevant environment."[10] But although most scholars agree that ethnic conflicts pose one of the severest challenges to the contemporary international order, they disagree as to how ethnic identity is formed and why it persists. Generally, one may speak of two schools of thought on this subject—the *primordialist* and the *instrumentalist,* or *constructivist.*

For the primordialists, ethnic identity is a "given" or "natural" phenomenon.[11] Understood in this sense, ethnic groups "constitute the network into which human individuals are born" and where "every human infant or young child finds itself a member of a kinship group and of a neighborhood" and therefore comes to share with the other group members certain common objective cultural attributes.[12] Some of these common objective cultural attributes are language, religion, customs, tradition, food, dress, and music.[13] Along with objective cultural markers, primordialists also stress the subjective or psychological aspects of a self- and group-related feeling of identity distinctiveness and its recognition by others as a crucial determinant of ethnic identity formation and its persistence.[14] The exact nature of these psychological feelings is not very clear. Rex, for instance, argues that in psychological terms three things are important for group creation: First is the emotional satisfaction, or warmth, that one receives from belonging to the group; second, a shared belief in a myth of origin or the history of the group is important because it sets the boundaries of the group; finally, group members must "regard the social relations, within which they live, as 'sacred' and as including not merely the living but the dead."[15] Ethnic identity from the primordialist perspective therefore is a "subjectively held sense of shared identity based on objective cultural . . . criteria."[16]

Anthony Smith exemplifies this approach when referring to six "bases" or "foundations" of ethnic identity. First, an ethnic group must have a name in order to be recognized as a distinct community both by its members and outsiders. The other five bases include belief or myth of common ancestry; presence of historical memories (as interpreted and diffused over generations by group members, often verbally) among group members; shared culture (including dress, food, music, crafts and architecture, laws, customs and institutions, religion, and language); attachment to a specific territory; and a sense of common solidarity.[17] Discussing the conditions that promote the formation and survival of ethnic groups, Smith pointed out that in premodern times, four factors favored ethnic crystallization and survival. The first condition was "the acquisition (or, later, the loss) of a particular piece of territory, which was felt to 'belong' to a people as they belonged to it."[18] Second, a history of struggle with various enemies not only led to a sense of community but also served (through historical myths and beliefs) as a source of inspiration for future generations. Third, some form of organized religion was necessary "for producing specialists in communications and record-keeping, as well as for generating the rituals and traditions that formed the channels of continuity for ethnic communities."[19] Finally, "the proximate cause of ethnic durability and survival was the rise and power of a myth of 'ethnic chosenness'."[20] Smith concluded that the factors that promote one's sense of ethnic identity have become more influential in modern times. Of crucial importance has been the increasing cultural and civic activities of the modern state, activities of intellectuals and intelligentsia within the ethnic group, and the development of the ideology of nationalism—particularly ethnic nationalism in contradistinction to a territorial or civic one.[21]

The instrumentalists, or constructivists, in turn, categorically reject the notion that ethnic identity is a natural or given phenomenon. Pointing out that the presumption of naturalness of ethnicity obscures the human hand and motivations behind its formation, constructivists contend that ethnic identity is a social construction—that is, it is the product of human actions and choices "rather than biologically given ideas whose meaning is dictated by nature."[22] Max Weber was one of the earlier writers who stressed the social construction of ethnic identity. Weber viewed ethnic groups as "human groups" whose belief in a common ancestry, in spite of its origins being mostly fictitious, is so strong that it leads to the creation of a community.[23] This led him to conclude that ethnic membership by itself "does not necessarily result in ethnic group formation but only provides the resources that may, under the right circumstances, be mobilized into a group by appropriate political action."[24]

In recent years, Charles Keyes has argued that ethnic identity derives from a cultural construction of descent. For Keyes, descent can be of two types—social descent and genetic descent.[25] Social descent is a form of kin selection by which human beings seek to create solidarity with those whom they recognize as being "of the same people." Genetic descent, on the other hand, consists of "biological characteristics transmitted through genetic inheritance."[26] Keyes argued that it is the cultural construction of social descent that leads to the formation of ethnic identity because it determines the characteristics that indicate who does or does not "belong to the same people as oneself."[27] He cautions, however, that there "is no invariable pattern as to which cultural differences will be seized upon by groups as emblematic of their ethnic differences."[28] Instead, the type of cultural markers that are put forward "as emblematic of ethnic identity depends upon the interpretations of the experiences and actions of mythical ancestors and/or historical forebears."[29] These interpretations often take the form of historically symbolic myths or legends that can be found in stories, music, artistic depictions, dramas, and rituals.[30] But no matter how these myths and legends are created and presented, "the symbols of ethnic identity must be appropriated and internalized by individuals before they can serve as the basis for orienting people to social action."[31]

Although they argue that ethnic identity is not biologically given but is socially constructed, instrumentalists, or constructivists, do recognize that the construction of ethnic identity and its internalization by individuals does not necessarily make it a variable of sociopolitical action. Rather, ethnic identity becomes a variable of sociopolitical action "only if access to the means of production, means of expropriation of the products of labor, or means of exchange between groups are determined by membership in groups defined in terms of nongenealogical descent."[32] At such moments, ethnicity can be "a device as much as a focus for group mobilization by its leadership through the select use of ethnic symbols for socio-cultural and politico-economic purposes."[33] Politicized ethnicity is thus the creation "of elites, who draw upon, distort, and sometimes fabricate materials from the cultures of the groups they wish to represent in order to protect their well-being or existence or to gain political and economic advantage for their groups as well as for themselves."[34]

From this discussion, it becomes clear that the most contentious issue between the primordialists and the constructivists concerns the role of culture in the formation of ethnic identity. Earlier primordialists, such as Geertz, Isaacs, Naroll, Gordon, Mitchell, Epstein, and Furnivall, considered ethnicity to be a biologically given phenomenon organized around objective markers such as common cultural attributes.[35] This viewpoint—assigning primacy to culture in the formation of ethnic identity— came under attack in the late 1960s. Kuper was one of the first scholars who questioned the primordialists' basic assumption that a dependency relationship exists between cultural and sociopolitical groupings, including ethnic groups.[36] Subsequently, Barth as well as Glazer and Moynihan analytically distinguished between the objective and the subjective bases of ethnicity.[37] Social constructivists, however, took their criticism of primordialism to extreme forms by relegating culture to a secondary position in the formation and persistence of ethnic identity. Some constructivists even suggested that cultural markers can be manipulated to rationalize the identity and existence of an ethnic group.[38]

DEFINITIONS

The controversy over the formation and persistence of ethnic identity presents definitional problems of key terms and concepts associated with ethnic politics because there is no unanimity among experts on this issue. But because the understanding of ethnic conflict depends on the prior understanding of key terms and concepts associated with it, we attempt to provide here working definitions of some of these key terms and concepts.

The term *ethnic group,* or *ethnic community,* refers to either a large or small group of people, in either backward or advanced societies, who are united by a common inherited culture (including language, music, food, dress, and customs and practices), racial similarity, common religion, and belief in common history and ancestry and who exhibit a strong psychological sentiment of belonging to the group. Ethnic groups can be of two main types—homeland societies and immigrant diasporas.[39] Homeland societies are longtime occupants of a particular territory and therefore claim an exclusive as well as a moral right to rule it. Often, such claims are backed by actual or fictive historical and archaeological evidence. The political aspirations behind such claims may also vary depending upon the numerical status of the homelands society and the type of state in which they are located. Thus, for instance, the political demands of a homelands society in a multinational state may exist between territorial autonomy and secession leading to independent statehood. Ethnic diaspora communities, on the other hand, are found in foreign countries and are caused as a result of population migrations. Whether such migrations are induced by oppression in their home state or by the lure of better economic opportunities, ethnic diasporas usually are "inclined to maintain their distinctive collective identities and customs, in part because they are excluded by virtue of these differences from participation and membership in the host society."[40] Ethnic diasporas can be of three types. First, there can be ethnic diasporas that, upon arrival in a foreign land, quickly manage—because of numerical, military, and technical superiority—to subordinate, exterminate, or expel the original inhabitants and take control of the territory, thereby transforming the status of the diasporas to "sons of the soil" or homelands society. Second, there may be bourgeois ethnic diasporas on foreign soil. Members of bourgeois ethnic diasporas usually possess high levels of educational and technical skills for which they are often the targets of the sons of the soil. Finally, there can also be labor diasporas, caused as "a result of large-scale migration from poor, overpopulated, labor-surplus countries to prosperous labor-scarce economies."[41] Both bourgeois and labor diasporas cannot claim territorial control in a foreign state, but they usually demand "nondiscriminatory participation as individuals in public affairs" along with "nondiscriminatory access to education, employment, housing, business opportunities, and public services" as well as "official recognition of their right to maintain institutions that perpetuate elements of their inherited culture."[42]

An ethnic group's transition to a *nation* occurs when political and statist ideas develop within it. The term *state* is "a legal concept describing a social group that occupies a defined territory and is organized under common political institutions and an effective government."[43] The state, furthermore, exercises sovereign authority and is recognized as such by other states. In theory, the state is considered to be a natural outgrowth of a nation's desire to maintain and govern itself independently of other nations.[44] Hence, it is logical to expect that the development of nations preceded the development of modern states.[45] The basis of such political and statist ideas in an ethnic group could be a belief in *national self-determination*—the right of nations to sovereign statehood[46]—based on common citizenship, a common judicial and administrative system, a central government, and popular sovereignty as the basis of state power. In that case the ethnic group could be said to have transformed into a *civic nation.*[47] As the famous French historian Ernest Renan pointed out in his famous lecture of 1882 entitled *"Qu'est-ce qu'une nation?"*("What is a nation?"), a civic nation is a "daily plebiscite," meaning that a civic nation comes into existence when the population of a given territory perceives itself to be a nation and equates citizenship with nationality.[48] The origins of the idea of the civic nation lie primarily in the evolution of the nation in France, England, and the United States. In these three states, political developments in the eighteenth and nineteenth centuries transformed the idea of a nation into "a community of politically aware citizens equal before the law irrespective of their social and economic status, ethnic origin and religious beliefs."[49] On the other hand, the basis of such political and statist ideas could be the spirit of the cultural community based on common ancestry, language, religion, customs, and history. In such an event, the ethnic group can be said to have transformed to an *ethnic nation.* An ethnic nation, therefore, leaves individuals with little choice as to which nation they can belong as an individual's membership in a nation is determined by nature and history.[50]

Although conceptual distinctions can be drawn between the civic nation and the ethnic nation, sometimes these distinctions can become blurred. For example, if one uses the ethnic nation idea, then Alsatians are a part of the German nation because of the commonality of culture, history, and language. If instead the civic nation idea is used, then Alsatians must be regarded as French "because of their desire to be citizens of the French state with which they have felt close ties since the Revolution of 1789 and the Napoleonic era, if not before."[51] The boundary between the civic nation and the ethnic nation can also be crossed in situations where one state includes many ethnic nations, not all of which may voluntarily give allegiance to the state based on civic ideas. Such states, an overwhelming majority in the world, are not *nation-states*—the congruence of the nation and the state—but rather *multinational states* because they incorporate more than one ethnic nation. Contrarily, many ethnic nations in the world overlap state borders. As the Kurds demonstrate, such *non-state nations,* due to a "lack of 'fit' between nations and states, is often a source of international conflict."[52]

An ethnic group that has transformed itself to a nation and exhibits loyalty and sentiment towards it can be said to demonstrate the spirit of *nationalism.* The term *nationalism* has been variously conceptualized and defined by scholars, so there is little unanimity regarding the exact meaning of the phenomenon. For instance, Ernst Haas saw nationalism as "the convergence of territorial and political loyalty irrespective of competing foci of affiliation, such as kinship, profession, religion, economic interest, race, or even language."[53] To Benedict Anderson, on the other hand, the term *nation* symbolized an imagined political community, whereas *nationalism* referred to an artificial linguistic identity.[54] For Dudley Seers, however, nationalism referred to particular types of economic policy (in his case, development planning) that promote state autonomy from the global economy.[55] On his part, Anthony Smith saw nationalism as an essentially political ideology of solidarity that competes with other ideologies such as liberalism, socialism, and fascism.[56]

The idea of *nationalism* as primarily a political principle is also endorsed by Ernest Gellner, who maintained that nationalism as a political doctrine requires the congruence of political and national units. Gellner further drew a distinction between nationalist *sentiment* and nationalist *movement.* Although the former is "the feeling of anger aroused by the violation of the principle, or the feeling of satisfaction aroused by its fulfillment," the latter is the actualization of such sentiment.[57]

Finally, Elie Kedourie believed that the idea of nationalism is logically absurd and illegitimate because it uses dubious cultural criteria—notably linguistic considerations—to demarcate political boundaries and to make decisions regarding political obligation.[58]

Most scholars would, however, agree with Hans Kohn that "Nationalism is first and foremost a state of mind, an act of consciousness."[59] In other words, nationalism is essentially emotional or sentimental in nature.[60] In our complex civilization, the number of groups to which an individual may belong has increased exponentially. Nevertheless, as Kohn noted, "Within these pluralistic, and sometimes conflicting, kinds of group-consciousness there is generally one which is recognized by man as the supreme and most important, to which therefore, in the case of conflict of group-loyalties, he owes supreme loyalty."[61] This supreme group is the nation, and one's consciousness of and loyalty to the nation represents the phenomenon of nationalism.

If nationalism is one's consciousness of and loyalty to the nation, then an ethnic group that has transformed itself to a nation can demonstrate two main types of nationalism: *civic nationalism* and *ethnic nationalism.* While ethnic nationalism defines an individual's membership in and loyalty to one nation in terms of lineage and vernacular culture, civic nationalism conceives of the nation and one's membership in, and loyalty to, it in terms of citizenship, common laws, and political participation.[62] Thus in a state, based on the idea of a particular ethnic nationalism, individuals belonging to different ethnicities, even if they reside in and are citizens of the state, "cannot become part of the national grouping."[63] Contrarily in a state, based on the idea of civic nationalism, any citizen "is a national, regardless of ethnicity and lineage."[64]

The transformation of an ethnic group into an *ethnic political movement* occurs when an ethnic community is converted "into a political competitor that seeks to combat ethnic antagonists or to impress ethnically defined interests on the agenda of the state."[65] Theoretically, an ethnic political movement tries to represent "the collective consciousness and aspirations of the entire community," but in practice, ethnic political movements "may be split into several tendencies or concrete organizations, each competing for the allegiance of the community and for the right to be its exclusive representative."[66] But on the whole, the strength of an ethnic political movement depends on the strength of ethnic identity and *ethnic solidarity*—the duties and responsibilities of members toward their ethnic group—within the ethnic community.

THE POLITICAL MOBILIZATION OF ETHNIC GROUPS

Ethnic politics and ethnic conflict take place mostly within the context of multiethnic societies. As Esman has correctly noted:

> The fundamental reality is that of ethnic pluralism within the boundaries of the great majority of political systems in the contemporary world. From this fundamental reality emerge the central problems—relationships and terms of coexistence, coercive or consensual—that are shaped and maintained by these ethnic communities and the rules and practices enforced by the political authorities that govern these states.[67]

Ethnic pluralism in most of today's states is attributable to four main factors. First, multiethnic societies developed as a result of conquest and annexation throughout human history. Second, European colonization in the eighteenth and nineteenth centuries and later decolonization in the twentieth century created ethnically plural states in Asia and Africa with arbitrarily drawn borders. Third, population movements and migrations throughout human history contributed significantly to the creation of ethnically plural states. Finally, the politicization of the principle of national self-determination in the aftermath of the First World War and its subsequent "domestication" after the Second World War froze the world's ethnopolitical map, thereby legitimating ethnically plural states and creating a direct impact on ethnic politics—especially when such politics centered on minority ethnic communities' claims for separate statehood.[68]

In spite of its salience, understanding of ethnic politics, ethnic conflict, and ethnosecessionist tendencies was not well developed in the immediate post–Second World War years. Because the idea of nationalism—which as we have seen is closely connected with ethnic politics—was seen to be associated with war and human suffering, the preoccupation of both social scientists and politicians, whether liberals or Marxists, was with the themes of *modernization* and *integration*. At the state level, modernization and integration were associated with state building and nation building whereby different ethnic groups could be brought together in multiethnic states into free, equal, and democratic association.[69] At the international level, integration called for the strengthening of economic and political ties between states and the creation of regional organizations for this end. The result was that by "the late 1950s it was assumed that there was a dynamic towards assimilation, an incessant trend heralding a new era of progress and prosperity across the world."[70]

The resilience and persistence of ethnic nationalism and the disintegrative tendencies that it fostered in many parts of the world—especially in the developing world—in the 1960s and 1970s gradually led to serious scholarly inquiry regarding conceptualization and explanation of this phenomenon. Yet, the initial theorizing about ethnic fragmentation in many multiethnic societies did not focus on ethnic political mobilization per se but rather tried to explain the failure of the modernization paradigm in the developing world and the resultant fragmentation of these societies. If these theories developed our understanding of ethnic political mobilization, then they did it *indirectly*—that is, by suggesting that certain factors associated with the modernization process lead to societal fragmentation and the rise of ethnic nationalism. The indirect theories of ethnic political mobilization can be grouped together as the negative theories of integration, the negative theories of cohesion, and the theories of disintegration and revolution.

TABLE 1.1 Theories of ethnic political mobilization and ethnic conflict.

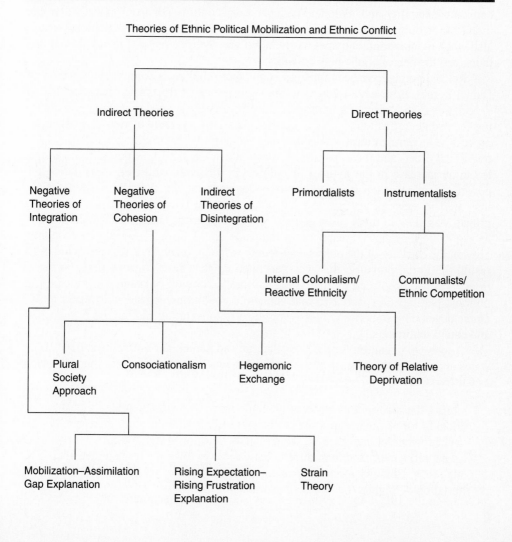

THEORIES OF ETHNIC POLITICAL MOBILIZATION AND CONFLICT

Negative Theories of Integration

One of the best-known and most influential theories in this category is that of Karl Deutsch. In his *Nationalism and Social Communication,* Deutsch constructed a paradigm of national integration in developing states employing two key concepts: mobilization and assimilation. His argument was that, first, modernization led to a greater political mobilization of the population and, second, that increasing urbanization and the spread of communication (a consequence of modernization) result in the assimilation of those who are politically mobilized. The outcome is national integration, the basis for (civic) nationalism. At the same time, Deutsch signaled the dangers of this integrative process. Using the same concepts of mobilization and assimilation, he argued that parochialism, or regionalism (including its ethnic forms), with its concomitant instability and national fragmentation, could result from situations where mobilization outpaced assimilation. Therefore, the mobilization–assimilation gap created when mobilization outpaced assimilation was the root cause of national fragmentation and the rise of ethnic nationalism.[71]

Related points have been made by such other scholars as Samuel Huntington and Daniel Lerner. Both have referred to the significance of the tension between "rising expectations" and "rising frustrations," caused primarily by modernization, in accounting for disintegrative tendencies in developing states. In many of these societies, the process of modernization by causing rapid social mobilization, the breakdown of the traditional order, and the expansion of communications and transportation networks, led to an increase in the number of political participants who were sensitive to the poverty in which they lived. Thereafter, demands on the political system greatly increased as new groups entered the political arena. However, because economic growth was slow in most cases and also because political elites were concerned that an equitable distributive response to demands could further slow down economic growth, the capacity of the political system to respond to demands was restricted. As a result, the initial euphoria that was generated by the "revolution of rising expectations" was soon replaced by the despair of the "revolution of rising frustrations." As political participation increased and economic conditions degenerated, many multiethnic developing societies witnessed political fragmentation and the rise of parochial and ethnic sentiments.[72]

Another explanation for the rise of ethnic and parochial sentiments in developing states undergoing the process of modernization was provided by strain theorists, such as Clifford Geertz, who argued that:

> during the disorienting process of modernization . . . unintegrated citizens, looking for an anchor in a sea of changes, will grab hold of an increasingly anachronistic ethnic identity, which bursts onto the scene and then recedes as the process of structural differentiation moves toward a reintegrated society. Thus, ethnicity might resurge temporarily, but like suicide, it is a manifestation of anomie that would inexorably disappear.[73]

So, from the strain theory perspective, the rise of ethnic sentiments in a developing and modernizing society was the outcome of the insecurity faced by individuals at a time of tremendous sociocultural, economic, and political upheaval and change. But such sentiments were considered to be temporary; therefore, ethnic political mobilization was expected to be short-lived. Following up on the strain theory perspective, Stein Rokkan highlighted the salience of three related factors—territorial concentration, social isolation, and economic isolation of ethnic groups during the process of modernization—in accounting for the rise of ethnonational sentiments and political fragmentation in developing states. These three factors indicated for Rokkan the failure of the state to draw ethnic groups into national life.[74] But the underlying assumption that ethnicity is a primordial sentiment and ethnic political mobilization an aberration that would disappear when the structural reintegration of society is completed remained in his analysis.

Negative Theories of Cohesion

Negative theories of cohesion include three models of control: the first is *incompatibility theory* or the *plural-society approach;* second, skepticism about the plural society approach led to the theory of *consociationalism;* finally, shortcomings in the consociational model produced the development of the theory of *hegemonic exchange.*

The Plural-Society Approach. The failure of the modernization paradigm and various assimilationist theories to account for growing ethnic fragmentation in multiethnic societies led to disillusionment with the optimistic predictions of nation-building theories and renewed interest "in the theory of the plural society, which posited that multi-ethnic societies could not remain both stable and democratic."[75] The earliest indications of the approach could be found in the seventeenth-century writings of both the Duke of Sully and John Stuart Mill, but the first systematic version of the plural-society approach was developed by the British economist J.S. Furnivall and later modified by the West Indian anthropologist M.G. Smith.

As elaborated by Furnivall, the central thesis of the plural-society approach is that in ethnically plural societies—where different ethnic groups live in close proximity to, but separately from, each other—intercommunal relations are characterized by unchecked economic competition. Because relations between the various groups remain confined to the marketplace, these societies fail to develop a sense of common loyalty that would overcome the cultural and ethnic differences between the various groups—in other words, a sense of civic nationalism. Unrestrained competition and competing nationalisms between different cultural groups that follow cause society to fragment. Furnivall argued that the only way such societies could be held together is through the application of external force. For him, such external force was provided by colonialism.[76]

M.G. Smith further modified the plural-society approach. He argued that a plural society could be created by incorporating members of different ethnic groups into a multiethnic state in one of three ways. First, a multiethnic state may be created through the *uniform* incorporation of individuals as equal citizens with equal civic and political status, irrespective of ethnic or cultural affiliation. Second, it could be created through the *equivalent* incorporation of different collectivities with equal or complimentary public rights and status, thus leading to a consociational democracy model. Finally, it could be created through *differential* incorporation whereby a dominant group comes to exercise and maintain power and superior position by excluding other groups from power.

Smith, however, harbored serious doubts about the stability and durability of such multiethnic states. Uniform incorporation, for example, could result in assimilative policies leading to resentment. Differential incorporation, on the other hand, was bound to create a dominant–subordinate relationship among the groups and exclude some groups from real power; therefore it could not lead to a stable and democratic multiethnic state. Finally, even equivalent incorporation, which seemed to hold the most hope, could not in practice produce stable and democratic multiethnic states because often "the components of a consociation are unequal in numbers, territory, and economic potential."[77] Consequently, real or perceived grievances could cause ethnic unrest and undermine the stability of the state.

The Theory of Consociationalism.   As a challenge to the bleak picture painted by the plural-society approach, two alternative explanations that addressed the issues of stability, harmony, and democracy in multiethnic states were developed: one was the consociational democracy approach pioneered by Arend Lijphart; the other was Donald Rothchild's theory of hegemonic exchange.

In his *Democracy in Plural Societies: A Comparative Exploration,* and *Democracies: Patterns of Majoritarian and Consensus Government in Twenty-One Countries,* Lijphart offered a framework and conditions that could lead to stable, democratic, multiethnic states. In so doing, Lijphart rejected the traditional Westminister majoritarian model with its "one-party cabinets, a two party system, a first past the post electoral system, a unitary and centralized government and an unwritten constitution."[78] Instead, he opted for a consociational framework involving executive power sharing and grand coalitions, formal and informal separation of powers, balanced bicameralism and special minority representation in the upper chamber, a multiparty system, proportional representation, territorial as well as nonterritorial federalism and decentralization, and a written constitution protecting minority rights through difficult procedures for amendment.[79] Although these criteria were important, Lijphart placed particular emphasis on the formation of grand coalitions of leaders representing all the communities, the provision of veto power to all communities on legislation affecting their vital interests, a system of proportional representation in parliament, and a high degree of autonomy for each community to run its own affairs as the key to building a stable and democratic multiethnic state. He also suggested a list of conditions that could promote elite cooperation in multiethnic states. These included a power balance between the various groups so that none could form a majority by itself, a multiparty system, small state size, crosscutting societal cleavages, feelings of patriotism or a common religion, clear group boundaries, and a tradition of cooperation among group elites. The relative stability of states such as Switzerland, Canada, Malaysia, Belgium, and Holland is seen by some scholars as the result of the implementation of the consociational model.

Some of Lijphart's conditions are clearly contradictory—such as the existence of crosscutting societal cleavages and clear group boundaries—while the sum of them is convoluted. Moreover, considering the fact that some of the worst cases of ethnic violence have occurred in such small states as Cyprus, Lebanon, and Sri Lanka, it is doubtful if small state size really promotes cooperation among elites. To be sure, Lijphart did emphasize that the presence or absence of these conditions was not decisive and that they were therefore neither necessary nor sufficient themselves to determine the success of consociational democracy.[80]

The absence of some or all of Lijphart's conditions may, however, unleash ethnonationalist sentiments and conflict in multiethnic states. The empirical evidence suggests that the record of consociational democracy has been mixed. Although it has produced relatively stable democracies in some multiethnic states such as Switzerland, Holland, and to a lesser degree Belgium and Canada, it has failed to prevent the outbreak of ethnic conflict elsewhere, such as in Sri Lanka, Cyprus, and Lebanon.

An attempt to refine the consociational democracy model of Lijphart was made by Eric Nordlinger in his *Conflict Regulation in Divided Societies.* Like Lijphart, Nordlinger also stressed elite cooperation and structured elite predominance as ways to prevent conflict in multiethnic societies.[81] He maintained that elite cooperation and conflict regulation is possible through any of the following strategies: stable coalition, the proportionality principle, depoliticization, mutual veto, mutual compromise, and concessions. He further observed that certain conditions may motivate elites to regulate conflict through cooperation. These include their desire to thwart external threats to the state, the presence of a sufficiently large commercial class dedicated to the promotion of economic values, the inability of any group to acquire political power and office without the support of others, and the threat of civil violence in the event of elite noncooperation.[82] But unlike Lijphart, Nordlinger was skeptical about the positive impact of either crosscutting cleavages or segmental isolation of groups on elite cooperation. He argued that there is simply not enough evidence to suggest that crosscutting cleavages positively reduce violence in divided societies. Moreover, because an individual's cultural identity is often more salient than cross-cultural ties, cross-cultural cleavages are more likely to be catalysts of ethnic violence rather than its moderators. Again, geographical isolation may actually "increase conflict by increasing unequal development and by encouraging calls for greater autonomy, which can raise the stakes of the conflict."[83]

The Theory of Hegemonic Exchange.   The inability of consociational arrangements to prevent ethnic conflict in some multiethnic states led to the development of the hegemonic-exchange theory, which supplemented consociational democratic ideas with control and dominance theory. This approach is associated primarily with Donald Rothchild, who has applied it to African states.

Rothchild found that although a number of African states were able to impose a limited amount of hegemony over some ethnic groups within their borders and thus prevent open ethnic conflict, these states were "soft" states because they lacked the capacity to impose solutions on all ethnic groups. So these states had to engage in a process of exchange with them. The result was a hegemonic-exchange system of state-group relations in which a quasi-autonomous state and various ethnoregional interests engaged, on the basis of commonly accepted procedural norms and rules, in a process of mutual accommodation.[84]

Like the consociational approach, the hegemonic-exchange system does not regard ethnic relations within a state as a clash of primordial identities. Instead, "it posits that ethnic groups have overt, tangible interests that can be pursued in a rational, utility maximizing manner [and hence] tradeoffs and bargaining are possible, and ethnic violence can be ended by changes in policies of allocation of power and wealth."[85] The role of the state in this scheme is not that of an "oppressor, but as a mediator and facilitator; and in order to play this role it must reject an exclusivist approach to access to power in favor of an inclusive strategy based on ethnic balancing."[86] Rothchild's examples of hegemonic exchange included post–civil-war Nigeria, Mauritius, Togo, Ivory Coast, Zambia, Kenya, and Zimbabwe after 1987.

The problem with theories of cohesion and control are threefold. First, as the theories of consociationalism and hegemonic exchange indicate, the maintenance of cohesion in multiethnic states is a difficult task, and cohesion, even when achieved, remains precarious. At any moment, it can be shattered by the emergence of new counterelites who cannot be incorporated into the system or by the emergence of new demands by groups that cannot be accommodated. Second, the existing balance of power between the various groups may change over time, thereby undermining cooperative arrangements arrived at by groups earlier. Finally, interethnic cohesion achieved through institutionalized control and domination is difficult to maintain when the legitimacy of state authority cannot be taken for granted. We are drawn to the conclusion, then, that not only are the various models of cohesion and control unlikely to preserve political stability in multiethnic states but that they might also actually facilitate the rise of ethnonationalist feelings.

Indirect Theories of Disintegration

The indirect theories of disintegration subsume "the various interpretations of revolution, inter-group conflict and aggression, all of which contain clues which can lead to a general theory of disintegration."[87] The most important explanations come from those theories of revolution that stress socioeconomic factors such as relative deprivation, resource scarcity, and the sudden rise in aspirations that are frustrated; and also political approaches dealing with interest group competition, mobilization, breakdown of institutions, and revolutionary organization and leadership.[88]

By far the most important theory in this category is that of relative deprivation developed by Gurr in *Why Men Rebel. Relative deprivation* refers to "the perceived discrepancy between value expectations and value expectancies in a society."[89] What this means is that "the inclination to revolt is most likely to be present when people perceive an inequity in the wretchedness of their condition—when they receive less (their expectations) than they feel they deserve (their expectancies)."[90] Gurr points to four stages in the process by which relative deprivation leads to revolt: First, people must recognize that deprivation exists; second, they must also become aware that the wretched conditions they experience are not universal and that others enjoy what they lack; third, people must develop the feeling that a situation of deprivation is unfair; the final step is the recognition that political action may be able to change the situation. This is the stage for mass political activity and revolution.[91]

The theory of relative deprivation is useful for explaining the rise of ethnic political mobilization not only among economically backward groups but also among relatively prosperous ethnic groups, such as the Sikhs in India or the Tamils in Sri Lanka. When such groups begin to perceive a threat to their privileged position or if they become victims of state discrimination, they too may undertake political action to rectify the situation. After all, as the theory suggests, it is the realization by a group that it is receiving less than it deserves and that others are receiving more that motivates the group to take political action. Applying this concept to ethnic conflict, as Gurr does in his later work, *Minorities at Risk,* it is easy to understand why perceived disadvantage or discrimination (real or imaginary) by a group regarding its status (sociocultural, economic, political) is an underlying cause for political action.[92]

DIRECT THEORIES OF ETHNIC POLITICAL MOBILIZATION AND CONFLICT

Direct theories of ethnic political mobilization—those theories that focused on ethnic political mobilization and not on developmental or modernization problems—were developed chiefly in the 1970s and 1980s as a result of dissatisfaction among scholars with inadequate conceptual tools with which to explain the persistence and proliferation of ethnic political mobilization. Thus the failure of strain theory to account for the persistence of ethnic conflict led to its eventual abandonment. Moreover, scholars realized that although the various indirect theories offered some insights regarding the causes of ethnic political mobilization, they did so more through inference and induction. Their primary focus remained modernization and its associated problems—stability and democracy in plural societies and the issues of violence and revolution. Particularly in the 1980s, scholars who were not yet prepared to discard the salience of the modernization process in the rise of ethnic nationalism tried to reformulate these theories. Two paradigms dealing directly with the causes of ethnic political mobilization thus emerged—the internal colonialism approach and the primordialist approach; a third, older approach—the communalist approach—also sought to explain ethnic political mobilization in underdeveloped societies.

The Primordialist Approach

The primary focus of the primordialist approach is on ethnic identity and consciousness that it treats as "the essential independent variable that leads to political assertiveness and militant separatism, regardless of the existence of inequality or dominance."[93] Primordialists argued that distinct communities prefer to be governed poorly by their ethnic brethren rather than wisely by aliens because rule by foreigners is degrading. Although the primordialists put more stress on cultural markers as sources of ethnic identity and consciousness, they nevertheless did not discount the role of socioeconomic variables and continued to recognize the salience of the modernization process in the rise of ethnonationalism. At the same time, they were unwilling to accept the general conclusion of the modernization approach that ethnicity is a vanishing tradition. In reformulating modernization theories, they acknowledged that socioeconomic factors may form the basis of discontent but that only discontent based on ethnocultural identity could lead to ethnonationalism and secessionist sentiments. This was a significant research breakthrough because unlike the indirect theories that regarded ethnic identity as a dependent variable, the primordialists claimed that ethnic identity is an independent or explanatory variable triggering political action in many societies. The primordialist approach is illustrated in the scholarship of Walker Connor, Nathan Glazer and Daniel Moynihan, Cynthia Enloe, Donald Horowitz, Anthony Smith, and John Armstrong.[94]

Connor, an early exponent of the primordialist perspective, has traced the etiology and manifestation of ethnic political mobilization. He contended that modernization, by increasing interaction and competition between ethnic groups for the same economic and political rewards, actually sharpened ethnic divisions in society in four ways. First, rapid social communication and mobilization increased cultural awareness and exacerbated interethnic conflict.[95] Second, improvements "in communications and transportation" increased "the cultural awareness of the [ethnic] minorities by making their members more aware of the distinctions between themselves and others."[96] Third, the rise of militant ethnic consciousness in many parts of both the developed and the developing worlds could be explained not in terms of the "nature or density of the communications media, but [of] the *message*."[97] The reference was to the doctrine of national self-determination that, in its pristine form, made ethnicity "the ultimate measure of political legitimacy, by holding that any self-differentiating people, simply because it *is* a people, has the right, should it so desire, to rule itself."[98] This doctrine not only provided justification but also acted as a catalyst for ethnic political movements. Finally, changes in the global political environment also contributed to the upsurge in ethnic consciousness by making it "much more unlikely that a militarily weak polity will be annexed by a larger power."[99] In this context, Connor pointed out that the achievement of nuclear parity between the superpowers caused "*independence* to appear as a more enduring prospect for even the weakest of units."[100]

In *The Ethnic Revival,* Anthony Smith posited that ethnic conflict is the outcome of incongruence between economic modernization and political development—processes associated with the birth of the modern state. Starting from the same perspective as Weber and Durkheim but arriving at a diametrically opposite conclusion, Smith concluded that the modern bureaucratic state seeks legitimacy in scientific rationality. When coupled with economic and educational modernization of society, the rationality imperative produces an expanding stratum of secular intelligentsia.

However, the inability of the state bureaucracy to absorb the entire body of secular intellectuals causes them to identify with their ethnic groups, which helps legitimate their perceptions of injustice.[101]

According to Saul Newman, a major shortcoming of Smith's argument was his failure to explain why secularizing intellectuals or elites, when faced with a lack of opportunities, should revert to their ethnic identities "instead of radical secular ideologies such as Marxism."[102] While it is true that cultural markers and primordial sentiments play a crucial role in the development of human personality, we can question whether ethnic identity alone constitutes a powerful factor triggering ethnopolitical movements because culture has a multiplicity of components that are given differentiated stress over time by individuals and groups. Another criticism of Smith's approach is that by concentrating on elites, his framework failed to address the question how such elites mobilize mass support. More important, he did not explain how the popular classes end up with a political agenda that suits the personal needs of a narrow elite. Finally, Smith paid little attention to the political obstacles faced by new ethnic movements and to such other factors as demographic, socioeconomic, and political power at the disposal of ethnic groups that often account for different levels and types of ethnic political activity.[103]

The Internal Colonialism Approach

Lack of agreement on the effect that modernization had on ethnic political mobilization led to the development of the internal colonialism approach. The main proponent of the internal colonialism approach is Michael Hechter, although the idea was derived from Marxist social theories expounded by Lenin and Gramsci.

At the crux of Hechter's argument is the concept of *exploitation,* which characterizes the relationship between members of a dominant cultural group and those of peripheral ethnic groups in advanced industrial states. Using the Celt minority in the United Kingdom as a case study, Hechter contended that such exploitation results in "a particularistic allocation of valued roles and resources to the dominant ethnic group," thereby causing political mobilization of the peripheral ethnic group.[104] Faced with infiltration of their region by the core group, its stunted development caused by its being treated as an appendage of the national economy, together with the destruction of the social fabric of the peripheral region as a result of modernization, cultural and ethnic differences become the basis of protests and separatist movements by the peripheral ethnic group. To be sure, Hechter pointed out that often the selective cooptation of potentially destructive or divisive leaders from such peripheral ethnic groups by the core ethnic group can weaken ethnopolitical movements, thereby ensuring the continuity of the cultural division of labor.[105]

Although Hechter studied the Celts in the United Kingdom, his theory can also explain ethnic political mobilization among peripheral minorities in many parts of the developing world. Good examples would include the Bengali and the Baluch nationalist movements in Pakistan, the various tribal movements in India (Nagas, Mizos, and Bodos to name a few), and the nationalist movements in the Central Asian republics of the former Soviet Union. Hechter further added an important dimension to the analysis of politicized ethnicity by combining economic explanations with cultural ones.

But the independent variable—the cultural division of labor—was in his view only a necessary and not sufficient condition for the formation of ethnic political movements.[106] His model also falls short in explaining ethnopolitical assertions on the part of economically privileged ethnic groups.

The Communalist Approach

The communalist approach is much older than others we have been considering here. It explains ethnic political mobilization by focusing on modernization, scarcity of resources, and elite competition. The process of modernization from this perspective affects both peripheral and core ethnic groups in two ways. First, it reduces ethnic diversity within both dominant and subordinate ethnic groups by eroding local identities. Second, as a result of this erosion of local identities, large-scale ethnic identity formation is promoted because of the altered conditions of political competition between groups and elites.[107] But although the communalist perspective posits that large-scale ethnic identity formation occurs when groups are forced to compete with each other for the same rewards and resources, the roots of ethnic political mobilization leading to ethnic violence and even ethnic separatism lie "in elite disputes over the direction of change and grievances linked with the scarcity of resources" and also "when previously acquired privileges are threatened or alternatively when underprivileged groups realize that the moment has come to redress inequality."[108] The communalists argue that this phenomenon is more pronounced in modern states, particularly those in the middle ranks of economic development. Such states, which may include India, Ukraine, Kazakhstan, Nigeria, and Brazil, often lack the capacity and resources to manage social mobilization and to satisfy the increased aspirations that mobilization creates. This being so, these states are particularly vulnerable to intense competition and conflict between ethnic elites and groups.

An important example of this approach to ethnic identity creation and to the rise of ethnic political mobilization as a result of elite competition in premodern and modern societies is the work of Paul Brass. Using case studies of ethnic and communal conflict from India, the former Soviet Union, and parts of Eastern Europe, Brass has shown how altered conditions of elite competition, the emergence of new elites, resource scarcity, and centralizing tendencies of states (all a result of modernization) have combined to generate intense elite competition and ethnic polarization in many of these societies.[109]

The communalist approach to ethnic political mobilization enhances our understanding of the causes of large-scale ethnic identity formation in modernizing societies, of the competition for resources that this process entails, and of the dynamics of elite interaction behind the politicization of ethnicity. But its major shortcoming is that it tends "to overemphasize the element of greedy elites and manipulative, power-seeking regional leaders who take advantage of the communal spirit for their own ends."[110] As a result, communalists often ignore "the element of inequality and communal identity as well as the degree of ingroup legitimization" that is required for ethnopolitical and secessionist sentiments to develop.[111]

Although the direct theories offer a wider variety of explanations for the rise of ethnonationalism than the indirect ones, they nevertheless, as our discussion suggests, suffer from major defects. Whereas the internal colonialism approach fails to account for the rise of separatist sentiments on the part of economically rich subnations, the primordialist approach is flawed by its minimalization of the significance of economic inequality as a source for the rise of ethnic separatist movements. In turn, the communalist perspective overemphasizes the role of manipulative elites driven by their own needs and aspirations, and it underestimates the importance of ethnic consciousness in the rise of separatist sentiments. It also fails to explain adequately why such movements at times acquire a high level of in-group legitimization for secession.[112]

ETHNIC POLITICAL MOBILIZATION: LINKING CAUSES AND OBJECTIVES

Most scholars agree that a fundamental distinction exists between ethnic politics and nationalist politics. Kellas, for example, points out that "Nationalism focuses on 'national self-determination,' or home rule in a national territory. Ethnic politics in contrast is largely concerned with the protection of rights for members of the group within the existing state, with no claim for a territorial 'homeland.'"[113] In similar fashion, Frye notes that "Ethnic groups may or may not feel a sense of nationalism, that is, they may or may not seek the creation of a nation-state that corresponds to a given territory. The sense of nation has a territorial aspect absent from ethnicity, since a member of an ethnic group living abroad can share a sense of identity with a co-ethnic in the home country quite apart from feeling an attachment to a nation-state."[114] But they disagree over the conditions when and if at all this distinction can be overcome and ethnic and nationalist politics can coincide.

We believe, however, that although ethnic and nationalist politics are differentiated, this differentiation can be overcome if the political goal of an ethnic group coincides with the political objective of the nationalist doctrine, namely self-determination. In other words, ethnic groups exhibit nationalist sentiment only when their political agenda hinges on "ethnic self-determination" and the creation of an ethnic nation-state corresponding with their territorial homelands. This interpretation also seems to be favored by Gurr when he defines *ethnonationalist groups* as large politicized groups of people who share a common language and ethnicity and who are territorially concentrated and exhibit a history of making demands for political autonomy or separate statehood.[115]

If we understand ethnonationalism as one specific type of ethnic politics—the movement by an ethnic group for self-determination in the form of political autonomy or the creation of a separate state corresponding to its ethnic homeland—then it becomes obvious that there can be different types of ethnic political movements. In his *Minorities at Risk,* Gurr has provided a detailed description of the various types of ethnic political movements currently active in the world. The aim of Gurr's project was to determine the cultural, economic, and political conditions that differentiated communal groups from each other. The project's purpose in classifying groups in terms of risk factors was at least in part policy oriented. Identifying group inequalities, however caused, could serve as an early warning system for potential ethnic conflicts about to erupt at some time in the future. International, state, and nongovernmental agencies might then undertake efforts to avert conflict at an early stage.

Gurr used the term *nonstate communal groups* to refer to peoples who share language, ethnicity, region of residence, and history but not necessarily constituting nations or states. Thus, "communal groups are cultural and psychological entities rather than bounded political communities."[116] Politically salient communal groups are those that either suffer or benefit from systematic discrimination and/or engage in political mobilization to promote self-defined interests. Gurr further subdivided politicized communal groups into national and minority peoples. National peoples can be ethnonationalist groups—large, regionally concentrated peoples with a history of organized political autonomy and separatist movements—as well as indigenous peoples—the conquered descendants of the original inhabitants of a region. In turn, minority peoples are made up of three groups: (a) ethnoclasses, that is, usually low-status ethnically distinct peoples; (b) militant sects, or groups focused on defense of their religious beliefs (reconceptualized in Gurr's book with Barbara Harff as the less pejorative-sounding, politically active religious minorities); and (c) communal contenders, or culturally distinct groups that aspire to exercise a share of state power. Communal contenders may be advantaged over other groups and therefore represent dominant minorities, or they may be disadvantaged, suffer various forms of discrimination, and be drawn into ethnic struggles of a particularly bloody kind.

Of 233 communal groups identified by Gurr as functioning between 1945 and 1989, more than two thirds were national groups: 81 (such as Croatians and Québécois) were ethnonationalist, and 83 (Native Americans, Australian aboriginals) were indigenous peoples. There were 45 ethnoclasses, ranging from African Americans in the United States and in 9 Latin American societies to Muslims in France and Koreans in Japan. Most of the 49 militant sects consisted of Muslim minorities (Turks in Germany, Malay in Thailand). There were 25 advantaged minorities (such as the Tutsis of Burundi and the Sunnis of Iraq) and 41 disadvantaged communal contenders (many of the tribal groups in sub–Saharan Africa).

To assess the extent to which disadvantages were the result of deliberate social policy and practice, Gurr distinguished between intergroup differentials and outright discrimination. Differentials were the traits that set each group apart in the larger society. Cultural differentials were measured in terms of six socially significant factors—ethnicity, language, religion, customs, origin, and rural or urban residence. Political differentials focused on how communal groups varied in terms of access to power and to the civil service, recruitment to military and police service, voting rights, right of purposeful association, and right to equal legal protection. Economic differentials were grounded in inequalities in income, in land and in other property, access to further education, and presence in business, the professions, and official positions. Based on his crossnational data base, Gurr concluded that generally "it has been easier for elites to give disadvantaged groups political rights and some access to power than to reduce economic inequalities."[117]

Cultural, political, and economic differentials may be created and reinforced by group discrimination, based on the deliberate social practice and policy of elites. Thus

Some economic and political inequalities in the modern world are the cumulative result of malign or neglectful social practices extended over a long period. Others . . . are not the result of deliberate agency at all but simply become salient when isolated groups on the periphery of modernizing societies are drawn, usually against their will, into closer contact with more powerful and technologically proficient groups.[118]

Economic discrimination was measured along two dimensions: substantial material inequality affecting a particular group and policies responsible for maintaining these inequalities. Similarly, political discrimination was evidenced in substantial underrepresentation in political participation and office holding of a group, and in policy fostering continued exclusion.

Finally, in addition to intergroup differentials and discrimination, the status of minority groups in a society was affected by what Gurr termed demographic and ecological stress. Demographic stress was assessed by the presence and severity of three conditions: a comparatively high birthrate, a relatively youthful population, and poor public health conditions. Ecological stress, in turn, measured the presence and severity of these three conditions: competition with other groups for settling vacant lands, dispossession from land by other groups, and forced resettlement within a country. Migration was measured by the presence and severity of substantial rural-to-urban population shift, significant emigration abroad, and influx of kindred groups from abroad, such as refugees.

Demographic stress was pronounced in the advanced industrial democracies, the product of high birthrates and poor public health among ethnoclasses. Ecological stress was greatest in Asia and Latin America, where the lands and resources of indigenous peoples were under threat from expanding dominant groups. Migration was most common in regions hit by famine and civil strife, such as Sudan and Ethiopia.

Gurr did not find a strong correlation between differentials and discrimination. By contrast, political and economic differentials were correlated; that is, a group's political status within a society was likely to be similar to its economic one. To some degree, cultural differences could be used to explain the unequal political and economic status of particular minorities. In particular, "wide cultural differences contribute more to minorities' poverty than to their lack of empowerment."[119] But Gurr was quick to make the general point that "there is no general empirical basis for arguing that inequalities affecting these kinds of groups are a function of cultural differences."[120] A stronger case could be made for attributing the persistence and growth of differentials to the impact of discrimination. As Gurr put it, "policies of neglect and deliberate exclusion are substantially responsible for the persistence of contemporary inequalities."[121]

A final issue that Gurr's study addressed and that is relevant to our discussion here is the linkage between objective disadvantages suffered by minorities and the political demands they make. As we noted earlier, ethnonationalism is a specific type of ethnic political movement where an ethnic group indulges in political activity with self-determination (in the form of political autonomy or the creation of a separate state corresponding to the ethnic territorial homeland) as its goal. If disadvantaged groups have been the victims of deliberate discrimination over a protracted time period by another group and if these groups have mobilized in self-defense, have sought redress of their legitimate grievances, and have failed to obtain them from the dominant group, this would appear to be the ideal-type case where secessionist claims would be made.

Yet, Gurr's empirical data indicate a different pattern of group demands for full political autonomy and for an expansion of political, economic, and social rights. Predictably, grievances about economic rights were greatest among indigenous peoples and ethnoclasses, both of which have suffered greatest economic disadvantages. Militant sects most often demanded social rights. Demands for political autonomy, in turn, were most often put forward by ethnonationalists. Disaggregating autonomy demands further, Gurr described how "The common denominator of almost all autonomy demands is the historical fact or belief that the group once governed its own affairs. . . . Sixty-three contemporary separatists justify their claims by descent from ancestors whose long-term autonomy ended when they were conquered by modern states."[122]

On the other hand, "Our most distinctive finding about separatism is that there is no global or regional correlation between the severity of either kind of discrimination and the intensity of separatist sentiments."[123] Just as paradoxically, there was little correlation between minority separatism and political or economic differentials. On the contrary, where differentials were relatively small, as between Québécois and English Canadians, Basques and Castilians, or Ukrainians and Russians, minority separatism was often at its strongest. The contemporary condition most strongly intensifying the demand for political autonomy turned out to be cultural differences and, taken globally, ecological stress (pressures on group lands and resources). Gurr concluded:

> The global evidence suggests that two different kinds of dynamics drive the political grievances of contemporary minorities. Political and economic disadvantages motivate communal groups to demand greater access to the political system and greater economic opportunities, whereas a history of political autonomy leads groups to attempt secession.[124]

In sum, strong group history and status tend to heighten a group's perception of the legitimacy of its grievances and to predispose it to act on them. In particular, the strength of group identity and cohesion, which affect the mobilization potential of a group, and repressive control exercised by a dominant group are the answer Gurr supplies to the question of why minorities rebel.[125] On the basis of his own empirical research, Alexis Heraclides has formulated a similar hypothesis:

> The more a group can be characterized as an ethnic group or nation, the more secondary is the role played by the factor of inequality or disadvantage in spurring active separatism (or, put differently, the lesser the degree of

inequality necessary to spawn secession). Conversely, the more a group lacks the trappings of ethnic or national identity, the more decisive is the role of inequality, and the higher the degree of inequality required. Most, but not all, separatist movements conform to one or other of the two variants of this hypothesis.[126]

Applying his oversimplified distinction between backward groups—those having poorer records in educational and occupational attainment and stereotyped as not achievement oriented—and advanced ones—whose members score above the mean in bureaucratic, professional, and commercial employment and in per capita income—Donald Horowitz comes up with a related conclusion about group makeup and the disposition to secede. Different criteria are used by the two groups to measure disadvantage. Thus "Backward groups tend to measure disadvantage in terms of deviation from some concept of proportionality in relation to population. Advanced groups gauge deprivation by discrimination, utilizing a standard of proportionality in relation to merit."[127] With most of his cases drawn from Africa and Asia, Horowitz provides a different profile of groups who are most anxious to secede from that of Gurr. Adding an additional continuum ranging from backward to advanced regions—measured by relative economic position of the region—Horowitz concludes: "By far the largest number of secessionists can be characterized as backward groups in backward regions" that have but a small stake in preserving the undivided state of which they form a part.[128] Examples of such groups include the Moros in the Philippines, the Nagas in India, and the Karens in Burma. But Horowitz's study corroborates one important finding made by Gurr: "Among the most frequent and precocious secessionists—backward groups in backward regions—economic loss or gain plays the smallest role, ethnic anxiety the largest."[129]

Ralph Premdas has also highlighted the role of cultural factors in engendering ethnic secessionist movements. He classifies the causes of secession into two categories—primordial and secondary. *Primordial causes,* which are based partly on fact and partly on myth, "refer to those cleavages in society that are deep and serve to define the very identity of the group."[130] These include "language, religion, race, values or culture, territory or homeland or region."[131] *Secondary factors,* which can be fabricated just like primordial ones, refer however to those politico-economic differentials and to discrimination that has been recently acquired or experienced by an ethnic group, such as "neglect, exploitation, domination and internal colonialism, repression and discrimination, and forced annexation."[132] Premdas observes that the mere "presence of primordial and secondary factors does not automatically transform" an ethnic movement into a separatist one. Rather, the transformation of the primordial factors into a "collective consciousness"—"when a group of people come to view themselves consciously as being endowed with a unique language, race, religion or region and see that this is threatened because of one of the secondary factors"—is needed to transform an ethnic political movement into a secessionist one.[133] Anthony Birch put similar emphasis on culture as a "constant factor" underlying ethnic secessionist movements.[134] But he also highlighted the salience of historical variables in the politicization of ethnicity and the emergence of secessionist movements.[135]

Not all scholars agree with the cultural interpretation of secessionism. Ivo Duchacek, for instance, has stressed the territorial aspect of separatism, especially in cases where separatists are hardly bound by ethnic, religious or communal links. Calling such secessionist movements "both ideological and territorial," he argues that the issue is not over which group's "policy should prevail in the nation; the very concept of the territorial community is at stake. The nation has already split into two or more groups, one of which desires to go it alone or at least achieve a high degree of territorial autonomy."[136] For Duchacek, territorial alienation of a group from the center not only leads to separatist feelings but also raises the "expectation of satisfaction in a new territorial community (an autonomous province or a sovereign state) that grants the people what the present territorial authority has refused or has proved unable to do."[137] The most usual and obvious reasons for a territorial group's discontent and search for a new territorial arrangement are "its sense of oppression, injustice, neglect . . . or simply a growing divergence of interests between the central government and the territorial groups."[138] Duchacek, however, agrees that when a secessionist movement breaks out, it usually acquires all the emotional trappings of nationalism.[139]

Although political scientists and interdisciplinary experts on nationalism have considered the issue of secession at length, economists have largely ignored the subject. One article published in 1995 puzzled over this: "Although freer trade and modern technology bind economies ever closer, political sentiments seem to be heading in the opposite direction."[140] Some twenty new countries were established between 1990 and 1994, and the desire for political independence clearly extended beyond the collapse of communism. Yet, there were no studies that could suggest what the economically optimal size for a country might be. For the international system, the question was: Does it make better economic sense to have a few large countries or a proliferation of smaller ones?

Two Italian economists made an attempt to answer these questions. Alberto Alesina and Enrico Spolaore argued that people who live close to each other generally have similar views about the role of government and the way it should spend its monies.[141] In larger countries, regions remote from each other display different preferences about government. Especially in democratic systems where majorities rule, the permanent minorities located on the peripheries have reason to establish their own governments. Thus "As the world becomes more democratic, so it splits into smaller political jurisdictions; in fact, from the perspective of overall economic efficiency, into too many small countries."[142]

Alesina and Spolaore contended that not only the global democratization trend but also international economic integration offered incentives to regions in existing states to seek secession. In the early years of GATT (the General Agreement on Trades and Tariffs) when trade barriers between countries were still high, it made economic sense for a region to remain in a large country with its large market. But with the World Trade Organization (WTO) regime created in 1995 after the successful completion of the Uruguay Round providing for freer trade, smaller regions could hope to become both politically independent and economically interdependent. The single

European market provides incentives for the Catalans in Spain, the Scots in Great Britain, and the Northern League in Italy to demand greater political autonomy. In Chapter 5 we describe the collapse of the USSR and the creation of fifteen new states—some very small—in its place. That these small states were a viable option at all is at least partially due to the existence of a world trade system that they could enter. As we also see in Chapter 6, Quebec's secession bid from Canada is predicated on its joining NAFTA immediately after independence. The Italian economists' conclusion is, therefore, that political democratization and economic globalization are likely to produce more rather than fewer independent countries. We may add that the wave of nationalism and secessionism that jarred international politics in the early 1990s was partially the product of such economic calculus.

A similar conclusion has also been reached by economist Gary Becker. Pointing out that the economic cost of independence has been significantly lowered by the rapid growth in international trade in the post–World War II period (between 5 percent and 10 percent per year), Becker contends that the economic prosperity of states is no longer dependent on having a large domestic economy. Rather, in today's international economy, small nations have four distinct advantages: First, for reasons of economic efficiency and in order to compete internationally for markets, a small nation, by concentrating on only a few products and services, often comes to specialize in niches that are too small for large nations to fill; second, small economies are more homogeneous and therefore less likely to be victims of internal clashes among special interests; third, the goods and services generated by a small nation tend to be less exposed to trade quotas and other restrictions because their volume and amount are usually not enough to affect producers in large countries; finally, a smaller nation is more likely to be admitted as a member into economic blocs and alliances, such as the European Union, because its products do not pose a competitive threat to existing members.[143]

Becker goes on to argue that the success stories of small economic entities such as Hong Kong, Singapore, Monaco, and Mauritius have provided encouragement to ethnonationalists and secessionists in many parts of the world. "Many of these groups concluded that they can do better economically by becoming separate nations and concentrating on producing specialized goods and services for the world economy."[144] As proof of this tendency, Becker offers the example of the Czech Republic where, after its split from Slovakia, economic growth has been rapid, unemployment significantly reduced, and exports increasingly reoriented toward the West. Similarly, challenging the assertion of many economists that French-speaking Quebec will decline economically if it secedes from the rest of Canada, Becker points out that this reasoning ignores or discounts the role international trade plays in economic success. His own prediction, therefore, is that "After perhaps a severe adjustment period, Quebec could find a prosperous place in the world economy by trading with Canada, the U.S., and Mexico as well as the rest of Latin America."[145]

Becker concludes that rather than being a handicap, small size can actually be advantageous to a nation in international economic competition. This realization is the source of the current proliferation of ethnonationalist and secessionist demands: "Smallness can be an asset in the division of labor in the modern world, where economies are linked through international transactions. Nationalism is merely riding the crest of world trade to forge new nations."[146]

Many of the findings reported in this chapter lead to the inescapable conclusion that more ethnonationalist groups will appear in the world and that a significant number of them will demand secession from existing states. To shed light on this tendency, let us return one final time to results from Gurr's study. His analysis brings out differences in the means employed by various types of minorities to achieve their demands. Gurr describes some of these differences:

> Most ethnonationalists and indigenous peoples aim at what we have called "exit" or greater autonomy from the state. The objective that typifies the other three categories of groups is "voice" or pressure to accommodate their interests within existing political systems. Among ethnoclasses, most of whom live in the western democracies and Latin America, nonviolent protest has consistently been the most common tactic.[147]

Nonviolent protest was the most common form of communal action in Western democracies, Latin America, Eastern Europe, and the former Soviet Union. Violence and rebellion became especially typical of communal contenders in the least developed states of Africa and several Middle East and Asian countries. An upsurge in violence by militant Muslim sects in non–Muslim ruled states had also become a trend by the end of the 1980s.

Based on the data set provided by the minorities at risk project, the profile of contemporary ethnonationalist movements displays a general lack of congruence between a group's status in society and its demands for separation. It has not been "the wretched of the earth," to employ Frantz Fanon's term, that have by and large made independence claims but rather large, relatively privileged, regionally based peoples that remain rueful over the loss of political autonomy they once enjoyed. Ethnonationalist leaders of peoples with cultural rather than economic claims— Catalans, northern Italians, Québécois—would also contend that being deprived of the historical right to determine their own affairs is as strong a moral basis for seeking independence as being systematically discriminated against, suffering persistent differentials, and undergoing disproportionate demographic and ecological stress. The means used to attain self-determination also affect the moral standing of an ethnonationalist movement, and these peoples would stress how their commitment to peaceful, constitutional change elevates the morality of their case further. On the other hand, in non–Western countries we frequently encounter the case of a group that has exhausted all peaceful means of reaching political accommodation with a dominant group. Such a group has inherently stronger moral claims than one that immediately turns to terrorist tactics.

On their own, none of the theoretical approaches can explain all cases of ethnic political mobilization. Our discussion has revealed the importance of diverse factors— cultural, economic, political—for the politicization of ethnicity. Attempting to combine these factors in one explanatory framework may allow for a better understanding of the reasons for the politicization of various ethnic groups in the world today.

ETHNIC CONFLICT AND INTERNATIONAL RELATIONS

Despite being a prominent feature of the global political landscape for nearly fifty years, ethnic movements and conflicts had not been given much attention by international relations specialists until recently. Reasons for this neglect are many. Myron Weiner pointed out that in the post–World War II years, scholars of international relations viewed "ethnicity and religious fundamentalism either as epiphenomena, that is, expressions of more fundamental group identities such as class, or as anachronisms which will soon disappear in an age of economic interdependence and secularization."[148] The paradigm assumed that increasing advancement in communications and transportation, industrialization, and urbanization would engender the assimilation of minority groups within the dominant culture, thereby creating a common identity uniting all inhabitants of the state and eliminating the sources of ethnic conflict. Ethnic identity and conflict was thus seen as nothing more than an "ephemeral nuisance."

The flaws of the modernization paradigm were not the only impediment to appreciating the scope of ethnic conflict. During the early 1970s, those international relations scholars interested in examining "ethnic revival" organized their research differently from development theorists. They focused on issues such as the impact of international capitalism on politics (dependency theorists), the impact of class structure on society (neo–Marxist theories), and the decision-making process within the governing elite structure ("policy studies" or domestic structures approach). As a result, "the roles of ethnicity and culture were relegated to the status of epiphenomena."[149]

Furthermore, operating within the context of the East-West ideological battle, both Western liberals and Soviet Marxists tended to be dismissive about the power of ethnic sentiments in the contemporary world. Ryan noted this: "The liberal has been wary of viewing the world in terms of cultural groups because it seems to contradict his emphasis on the individual. . . . The Marxist has tended to see nationalism as nothing more than an unfortunate diversion on the road to a communist society."[150] Ideological predispositions, therefore, resulted in the neglect of scholarly research on issues of ethnicity and nationalism.

A further reason for the relegation of ethnicity and ethnic conflict to the periphery of mainstream international relations was that until recently international relations experts were mainly concerned with other issues that were considered to be more urgent: East–West and North–South disputes, interstate conflicts, disarmament and strategic issues, revolutions and anticolonial liberation movements, and issues pertaining to a global economy.[151] Also, the preoccupation with the issue of integration between states and the emphasis on what were viewed as far weightier processes of functionalism, federalism, and supranationalism prevented attention from being "given to the possibility that the state could *break up from within* because of ethnic particularism."[152] As a result, scholars of international relations said little about the subject of ethnic conflicts, secessionist movements, or refugee and migration flows.

Finally, epistemological and methodological divergence between the English and American traditions in international relations studies was also partly responsible for the neglect of ethnicity and nationalism. Although American scholars focused their attention on issues of integration and interdependence, the "English tradition" made interstate relations the main focus of the discipline, leaving intrastate problems to be studied by comparative or area studies political research. Ryan noted the problem with such a division: "Many ethnic conflicts do not fit easily into either category and so defy neat systems of classifications."[153]

Due to the explosion of ethnic movements and conflicts in the post–bipolar period, international relations scholars have now confronted these phenomena. Because ethnic conflict is ultimately connected with issues of war and peace, human rights, democratization, and overall global order, it has now become a core subject of study and analysis within the international relations discipline. As we see it, the resurgence of ethnic conflict poses three interrelated sets of "problems" or "dilemmas" before the international community. Each of these problems or dilemmas is discussed in detail in the next three chapters. Here, it will suffice to provide a brief introduction to these problems so that our logic in organizing the next three chapters and the case studies that follow them will be easily understandable.

First, the resurgence of ethnic conflict raises certain fundamental normative questions before the international community. The international community, it must be remembered, is primarily (but not exclusively) a community of states and, therefore, the international normative regime—the legal rules and regulations of the international system that guide membership and interaction in that system—reflect this fundamental fact. As such, this is not a problem. It becomes a problem when we consider that more and more nonstate actors (such as ethnic groups) are seeking to enter the international community of states as members but that there does not exist any standard international legal criteria for deciding who could be admitted and who could not be. In the absence of such criteria, the international community has generally taken a pro-state stand in ethnic conflicts; that is, it has supported the states and their governments against the ethnic insurgents. In those rare cases, such as the conferral of state status on the Palestine Liberation Organization (PLO), where the international community went against the interest of one of its member states and supported the state's domestic ethnic challengers, political considerations—and not any uniform legal criteria—guided such decisions. But this pro-state bias of existing international norms, if applied uniformly, can become unfair especially to those ethnosecessionists whose reasons for desiring to separate from an existing state are justified from a moral standpoint. This is the crux of the normative dilemmas associated with ethnosecessionist movements that the international community will have to address soon as more and more claimants to statehood appear before it. Already, the way the collapse of the USSR, Yugoslavia, and Czechoslovakia was handled by the international community has fueled rather than dampened the self-determination aspirations and expectations of many other ethnic nationalities. International relations scholars have, therefore, started to develop some answers to this normative puzzle. We explore these issues—particularly the morality of secession—in detail in Chapter 2.

Second, the resurgence of ethnic and secessionist conflicts presents certain practical problems or challenges before the international community, especially those connected to the broader issues of war and peace and the maintenance of international stability and order. Whether these challenges take the form of ethnic terrorism, outside intervention in ethnic conflicts, or an ever-growing global refugee crisis, the international community must devise ways to deal with them. In Chapter 3, therefore, we try to explain the various ways through which ethnic conflicts become international problems, the causes and consequences of such internationalization, and the ways of dealing with these consequences. Again, an ever-growing scholarly literature bears testimony to the importance given to these issues by international relations specialists.

Finally, influenced by the first two sets of problems, a debate has developed within the international relations discipline regarding the question of finding "solutions" to ethnic and secessionist conflicts. As more and more ethnosecessionist conflicts break upon the world political scene, this issue will acquire a degree of urgency because not all claims to statehood can be accommodated, nor can the destructive and evil effects of these conflicts be tolerated. So mechanisms must be devised whereby some of these conflicts can be resolved within the current state structures but in ways that they do not reemerge anytime soon. Because disputants are hardly likely by themselves to be the agents of such conflict resolution, international third-party actions are likely to be of importance in the foreseeable future. In Chapter 4, we devote attention to this issue in some detail.

DISCUSSION QUESTIONS

1. Discuss the different manifestations of ethnic conflict in the world today. Are some more dangerous than others?
2. What are the main differences between a civic nation and ethnic nation? Why is the civic nation more conducive to building stable multiethnic societies?
3. Identify the main schools of thought regarding the formation and persistence of ethnic identity, and point out their central arguments. In your opinion, which school of thought can better predict the rise of ethnonationalism in the world today?
4. In what way are the direct theories of ethnic political mobilization different from the indirect theories? Which theoretical frameworks could be applied to explain why economically prosperous ethnic groups often demand regional autonomy or independence?
5. Although many ethnic groups in the contemporary period show signs of political mobilization, not all desire to secede from the state in which they are located. What factors determine why some ethnic groups desire secession and independence while others do not?

NOTES

1. William R. Keylor, *The Twentieth Century World: An International History.* (New York: Oxford University Press, 1996), p. 451.
2. Fen Osler Hampson and Brian S. Mandell, "Managing Regional Conflict: Security Cooperation and Third Party Mediators." *International Journal,* 45, 2, Spring 1990, p. 191.

3. "'New World Order' or Utopia? Prospects for Democratization after the Cold War," *In Brief...*, (Washington, DC: United States Institute of Peace), May 30, 1991, no page number.

4. While it is an imperfect and imprecise term, *fin-de-sièclism* can be used to connote a period in which societies search for identity and order at what they perceive to be a psychological caesura that is linked to the chronological one. Such usage can be found to depict turmoil in society in the late nineteenth century. Because of its depiction of a world in search of its real self, it seems preferable to the concept of the post–cold war world, which is both self-evident and a negative definition (what the world is not).

5. Milton J. Esman, *Ethnic Politics.* (Ithaca, NY: Cornell University Press, 1994), p. 2.

6. Stephen Ryan, *Ethnic Conflict and International Relations.* (Aldershot: Dartmouth, 1990), pp. x–xi.

7. Ray Taras, "Making Sense of Matrioshka Nationalism," in Ian Bremmer and Ray Taras, eds., *Nations and Politics in the Soviet Successor States.* (New York: Cambridge University Press, 1993), p. 516.

8. Ryan, *Ethnic Conflict and International Relations,* pp. x–xi.

9. Ted Robert Gurr and Barbara Harff, *Ethnic Conflict in World Politics.* (Boulder, CO: Westview Press, 1994), p. 13.

10. Esman, *Ethnic Politics,* p. 27.

11. For the primordialist approach, see Clifford Geertz, *Old Societies and New States: The Quest for Modernity in Asia and Africa.* (Glencoe, IL: Free Press, 1963); and Harold Isaacs, "Basic Group Identity: The Idols of the Tribe." *Ethnicity,* 1, 1974, pp. 15–42.

12. John Rex, "Ethnic Identity and the Nation State: The Political Sociology of Multi-Cultural Societies." *Social Identities,* 1, 1, 1995, pp. 24–25. See also, Judith Nagata, "In Defense of Ethnic Boundaries: The Changing Myths and Charters of Malay Identity," in Charles F. Keyes, ed., *Ethnic Change.* (Seattle, WA: University of Washington Press, 1981), p. 89.

13. See Anthony H. Richmond, "Migration, and Race Relations." *Ethnic and Racial Studies,* 1, January 1978, p. 60; and Anthony Smith, *Theories of Nationalism,* 2nd. ed. (New York: Holmes and Meier, 1983), p. 180. For a stimulating discussion on the role of food in the formation and, more importantly, the stereotyping of ethnic identity, see Uma Narayan, "Eating Cultures: Incorporation, Identity and Indian Food." *Social Identities,* 1, 1, 1995, pp. 63–86.

14. See, for example, Nathan Glazer and Daniel P. Moynihan, *Beyond the Melting Pot: The Negroes, Puerto Ricans, Jews, Italians and Irish of New York.* (Cambridge, MA: MIT and Harvard University Presses, 1963), pp. 13–14.

15. Rex, "Ethnic Identity and the Nation-State," p. 25.

16. Timothy M. Frye, "Ethnicity, Sovereignty and Transitions from Non-Democratic Rule." *Journal of International Affairs,* 45, 2, Winter 1992, p. 602.

17. See Anthony D. Smith, "The Ethnic Sources of Nationalism." *Survival,* 35, 1, Spring 1993, pp. 50–51.

18. *Ibid.,* p. 52.

19. *Ibid.,* p. 53.

20. *Ibid.*

21. *Ibid.,* pp. 53–55.

22. Peter Jackson and Jan Penrose, "Introduction: Placing 'Race' and Nation," in Jackson and Penrose, eds., *Constructions of Race, Place and Nation.* (London: UCL Press, 1993), p. 1. See also Jan Penrose, "Reification in the Name of Change: The Impact of Nationalism on Social Constructions of Nations, People and Place in Scotland and the United Kingdom," in Jackson and Penrose, eds., *Constructions of Race, Place and Nation,* p. 28.

23. John Stone, "Race, Ethnicity, and the Weberian Legacy." *American Behavioral Scientist*, 38, 3, January 1995, p. 396.
24. *Ibid.*
25. Charles F. Keyes, "The Dialectics of Ethnic Change," in Keyes, ed., *Ethnic Change*, p. 5.
26. *Ibid.*, p. 5.
27. *Ibid.*, p. 6.
28. *Ibid.*, p. 7.
29. *Ibid.*
30. *Ibid.*, p. 9.
31. *Ibid.*
32. *Ibid.*, p. 11.
33. Urmila Phadnis, *Ethnicity and Nation-building in South Asia,* (Newbury Park, CA: Sage, 1990), p. 16.
34. Paul R. Brass, *Ethnicity and Nationalism: Theory and Comparison.* (Newbury Park, CA: Sage, 1991), p. 8.
35. See Geertz, *Old Societies and New States;* Isaacs, "Basic Group Identity," pp. 15–42; Raoul Naroll, "On Ethnic Unit Classification," *Current Anthropology* 5, October 1964, pp. 283–312; Milton Gordon, *Assimilation in American Life: The Role of Race, Religion and National Origins.* (New York: Oxford University Press, 1964); J. Clyde Mitchell, *The Kalela Dance: Aspects of Social Relationships among Urban Africans of Northern Rhodesia.* (Manchester: Manchester University Press, 1956); A.L. Epstein, *Politics in an Urban African Community.* (Manchester: Manchester University Press, 1958); and J.S. Furnivall, *Netherlands India: A Study of Plural Economy.* (New York: Macmillan, 1944).
36. For details of Kuper's criticism of primordialism, see Leo Kuper, "Plural Societies: Perspectives and Problems," in Leo Kuper and M.G. Smith, eds., *Pluralism in Africa.* (Berkeley, CA: University of California Press, 1969), pp. 7–26.
37. See Frederick Barth, *Ethnic Groups and Boundaries: The Social Organization of Cultural Difference.* (London: Allen and Unwin, 1970); and Nathan Glazer and Daniel P. Moynihan, eds., *Ethnicity: Theory and Experience.* (Cambridge, MA: Harvard University Press, 1975).
38. Nagata, "In Defense of Ethnic Boundaries," p. 90.
39. Esman, *Ethnic Politics,* p. 6.
40. *Ibid.*, p. 7.
41. *Ibid.*, p. 8.
42. *Ibid.*, p. 9.
43. Jack C. Plano and Roy Olton, *The International Relations Dictionary.* 4th ed. (Santa Barbara, CA: ABC-Clio, 1988), p. 366.
44. John T. Rourke, *International Politics on the World Stage,* 3rd ed. (Guilford, CT: Dushkin, 1991), p. 142.
45. As far as Europe is concerned, nation building preceded state building. Historically in Europe, the formation of the ethnic nation was followed by the formation of the civic nation, which in turn led to the creation of modern states. But in Asia and Africa, state building generally preceded attempts at nation building. In Africa and Asia, colonization created states with artificial boundaries, without regard to ethnic enclaves and also without ascertaining the political aspirations of ethnic groups. Therefore, when anticolonial sentiments arose in these states and became instrumental in achieving political independence, such sentiments were more a function of colonial exploitation and dominance rather than expressions of the political will of nations. Hence, decolonization did not change state boundaries in Asia and Africa to make them coincide with ethnic and national boundaries.

The result was the continuation of a state structure incorporating different tribal, ethnic, and national groups who found little to bind them together once independence was achieved and the common enemy (the colonial power) had departed. These states therefore were born with a lack of internal cohesion and with civil discord and regime instability, which made the task of nation-building very difficult.

46. Carlton J. H. Hayes, *The Historical Evolution of Modern Nationalism.* (New York: R.R. Smith, 1931), pp. 10–11.

47. Peter Alter, *Nationalism,* Translated by Stuart McKinnon-Evans. (London: Edward Arnold, 1989), p. 15.

48. *Ibid.,* p. 14.

49. *Ibid.,* p. 15.

50. *Ibid.*

51. *Ibid.,* p. 16.

52. Rourke, *International Politics on the World Stage,* pp. 142–143.

53. Ernst B. Haas, "What Is Nationalism And Why Should We Study It?" *International Organization,* 40, 3, Summer 1986, p. 709.

54. Benedict Anderson, *Imagined Communities: Reflections on the Origin and Spread of Nationalism.* (London: Verso Editions & NLB, 1983).

55. Dudley Seers, *The Political Economy of Nationalism.* (New York: Oxford University Press, 1979).

56. See Anthony D. Smith, *Nationalism in the Twentieth Century.* (New York: New York University Press, 1979); and *Theories of Nationalism.*

57. Ernest Gellner, *Nations and Nationalism.* (Ithaca, NY: Cornell University Press, 1983), p. 11.

58. For a detailed exposition of Kedourie's views on nationalism, see Elie Kedourie, *Nationalism,* 3rd ed. (London: Hutchinson, 1966).

59. Hans Kohn, *The Idea of Nationalism: A Study in its Origins and Background.* (New York: Macmillan, 1951), p. 8. See also, Kohn, *Nationalism: Its Meaning and History.* (Princeton, NJ: D. Van Nostrand, 1955), p. 9.

60. The emotional or sentimental nature of nationalism is also reflected in the writings of two other prominent experts on the subject, Carlton Hayes and Boyd Shafer. For details of their ideas on nationalism, see Carlton J. H. Hayes, *Essays on Nationalism.* (New York: Macmillan, 1928); and Boyd C. Shafer, *Nationalism: Myth and Reality.* (New York: Harcourt, Brace and World, 1955), and *Faces of Nationalism.* (New York: Harcourt, Brace, and Jovanovich, 1972).

61. Kohn, *The Idea of Nationalism,* p. 11.

62. See Smith, "The Ethnic Sources of Nationalism," p. 55; and Charles A. Kupchan, "Introduction: Nationalism Resurgent," in Kupchan, ed., *Nationalism and Nationalities in the New Europe.* (Ithaca, NY: Cornell University Press, 1995), p. 4.

63. Kupchan, "Introduction: Nationalism Resurgent," p. 4.

64. *Ibid.*

65. Esman, *Ethnic Politics,* p. 27.

66. *Ibid.*

67. *Ibid.,* p. 2.

68. We discuss the concept of national self-determination in detail in the next chapter.

69. Some of the major works that represent the modernization, development, and national integration paradigms are: Gabriel A. Almond and G. Bingham Powell, *Comparative Politics: A Developmental Approach.* (Boston, MA: Little, Brown, 1966); David Apter, *The Politics of Modernization.* (Chicago: University of Chicago Press, 1965); Gabriel A. Almond and Sidney Verba, *The Civic Culture,* (Princeton, NJ: Princeton University Press, 1963);

Gabriel A. Almond and James S. Coleman, eds., *The Politics of Developing Areas.* (Princeton, NJ: Princeton University Press, 1960); Lucian W. Pye, *Aspects of Political Development.* (Boston, MA: Little, Brown, 1966); Lucian W. Pye and Sidney Verba, eds., *Political Culture and Political Development.* (Princeton, NJ: Princeton University Press, 1965); Lucian W. Pye, ed., *Communications and Political Development.* (Princeton, NJ: Princeton University Press, 1963); Karl W. Deutsch, *Nationalism and Social Communication.* (Cambridge, MA: MIT Press, 1953); and Karl W. Deutsch and William Foltz, eds., *Nation-Building.* (New York: Atherton, 1963).

70. Alexis Heraclides, *The Self-determination of Minorities in International Politics.* (London: Frank Cass, 1991), p. 3.

71. Deutsch, *Nationalism and Social Communication,* pp. 86–130.

72. See, for example, Samuel P. Huntington, *Political Order in Changing Societies.* (New Haven, CT: Yale University Press, 1968); and Daniel Lerner, "Communications and the Prospects of Innovative Development," in Lerner and Wilbur Schramm, eds., *Communication and Change in the Developing Countries.* (Honolulu: East-West Center Press, 1967), pp. 305–317.

73. Saul Newman, "Does Modernization Breed Ethnic Political Conflict?" *World Politics,* 43, 3, April 1991, pp. 454–455. See also Geertz, *Old Societies and New States.*

74. See Stein Rokkan, *Citizens, Elections, Parties.* (New York: McKay, 1970).

75. Ryan, *Ethnic Conflict and International Relations.* p. 1.

76. For details of Furnivall's idea on plural societies, see J. S. Furnivall, *Netherlands India: A Study of Plural Economy.* (New York: Macmillan, 1944), pp. 446–469.

77. M. G. Smith, "Some Developments in the Analytic Study of Pluralism," in L. Kuper and Smith, eds., *Pluralism in Africa.* (Berkeley, CA: University of California Press, 1971), p. 442.

78. Ryan, *Ethnic Conflict and International Relations,* p. 16.

79. See Arend Lijphart, *Democracy in Plural Societies: A Comparative Exploration.* (New Haven, CT: Yale University Press, 1977); and *Democracies: Patterns of Majoritarian and Consensus Government in Twenty-One Countries.* (New Haven, CT: Yale University Press, 1984), especially pp. 23–30.

80. Ryan, *Ethnic Conflict and International Relations,* p. 17.

81. E. A. Nordlinger, *Conflict Regulation in Divided Societies.* (Cambridge, MA: Harvard Center for International Affairs, 1972), p. 87.

82. Ryan, *Ethnic Conflict and International Relations,* p. 17.

83. *Ibid.,* p. 18.

84. Donald Rothchild, "Hegemonic Exchange: An Alternative Model for Managing Conflict in Middle Africa," in D. L. Thompson and D. Ronen, eds., *Ethnicity, Politics and Development.* (Boulder, CO: Lynne Rienner, 1986), p. 72.

85. Ryan, *Ethnic Conflict and International Relations,* pp. 19–20.

86. *Ibid.,* p. 20.

87. Heraclides, *The Self-determination of Minorities in International Politics,* p. 6.

88. Some of the most important works in this area include: Ted Robert Gurr, *Why Men Rebel.* (Princeton, NJ: Princeton University Press, 1970); James C. Davis, "Toward a Theory of Revolution." *American Sociological Review,* 27, February 1962, pp. 5–19; Mancur Olson, *The Logic Of Collective Action.* (Cambridge, MA: Harvard University Press, 1965); Chalmers Johnson, *Revolutionary Change.* (Boston, MA: Little Brown, 1966); Huntington, *Political Order in Changing Societies;* Charles Tilly, *From Mobilization to Revolution.* (Reading, MA: Addison-Wesley, 1978); and Theda Skocpol, *States and Social Revolutions.* (Cambridge, NY: Cambridge University Press, 1979).

89. Donald M. Snow, *Distant Thunder.* (New York: St. Martin's, 1993), p. 60.

90. *Ibid.*
91. For details, see Gurr, *Why Men Rebel.*
92. See Ted Robert Gurr, *Minorities at Risk: A Global View of Ethnopolitical Conflicts.* (Washington, DC: United States Institute of Peace Press, 1993).
93. Heraclides, *The Self-determination of Minorities in International Politics,* p. 8.
94. See, for example, Walker Connor, "Nation-Building or Nation-Destroying?" *World Politics,* 24, 3, April 1972, pp. 319–355 and "The Politics of Ethnonationalism." *Journal of International Affairs,* 27, January 1973 pp. 1–21; Glazer and Moynihan, *Ethnicity: Theory and Experience;* Cynthia H. Enloe, *Ethnic Conflict and Political Development.* (Boston, MA: Little Brown, 1973); Donald L. Horowitz, *Ethnic Groups in Conflict.* (Berkeley and Los Angeles, CA: University of California Press, 1985); Anthony D. Smith, *The Ethnic Origins of Nations.* (Oxford: Basil Blackwell, 1986); and John A. Armstrong, *Nations Before Nationalism.* (Chapel Hill, NC: University of North Carolina Press, 1982).
95. Connor, "Nation-Building or Nation-Destroying?" p. 328. Similar views can be found in Connor, "The Politics of Ethnonationalism," pp. 1–21.
96. *Ibid.,* p. 329.
97. *Ibid.,* p. 331. Emphasis added.
98. *Ibid.,* emphasis in original. For a detailed exposition of Walker Connor's views on the doctrine of national self-determination, see Walker Connor, "Self-Determination: The New Phase." *World Politics,* 20, 1, October 1967, pp. 30–53.
99. *Ibid.,* pp. 331–332.
100. *Ibid.,* p. 332, emphasis added.
101. For details, see Anthony D. Smith, *The Ethnic Revival.* (Cambridge: Cambridge University Press, 1981).
102. Saul Newman, "Does Modernization Breed Ethnic Political Conflict?" p. 458.
103. *Ibid.,* pp. 458–459.
104. Charles Ragin, *The Comparative Method.* (Berkeley and Los Angeles, CA: University of California Press, 1987), p. 135.
105. See Michael Hechter, *Internal Colonialism: The Celtic Fringe in British National Development, 1536–1966.* (London: Routledge and Kegan Paul, 1975), p. 41.
106. See Michael Hechter and Margaret Levi, "The Comparative Analysis of Ethnoregional Movements." *Ethnic and Racial Studies,* 2, July 1979, p. 272.
107. For a detailed exposition of how the process of modernization affects core and peripheral ethnic groups under this perspective, see Michael Hannan, "The Dynamics of Ethnic Boundaries in Modern States," in Hannan and John Meyer, eds., *National Development and the World System: Educational, Economic and Political Change, 1950–1970.* (Chicago: University of Chicago Press, 1979), pp. 253–277; Francois Nielsen, "The Flemish Movement in Belgium after World War II: A Dynamic Analysis." *American Sociological Review,* 45, 1980, pp. 76–94; and "Toward a Theory of Ethnic Solidarity in Modern Societies." *American Sociological Review,* 50, 1985, pp. 133–149; and Charles C. Ragin, "Class, Status, and 'Reactive Ethnic Cleavages': The Social Bases of Political Regionalism." *American Sociological Review,* 42, 1977, pp. 438–450; and "Ethnic Political Mobilization: The Welsh Case." *American Sociological Review,* 44, 1979, pp. 619–635.
108. Heraclides, *The Self-determination of Minorities in International Politics,* p. 9.
109. See Brass, *Ethnicity and Nationalism.*
110. Heraclides, *The Self-determination of Minorities in International Politics,* p. 9.
111. *Ibid.*
112. *Ibid.,* pp. 8–9.

113. James G. Kellas, *The Politics of Nationalism and Ethnicity,* (New York: St Martin's Press, 1991) p. 6.
114. Frye, "Ethnicity, Sovereignty and Transitions from Non-Democratic Rule," pp. 602–603.
115. Gurr, *Minorities at Risk: A Global View of Ethnopolitical Conflicts.*
116. *Ibid.,* p. 10.
117. *Ibid.,* p. 42.
118. *Ibid.*
119. *Ibid.,* p. 58.
120. *Ibid.*
121. *Ibid.,* p. 59.
122. *Ibid.,* p. 76.
123. *Ibid.,* p. 79.
124. *Ibid.,* p. 86.
125. As another predisposing factor for a group to rebel, Gurr adds the extent of a group's collective disadvantage (that is, differentials, discrimination, and stress) compared to other groups. In identifying this reason (p. 126), he appears to ignore the results of his disaggregated analysis of the respective impact of differentials, discrimination, and stress provided earlier in *Minorities at Risk.* Furthermore, the framework for explaining ethnopolitical violence depicted in Ted Robert Gurr and Barbara Harff, *Ethnic Conflict in World Politics.* p. 86, Figure 5.1, seems in some parts inconsistent with the framework outlined in *Minorities at Risk.*
126. Heraclides, *The Self-determination of Minorities in International Politics,* p. 19.
127. Horowitz, *Ethnic Groups in Conflict,* p. 259.
128. *Ibid.,* p. 236.
129. *Ibid.,* p. 259.
130. Ralph R. Premdas, "Secessionist Movements in Comparative Perspective," in Premdas, S. W. R. de A. Samarasinghe, and Alan B. Anderson, eds., *Secessionist Movements in Comparative Perspective.* (New York: St. Martin's Press, 1990), p. 22.
131. *Ibid.*
132. *Ibid.*
133. *Ibid.,* pp. 22–23.
134. Anthony H. Birch, *Nationalism and National Integration.* (London: Unwin Hyman, 1989), p. 69.
135. *Ibid.* See also Anthony H. Birch, "Minority Nationalist Movements and Theories of Political Integration." *World Politics,* 30, 3, April 1978, pp. 325–344.
136. Ivo D. Duchacek, *Comparative Federalism: The Territorial Dimension of Politics.* (Lanham, MD: University Press of America, 1987), p. 67.
137. *Ibid.*
138. *Ibid.*
139. For details of Duchacek's ideas on secessionist movements, see also Ivo D. Duchacek, "Antagonistic Cooperation: Territorial and Ethnic Communities." *Publius,* 7, 4, 1977, pp. 3–29; and "Federalist Responses to Ethnic Demands: An Overview," in Daniel J. Elazar, ed., *Federalism and Political Integration.* (Lanham, MD: University Press of America, 1984), pp. 59–71.
140. "A Wealth of Nations." *The Economist,* April 29, 1995, p. 90.
141. Alberto Alesina and Enrico Spolaore, "On the Number and Size of Nations." (Cambridge, MA: National Bureau of Economic Research, Working Paper No. 5050, March 1995). Cited in "A Wealth of Nations," p. 90.
142. "A Wealth of Nations," p. 90.

143. Gary S. Becker, "Why So Many Mice are Roaring." *Business Week,* November 7, 1994, p. 20.
144. *Ibid.*
145. *Ibid.*
146. *Ibid.*
147. Gurr, *Minorities at Risk,* p. 115.
148. Myron Weiner, "Peoples and States in a New Ethnic Order?" *Third World Quarterly,* 13, 2, 1992, p. 317.
149. David Brown, "Ethnic Revival: Perspectives on State and Society." *Third World Quarterly,* 11, 4, October 1989, p. 2.
150. Ryan, *Ethnic Conflict and International Relations,* p. xix.
151. See Weiner, "Peoples and States In a New Ethnic Order?" p. 317; and Heraclides, *The Self-determination of Minorities in International Politics,* p. xv.
152. Ryan, *Ethnic Conflict and International Relations,* p. xxi. Emphasis added.
153. *Ibid.*

chapter 2

Ethnic Conflict and International Norms

INTRODUCTION

One of the areas of recent scholarship on ethnic conflict in international relations is the study of the interrelationship between universally recognized norms of behavior within the international system—the so-called *international normative regime*—and ethnonationalist and secessionist movements. When Woodrow Wilson sought international acceptance in 1918 of his Fourteen Points, several of which concerned the exercise of the right of self-determination, his intention was the adoption of that principle as an international norm. When Bill Clinton signed a treaty in 1996 banning the testing of nuclear weapons, he explicitly referred to the renunciation of testing as part of the international normative regime. The international normative regime consists, then, of the legal and political principles that govern the interstate system and membership in that system.

In this chapter, we examine international norms that govern the outbreak of ethnic conflicts. We point out that although the international system is anchored by the principles of national self-determination and the nation-state, the international normative regime is biased against ethnonationalists and secessionists, who invoke these same principles to justify their causes. We consider whether, in the face of a proliferation of ethnic conflicts, the international normative framework is reformable so as to accommodate legitimate ethnic demands. In the second part of the chapter, we analyze the debate surrounding the morality of secessionist movements. We identify the moral grounds that are advanced for justifying a group's right to secede from an existing state and to form a separate one. We link this discussion to the prevailing international system that is largely hostile to change, however morally justified it may be.

INTERNATIONAL NORMS AFFECTING ETHNONATIONALISM

Ethnonationalists may or may not be secessionists. As William Safran has shown, there are many nonseparatist options available to accommodate ethnonationalist demands: corporatist arrangements, communalism, multiculturalism, ethnic cooptation, affirmative action.[1] For many ethnonationalists, however, the jackpot is separation and independent statehood rather than the above "satisficing" strategies. We can call such movements aiming at statehood *ethnosecessionist.*

Ethnosecessionists are confronted by two fundamental principles of the international system. These principles are: (1) the doctrine of state sovereignty and (2) the concept of self-determination. Whereas existing states invoke the first doctrine to justify their survival as a unified state, ethnonationalists seeking secession and independence refer to the second principle to justify their case for statehood.[2]

The Doctrine of Sovereignty

The current international system comprised of sovereign states came into existence after the Peace of Westphalia in 1648, an agreement that ended the Thirty Years' War in Europe and marked the breakup of medieval Christiandom. At first this state system was confined to Europe. The main principle on which the Westphalian system rested was *sovereignty.* According to Alan James, sovereignty "is a legal, absolute, and unitary condition."[3] It is legal in that under international law a sovereign state is not subordinate to any other state. Sovereignty is also absolute because it "is either present or absent" and "there is no intermediate category."[4] Sovereignty is, finally, unitary because a sovereign state exercises "supreme authority within its jurisdiction."[5]

Under the Westphalian system, sovereignty was closely equated with state power. The tendency of the Westphalian system was "to free the state from any form of limitation, both legal and moral, as well as an inclination to identify sovereignty with force."[6] At the same time, because each state enjoyed sovereign power within its borders, the Westphalian system repudiated the principle of hierarchy in interstate relations and replaced it with the principle of sovereign equality of states.[7]

Recently, some scholars have questioned the usefulness of treating sovereignty as the cornerstone of the international system. Nicholas Onuf raised the question starkly: "The cold war has come to an end; and so, perhaps, has the long period of sovereignty's conceptual stability." He contrasted how nineteenth-century nationalism fostered an identity between state and nation, with the state expected to be the champion of the national idea. But "In our own time nationalism tends to promote a contrary sensibility. The well-formed nation–state is a rarity. When states and nations fail to coincide, popular opinion favors the nation with a measure of majesty no longer available to the state. Increasingly the nation as people, not land, delimits the span of rule."[8]

This may be cold comfort to many an ethnosecessionist movement that has failed to attain sovereignty. There are three features of the still generally accepted principle of the sovereign equality of states that create trouble for secessionists. The first concerns international legal norms on the territorial sovereignty of states and the creation of new states. The second deals with the need for all units of the system to recognize each other as sovereign; obtaining recognition of sovereign statehood from established states has proved difficult for secessionists. The third feature of the inter-state system hindering ethnosecessionists "is the requirement of non-interference in the domestic affairs of other states."9 Let us consider each of these obstacles to seces-sion in turn.

State Formation and Territory.   In *The Law of Nations,* Brierly noted that a new state is formed "when a community acquires, with a reasonable probability of permanence, the essential characteristics of a state, namely an organized government, a defined ter-ritory, and such a degree of independence of control by any other state as to be capa-ble of conducting its own international relations."10 This can be achieved, as Heraclides pointed out, through "the granting of independence, by the acknowledg-ment of already existing *de facto* independence, from the dissolution of an empire or federation, by the merger of two or more units (former colonies or parts of empires) or states, by partition (the formation of two or more states by mutual consent) and by the seizure of independence."11

For those ethnonationalist movements whose goal is the creation of new sover-eign states, the most direct way to separate statehood is either through the partition of an existing state (by mutual consent) or through the forcible seizure of independence. As long as the creation of a separate state is the result of a mutually agreeable parti-tion, it is acceptable under international law. But with few exceptions, the interna-tional normative regime condemns the forcible seizure of independence. So, while it seems that international law provides for a simple way for ethnosecessionists to acquire separate statehood, in practice this is not so. The major difficulty is distin-guishing between forcible secession and mutually agreeable partition.

In medieval society with its vast empires, the main political objective was, as Mayall put it, to have power over people. But with the emergence of the Westphalian international system based on the principle of state sovereignty, territory or land became "the ultimate object of political life."12 In this system, the value that sovereign states cannot sacrifice is their political independence. In practice, this means that states cannot surrender their territorial integrity except under special circumstances.13 Therefore hardly any existing sovereign state would acquiesce to loss of territory to ethnonationalists because to do so would violate a basic condition of state sover-eignty—the territorial integrity of states.

Along with this practical difficulty, international legal principles pertaining to the acquisition of territorial sovereignty—the exercise of authority over a piece of terri-tory in a way that demonstrates the fullest right to that territory—is stacked against ethnosecessionists. International law identifies five principal ways of acquiring sover-eignty over a territory: through occupation, prescription, cession, conquest, or accre-tion. Of these five, only physical occupation of territory as a means of acquiring terri-torial sovereignty is relevant to the case of secession.

Occupation generally means the acquisition of territory that is not already a part of another state. Titles to territory by occupation are now impossible, however, because the entire global landmass has been carved up into states. But international legal principles pertaining to territorial acquisition by occupation continue to be important "because the occupations of the past often give rise to the boundary disputes of the present."[14]

The law pertaining to title to territory through occupation has been set by the Permanent Court of International Justice under the League of Nations system. In the *Legal Status of Eastern Greenland* case (involving Norway and Denmark), the permanent court ruled that a claim to territorial sovereignty must be based on two elements: first, the claimant must demonstrate its intention and will to act as sovereign over the territory and, second, the claimant must show evidence of some actual exercise or display of sovereign authority in the territory.[15]

The first part of the test is not a major hurdle for ethnosecessionists because they demonstrate the intention and political will to act as sovereign over a territory they consider to be their homeland. The problematic aspect is the second part of the test. As the permanent court observed in the *Eastern Greenland* case, in the absence of any competing claim by another party, only a slight exercise of authority would be sufficient to grant title to territorial sovereignty.[16] However, barring exceptional circumstances, a territorial claim made by an ethnonationalist movement is unlikely to go unchallenged by the state. In such circumstances, the evidence of actual exercise of authority by ethnosecessionists over the claimed territory has to be substantial. This is unlikely because, compared to ethnosecessionists, an existing state has more power to demonstrate its sovereign authority over territory. It seems that the only way for ethnonationalists to pass this second test is to win a decisive military victory against the state, control and exercise real authority in the claimed territory, and do so for a considerable length of time. Such cases are extremely rare, and even with territorial seizures, there is no guarantee that statehood will result.

The Problem of Recognition.   Recognition of a state is the act by which another state acknowledges that the political entity in question possesses the attributes of statehood. Recognition confers an international legal personality on a state and allows it to join the family of nations with full rights, privileges, and duties. In their quest for separate statehood, ethnonationalists must obtain international recognition; otherwise they are a rogue state. International legal principles dealing with recognition can prove to be major obstacles to this quest.

Three politico-legal principles are used to determine the entities that are to be accorded recognition as sovereign states. The first involves *ideological criteria* that determine whether a new state or its government can pass a political eligibility test. In practice, recognition is dependent on whether a would-be state is likely to prove to be a friendly government to the recognizing party. For three decades after World War II, the United States refused to recognize the People's Republic of China. The reason was neither constitutive nor declarative (described below) but ideological—the refusal to recognize a communist government that seized power through revolution. Only Henry Kissinger's Realpolitik in the 1970s overcame the ideological blockage and extended recognition to communist leader Mao Zedong's government.

According to the *constitutive theory* of recognition, the act of recognition itself creates statehood and confers authority on a government. States acquire a legal personality in international law only through the act of recognition. The act of recognition is not only constitutive but reciprocal; that is, it creates rights and obligations of statehood where none existed before. The recognition of Poland and Czechoslovakia as independent states in 1918 offers a good example of the constitutive theory of recognition.

The constitutive approach leaves unclear the minimun threshhold needed to obtain statehood. How many states have to confer recognition for a state to acquire legal existence is, therefore, uncertain. Iceland was the first country to recognize officially the independence of the Baltic states in 1991, but this was meaningless until a host of other Western states did likewise. This can be a difficult obstacle for ethnosecessionists to overcome. The constitutive theory's inflexibility is an obstacle to breakaway ethnic groups. Thus Brierly noted that a strict application of the constitutive theory would signify "that an unrecognized state has neither rights nor duties in international law."[17] This is absurd because states like the Baltic ones did have a shaky but legal existence before they were widely recognized. The recognition requirement can frustrate ethnonationalists who are able to demonstrate all the other attributes of statehood. They can even win modern-day battles of Gettysburg and still be denied recognition.

Given the weaknesses in the constitutive theory of recognition, some international legal experts accept the view that the act of recognition is not a constitutive but a *declaratory act*. The declarative theory of recognition centers on the ability of a state or government to govern and control its population and territory, but this legalist approach is also fraught with difficulties. For example, how is "control" to be measured? The formal recognition of statehood "does not bring into legal existence a state which did not exist before."[18] Rather, the declaratory theory posits that a state may de facto exist prior to being recognized and if it does, then irrespective of whether it has been formally recognized by other states or not, "it has the right to be treated by them *as* a state."[19] The main purpose of recognition from the declaratory approach

> is to acknowledge as a fact something which has hitherto been uncertain, namely the independence of the body claiming to be a state, and to declare the recognizing state's readiness to accept the normal consequences of that fact, namely the usual courtesies of international intercourse.[20]

Although the declaratory approach regards recognition of states as a political act on the part of other states in the international system, in practice this question is often both "difficult and delicate, especially when part of an existing state is forcibly endeavoring to separate itself from the rest."[21] In the absence of fixed rules, recognition of the independence of a region in revolt while conflict is ongoing, as in Chechnya between 1994 and 1996, would be premature and regarded as unjustified intervention in the internal affairs of the other state.

On the other hand, the mere persistence of the old state in the struggle where ethnosecessionists are clearly winning is not sufficient cause for withholding recognition of the seceding new state.[22] Heraclides notes that "even though recognition is an optional act, if an entity bears the usual marks of statehood, in particular if there is *de facto* control of a territory and its inhabitants by an organized government, other states put themselves at risk legally if they choose to ignore the basic obligations of state relations."[23] But under "normal circumstances, the existence of a rebellion within a state is a domestic matter with which other states have no concern."[24]

There are two exceptional situations in which other states seek to avoid charges of taking sides in a conflict while recognizing political and military realities. Under international law, conferring the status of *insurgency* or the status of *belligerency* offers ethnosecessionists a "halfway house recognition" of their claims.[25] For Richard Falk, both these situations reflect an "international acknowledgment of the existence of an internal war."[26] The acknowledgment by the international community of a state of internal war also means that the international legal principles pertaining to warfare apply.[27]

Conferring insurgent status on a group involved in an internal war with the state, whether done tacitly or explicitly, is an indication that the recognizing state regards the insurgents as legal contestants, and not as mere lawbreakers. To be sure, it does not automatically "entail the legal burdens of a neutral—possibly the recognizing state is still free to assist the legal government, and would be illegally intervening if it materially assisted the insurgents."[28] Therefore, although it shields insurgents from being treated as mere lawbreakers, the granting of insurgent status in no way confers on the insurgents the status of a state.

In turn, to qualify for belligerent status, rebel groups must meet a number of criteria—a so-called factual test: First, an armed conflict must exist within a state; second, the rebels must physically occupy and govern over a substantial portion of national territory; third, the rebels must carry out hostilities in accordance with the laws of war and through an organized armed force operating under a clear chain of command; fourth, outside states must recognize the rebels as belligerents.[29]

But recognition of belligerency, too, does not translate into recognition of the breakaway group as a state. Conferring this status is "purely provisional" because "it puts both belligerent parties in the position of states; but only for the purposes and for the duration of the war."[30] At one level, the recognition of belligerency of the rebels by other states may be advantageous to the state facing the rebellion because this act automatically relieves the state "of responsibility for the acts of its own rebellious subjects towards other states."[31] At another level, however, "the granting of recognition of belligerency to rebels is a step often resented by the state to which they belong, and its judgment of the propriety of the recognition is likely to differ from that of the recognizing state."[32] Although provisional in nature, granting belligerency status does accord rebels a degree of international legitimacy. Hardly any state, faced with a movement that is trying to undermine its territorial integrity, would want any type of legitimacy to be conferred on such a movement, even if for the limited purposes and duration of the conflict.

As with title to territory, so too recognition—whether of full statehood or of the more circumscribed status of insurgency or belligerency—has proved to be a nearly insurmountable hurdle, designed by the international system, for ethnosecessionists to overcome.

Nonintervention and Nonuse of Force.   In an international system based on the principle of sovereign equality of states, where only states can claim a monopoly of jurisdiction within their borders and where this right is recognized by all states in the system, it is logical that states be allowed to exercise this right within their territory free of outside interference. To do otherwise would make sovereignty meaningless. Thus, the principle of nonintervention in the internal affairs of states "is one of the cardinal principles of international law and can be seen as complimentary to the non-use of force prohibition."[33] Because intervention implies the use of, or the threat to use, force, it violates the principle of territorial supremacy of states and thus comes into conflict with international law.

The duty of states not to intervene in the internal or external affairs of another state received recognition in Articles 1 and 3 of the draft *Declaration on the Rights and Duties of States* adopted in 1949 by the United Nations International Law Commission. In Article 2, paragraphs 4 and 7, the United Nations Charter also prohibited intervention by calling on all member states to refrain from threatening or using force against the territorial integrity or political independence of any state. International law allows for departures from this fundamental norm

> in exceptional circumstances, and for such reasons as defense, peace and security (in which case there is collective intervention by an IGO or by its members following a specific resolution), and in rare cases for humanitarian considerations, in particular in flagrant instances of institutionalized racism and violence against a majority, and in classical colonialism (there is also, in theory at least, the case of belligerency).[34]

Recently, more reasons have been found to justify international intervention. They range from pure realist (power) considerations such as "might makes right" and the need to protect oneself by such intervention, to internationally accepted justifications (consent given by the subject government; collapse of governing authority in the subject country; consensus in the international community), to pure globalist explanations such as conforming with universal principles or decisions taken by supranational authorities.[35] One study concluded that "In the short term, we are likely to witness continued attempts by the international community to 'chip away' at the sovereign autonomy of states."[36]

Nevertheless, nonintervention and nonuse of force remain fundamental principles of international law, and as a result, under a traditional interpretation of the law, ethnosecessionist movements do not have the legal right to seek external support, even from ethnic kin in neighboring states. For, sensu stricto, "non-intervention means non-interference against a state and not non-intervention in its support."[37] A sovereign independent state, therefore, has the right to seek support from any third state, but "third states cannot assist secessionists, for they would in effect be using force against the territorial integrity of an independent state."[38] Under traditional international law, "in relations with third states a lawful government is in a privileged position compared with the insurgents, at least until there has been recognition of belligerency."[39] The recognition of belligerency is extremely rare, however, is provisional in nature, and at best may create parity between the secessionists and the state.[40]

The normative principles of nonintervention and nonuse of force put secessionists at a great disadvantage in acquiring external support compared to the lawful government. The reason for this unfairness is transparent. Falk emphasized how in a system of states "governments have a mutual interest in their security of tenure," and therefore "the bias of the system against revolutionary challenge is a logical expression of the basic idea of sovereign states exercising exclusive control over territory."[41] As if these legal norms and Realpolitik factors were not enough, the world of mutual treaty obligations and strategic considerations have also contributed to the creation of an international system heavily biased against secessionists.

Self-Determination and Ethnosecessionist Movements

The Origins of the Principle.   Although it established the legal principle of sovereignty to govern interstate relations, the Westphalian system left unanswered the crucial question of where sovereignty lay in a state.[42] The dynastic principle of legitimacy was left intact, as was "the right of *rulers* to determine the sovereignty and form of government of 'their' territories."[43]

The rise of nationalism in the eighteenth century modified the original model. Under the impact of nationalism the dynastic principle of sovereignty was replaced by that of popular sovereignty, which meant that, in theory at least, "the question of government ought to be determined by the governed."[44] The idea of popular sovereignty emanated from the principle of self-determination, which proclaimed that "government should be based on the will of the people, not on that of the monarch, and people not content with the government of the country to which they belong should be able to secede and organize themselves as they wish."[45]

The principle of self-determination subsequently coalesced with the idea of nationalism to give rise to the principle of *national self-determination* where a people, collectively, because they formed a nation, had a right to determine their own political fate. As Neuberger noted, in Europe in the nineteenth century

> The cry for national self-determination arose as a protest against national oppression, against empires which were "prisons of nations," and against "artificial" borders which cut across "natural" ethnocultural nations. Behind the principle of national self-determination was the vision of a new order in which political and ethnic borders would coincide and in which a system based on natural nation-states would assure international peace and stability.[46]

The impact of the idea of national self-determination was felt in Europe first and then elsewhere. In the first half of the nineteenth century, national liberation movements struggled to take power in Latin America while, in the second half, within the British Empire, Canada and Australia became sovereign dominions.

During the First World War, the principle of national self-determination was reaffirmed when President Wilson "led the United States into the war in order to make the world safe for democracy and national self-determination, while Lenin led the Soviet Union out of the war proclaiming the principle of nationalities as a new guiding principle for a socialist world order."[47] To both Wilson and Lenin, the principle of national self-determination conferred a right to people to decide their own fate, irrespective of existing state boundaries and political structures. National self-determination thus comprised two essential elements: the right to secession and the right to create independent states. But although Lenin enunciated the doctrine in the *Declaration on the Rights of the Peoples of Russia* to justify the October revolution, Wilson saw

> no gap between national self-determination and democracy (for what other purpose would a people claim the right to self-determination if not to rule themselves?) and between both these concepts and the idea of a self-policing system of collective security to replace the discredited system of international power politics (for if all legitimate national and democratic aspirations had been met would not all have a joint interest in deterring any disturbance of the peace?).[48]

Wilson's vision of giving the principle of national self-determination a universal significance collided with three obstacles, none of which it was able to overcome fully. First, a strict implementation of the principle of national self-determination required the breakup of existing states and needed the acquiescence of the major powers. Although the victorious powers in Europe, notably England and France, were willing to accept national self-determination in principle, they were unwilling to extend this as a right applicable in their own territory or possessions. The British government, for instance, was unwilling to grant full self-determination to the Irish, contending that it would violate state integrity, security, and sovereignty. Only in 1922, six years after the Easter Uprising in Dublin, was Britain prepared to recognize an emasculated Irish Free State, not fully sovereign and missing six Irish counties in the north.

A second problem that the principle of national self-determination was unable to resolve was the status of ethnic minorities. The minorities question was bound to emerge because, irrespective of how political maps were drawn, dissatisfied minority populations would emerge in each state. Additionally, because nationalities in Europe were scattered across many countries, strict implementation of the principle of national self-determination would have required either a great proliferation of new states or massive population migrations.

A third obstacle in the path of universalizing the principle of national self-determination was the desire of European powers to hold onto their colonies in Asia and Africa. Granting national self-determination to the various nationalities in the colonies went against the self-interest of European powers; they favored a narrower formulation of the principle so that national self-determination would be confined to Europe.[49]

After the First World War, then, the major powers used the language of national self-determination—that is, they accepted it as a principle rather than as a right—but redrew "the map of Europe so that it roughly reflected the nationality principle but without any fixed procedure and subject to considerations of practicality and political interests."[50] Thereafter, the principle of self-determination was not even included in the Covenant of the League of Nations. The net effect was that the principle was removed "from the realm of choice to that of nature or essence," and "the idea of an act of self-determination" was replaced by "the idea of national determinism."[51]

Until the end of the Second World War, national self-determination was not extended to colonial possessions, which created a transparent paradox. Britain and France, the major powers after 1918, were both seats of far-flung empires and "were also the countries in which liberal constitutionalism was most securely anchored and where national unification had proceeded furthest."[52] Initially, liberal imperialists tried to resolve this contradiction between the political values of liberal democracy and the idea of a nationally, and ultimately racially, defined imperial order by conceptually dividing the world between civilized powers and barbarians. But, as Mayall noted, "since liberal values were ultimately grounded in the Enlightenment discovery of universal human rights, this distinction could no longer be regarded as part of the natural order." Therefore "it was necessary to envisage a process whereby barbarian states could graduate into 'civilized' international society after a period of enlightened education and preparation for self-government."[53] This, then, was the classic "white man's burden" argument.

National Self-Determination Under the United Nations.   As a basic democratic principle of international life, national self-determination received considerable attention under the United Nations system that came into existence in 1945. To be sure, the right of self-determination was not included in the original draft of the charter as drawn up by the major powers at Dumbarton Oaks. But at the San Francisco Conference, under pressure from the Soviet delegation as well as from Latin America and the Arab world, "the right of self-determination was introduced into Article 1 (2) among the purposes of the United Nations and the section on economic and social cooperation (Article 55)."[54]

Self-determination is thus mentioned twice in the UN Charter. First, under Article 1 (2), the charter states that one of the main purposes of the United Nations is "To develop friendly relations among nations based on respect for the principle of equal rights and self-determination of peoples, and to take other appropriate measures to strengthen universal peace." Second, under Article 55, the charter lays down general social, economic, and human rights based on the principles enunciated in Article 1 (2).

Although self-determination was affirmed under the UN Charter, the issue remained contentious. As during the interwar period, it was unclear whether self-determination was to be applied as a "political principle" or as a "legal right." The UN preferred to treat self-determination as a political principle and went on to identify its role: (1) to expound on the basic principles of the charter, carried out primarily through UN resolutions (such as the Friendly Relations Declaration of 1970) and the advisory opinions of the International Court of Justice (such as on Namibia and Western Sahara); (2) to elaborate a system of universal human rights, enacted in 1966 in the form of the Covenants on Human Rights; and (3) to address the problem of colonialism, the decisive resolution being the Declaration on the Granting of Independence to Colonial Countries and Peoples in 1960. Although Resolution 1514 asserted that "all peoples have the right to self-determination," paragraph 6 drew a caveat: any disruption in "the national unity and the territorial integrity of a country is incompatible with the purposes and principles of the Charter of the United Nations."

If in theory the principle of self-determination extended to all people, in practice it could be exercised only by those under colonial rule. Heraclides pointed out that these people "can exercise this right once and for all and never again, without disrupting the territorial integrity of the colonial entity."[55] Lee Buchheit challenged the arbitrariness of the measure and asked

> why a colonial people wishing to cast off the domination of its governors has every moral and legal right to do so, but a manifestly indistinguishable minority which happens to find itself, pursuant to a paragraph in some medieval territorial settlement or through a fiat of the cartographers, annexed to an independent State must forever remain without the scope of the principle of self-determination.[56]

An unstated UN objective was, clearly, to freeze the political and territorial map of the world once the process of decolonization was over.[57] This objective was supported by the African and Asian successor states to the Western colonies and by other international and regional political organizations. For the UN and regional intergovernmental organizations (IGOs), the rationale for pursuing such a policy was obvious: "They would be placing themselves in an almost untenable position if they were to interpret self-determination in such a way as to invite or justify attacks on the unity and integrity of their own member states."[58] Similarly, for the African and Asian successor states, imperatives of sovereignty, territorial integrity, and national security prevented them from implementing self-determination along ethnic or cultural lines. So although many African and Asian nationalists had earlier argued for the necessity of revising "artificial boundaries" created by the Western colonial powers, they became ardent supporters of maintaining the territorial status quo once independence was achieved.

The UN's policy thus opposed noncolonial secessionists' efforts to break away from existing independent states. The Friendly Relations Declaration of 1970 categorically rejected and denounced any secessionist movement threatening the national unity and territorial integrity of an independent state. "Apart from colonies, and other similar non–self-governing territories, the right of self-determination is extended only to territories under occupation . . . and to *majorities* subjected to institutionalized racism (segregation, apartheid) but not *minorities* that are victims of similar policies."[59] In short, the basis of self-determination had become "territorial instead of ethnic or cultural" and in practice it "came to mean only *independence from Western colonial rule.*"[60]

Heraclides drew the connection between this circumscribed interpretation of self-determination and secession:

> Self-determination is defined in international law basically as anti-colonial self-determination ("external" aspect) and as majority rule ("internal"

aspect) as well as anti-racist (basically not racism against the majority) and anti-occupation self-determination—not as secessionist or "national" (ethnic) self-determination on the part of a numerical minority. As a consequence, recognition of a secessionist entity is not permissible; secession—contrary to partition—is not creative of statehood.[61]

Allen Buchanan, too, described how "Fears that secession would mean international anarchy led to attempts to dissociate endorsement of the right of self-determination from recognition of a right to secede."[62] In practice, this often meant disconnecting minority rights from a minority's political objectives.

The United Nations made an effort to update norms governing the status of minorities in the contemporary state system by enacting resolution 47/135 in December 1992. Titled "Declaration on the Rights of Persons Belonging to National or Ethnic, Religious and Linguistic Minorities," it set international minimum standards for securing minority rights, for example, recommending measures for native-tongue instruction for minorities and for promoting knowledge about minority cultures. But as with most UN resolutions, piously expressed objectives may have little bearing on actual rights provided by member states.[63] By ignoring the issue of minorities' possible desire to build their own state, the 1992 resolution reflected the persistence of the ethos of antisecessionism.

This historical background helps us understand further why the current international normative regime is biased against ethnosecessionists. The international legal framework of state formation and recognition, the norm of nonintervention, and the interpretation of the principle of self-determination all conspire against them. Furthermore, as Heraclides pointed out, "Constitutional law operates in a way almost equally adverse to secession as international law . . . only three post-war constitutions have recognized a right of secession: those of Burma between 1947 and 1974, Yugoslavia and the Soviet Union."[64]

Some exceptions to the international normative regime on secession can be identified, but they only serve to underscore the existing rules. Although most states support the contemporary interpretation of the right of self-determination, some, like Somalia, officially recognize secession to be part of this right. Some Islamic states have also done the same, especially in cases where Muslim groups are fighting for self-determination.[65] Similarly, India's recognition of Bangladesh's secession in 1971, the recognition given to Biafra by some African states in 1968, and the relatively quick recognition given to the Soviet and Yugoslav successor states by Western European countries are exceptions to the rule.

The exceptionalism of recognized secession is clearly seen when we realize how few cases of successful secession there are. Between 1945 and 1990, many separatist movements existed but only one successful secession—that of Bangladesh—occurred. It is true that in the early 1990s a number of successful secessions took place, but they were concentrated in communist regimes that were organized as federal systems and were in the throes of collapse. The line was drawn clearly so as to preclude legal recognition of other secessions even when they had won military victories, as in the case of Chechnya in Russia, Trans-Dniester (a Russian region) in Moldova, Abkhazia in Georgia, and Karabakh (an Armenian enclave) in Azerbaijan.

So the spate of successful secessions in the 1990s signaled a modification of the international normative regime on secession only to the degree that it formally recognized the consequences of a political bloc losing the cold war.

This section has argued that the international legal framework, norms, and actual state practice are stacked against ethnosecessionists. In the next section, we consider strong moral cases that ethnonationalist groups often muster for seceding from a country. We focus on the question of whether the international normative regime should exhibit sensitivity to particularly egregious cases of oppression of nationalities and minorities engendering ethnosecessionist sentiment, or whether it should follow established practice and give a blanket rejection to all ethnosecessionist claims, regardless of the circumstances involved.

THE GENERAL CASE FOR SECESSION: OBSOLESCENCE OF THE STATE

We can agree that the goal of secession pursued by a particular ethnonationalist movement is unlikely to find support in the international community. At the same time, it is also probable that the portrayal of minorities as being at-risk will evoke considerable international sympathy for such groups. The moral case for secession, separation, sovereignty, and statehood—describing not always mutually distinguishable phases of a group's drive for political independence—would seemingly be the stronger and the more worthy of international support the more at-risk a minority is, the more serious its grievances are, and the more realistic, flexible, and accommodating its demands have been over time.[66] We know that the outcome of struggles for secession and statehood is usually determined by armed struggle, but it is important to consider the competing moral worlds of separatist movements and the international system into which they wish to be admitted as independent states.

In recent years an important body of literature that addresses the topic of the morality of secession has emerged. Even moral philosophers have become alerted to the beleaguered status of ethnonationalist movements that are fighting the power of the existing state. This literature has framed the issue in terms of the morality of secession—a notion referring to the efforts by a national group to undo a political union as a prelude to pursuing its own sovereignty. To be sure, the grounds for leaving a union may not always be the same as those for claiming statehood. Claims of discrimination are more persuasive for the first case; claims of historical destiny for the second. Generally, however, groups seek to advance the most morally persuasive case justifying its actions and objectives.

Explicit demands for secession and statehood are partly a consequence of the notion of self-determination having become too ephemeral and arbitrary. Indeed, an indirect cause for the increase in ethnosecessionist movements is that self-determination, as evidenced in the legal framework described above, has become diluted and without practical implications. One writer traced the discrediting of the principle to Hitler's appropriation of it in the 1930s to justify Third Reich military aggression in defense of the purported national aspirations of Germans in Austria and Czechoslovakia. Thus "From its Wilsonian origins, the concept of self-determination has been more an instrument of international politics than a humanitarian principle associated with the law of nations."[67] Today the moral grounds for secession resemble the moral case behind self-determination in the colonial era.

As we have indicated above, the most compelling case for secession seems to concern a minority population that is at-risk, but both what a minority is and when it is at genuine risk are ambiguous notions. Heraclides claimed that

> there is no generally acceptable normative definition of ethnic or national minorities. On this basis many a state does not recognize the existence of distinct minority groups with corresponding minority rights, and of the minorities in question as they choose to define themselves. Another problem is that few states are prepared to regard such rights as "group rights."[68]

Taxonomies of at-risk groups have little practical significance, then, if states dispute the very existence of distinct minority groups on the territory they govern.

Legal and political scholars, too, disagree about the conditions under which a group would be entitled to exercise self-determination. In *The Power of Legitimacy Among Nations,* Thomas Franck advanced the broad principle of "entitlement to equality" as a basis for self-determination. In his view, "self-determination is a right applicable to any distinct region in which the inhabitants do not enjoy rights equal to those accorded all people in other parts of the same state."[69] Franck thus avoided the conceptual difficulties associated with defining minority groups and drew attention instead to the fundamental condition of inequality.

In his pioneering study, *Secession: The Legitimacy of Self-determination,* Buchheit examined whether self-determination constituted a natural right derived from natural law and representing a universal humanist principle. Studying such natural-rights theorists as Thomas Hobbes, Hugo Grotius, Emmerich von Vattel, and John Locke, the author concluded that "at no point in the evolution of natural rights thinking has the doctrine of a right to resistance on the part of individuals or groups of individuals been affirmed in an unqualified manner." He added: "Nor has this inherent right of resistance generally been viewed as including a group right of secession."[70]

Buchheit was persuaded, however, that a highly qualified right of secession had emerged under positive international law. The Congress of Vienna in 1815—in that part of its declaration promising national institutions for partioned Poland—as well as the post–World War I treaties of Versailles (in 1919 between the Allies and Germany), Trianon (in 1920 with Hungary), Sèvres (in 1920 with Turkey), and others with both defeated and emergent states—especially those parts specifying the obligations of states to their minorities—constituted empirical evidence of the right to self-determination. The 1960 UN Declaration on the Granting of Independence to Colonial Countries and Peoples and the Friendly Relations Declaration of 1970 reinstated the importance of self-determination as a desideratum, if not a legal right. Writing in 1978, Buchheit concluded that "the evolution of an international legal recognition of secessionist self-determination, although cautious and uniformly conservative, is nevertheless perceptible."[71]

The author then sought to integrate this limited opportunity structure for secessionists with normative-based models that could justify secession in the contemporary world. One was *remedial* secession—"a scheme by which, corresponding to the various degrees of oppression inflicted upon a particular group by its governing State, international law recognizes a continuum of remedies ranging from protection of individual rights, to minority rights, and ending with secession as the ultimate remedy."[72] A second model was the *parochialist,* which contends that "the only really inescapable requirement for a legitimate claim to self-determination is the existence of a genuine 'self' wanting to control its own political destiny."[73] The merits of the latter claim rested on two questions: (a) the extent to which a group is in fact a self capable of independent existence, and (b) the likelihood that a greater degree of harmony, or less social disruption, would follow if an existing union was dismantled to accommodate secession. Effects of a successful secession had to be measured both on the remaining state as well as on the general international order. Buchheit arrived at a persuasive calculus of the legitimacy of secession:

> Where the disruption factor is high, the claimant must make out an extraordinarily good case for its entitlement to self-determination. In other words, the higher the disruption factor, the more will be required by way of demonstrating selfness and future viability. Where little disruption is liable to ensue from the secession, or where the amount of current disruption outweighs the future risk, the community can afford to be less strict in its requirements for selfhood. . . . It may therefore accommodate to a greater extent the self-governing wishes of a particular people who cannot offer overwhelming proof of their racial, historical, or linguistic distinctness.[74]

Although it is a well-conceived formula, the fact that the international state system has generally exaggerated the degree of disruption that would result from even a small or inconsequential actor (let us say, Chechnya) being awarded statehood suggests that Buchheit's calculus has more scholastic than practical implications.

Recognizing the limitations on measuring the legitimacy or morality of separatism, Ruth Lapidoth's approach focused on bending the definition of *sovereignty.* "In a case of diffusion of power, both the central government and the regional or autonomous authorities could be the lawful bearer of a share of sovereignty, without necessarily leading to the disappearance or dismemberment of the state."[75] But here, too, merely broadening the meaning of *sovereignty* so that it might subsume disadvantaged groups seemed unlikely to satisfy the demands of ethnosecessionist movements.

An ambitious attempt to accommodate separatist demands by opening up new political space was made by Gidon Gottlieb. This legal scholar proposed the creation of "new space for nations," which entailed the need "to deconstruct the notion of sovereignty into two initial components: sovereignty as power over people and sovereignty as power over territory."[76] Alongside the established system of states, Gottlieb proposed setting up a system of non–territorially based nations and peoples. The extension of a legal personality to instrumentalities other than states would allow populations to enjoy a full range of political and civil rights without territorial definition. Thus, while being citizens of a sovereign state, people could simultaneously be inhabitants of a national home, including one that might stretch across existing state boundaries.

The idea of a national home regime was a solution to competing ethnic claims. It would be designed "to reconcile the integrity and sovereignty of states with the claims of national groups within them; to provide a context for common nationality links for nations that are divided by state boundaries; to address their yearning for national identity; and to do so without undermining the cohesion of multinational societies."[77] Such a functional approach to organizing peoples is utopian, as Gottlieb recognized. Mixing state entities with nonstate ones while not ordering them in a hierarchy seemed both good common sense and an unrealistic expectation. The case of failed UN blueprints for establishing a Jewish homeland within a Palestinian state after World War II indicates the overwhelming power of the traditional idea of sovereignty. On the other hand, imagining new structures of organizing peoples is not without merit in the face of intractable ethnic conflicts.

Mayall, an active contributor to the debate on self-determination, proposed the creation of a new transnational regime to cope with the proliferation of ethnosecessionist movements. Although designed for Europe, what Mayall termed the "Maastricht option" could have a broader application: "A form of European unification in which some powers are progressively transferred to the center while others are devolved to the regions could possibly provide a way by which minorities could gain autonomy without opting out of either the state or the open economy."[78] Again, the criticism of such a proposal is the unrealistic expectation it has of existing states being willing to cede powers to both higher and lower authorities.

An unassailable conclusion about the difficulties of achieving new political structures was drawn by Myron Weiner: "We end the twentieth century with the same unresolved issue with which the century began: how can we reconcile the claims for self-determination with the sovereign claims of states that their borders remain sacrosanct?" The author underscored the need to "find an imaginative solution to this problem by devising autonomy arrangements for ethnic groups that are short of state sovereignty, but which assure communities of greater self government within their own territories." He reviewed the traditional institutional arrangements employed for mitigating ethnic conflict:

> federalism, the principle of dividing powers of a state between a central government and its territorial subdivisions; cultural autonomy for communities with established historical relations within a territory; guarantees for the rights of national minorities including representation in elected bodies; condominium, the principle of two states sharing sovereignty over a territory; and guarantees of religious freedom.[79]

Although he suggested that these arrangements continued to provide the most viable solution to situations of ethnic conflict within a state, Weiner added that "Part of the solution lies in legitimizing the idea that modern states need not be centralized, that centralism has outlived its usefulness."[80] Both the state and the potential ethnosecessionists had to learn that the modern centralized state is not a goal in itself. Apart from pressure from below—exerted by minorities and regions—the centralized state is today also eroded by functional imperatives from above—adapting to an increasingly interdependent global economy and to new international regimes.

The same goals that separation might achieve for disaffected groups could equally be realized in a system of more responsible and responsive government. According to Amitai Etzioni, "Since the ultimate purpose of self-determination is not self-determination per se but responsive government, mutual tolerance might be what many countries and ethnic groups need most and first."[81] As an example of this approach, "The peoples of India desire and deserve a government that is responsive to them, but not necessarily a separatist one."[82] Indeed, Etzioni made the questionable claim that "Self-determination movements gained support because they fought against oppression, not because they fought for separatism."[83] The fact is that many national liberation movements had no alternative but to strive for both objectives simultaneously.

Excessive self-determination may work against democratization, however. "What meaning does self-determination have when miniscule countries are at the economic and military mercy, even whim, of larger states—states in whose government they have no representation at all?"[84] Similar logic has been used by radical third-world leaders such as Fidel Castro to cast a pale on the utility of liberal democracy and free enterprise. When the crucial decisions affecting smaller countries are taken by international lending institutions and multinational corporations located in the advanced states of the West, neither self-determination nor democracy really exist, according to the Cuban leader.

For Etzioni, "Only when secessionist movements seek to break out of empires— and only when those empires refuse to democratize—does self-determination deserve our support. Otherwise, democratic government and community building, not fragmentation, should be accorded the highest standing."[85] Liberals may sympathize with the motives and moral claims that separatist movements embody, but they insist that other ways are available to satisfy their demands short of recognizing their right of secession.

The stark choice available to state actors confronting outbreaks of secession is "abandoning the weather-beaten (anti-secessionist) normative ship and permitting unilateral independence at least for those who can achieve it on the ground," such as the case of Eritrea, or returning to the original normative regime so as to "shut the 'window of opportunity' for secessionist attempts."[86] Heraclides listed the dangers of following only the first alternative:

> the fear of indefinite divisibility (internal as well as regional), otherwise known as the domino effect; the issue of stranded majorities or trapped minorities; the non-viability of the rump state; the danger of giving birth to unviable entities that would be a burden internationally; the damage done to the will of the majority and the resultant ability of a minority to constantly blackmail the majority with secession; and, above all, the opening up of a Pandora's box of self-determination *ad absurdum.*[87]

We have considered the competing arguments addressing the question of whether the modern state is reaching obsolescence and, in consequence, if its breakup is justified. Let us turn to explicit moral grounds given for breaking up the state.

MORAL GROUNDS THAT JUSTIFY SECESSION

A leading contributor to the debate on the morality of secession has been political philosopher Allen Buchanan. Like political scientists, he recognizes that secession is a messy affair: "Secession can shatter old alliances, stimulate the forging of new ones, tip balances of power, create refugee populations, and disrupt international commerce. It can also result in great loss of human life."[88] It is identifying the contingent conditions that justify secession that Buchanan set out to discover.

Drawing on an obvious parallel, he noted that political union, like marriage, is a human creation designed to satisfy mutual needs, and it may be dismantled when such needs are not being served. As with divorce, one can conceive of "no-fault secession," where no injustice has been committed or wronged party found. The velvet divorce that put an end to the Czechoslovak federation in 1991 is as good an example as we have of a no-fault breakup of a political union.

What does the moral right to secede entail? For Buchanan, "To say that there is a moral right to secede is to say at least two things: (1) that it is morally permissible for those who have this right to secede, and (2) that others are morally obligated not to interfere with their seceding."[89] As an example, Lithuania's unilateral declarations of sovereignty and then independence in 1990–1991 were morally permissible, given how Lithuania was incorporated into the Soviet Union during World War II. It is worth considering the converse of these propositions. For even if some course of action, like secession, may be morally wrong, it does *not* follow that it is morally permissible to prohibit it by force. Thus Gorbachev was morally obliged not to dispatch black berets to quash the secessionist movement in Vilnius. Another example illustrates this logic. Even if Chechnya had weak moral claims to justify its pursuit of independence from the Russian Federation after 1991, this did not provide President Yeltsin with a moral carte blanche to use force—especially brutal and indiscriminate force against both civilians and soldiers—to prevent its breakaway, as he did from 1994 to 1996.

Buchanan chided liberal theorists for having little to say about secession. In theory, liberalism countenances secession because it holds that legitimate political authority rests on the consent of the governed. Where that consent is withdrawn, as through an ethnosecessionist movement, political authority becomes illegitimate. Buchanan attacked liberalism not only for being largely silent on secession but also on assigning low value to collective rights and the communal life of a group. Protecting a group's culture assures its individual members of a meaningful context for choice—a goal liberalism would readily embrace. It follows that opposition to political authority is justified for reasons not usually envisaged by classical liberalism. Moral grounds for opposing rulers include not merely violations of individual rights but also situations where a group is a victim of systematic discrimination.

Following Buchanan, let us identify twelve prosecession arguments based on moral claims. A first reason can be the defense of liberty. Just as it is impermissible to interfere with the individual's liberty so long as that individual's choice does no harm to others, so it may be immoral to interfere with a group's exercise of liberty where no one is harmed. Of course, the secession of a group is likely to disrupt the national life of a state and may have an adverse impact on the state's resources, territory, and fiscal base. Justifying separation (or revolution, for that matter) in the name of liberty has occurred regularly in world history, but usually the harm principle is studiously ignored by moralists who seek to legitimate political independence.

A second moral case is the promotion of diversity. Here, a circuitous logic is at work to justify separation. The best guarantor of cultural diversity is the creation of independent political units that then will freely interact with each other. Yet, in the real world, relations are invariably soured by parties to a divorce. France's relations with Algeria, Russia's with Lithuania, or Bangladesh's with Pakistan have been troubled ones after the separation decision. It is questionable whether promoting diversity under all circumstances is a good in itself. Fragmented states in Africa, for instance, might suffer more from diversity policies than from centripetal ones.

Third, in order to safeguard liberalism, it is in the interest of a liberal state to permit illiberal groups to secede. Tolerance for various communal lifestyles may, on occasion, backfire on the liberal state, as when militant religious sects take up arms. For its own protection, the state should grant illiberal groups the right to secede. Indeed, there may even be an obligation for such groups to part ways with a state whose philosophic principles they do not share. Needless to say, this is an esoteric moral ground for secession: Few ethnosecessionist movements would want to claim as their moral basis for secession the fact that they have no tolerance for a tolerant state.

A fourth case for secession evolves when the original goals for setting up a political union have become obsolete or irrelevant. Considerations that previously necessitated a common association of various groups no longer hold, and contracting parties are freed from the time-specific and delimited obligations imposed on them. Buchanan considered that states bound together by the Articles of Confederation so as to achieve independence from Britain were not necessarily bound to each other once this goal was achieved.

Related to this case, a fifth reason occurs when the right of secession is included in a constitution in order to attract new members, and at some later date a member reconsiders its entry decision and decides to avail itself of the constitutional provision for exit. Thus, a country that joins the European Union but becomes disenchanted with its political evolution would have moral and legal justification for leaving it. These two grounds are very uncommon and, in political practice, also unrealistic.

In contrast, the sixth reason for secession is widely used by breakaway ethnonationalist groups today who claim that they wish to escape discriminatory redistribution at the hands of the existing state. Where a national government does not operate for genuine mutual advantage and discriminates against or exploits certain groups, then this "in effect voids the state's claim to the territory in which the victims reside."[90] Inequalities, or differentials (to use Gurr's concept), may exist among groups, but only when ruling elites skew benefits to favor some and disadvantage others in unjustified ways does this powerful moral argument in favor of secession become irrefutable. Whether inequalities constitute injustice depends on whether the redistributive pattern is morally arbitrary. Cases exist where "if a stark disadvantage does not exist in the first place it has to be invented."[91] However, as Gurr found, it is relatively uncommon for the victims of unjust, systematic discrimination to assert ethnosecessionist demands, even though they would be morally justified in doing so. On the other hand, victims of perceived discrimination often couple this reason—

intended more for mass consumption than as a bargaining resource with the ruling elite—with cultural preservation rhetoric, described below.

A seventh case marries efficiency considerations to morality. Applying the principle of Pareto optimality, so long as one individual would be better off and everyone else no worse off if secession occurred, then such a course of action is justified. This logic is often embedded in peaceful breakups of political unions. Curiously, though, it is probably more often advanced to justify unification of separate units and of centralization of decision making.

The normative principle of nationalism consisting in the notion that every people is entitled to have its own state is a further reason given to justify secession. The belief that political boundaries should coincide with cultural ones is widespread but, in reality, it is an unviable proposition in most cases. Buchanan took aim at this argument and found it among the least plausible grounds to justify political divorce for it implies that multicultural, pluralist states are an inferior arrangement to ones that embody the pure nationalist principle. Although it is more valid to invoke this normative principle when a group's culture or its economic opportunities are under severe threat, generally to argue this case is to become vulnerable to Ernest Gellner's caustic critique: "It follows that a territorial political unit can only become ethnically homogeneous, in such cases, if it either kills, or expels, or assimilates all non-nationals."[92]

Instead of focusing on an often spurious national principle, the ninth possible case for secession directs attention to the preservation of a culture. Separatism can best enhance the flourishing of a culture and, in this way, separatism contributes to the lives of the individuals whose culture it is. Important ethnonationalist groups in the West—Basques, Flemish, Quebecers—often cite cultural factors as the main reason for wishing to have political sovereignty. Buchanan would not dispute such claims, but he did regard efforts made to prolong the life of a moribund culture or to prevent their members' assimilation into a more dynamic culture as unjustified. Thus, a culture may be pernicious to its own members and not worth saving, or it may both erode another culture *and* prevent assimilation of its members into the dominant one. Referring to Native North Americans, Buchanan wrote of the double jeopardy suffered when "those whose cultures have been most severely damaged also have been barred from genuine assimilation into the culture the whites brought."[93]

With regard to creating states in order to safeguard cultures, then, the most compelling counterargument is the practical consideration that there is simply not enough space and resources for every group to have its own territorial state. Just as persuasive a pragmatic consideration is that the domino effect may lead to no end of self-determination struggles. As Etzioni noted, "new ethnic 'selves' can be generated quite readily, drawing on fracture lines now barely noticeable. Subtle differences in geography, religion, culture, and loyalty can be fanned into new separatist movements, each seeking their own symbols and powers of statehood."[94]

The intrinsic value of protecting a culture, especially where it is under threat, led Buchanan to stipulate conditions where invoking the cultural-preservation principle in order to seek separation would be justified. The five conditions include that: (a) the culture really is in peril; (b) less-disruptive ways of preserving the culture do not exist;

(c) the imperiled culture meets minimal standards of justice itself (that is, it does not represent a Khmer Rouge–type culture bent on genocide); (d) secession should not lead to the building of an illiberal state; and (e) neither the extant state nor any third party has a historic claim to the seceding territory. Positing these as prerequisite conditions that justify separation on the grounds of cultural preservation severely limits the universe of morally sound ethnosecessionist claims.

Rather than self-preservation, self-defense can be given as a tenth reason to justify a separate state. Fear of extermination from either the existing state or a third party from whom the extant state cannot offer viable protection would be variants of the self-defense justification. Thus in the first case, whatever legitimate claims the state has to the seceding territory becomes outweighed by the claims of victims of genocidal policy. In the second case, Buchanan speculated about the moral grounds Jewish groups had to create a separate Jewish state in central European countries occupied by Germans who were perpetrating the holocaust. More recently, Palestinian Arabs who feel that neither Israel nor Jordan safeguard their interests are driven to build their own state.

An eleventh reason, as persuasive as the case of discriminatory injustice, concerns rectification of past injustices. As Buchanan emphasized, "The argument's power stems from the assumption that secession is simply the reappropriation, by the legitimate owners, of stolen property."[95] The argument for rectificatory justice subsumes the historical grievance claim that is grounded in a valid claim to territory: "The valid claim to territory that every sound justification for secession includes must be grounded in a historical grievance concerning the violation of a preexisting right to territory."[96] The best-known instances of historical grievance claims originated in the secret protocol of the August 1939 Ribbentrop–Molotov pact that led to the incorporation of the Baltic states and northern Romania into the USSR. Especially, as in this case, where groups can claim unjust loss of their territory, the right to secession is legitimate. We should be aware, however, of the sheer proliferation of historical grievances over loss of territory (see Table 2.1 [Part 2]), ranging from the random, colonially imposed borders of African and Asian states, to Austria's claim on South Tyrol, to Guatemala's belief of jurisdiction over Belize. Rectifying demonstrated cases of past injustices, especially illegitimate incorporation into a larger state or empire, is as compelling a moral argument for separation as there can be.

Finally, adopting the liberal basis for legitimate authority and political obligation—consent—a twelfth reason why secession can be justified is the disappearance of the fair play of the liberal system. Where fairness vanishes, consent can be withdrawn and political obligations cease. This logic is often used as an ancillary reason in favor of secession by an ethnonationalist movement claiming discrimination.

More parsimonious approaches to justifying secession than this twelve-point typology exist. Heraclides advanced a tautological one: "Potential separatist groups are all those that have the ability to generate a secessionist movement, that is, a legitimized secessionist organization that can engage the Center in a secessionist conflict, be it armed or peaceful."[97] This explanation is associated with the "heroic" argument: "That if a group is willing to suffer in order to gain its coveted goal of independence then it is such a movement."[98]

TABLE 2.1 (PART 1)   Secessionist and Irredentist Movements in the 1990s.

Secessionist Region	Existing State	Assistance From
Abkhazia	Georgia	Russia
Assam	India	
Basques	Spain	
Cabinda	Angola	Zaire
Catalonia	Spain	
Chechnya	Russia	
Corsica	France	
Crimea	Ukraine	Russia
East Timor	Indonesia	
Irian Jaya (West Papua)	Indonesia	
Karen	Myanmar	
Kashmir	India	Pakistan
Kosovo	Yugoslavia	Albania
Kurdistan	Iran, Iraq, Turkey	
Mindanao	Philippines	
Mohajir	Pakistan	India
Nagaland	India	China, Myanmar
Nagorno Karabagh	Azerbaijan	Armenia
Northern Italy	Italy	
Northern Kazakhstan	Kazakhstan	Russia
Ogaden	Ethiopia	Somalia
Ogun	Nigeria	
Oromo	Ethiopia	
Puerto Rico	U.S.	
Punjab	India	Pakistan
Quebec	Canada	
Scotland	Great Britain	
Serbs	Bosnia Herzegovina, Croatia	Yugoslavia
South Ossetia	Georgia	Russia
Southern Sudan	Sudan	
Tamils	Sri Lanka	
Tibet	China	
Trans-Dniester	Moldova	Russia
Western Sahara	Morocco	Algeria
Xinjiang	China	
Zanzibar	Tanzania	
Zulu	South Africa	

Heraclides spoke of "the two main pillars of the secessionist self-determination rationale—namely 'nationhood' and 'alien domination'" (approximating Buchheit's distinction between parochial and remedial secessionist claims). He was more persuaded by the rationale offered in the second case and went on to identify four prerequisites for accepting secession as a solution to intercommunal conflict: (1) the existence of a sizeable, distinct, and compact community (not necessarily nation or national minority) that overwhelmingly supports statehood and demonstrates it by recruitment

TABLE 2.1 (PART 2) Secessionist and Irredentist Movements in the 1990s.

Irredentist Claims On	Irredentist Claims By	Current Sovereignty
Aegean Sea Islands	Greece, Turkey	Turkey, Greece
Arunachal Pradesh	China	India
Baluchistan	Iran, Afghanistan	Pakistan
Belize	Guatemala	Belize
Bosnia Herzegovina	Croatia, Yugoslavia	Bosnia Herzegovina
Cyprus	Greece, Turkey	Cyprus
Diego Garcia	Mauritius	U.K.
Djibouti	Somalia	Djibouti
Falklands/Malvinas	Argentina	U.K.
Gibraltar	Spain	U.K.
Hatay	Syria	Turkey
Israel	Palestine, Syria	Israel
Kashmir	Pakistan	India
Kurile Islands	Japan	Russia
Kuwait	Iraq	Kuwait
Moldova	Romania, Russia	Moldova
Northern Ireland	Ireland	U.K.
North Ossetia	Ingushetia	Russia
North West Frontier Province	Afghanistan	Pakistan
Sabah	Philippines	Malaysia
South Tyrol	Austria	Italy
Taiwan	China	Taiwan
Transylvania	Hungary	Romania
Ukraine	Russia	Ukraine
Uzbekistan	Kazakhstan, Kyrgyzstan	Uzbekistan

SOURCE: Adapted from Karin von Hippel, "The Resurgence of Nationalism and Its International Implications," *The Washington Quarterly*, 17, 4, Autumn 1994, pp. 192–193. The Table identifies the best known secessionist and irredentist conflicts. There are many others.

into the ranks of the separatists; (2) a pattern of systematic discrimination, exploitation, or domination against the community; (3) a policy of cultural domination (Buchanan's cultural threat argument) seeking erosion of the disadvantaged group's culture or assimilation of its members into the dominant culture; and (4) the state's rejection of dialogue with the aggrieved community. Two additional "floating criteria" lending support to the separatist cause are a realistic prospect of conflict resolution and peace as a result of secession and liberal, tolerant policies to be pursued by the prospective state (corresponding roughly to Buchanan's second condition). Implicit in the foregoing set of conditions was Heraclides' recognition that an "oppressed non-nation" might have a stronger moral case for separatism than a partially disadvantaged nation.[99]

But the author recognized that there are cases where "it would be hair-splitting to tell whose case is more sound—that of the state, or of the secessionists."[100] He offered three examples of such moral deadlock: (1) when both parties to the conflict are opposed to fundamental principles of political liberalism (Tamils and Sinhalese in Sri Lanka, Serbs and Albanians in Kosovo, and Azerbaijanis and Armenians in Nagorno-Karabakh); (2) when the moral arguments of the state and the secessionists seem of equal weight (Nigeria in seeking to preserve a federal state, and its eastern region in seeking to create an independent Biafra around an entrepreneurial community); and (3) when the state is committed to pluralism and tolerance but the ethnosecessionist group demands nothing short of independence (radical Sikhs in India, ultranationalist Basques in Spain, and their Quebec counterparts in Canada).[101]

CONCLUSION

We have surveyed the wide range of moral arguments that can be advanced to justify secession. In today's world of ethnic conflicts, some of these arguments are more persuasive and relevant than others. But as we argued in the first part of this chapter, the international normative framework generally overrides moral considerations in prioritizing continuity and stability in the state system.

Whether it desires this or not, at the turn of the twenty-first century the international system is increasingly drawn into localized ethnonationalist conflicts. The next chapter describes how internationalization of such conflicts occurs.

DISCUSSION QUESTIONS

1. What is meant by the concept of *international normative regime*? In what way is the international normative regime biased against ethnonationalists?
2. It is often argued by scholars that implementing the idea of *national self-determination* is dangerous for the international system. Why?
3. Examine the relevance of the principles of nonintervention in the internal affairs of a state and of nonuse of force to the study of secessionism. Which party to an ethnic conflict is favored by international adherence to these principles?
4. Why is international recognition so crucial for ethnosecessionists? What criteria should the international community use to decide which secessionist claims to accept and which to reject?
5. While it is true that the international normative regime is biased against ethnonationalists, it is also true that under certain special circumstances, ethnosecessionist demands may be legitimate. How can they be accommodated by the international system?
6. Of the many moral arguments that are advanced to justify secessionism, which in your view carry most weight? Why?

NOTES

1. William Safran, "Non-separatist Policies Regarding Ethnic Minorities: Positive Approaches and Ambiguous Consequences." *International Political Science Review,* 15, 1 January 1994, pp. 61–80.
2. Alexis Heraclides, *The Self-determination of Minorities in International Politics,* (London: Frank Cass, 1991), p. 21.

3. Alan James, *Sovereign Statehood*. (London, 1986), p. 25. Quoted in Robert H. Jackson, *Quasi-States: Sovereignty, International Relations, and the Third World*. (Cambridge: Cambridge University Press, 1990), p. 32.
4. *Ibid.*
5. *Ibid.*
6. Djura Nincic, *The Problem of Sovereignty in the Charter and in the Practice of the United Nations*. (The Hague, Netherlands: Martinus Nijhoff, 1970), p. 2.
7. James Mayall, *Nationalism and International Society*. (Cambridge: Cambridge University Press, 1990), p. 18.
8. Nicholas Onuf, "Intervention for the Common Good," in Gene M. Lyons and Michael Mastanduno, eds., *Beyond Westphalia? State Sovereignty and International Intervention*. (Baltimore, MD: Johns Hopkins University Press, 1995), p. 52.
9. Heraclides, *The Self-determination of Minorities in International Politics*. p. 20.
10. J.L. Brierly, *The Laws of Nations: An Introduction to the International Law of Peace*. 6th ed. Edited by Sir Humphrey Waldock. (London: Oxford University Press, 1963), p. 137.
11. Heraclides, *The Self-determination of Minorities in International Politics*, p. 24.
12. Mayall, *Nationalism and International Society*, p. 19.
13. *Ibid.*, p. 20.
14. Brierly, *The Law of Nations*, p. 163.
15. *Ibid.*
16. *Ibid.*, p. 164.
17. *Ibid.*, p. 138.
18. *Ibid.*, p. 139.
19. *Ibid.* Emphasis in original.
20. *Ibid.*
21. *Ibid.*, p. 138.
22. *Ibid.*
23. Heraclides, *The Self-determination of Minorities in International Politics*, p. 25. Emphasis in original.
24. Brierly, *The Law of Nations*, p. 141.
25. Heraclides, *The Self-determination of Minorities in International Politics*, p. 25.
26. Rosalyn Higgins, "Internal War and International Law," in Cyril E. Black and Richard A. Falk, eds., *The Future of the International Legal Order*. Vol. III: *Conflict Management*. (Princeton, NJ: Princeton University Press, 1971), p. 88.
27. James E. Bond, *The Rules of Riot: Internal Conflict and the Law of War*. (Princeton, NJ: Princeton University Press, 1974), p. 49.
28. Higgins, "Internal War and International Law," p. 88.
29. Higgins, "Internal War and International Law," p. 88; and Bond, *The Rules of Riot*, p. 34.
30. Brierly, *The Law of Nations*, p. 142.
31. *Ibid.*
32. *Ibid.*, p. 143.
33. Heraclides, *The Self-determination of Minorities in International Politics*, p. 26.
34. *Ibid.*
35. Gene M. Lyons and Michael Mastanduno, "State Sovereignty and International Intervention: Reflections on the Present and Prospects for the Future," in Lyons and Mastanduno, *Beyond Westphalia*, p. 261.
36. *Ibid.*, p. 264.
37. *Ibid.*
38. *Ibid.*

39. Higgins, "Internal War and International Law," pp. 93–94.
40. Richard A. Falk, ed., *The International Law of Civil War.* (Baltimore, MD: Johns Hopkins University Press, 1971), p. 12.
41. *Ibid.,* p. 13.
42. Mayall, *Nationalism and International Society,* p. 26.
43. Benjamin Neuberger, *National Self-determination in Postcolonial Africa.* (Boulder, CO: Lynne Rienner, 1986), p. 4.
44. John Stuart Mill, *Utilitarianism, Liberty, Representative Government.* Quoted in Mayall, *Nationalism and International Society,* p. 27.
45. A. Rigo Sureda, *The Evolution of the Right of Self-determination: A Study of United Nations Practice.* (Leiden, The Netherlands: A.W. Sijthoff, 1973), p. 17.
46. Neuberger, *National Self-determination in Postcolonial Africa,* p. 4.
47. *Ibid.,* p. 5.
48. Mayall, *Nationalism and International Society,* p. 44.
49. *Ibid.,* pp. 44–45.
50. *Ibid.,* p. 54.
51. *Ibid.*
52. *Ibid.,* p. 45.
53. *Ibid.,* pp. 45–46.
54. Nincic, *The Problem of Sovereignty in the Charter and in the Practice of the United Nations,* p. 221.
55. Heraclides, *The Self-determination of Minorities in International Politics,* pp. 21–22.
56. Lee C. Buchheit, *Secession: The Legitimacy of Self-determination.* (New Haven, CT: Yale University Press, 1978), p. 17.
57. Mayall, *Nationalism and International Society,* p. 56.
58. Heraclides, *The Self-determination of Minorities in International Politics,* p. 23.
59. Alexis Heraclides, "Secession, Self-determination and Nonintervention: In Quest of a Normative Symbiosis." *Journal of International Affairs,* 45, 2, Winter 1992, pp. 404–405.
60. Heraclides, *The Self-determination of Minorities in International Politics,* p. 22. Emphasis added.
61. Alexis Heraclides, "Secessionist Conflagration: What is to be Done?" *Security Dialogue,* 25, 3, 1994, p. 284.
62. Allen Buchanan, "Self-determination and the Right to Secede." *Journal of International Affairs,* 45, 2, Winter 1992, p. 350.
63. For a summary and critique of the resolution, see Patrick Thornberry, "International and European Standards on Minority Rights," in Hugh Miall, ed., *Minority Rights in Europe: Prospects for a Transitional Regime.* (New York: Council on Foreign Relations Press, 1995), pp. 14–21.
64. Heraclides, *The Self-determination of Minorities in International Politics,* p. 23.
65. *Ibid.*
66. On the notion of sovereignty and its distinction from self-determination, see Ruth Lapidoth, "Sovereignty in Transition." *Journal of International Affairs,* 45, 2, Winter 1992, pp. 325–346.
67. Robert A. Friedlander, "Self-determination: A Legal-Political Inquiry," in Yonah Alexander and Friedlander, eds., *Self-determination: National, Regional, and Global Dimensions.* (Boulder, CO: Westview Press, 1980), p. 318.
68. Heraclides, "Secessionist Conflagration," p. 287.
69. Thomas M. Franck, *The Power of Legitimacy Among Nations.* (Oxford: Clarendon Press, 1990), p. 168.

70. Buchheit, *Secession,* p. 55.
71. *Ibid.,* p. 97.
72. *Ibid.,* p. 222.
73. *Ibid.,* p. 223.
74. *Ibid.,* p. 241.
75. Lapidoth, "Sovereignty in Transition," p. 345. For a further elaboration of Lapidoth's views on sovereignty and self-determination, see Lapidoth, "Redefining Authority: The Past, Present, and Future of Sovereignty." *Harvard International Review,* 17, 3, Summer 1995, pp. 8–11 and 70–71.
76. Gidon Gottlieb, *Nation Against State: A New Approach to Ethnic Conflicts and the Decline of Sovereignty.* (New York: Council on Foreign Relations Press, 1993), pp. 36–37.
77. *Ibid.,* pp. 42–43.
78. James Mayall, "Sovereignty and Self-determination in the New Europe," in Miall, ed., *Minority Rights in Europe,* p. 12.
79. Myron Weiner, "Peoples and States in a New Ethnic Order?" *Third World Quarterly,* 13, 2, 1992, p. 332.
80. *Ibid.*
81. Amitai Etzioni, "The Evils of Self-determination." *Foreign Policy,* 89, Winter 1992–1993, p. 33.
82. *Ibid.,* p. 25.
83. *Ibid.,* p. 35.
84. *Ibid.,* p. 28.
85. *Ibid.,* p. 35.
86. Heraclides, "Secessionist Conflagration," pp. 285–286.
87. Heraclides, "Secession, Self-determination and Nonintervention," p. 408.
88. Allen Buchanan, *Secession: The Morality of Political Divorce From Fort Sumter to Lithuania and Quebec.* (Boulder, CO: Westview Press, 1991), p. 2.
89. *Ibid.,* p. 27.
90. *Ibid.,* p. 44.
91. Heraclides, *The Self-determination of Minorities in International Politics,* p. 17.
92. Ernest Gellner, *Nations and Nationalism.* (Oxford: Blackwell, 1983), p. 2.
93. Buchanan, *Secession,* p. 54.
94. Etzioni, "The Evils of Self-determination," p. 27.
95. Buchanan, "Self-determination and the Right to Secede," p. 353.
96. Buchanan, *Secession,* p. 68.
97. Heraclides, *The Self-determination of Minorities in International Politics,* pp. 14–15.
98. *Ibid.,* p. 15.
99. Heraclides, "Secession, Self-determination and Nonintervention," p. 409.
100. Heraclides, "Secessionist Conflagration," p. 290.
101. *Ibid.*

chapter 3

Ethnic Conflict as an International Problem

INTRODUCTION

Ethnic conflicts usually, but not always, occur within states, but few of these conflicts remain confined within the national level for long. Most quickly transform themselves into international problems. In the previous chapter, we discussed some of the normative problems that ethnic conflicts raise before the international community. In this chapter, we focus on the practical difficulties that ethnic conflicts generate internationally.

The transformation of ethnic conflicts from the national to the international level may occur in one of two ways. First, ethnic conflicts at the national level may generate actors and consequences whose operation and effects are felt at the international level. We may call this process the *internationalization* of ethnic conflicts. Second, developments occurring in the international system may, in turn, affect domestic ethnic conflict, thereby lending it an international character. This process may be termed the *ethnicization* of international politics.

THE INTERNATIONALIZATION OF ETHNIC CONFLICT

Four alternative processes may lead to the internationalization of ethnic conflict, not all of them, however, being of the same level of salience. One common way that domestic ethnic conflict can become internationalized is through the international diplomatic activity of ethnosecessionists and states confronted with ethnic conflict. The main purpose of such international activity is to elicit supportive reaction from the targeted international actors. To that extent, a linkage may be established between the conflict in question and the international system.

Partisan intervention by outside states in a domestic ethnic conflict is another common way for such conflicts to acquire an international dimension. Also, in most cases, partisan intervention produces certain negative consequences that may threaten international peace and stability. Outside intervention in an ethnic conflict may be direct; that is, the intervenor is physically involved in the conflict as a direct participant in some capacity. Outside intervention in an ethnic conflict may be instead indirect; that is, the intervenor does not physically participate in the conflict but reacts in ways that have some effect on the conflict.

A third process that often leads to the internationalization of an ethnic conflict is international terrorism. The use of terrorist tactics and methods by disaffected groups in many societies is not a new phenomenon. Its use by ethnonationalists and secessionists internationally makes them direct participants at the international level and intensifies an existing problem for the international community.

A final way that domestic ethnic conflicts come to acquire an international character is through the flow of refugees. The biggest casualty of ethnic conflict, as recent events demonstrate, are civilians. Whether it be in Bosnia, Somalia, Rwanda, Sri Lanka, or Iraq or Turkey (the Kurds), ethnic conflict and violence inevitably result in the flow of people across borders, causing enormous human suffering and putting tremendous pressures on states that receive them. To the international community, therefore, refugees generated by ongoing ethnic conflicts have emerged as a serious problem.

Diplomatic Activity of Ethnosecessionists and States Confronted with Ethnic Conflict

International diplomatic activity by ethnosecessionists as well as by states confronted with ethnic conflict is a conspicuous way through which a domestic ethnic conflict may come to acquire an international character. As Modelski has correctly pointed out, in internal wars the "incumbents always and by definition have international connections, simply because they are in charge of the legitimate machinery of the state, which includes the diplomatic and other international networks; the insurgents, by virtue of having to approximate the incumbents as closely as possible in order to supplant them, must develop the same machinery."[1]

Motives for Undertaking International Diplomatic Activity. Ethnonationalists undertake international diplomatic activity to maintain physical durability and to acquire international acceptability.[2] The first aim—maintaining physical durability—refers to the ethnonationalists' desire to exist as a group and as a political movement, especially in the face of oppression and repression by the state. For example, threats to a hitherto amorphous group's well being and even existence may activate latent group identity and interests and cause it to mobilize in its self-defense and self-interest. This is what David Carment and other rational choice theorists refer to as the collective action phenomenon.[3] Additionally, to survive state oppression and achieve success as a political movement, ethnonationalists need to be audible—to be heard—

internationally to attract external allies and sympathizers.[4] Moreover, ethnonationalists may seek to attract international mediators to the conflict if they perceive that such mediation will help them to acquire more concessions at the negotiating table than they alone could hope to achieve.

Ethnonationalists, therefore, undertake diplomatic activity at the international level to gain external supporters and sympathizers who can provide them with both material and diplomatic support. Diplomatic support may include the extension of recognition, verbal encouragement and advice, provision of safe havens for exiles and refugees, and propaganda activities in international forums. Material support, on the other hand, may consist of financial backing and such military help as providing weapons, ammunition, supplies, base of operations, training facilities, and intelligence information. In rare cases, even armed intervention may be provided.

Although these strategic aims can be pursued simultaneously, it stands to reason that attracting external allies who can provide diplomatic, moral, financial, and military support is the ethnonationalists' first priority: Unless they are able to raise the stakes of the conflict, they may find it difficult to either persuade the state to enter into political negotiations with them (because, being usually more powerful militarily, the natural inclination of states when confronted with ethnic movements is to seek a military solution) or to negotiate from a position of strength themselves.[5] Moreover, if the aim of ethnonationalists is to secede from the state, then the need for diplomatic, financial, and military assistance is all the more urgent. Further, as Bertelsen notes, an ethnic group that is "losing battles within the domestic context of its nation–state may seek to widen the scope of the conflict by moving into an arena that offers more allies or different rules of the game—and therefore perhaps better opportunities for success."[6]

In this search for partisan external support, a number of factors are crucial for success. First, ethnic groups must be pragmatic in selecting and accepting aid from external third parties. This may require the movement to adopt a diffuse or flexible ideology. While this may help the group acquire aid from different quarters, its overall international, as well as internal, image may suffer from its flexible ideological stance.[7] Second, to be able to make a strong international impact, ethnonationalists must be able to present their case articulately and persuasively before the international community.[8] This may call for the effective use of propaganda, as well as considerable diplomatic and debating skills of group leaders and representatives. Finally, the ability to use effectively positive inducements (rewards for services and support) as well as negative sanctions (credible threats against noncompliance of ethnonationalists' demands by third parties) may also prove pivotal in attracting partisan support from external parties.[9]

A principal reason for states confronted with ethnic conflicts to engage in international diplomatic activity is, of course, to counter the ethnonationalists' diplomatic activity. Toward this end, a state may become active in international forums to explain its position on the conflict to other international-community members and to demonstrate the unjust nature of the ethnonationalists' demands. This can reduce the amount of international sympathy for the ethnonationalists. Another reason that could lead a state to undertake diplomatic activity is to seek international support for the state's territorial integrity and sovereignty, especially if the ethnonationalists are powerful secessionist challengers. A state confronted with ethnic conflict may also seek international support to bolster its security. For example, it is not surprising to find states that are fighting ethnic insurgents to be seeking arms and weapons from the international community. Finally, when states respond to ethnic and other internal challenges through military repression, it often leads to human rights violations, killing of innocent civilians, and other abuses. This is the cost that states usually pay for fighting a war where the adversaries are not easily identifiable. But consistent and serious human rights abuses may cause grave harm to a state's international reputation, prestige, and standing. This may lead to international politico-economic sanctions. Such states may try to use diplomacy to escape censure and condemnation from the international community and to improve their international image.

Targets of International Diplomatic Activity.   International diplomatic activity of ethnonationalists and states involved in ethnic conflict may be undertaken at four different levels—individual, group, state, and systemic. At the individual level, the targets of lobbying are usually prominent international personalities. The list of such personalities is varied; for example, both ethnic groups as well as states may approach a former U.S. president to present their case to the U.S. administration. Along with this role, the former president may become involved in the conflict as a third party interested in helping the disputants to reach a political settlement. President Jimmy Carter's role as an intermediary between adversaries in a number of domestic conflicts is a case in point. Ethnic groups as well as states may also try to reach influential foreign intellectuals, creative artists, religious figures, and media personalities who may be able to publicize their clients' case in their own countries, carry out fund-raising activities for their clients, and act generally as spokespersons for their clients in their countries. For example, American film actor Richard Gere has been instrumental in publicizing, in the United States and in other Western countries, the Tibetan people's plight under Chinese occupation. A means often used by ethnic groups and states in seeking to win over important foreign personalities is to encourage them to visit the conflict area on fact-finding missions. Moreover, international arms merchants, prominent underworld leaders, and bankers and financiers may also be "targets of opportunity" of ethnic groups because of their ability to provide weapons, ammunition, and money for insurgent warfare.

At the group level, the most common targets of ethnonationalists are co-nationals in neighboring states who may be eager supporters of the ethnonationalists because of common ethnicity ties. Such partisan support may consist of military and financial aid, training, sanctuary, and base facilities, as well as publicity for the ethnonationalists' cause. The co-nationals' ability to provide such support actively and consistently is likely to increase if they are their own state's dominant group, if they have an irredentist claim vis-à-vis the ethnonationalists, and if their influence on their government (especially if the co-nationals are not their own state's dominant group) is strong.

Ethnic diasporas are also a target of ethnonationalists' lobbying, especially if their economic and political clout is considerable. States, too, may try to reach well-known expatriates who can help shape favorable opinion in a foreign country for the state's position vis-à-vis ethnonationalists or who may be able to provide financial help to the state.

Neighboring ethnic groups (either in their own state or in a neighboring state) who are not co-nationals but are engaged in similar struggles with their central governments are often approached by ethnic groups for help. Such groups may be able to provide valuable services—such as providing military assistance, information, base facilities to be used for training, regrouping, and bunkering down purposes—provided they control substantial territory, have the necessary resources, and are not hostile toward the support-seeking ethnic group for ideological or other reasons. Such groups may also be approached by states confronted with ethnic and secessionist activities with an offer of rewards in return for cooperation in tracking down ethnonationalists and secessionists operating from their regions.

Another likely target of ethnonationalists in their quest for international support and sympathy are ideological and religious "brothers"—those groups or political parties (or in some cases, states) with whom the ethnonationalists share a common ideology or religion.[10] Ethnic groups who profess communist ideology regularly provide support to other ethnic movements who have a similar ideological orientation. Groups with Islamic fundamentalist ideologies also support each other's cause.

Because states are the principal actors in international politics, they are the most likely targets of ethnonationalists' lobbying. One type of state that is likely to be solicited by ethnonationalists is one that is supportive of the central government. At a minimum, ethnonationalists may attempt to convince such states not to provide support to the central government. If successful, it could change the balance of forces in the conflict. A more obvious target of ethnonationalists' lobbying is those states that are the staunch enemies of the center. Support from such states may be more likely because they may want to exploit the situation for their own gain. Another type of state that might be approached is one that is already providing some support to the movement as a whole, to some factions within the movement, or to rival fronts within the group. States that in the past have championed similar movements elsewhere are also likely to be on the ethnonationalists' potential-supporters list. Former colonial powers (if one is present) and major powers are yet another category of states that may be asked for assistance, for recognition, or for serving as a third-party manager of the conflict. Finally, neighboring countries, especially those that contain co-nationals, are likely targets of ethnonationalists in their quest for diplomatic, financial, and military assistance. Foreign states are also the principal targets of states threatened by ethnic and secessionist groups. They may approach their traditional allies for diplomatic, financial, and military support, or they may contact their adversaries with promises of substantial concessions if such states refrain from supporting the ethnonationalists. Those states facing similar ethnic problems or sharing a similar ideology may be approached for diplomatic, moral, financial, and military support.

At the systemic level, international governmental organizations (IGOs), whether regional (such as the European Union, the Organization of African Unity, and the Arab League) or global (such as the United Nations), are the most likely targets of ethnonationalists. IGOs are primarily organizations of states, and they are therefore unlikely to be supportive of secessionists against one of their members. Moreover, because most IGOs are created to deal only with interstate disputes and conflicts, ethnic groups, especially those that are nondominant within a state, find it difficult to convey their views to such bodies.[11] The only way that ethnic groups can present their grievances to an IGO is to find a state sponsor that is a member of that particular organization; the Turkish Cypriots, for instance, have relied on Turkey to raise their case in the UN. Not all ethnic groups find state sponsors that are willing to raise their case before IGOs; for instance, the Kurds, who are scattered across four states in the Middle East—Iran, Iraq, Turkey, and Syria—have often failed to find a state sponsor willing to promote their case.

Why, then, do ethnonationalists seek to present their grievances to IGOs? Considering that IGOs are mainly organizations of states and are normatively biased against ethnonationalists, even limited success that ethnic groups achieve in presenting their grievances in an international forum of states lends a degree of legitimacy to their movement. Psychologically, it may boost their members' morale and provide prestige to their leaders. IGOs also provide a forum from where the group can reach a wider international audience. A convincing argument regarding the legitimacy of their grievances, the suffering of their members, and the justness of their demands may help ethnonationalists win external allies, sway international public opinion in their favor, and bring international condemnation and pressure on the state. The persistent attempts of the Palestine Liberation Organization (PLO) under its chairman, Yasir Arafat, to legitimize its political claims and aspirations in the UN and other international organizations is a good example. The PLO recorded a breakthrough in the aftermath of the 1973 Arab–Israeli War when the Rabat Conference accepted its claim as the only legitimate representative of the Palestinian people. Subsequently, the PLO was granted observer status within the UN and other UN specialized agencies, and the General Assembly invited Arafat to address the body on November 13, 1974. The consequences of these actions is concisely noted by Stack: "The granting of observer status to the PLO at the UN and at several specialized agencies has enhanced the organization's position and has accelerated the process by which its legitimacy has been acknowledged by such other political actors as the European Economic Community."[12] Along with the UN, approval by other regional organizations such as the Organization of African Unity and the Arab League further legitimized the PLO's status and political goals.

Second, if the ethnonationalists are seeking to reach a peaceful settlement of the conflict with the center, they may wish to involve an IGO such as the UN in the settlement process as a third-party mediator because of its prestige and impartial image, its disinclination to exploit the situation for its own gain, and its ability to deintensify and deinternationalize the conflict by preventing external states from intervening or counterintervening in the conflict.[13] Ethnonationalists may decide to seek a negotiated settlement to the conflict for a number of reasons: significant losses on the battlefield; loss of external support; lack of international sympathy for their cause; exhaustion from prolonged conflict; death, imprisonment, or exile of top leaders; factionalism or dissension within their ranks; erosion of popular support; acceptance by the government of some of their main demands; and so on. In such situations, they may decide to initiate political negotiations with the center under a third party's auspices in the belief that a settlement reached under an impartial third-party's auspices could be more equitable and get them more concessions than they could get by themselves.

Most states prefer not to take their domestic ethnic problems to IGOs because of the fear that such action will internationalize the conflict and bestow a degree of legitimacy to the ethnonationalists. They also run the risk of incurring international condemnation of their policies toward ethnic minorities, especially if they have chosen to use the military option, as most states do. But some states do take their ethnic problems to IGOs on the assumption that their long-term interests are better served this way or on the basis that their moral claims are unassailable. Moreover as organizations of states, an ethnically troubled state may calculate that an IGO will be supportive of the its position. This may indeed occur if the claims of ethnonationalists are seen as unfounded, if their method of operation is considered brutal and in violation of accepted international norms of conduct, or if they are in league with actors of unsavory reputation. States may also decide to take their ethnic problems to an IGO if they are losing their fight with the secessionists and want a third-party-mediated settlement to preserve their sovereign existence and territorial integrity. Finally, some states have taken their ethnic problem to IGOs out of their moral conviction; for instance, one reason why Prime Minister Nehru of India wished to involve the UN in the India-Pakistan dispute over Kashmir was his belief that the issue of Kashmir's accession to India or Pakistan had to be decided by a UN-sponsored plebiscite in order to ascertain the political desire of the Kashmiri people.

International nongovernmental organizations (INGOs), such as Amnesty International, Doctors Without Frontiers, and the Red Cross, are also frequent targets of lobbying by ethnonationalists. INGOs mainly become involved in internal conflicts to monitor the situation and to provide humanitarian relief to combatants as well as noncombatants. As a result, they may come to acquire firsthand knowledge about the conflict that they can share with other international actors. Moreover, some INGOs are powerful international actors in the sense that their work is internationally significant, their reach is global, and their influence on states and international governmental organizations are substantial. Reaching such INGOs is important for ethnonationalists for the sake of publicity and to induce more favorable reaction from the international community.

Another target of ethnonationalists' lobbying are multinational companies (MNCs). In contrast to foreign states and international organizations, which are often restricted by sovereignty and territoriality considerations from reaching ethnic groups directly, freewheeling and globally active MNCs can directly contact ethnic groups in the states where they do business. MNCs are also the target of lobbying by the government because their activities may have important "consequences for ethnic identities and interethnic distribution of power."[14] For instance, if a state is dominated by a particular ethnic group, then the MNC can become an instrument for perpetuating that group's economic and political dominance of the state. MNCs can help governments to expand their control over remote regions of the country by establishing lines of economic, demographic, and technological communication between the center and far-flung regions. This may further augment the center's political and economic power vis-à-vis other ethnic groups.[15]

Partisan Intervention in Ethnic Conflicts

Given the "self-help" nature of our international system, the outbreak of ethnic conflict within a state opens up considerable opportunities for outside partisan intervention into the conflict, thereby transforming such conflicts into international ones having consequences for international peace and stability.

Theoretically, two types of partisan external interventions are possible in ethnic conflicts. First, an outside intervenor can pursue a policy of *diffusion and encouragement.* In this case, the intervenor chooses to help the weaker side (usually, but not always, the ethnic insurgents) by becoming a partisan supporter of the ethnic insurgents. Partisan support may be of two kinds. It may consist of *tangible support* such as military and material aid; access to transportation, media, communications, and intelligence networks; and services rendered either within or outside the secessionist region. When it offers tangible aid to the ethnosecessionists, the intervenor's role in the conflict may be regarded as direct; that is, the intervenor is physically involved in the conflict as a direct participant in some capacity. On the other hand, the intervenor may provide the ethnosecessionists with *politico-diplomatic support* including statements of concern, support in IGOs, diplomatic pressure, publicity campaigns for the secessionists' cause, and diplomatic recognition. In such cases, its intervention may be regarded as indirect—the intervenor does not physically participate in the conflict but reacts to the conflict in ways that impact it.

Second, an outside intervenor can pursue a policy of *isolation and suppression.* In this case, the intervenor allies against the ethnic insurgents and strengthens the state's forces. Such action may involve providing politico-diplomatic aid to the state. The intervenor can also mobilize the international community to undertake collective action on the state's behalf. In cases where the victory of the ethnic separatists is a fait accompli, the intervenor may take action to ostracize the new state by refusing recognition or blocking its admission to international organizations. Finally, the intervenor may cut off all support to the secessionists (if such support was being provided earlier) and even undertake joint military action with the state's forces against the secessionists. It is important to note that in following a policy of either diffusion or isolation, the intervenor becomes a partisan supporter of one side in the conflict.

Reasons for Partisan External Intervention in Ethnic Conflicts.   Partisan external intervention in ethnic conflicts occurs as a result of two main factors. First, as we have seen, both ethnosecessionists and states confronted with such movements often seek such intervention in order to tip the balance of power in the conflict in their favor. Second, external intervenors may also have their own reasons for becoming involved in such conflicts. An external party may intervene in ethnic conflicts as partisan supporters of either the insurgents or the center for both affective and instrumental motives.[16] Affective motives include reasons of justice, humanitarian considerations, ethnic, religious, racial, or ideological affinity with one of the disputants, and even "personal friendships between top protagonists."[17] Instrumental motives, on the other hand, are rooted in Realpolitik and may include "international political (including general strategic) considerations, short-term and longer-term economic motives, domestic motives (internal political reasons including the demonstration effect fears) and short-term military gains."[18]

An external party may become a partisan intervenor in an ethnic conflict for reasons of justice only if it is convinced of one of the adversaries' moral and legal position. If the state's case seems morally and legally just, an external party may intervene to bolster its strength and to isolate and suppress the ethnonationalists. In Bosnia, for instance, few international actors believe in the moral and legal justness of the Serbs' position; consequently, the external intervenors (such as the UN and NATO) came to the aid of the Muslim-dominated Bosnian government in order to isolate and suppress the Bosnian Serb forces. On the other hand, if the ethnosecessionists' legal and moral case appears more just, then the external party may decide to provide partisan support to them. The overwhelming demonstration of international sympathy and support for the Bengalis during their attempted (and ultimately successful) secession from Pakistan in 1971 is a good example. For ethnic insurgents as well as for the state, therefore, a convincing presentation of their legal and moral position in international circles is crucial. External parties most likely to intervene for reasons of justice are international organizations, major powers, and regional states.

Humanitarian considerations—saving civilian lives; delivering food, medicine, and aid; preventing ethnic cleansing and other form of human rights abuses—as the principal motivating factor for partisan external intervention have increased in importance in the 1990s. The conflicts in Bosnia, Somalia, and Rwanda showed that the role and power of IGOs in ethnic disputes had changed. The international community decided that the principles of state sovereignty and nonintervention in the internal affairs of states would no longer prevent it from intervening in internal conflicts on humanitarian grounds.

International organizations are not the only external party to intervene for humanitarian reasons. States—both major and regional powers—may also intervene in a partisan manner for humanitarian reasons. Whose side they choose depends primarily on which side in the dispute is more responsible for perpetrating a humanitarian crisis. External intervenors may follow a policy of isolation and suppression of the ethnosecessionists if they are convinced that stopping the conflict immediately is essential for the assuagement of civilian suffering, repatriation of refugees, and punishment of criminal elements within the secessionist movement.

Ethnic affinity of the intervenor with one of the disputants may lead to partisan support for that side. Shiels has pointed out that ethnosecessionists are more likely to receive aid from a neighboring state if that state is strongly influenced by their ethnic kin or co-nationals.[19] In such cases, the ethnic kin state may start to provide partisan support to the ethnosecessionists (as India did for the Tamil secessionists in Sri Lanka) or may even pursue an aggressive irredentist policy with the aim of redeeming its lost co-nationals (as seen from Somalia's policy toward the Ogaden region of Ethiopia and Pakistan's policy toward Kashmir).[20] However, in some instances, attempts by ethnic insurgents to attract partisan support from their ethnic kin in a neighboring state who are a small minority in that state and, more important, who are seen as a security risk by the government of that state, may backfire on them. The ethnic kin state may then begin to fear the possibility of a "demonstration effect" on its own ethnic minority and decide to isolate and suppress the secessionists by cooperating with the state forces. It may also start to repress its own ethnic minority.[21] For example, the outbreak of the Baluch insurgency in Pakistan in 1973 had the effect of producing greater cooperation between Pakistan and Iran, which was suspicious about the political ambitions of its own Baluch minority. Iranian armed forces not only massacred the Iranian Baluch population but also provided support to the Pakistani military in its operations against the Pakistani Baluch separatist organizations. Like Iran, Turkey has suppressed its own Kurdish minority and, at times, has taken military action against the Kurds of Iraq on the suspicion that they are providing support to the Kurds in Turkey.

Religious-ideological ties may also lead an external party to become partisan supporters of the ethnic insurgents or the state forces. For instance, many insurgent groups in

India and Israel who profess an Islamic fundamentalist ideology have received support from neighboring groups and states with similar religio-ideological orientation. In recent years militant Islamic *mujahideen* (soldiers of God), who were once active in Afghanistan and still maintain close ties with that country, have infiltrated into Indian-held Kashmir to aid local ethnic insurgents. Islamic *mujahideen* and volunteers are also reported to have come to Kashmir from Bahrain, Saudi Arabia, Sudan, Indonesia, and Malaysia.[22] Israel has also faced a similar predicament: Some factions of the PLO have long enjoyed the sympathy and often direct support of a variety of guerilla and terrorist groups around the world—the Japanese Red Army's massacre at Tel Aviv's Lod international airport in May 1972 is an early and dramatic illustration of this point. Militant factions within the PLO and more recent militant Islamic groups such as the Hamas and the Hizbollah militia in Lebanon have also received substantial support from similar religio-ideologically oriented groups in Lebanon, Iran, Iraq, Jordan, Egypt, Saudi Arabia, and Syria. But there might be situations also where an external party decides to pursue a policy of isolation and suppression of the secessionists because the ideology and aims of the secessionist movement may be incompatible with or a threat to its own ideological position.

Generally, partisan external intervenors who decide to isolate and suppress the ethnosecessionists for affective reasons will do so mainly through nonmilitary means. Nonmilitary means may include providing economic aid and intelligence information to the victimized state, demonstrating diplomatic solidarity with and sympathy for the state forces against the secessionists, cooperating with the state forces and other international actors to undercut the appeal of the secessionists, and blocking all assistance to the secessionists.

Compared to affective motives, which are supposedly driven by empathy, kinship, and at times the strength of moral and legal claims, instrumental motives for partisan external intervention are rooted in Realpolitik. In other words, ethnic conflicts within states may tempt outside powers to intervene to promote their self-interest.[23] For such instrumentally driven intervention to occur, "gains should outweigh costs." Put another way, "gains should be as cheap as possible, that is, a large return for a small outlay."[24]

Gains can be of different kinds and can be both short- as well as long-term. Where economic gains are concerned, states have a natural advantage over ethnic groups in being able to offer economic inducements in return for partisan external support. But there are cases where ethnic groups, depending on where they are located, can offer attractive economic incentives to external parties. For example, the Kurd homeland in Iraq includes vast deposits of oil. Kurdish secessionists may be able to offer future access to that oil as an inducement to an external party for its support for Kurdish independence. But generally, as Gurr and Harff contend, the more resources a state has, the more is the likelihood of its receiving support from external actors during instances of internal ethnic conflicts.[25]

Sometimes, external parties may decide to support the ethnic separatists precisely so as to prolong the conflict and drain its enemy's economic, technical, human, and military resources, thereby weakening it from within. For this reason, the longer an internal conflict lasts, the greater the possibility of partisan intervention by outside parties (especially the enemies of the state) on behalf of the insurgents. At times, an external intervenor may use its support for ethnic separatists as bargaining leverage in negotiations with the state over other more vital issues. In either case, support for ethnic separatists may be a means to an end for the intervenor.

Instrumental motives may also induce external parties to pursue a policy of isolation and suppression of the ethnosecessionists. For instance, an external state that at one time was a partisan supporter of secessionists may decide to alter course and pursue a policy of isolation and suppression if it calculates that its earlier course of action may lead to serious negative consequences for its internal security (demonstration or contagion effect), external security (raising the possibility of counterintervention), and national reputation, prestige, and economy (as a result of international sanctions). It may then distance itself from the secessionists and begin to cooperate with the state forces.

Characteristics of Partisan External Intervention in Ethnic Conflicts.   There is an overwhelming tendency among scholars to regard instrumental motives for partisan external intervention in ethnic conflicts as taking precedence over affective motives. For many writers, affective motives devoid of instrumental considerations will never lead to intervention. Only where affective and instrumental motives are combined, do direct interventions in the internal affairs of sovereign states occur.[26] But as Heraclides has shown in his comparative analysis of seven cases of attempted secession, instrumental motives were less common than affective ones. Moreover, small states (the exception being Israel, which is an anomalous small state) usually became involved for affective reasons, while medium states, regional powers, and superpowers intervened mainly for instrumental reasons.[27]

A second assumption made by some scholars about external intervention in ethnic conflicts pertains to the level of and motives for intervention. It is generally assumed that high levels of military as well as politico-diplomatic support are usually provided by the intervenor only if expectations of instrumental gains are involved.[28] This assumption was confirmed by Heraclides' findings only insofar as material support was concerned. High levels of politico-diplomatic support were provided mainly for affective motives or a combination of affective and instrumental motives.[29]

A third assumption concerns the type of external support and its degree of availability. Of the two kinds of external support, it is generally believed that high levels of politico-diplomatic support may be readily available—because words are supposed to be cheaper than material aid—to secessionists than material support.[30] But Heraclides's study found that although politico-diplomatic support for secessionists was usually low and of limited extent in most cases, material support was much greater.[31] So, words were not cheap as might be expected.

A fourth assumption about partisan external intervention is that it is likely to be unreliable because dissident ethnic groups are often "perceived as instrumentalities in the foreign policy armamentatium of one state to disrupt the internal affairs of another state."[32] Although Heraclides's study confirmed this assumption, it showed that external parties who intervened in ethnosecessionist conflicts for instrumental reasons tended to be more reliable compared to those who intervened for affective reasons.[33] Within the category of affective motives, those that intervened for reasons of justice or empathy tended to be more reliable than those intervening for ideological or religious solidarity.[34]

Heraclides's study also discovered significant correlations between the type of states that intervened in secessionist conflicts and the type of support that was provided. One finding was that Western states as well as less-developed countries (LDCs) of a Western orientation usually provided ethnosecessionists with tangible support. Nonaligned LDCs usually provided politico-diplomatic support, especially of an open, verbal kind. A second finding was that neighboring states adjacent to government-held territory (and not to that held by the secessionists) generally supported the state forces. Those neighboring states that bordered both government- and rebel-held territory tended to support the ethnosecessionists. Neighboring states that were adjacent to only the secessionist-held territory tended to support the secessionists even more. Third, regional states rarely intervened militarily on behalf of ethnosecessionists (two exceptions were Indian military intervention in Bangladesh and Iranian border raids on behalf of the Iraqi Kurds). A fourth finding, belying the expectations of bipolar politics, was that superpowers were rarely interested in becoming involved in ethnosecessionist conflicts on opposing sides. Finally, the assumption that a state that is the center's traditional enemy is more likely to support the secessionists was found to be valid for both tangible and, especially, politico-diplomatic support.[35]

Constraints on Partisan External Intervention.   To be sure, partisan external intervention in ethnic conflicts is a rule-of-thumb in international relations. But exceptions to this rule are possible because of certain constraints on intervention. The first constraint is the international normative regime, especially the principles of state sovereignty and non-intervention in the internal affairs of sovereign states. In spite of these international norms, external intervention in internal wars has taken place because another basic characteristic of the international system is its "self-help" nature in the absence of any central authority. But by and large in the post–1945 period, direct intervention in communal and separatist conflicts has been less frequent than classic civil wars.[36] Even in those rare cases of intervention in secessionist conflicts, "incumbent governments have tended to attract more support than insurgents have."[37]

Certain characteristics of internal conflicts may also act as constraints on intervention. Deutsch has suggested that four specific characteristics of internal conflicts—their duration, extent or scope, degree of recruitment and attrition, and morale and intensity of motivation of each side—may have a bearing on external intervention. For external intervention to become a realistic possibility—especially high-level tangible involvement—an internal conflict must be protracted. Conflicts that last for only a few days or weeks provide little opportunity for external intervention, but prolonged internal conflicts, by generating a military balance between the adversaries, open up considerable opportunities for external intervention because the adversaries may seek to tip the military balance in their favor and to acquire the resources and capacity needed to engage in a long war through external intervention. Duration of the conflict is itself heavily dependent on the extent or scope of the conflict—how large a population is involved over how large a territory. If the extent or scope of the conflict is large, its prolongation increases the possibilities of external intervention. Similarly, the ability of adversaries to recruit new troops and to continue the conflict until one side emerges victorious also determines the duration of hostilities.[38]

Lack of capability, funds, and calculations of gains and losses by an external party may also act as constraints on intervention. External intervention is unlikely if the potential intervenor lacks the resources to carry it out. Moreover, the potential intervenor's belief that its losses would outweigh its gains and that intervention may be untimely or imprudent may act as further constraints on intervention.[39]

Partisan external intervention on behalf of ethnic separatists can also come at a high cost for the intervenor and thus act as a constraint. For example, if a state intervenes in an ethnic conflict for affective reasons, such as sympathy for fellow nationals, it may expose itself to the risk that if the level of support proves insufficient to ensure success of its separatist ethnic kin or if it fails to satisfy its fellow nationals, then the anger of its fellow nationals (and even some of its own population) may be directed toward itself for a poorly conceived adventure. The failure of Serbian President Slobodan Milosevic to come to the Krajina Serbs' rescue when they were attacked by Croatia stimulated Serb anger toward him. Some Krajina Serbs even swore vengeance on Milosevic, the man they once depended on but who now was considered a traitor.[40]

Finally, external parties may decline to intervene on behalf of the secessionists if they are opposed to the movement, are opposed to secession and armed conflict on principle, are supporters of the center, or are not convinced about the merits or justness of the secessionist claim. International political considerations (fear of reprisal from the incumbents, adverse reaction of the international community), domestic political and security imperatives, and apprehension about negative economic effects (the financial drain of providing support) may all act to prevent an external state from intervening on behalf of the secessionists. In addition, "bystander apathy"—that is, "the greater the number of onlookers in a situation in which a suffering or victimized person requires urgent assistance, the greater is the diffusion of responsibility"—may also act as a check on intervention.[41]

Consequences of Partisan External Intervention.   Partisan external intervention in ethnic conflict, when it occurs, may pose certain problems before the international community. For one, if ethnonationalists score substantial gains in their quest to secure support from external parties, it almost always increases the level of their repression at the hands of state forces, especially if the state's territorial integrity is under threat.[42] This happens because the natural tendency of governments faced with an ethnic insurgency is to define the conflict purely in legalistic terms—as a law-and-order problem—and to treat ethnic insurgents as criminals. In doing so, governments seek "a total solution and to insist that the insurgent organization be completely destroyed and all those who have violated any laws be punished."[43] Faced with harsh state repression, ethnic insurgents may be forced underground to survive, as a result of which their international audibility is sure to decrease.[44] More important, perhaps, harsher repression by the state may actually exacerbate the humanitarian crises usually generated by such conflicts, to which the international community cannot turn a blind eye. The Zapatista National Liberation Army in the southern Mexican state of Chiapas furnishes an example of this phenomenon: Employing modern communications technology such as electronic mail and faxes, this movement, representing the impoverished indigenous population of Mayan stock, quickly became an international cause célèbre in 1994 from the affluent in San Francisco to the salons of Paris. But the Zapatistas paid a price for such audibility as Mexican President Ernesto Zedillo resorted to counterinsurgency to take back rebel-held villages.

Second, external support for ethnonationalists is rarely on the scale that would enable them to win a decisive military victory against the state. What ethnic insurgents need most for a decisive victory is direct partisan military intervention by their external supporters. Very rarely are states willing to assume such a risk. Although there are notable exceptions to the rule—the Indian military intervention on behalf of Bengali secessionists in Pakistan in 1971 being one—partisan external support usually augments ethnonationalist strength in the short run, thereby resulting in military stalemates and an increase in human suffering.

Another problem may result when ethnic groups' capability to wage war is substantially dependent on partisan external support. In those instances, ethnic groups may become pawns in a wider political game played between states. For instance, the dependence of the PLO on Syria's support resulted for a time in its giving up more control than it got back in terms of capability.[45] Similarly, in their fight against the Iraqi government, the Kurds depended heavily on support from Iran (and secretly from the United States). Consequently, it was the Iranians and the Americans who came to acquire control over the conflict's intensity and duration. They could prolong the conflict and raise its level of intensity by providing more material support to the Kurds, or they could halt or lower the intensity by reducing the Kurds' fighting capability through aid cutoffs. In such cases, an ethnic group may become "a tool by which a nation-state may (indirectly) perpetrate violence against another state at reduced cost to itself."[46]

Partisan external intervention in an ethnic conflict may also, by inducing counterintervention, lead to an intensification and prolongation of the conflict.[47] When that happens, ethnic groups may no longer find themselves as disputants in an internal conflict but as victims of a much wider international war. In turn, this may lead to the marginalization of those issues that had led to the conflict's outbreak in the first place and to the introduction of new issues, actors, and solutions that transform the conflict's entire character, scope, and intensity. Conflicts such as those in Lebanon, Cyprus, and Angola all became protracted and more violent following external intervention and counterintervention.

Ethnic Conflict and International Terrorism

A very common way by which an ethnic conflict can become an "international problem" is the use of terrorist methods by ethnic insurgents. Lacking the resources needed for conventional military warfare, ethnic separatists often resort to terrorism because it is cheaper and easier to get away with. In addition, if the goal of ethnic separatists is to reach a global audience to publicize their cause, terrorism is an effective means due to media globalization—the so-called "CNN Factor."[48] In this context, Bertelsen has noted that "In order to avoid being dismissed as the domestic problem of an established nationstate and in order to prevent nation–states from imposing solutions upon them, (ethnic groups or nonstate nations) may direct violence against nation–states other than the ones in which they reside."[49] Some Palestinian groups residing in Syria, Libya, and Lebanon have used violence and terrorism against Israel, Western states supporting Israel, and other foreign targets. This has raised the cost of involvement of third parties in the dispute and has also prevented the maintenance of stable ceasefires between Israel and its Arab neighbors. The Sri Lankan Tamils guerrillas, too, have carried out terrorist attacks against foreign governments and leaders unsympathetic toward their cause. The assassination of Indian prime minister Rajiv Gandhi by Sri Lankan Tamil terrorists is an example.

The international targets of ethnoterrorism are not exclusively foreign governments or leaders. Ethnoterrorism is most frequently directed against the group's own government—whether its property and personnel at home or abroad. It can also claim victims among private businesspeople and citizens of one's own state abroad. Terrorism against foreign nationals located in one's own state also internationalizes ethnic conflict, often drawing reprisals from the state of the foreign nationals. The taking of foreign hostages by Kashmiri separatists illustrates how domestic acts of terrorism may come to acquire an international dimension. Further, as Said and Simmons have pointed out, dissatisfied ethnic groups "have begun to pirate international passenger flights, assassinate diplomats in foreign lands, and even to extort ranson from multinational giants such as Ford Motor Co. Kidnappings of businessmen and diplomats have become a familiar feature in international politics."[50]

Ethnic Conflict and Refugee Flows

Internal ethnic conflicts can be internationalized through refugee flows. A massive influx of refugees fleeing their own state for fear of persecution or prompted to leave as part of a state's effort to create an ethnically homogeneous state creates two different kinds of problems for the receiving state. "To grant a refugee political asylum on the grounds of persecution is, of course, to condemn the state which has been persecuting its citizens. But far more conflictual is the massive refugee influx which imposes a large economic and political burden upon the receiving country."[51] This may at times lead to war between refugee-generating and refugee-receiving countries.

A more profound problem for the international community is the humanitarian crises generated by refugee flows. Receiving states may seal their borders but, more often, allow refugees in but place them in inhospitable camps. The aim of such treatment, as Weiner reports, is to use the condition of the refugees as a policy of "human deterrence." In other words, inhospitable conditions of refugee camps, it is believed, can stem the further flight of refugees from their homeland.[52]

These two aspects of the refugee problem—that the number of refugees will multiply as more civil wars, ethnic conflict, state collapse, and forcible displacements occur, and that this will lead to increasingly hostile responses from receiving states—make it one of the most serious challenges facing the international community in the years to come.

THE ETHNICIZATION OF INTERNATIONAL POLITICS

Ethnicization of international politics refers to those processes or events that occur at the international level but that may have repercussions on ethnic conflicts at the national level. In this way, developments that originate at one systemic level may come to be linked with behavior in another system.

Globalization, Interdependence, and Ethnic Conflicts

Over the past four or five decades, technological advances in transportation and communication, the globalization of the mass media, and the development of an integrated global economy, have resulted in a drastic shrinkage of the world. The world, as some experts have noted, has truly become a "global village" with ever-increasing lines of interaction between the international system and a country's domestic economy, polity, and society, as well as between the international system and nonstate actors. Consequently, the ability of states to control their internal environment has been substantially reduced. One area in which this phenomenon can be seen is the proliferation of networks of transnational ties among ethnic groups across the globe. The establishment of such transnational networks has allowed "ethnic groups with greater opportunities for transnational interactions: the exchange of ideas, information, wealth, and political strategies."[53]

Undoubtedly, technological progress by continuously shrinking the world and increasing the frequency of intergroup contact provide the basis for powerful "demonstration effects" to occur.[54] An early manifestation of such demonstration effect could be seen during the student protest movements in the 1960s as student protests spread from one Western country to another and beyond. Indeed, the chant of demonstrators from Chicago to Prague became "The Whole World is Watching." In today's context, the outbreak of ethnic conflict in one part of the world may produce similar demonstration effects on ethnic movements in other regions. Such demonstration effects may engender analyses of the causes of success or failure of similar ethnic movements elsewhere. The "mistakes" committed by other ethnic groups will be noted, and the lessons of successful ethnic movements will be absorbed and even emulated. The linkages that such demonstration effects allow between ethnic movements in different geographical regions have, therefore, introduced a distinct international dimension to some of these movements.

An area where the globalization of the mass media and advances in communication technology has aided ethnic groups is international terrorism.[55] As Pierre has observed:

> Television gives the terrorist instant access to the world's living rooms, thereby enabling him to draw global attention to his cause. The mobility offered by the modern jet aircraft allows him to strike at will almost anywhere in the world and then move on to safe asylum. Hence, advances in technology has made it possible for a large society to be directly affected by a small band of terrorists.[56]

Technological advancements in worldwide communication and transportation may also stimulate and reinforce ethnic identities across state boundaries. "Highly politicized communication networks provide groups with the attributes of ethnicity, not through a common historical tradition that usually includes the immigration experience, but through a more synthetic process of rapid ideological and political conversion."[57] This may result in the establishment of ties between ethnic groups in one country and ethnic and other sub-state groups in another, not only on the basis of ethnicity but also ideology, strategy, and politico-economic goals. The collaborative relationships forged at one time between the Japanese Red Army and the PLO, the Croatian Ustasha and the Macedonian IRMO, the Sri Lankan Tamils and the Colombian drug lords, the Shi'a Hizbollah militia in Lebanon and the Iranian Revolutionary Guards, and the Hamas in the Israeli Occupied Territories and the Muslim Brotherhood in neighboring Arab countries, all dramatize this point.[58] Furthermore, innovations in communications and transportation technologies bind states more closely together, thereby increasing the scope and intensity of intrasocietal penetration. The impact of such intrasocietal penetration has been noted by Stack: "Intrasocietal penetration contributes to the strengthening of ethnicity throughout the global environment. French-Canadian separatists are not unmindful of the battles waged by Basque, Welsh, or Irish nationalists."[59] The emulation of tactics, strategies, and goals of one ethnic movement by another has thus become a common occurrence in international politics. The gains recorded by ethnic insurgents in one country may even reinforce the legitimacy and feed the ambitions of ethnic groups in another.

International Conflict and Its Ethnic Fallout

Can certain types of interstate conflicts generate repercussions for intrastate ethnic relations? Myron Weiner certainly thinks so when he argues that an international conflict between states of an irredentist versus antiirredentist nature that involves an overlapping ethnic group can have serious repercussions for interethnic relations and national integration in both the revisionist (that is, irredentist) and status-quo (antiirredentist) states.

In the status-quo state, the onset of an irredentist—antiirredentist struggle with a neighboring state may create tensions in interethnic relations in three ways. First, as the neighboring irredentist power presses its claim and expresses concern for the condition of its ethnic kin in the status-quo state, hopes of ethnic kin are raised that "it will be incorporated into the revisionist state or that, with the support of the revisionist power, it may achieve separate statehood."[60] There may be hostility toward any attempt by the status-quo state to integrate the ethnic group even more firmly within the state. Consequently, antagonistic relations between the ethnic group and the government of the status-quo state are likely to worsen.

Second, as demands for revising boundaries persist on the part of the irredentist state, the status-quo state may start to view the ethnic group as a trojan horse, a grave risk to the territorial integrity of the state. In that case, the status-quo state may be tempted to move in two directions simultaneously: It will try to accelerate programs to "nationalize" schoolchildren belonging to the ethnic group, to press the members of the ethnic group to learn the national language, and in various ways to demand expressions of identification and loyalty by the members of the ethnic group toward the national government. It will also increase police surveillance of the ethnic group, seal the border with border patrols, and in general impose more controls over the members of the ethnic group.[61]

Third, as a result of the status-quo state's crackdown, significant numbers within the ethnic group may come to regard the status-quo state as the oppressor and an obstacle in the path to its merger with the revisionist state (that contains its co-nationals) or to full independence. In such situations, as noted by Weiner, the ethnic group has to choose between one of three alternatives: The ethnic group could, for one, accept the existing boundaries and strive to improve its status within the status-quo state; or it could support the irredentist claim of the revisionist state, thus clearly stating its preference for merger with that state; or if the ethnic group happens to be a minority in both the revisionist and status-quo states, it could choose to join its co-nationals in a struggle to break free of both states.[62] Which option it selects will depend on the outcome of intense debates within the ethnic group regarding "the character of its own identity and its affinity or lack of affinity with other ethnic communities."[63]

Unless the ethnic group chooses the first option, its repression at the hands of the status-quo state is likely to increase. In that event, segments within the ethnic group (especially youth and students) may feel sufficiently threatened to organize an insurgency movement against the status-quo state. Such a movement is sure to receive substantial help from the revisionist state. Faced with a mounting insurgency, the status-quo state may have no choice but to respond with severe repression. This may prompt the revisionist power to intervene militarily to protect its ethnic kin from slaughter. The upward spiral of violence could easily lead to a full-fledged war.

Weiner notes that this type of irredentist–antiirredentist conflict between two states with an overlapping ethnic group may also lead to internal ethnic fragmentation in the revisionist state. Faced with persecution of its co-nationals in the status-quo state, a revisionist state may become fixated with boundary modification. The country's economic and political development may suffer as a result. When boundary modification becomes the obsession of the revisionist state's leaders, it will also affect the state's political culture. Loyalty and patriotism would become the most cherished values, and the public mood is likely to turn militant. Tolerance of the regime for disagreement would also be low, and it would most likely respond with repression toward those who disagreed with its policies.[64]

If the status-quo power stands firm on the boundary issue, frustration may eventually overwhelm both the leaders and the masses of the revisionist state. The latter may take preparatory measures for war and arm the people living on the disputed border. Caught in the vise of militant irredentism, the revisionist power may even launch an attack on the status-quo state. If the military campaign fails, public discontent may peak in the revisionist state and overspill into domestic conflict.[65] Moreover, "If the irredentist government has armed its border people and exiles from the disputed territory, or allowed outsiders to provide them with arms, there is a high probability that this armed minority will turn their arms against [the revisionist state] if in their judgement [the state] fails to pursue a sufficiently aggressive expansionist policy."[66]

Frustrated irredentist claims, as in the case of Argentina's defeat in 1982 when attempting to capture the Falkland/Malvinas islands in the South Atlantic from Britain, can even produce regime change. The United States was banking that frustrated irredentism would lead to Saddam Hussein's overthrow after his failure to hold on to Kuwait—Iraq's alleged eighteenth province—in 1991, but in this case anti–Westernism in Iraqi society eclipsed frustrated irredentism.

Ethnic Conflict as a Consequence of Empire and State Collapse

A growing phenomenon of the post–cold war world is empire and state collapse. Already the Soviet Empire has collapsed into fifteen different independent states. Subsequently, some of these states that emerged out of the wreckage of the Soviet Union are under threats of collapse. Elsewhere, notably in Africa, several states, such as Somalia, Liberia, Ethiopia, Angola, and Algeria have either completely collapsed or are under the threat of collapse. Several other states—such as Afghanistan, Tajikistan, and Iraq—face a similar challenge. In Eastern Europe, the collapse of the Yugoslavian state also went hand-in-hand with the demise of the cold war. Empire or state collapse is a deeper phenomenon than revolt, coup, or riots and other types of political violence. It has been defined by Zartman as "a situation where the structure, authority (legitimate power), law, and political order have fallen apart and must be reconstituted in some form, old or new."[67] But do collapsed states or empires create situations where intense conflict is possible among ethnic groups that emerge from the wreckage of these states or empires?

Using the realist concept of the *security dilemma,* Barry Posen argues that intense military conflict among ethnic groups emerging from the wreckage of empires or states is highly probable.[68] Writing after the fall of communism in the Soviet Union and Eastern Europe, Posen's starting argument is that in a situation of emerging anarchy (which the breakup of the imperial communist regimes created in the Eurasian region), the primary concern of the successor "entities" (states as well as ethnic groups aspiring for statehood) is security. Because the key to security is power, these entities are pushed into a natural competition for power. This competition for power in turn creates the security dilemma and triggers ethnic conflict between the successor entities.[69]

The security dilemma is intensified due to two factors. First, it becomes difficult for the successor entities to signal their defensive intention (that is, limited objectives) when their offensive and defensive military forces appear to be identical. Because military technology and military organization (often taken as the main factor distinguishing offense and defense) of the successor groups is likely to be rudimentary, their military strength becomes largely a function of their "groupness" or "cohesion." However, because the groupness of the successor entities is likely to be greater than the empires or states they emerge from, it may provide them with an inherent offensive military capability. But because all sides now stress their groupness and cohesion, each appears threatening to the other. Under these conditions, the only way to assess the intentions of other groups is to use history. But prevailing political conditions may lead groups to interpret history in a way that would not meet objective scholarly standards. The result, as Posen argues, is a "worst-case analysis" where every group thinks the other is the enemy.[70]

The second factor that intensifies the security dilemma is the belief in the superiority of offensive over defensive action. This is affected by technology and geography. Technology is a crucial variable in the offense–defense balance. Political geography is a situational variable that often provides an offensive advantage and an incentive for preventive war. In the context of the collapse of empires and states, recovering ethnic enclaves inhabited by one's ethnic kin (Armenia's link with Nagorno-Karabakh, located in Azerbaijan) might provide the incentive for rapid offensive military action. At the same time, the tactical offensive advantage that having a homogeneous population provides may induce a group to "ethnically cleanse" (that is, induce the other group's population to leave) areas that it controls.[71]

This intense security dilemma is further linked to groups' sense of opportunity or vulnerability. Whichever it is, launching a military offensive can either press home one side's temporary military advantage, or it may achieve a military advantage before the other side has time to shore up its forces. The preoccupation of great powers and international organizations with other trouble spots might provide further incentive for offensive military action.[72]

As a result of this intense security dilemma in the aftermath of the fall of empires, ethnic conflict among the successor entities breaks out. Posen adds a caveat to the model: nuclear weapons. If "a group inherits a nuclear deterrent, and its neighbors do as well, 'groupness' is not likely to affect the security dilemma with as much intensity as would be the case in non-nuclear cases. Because group solidarity would not contribute to the ability of either side to mount a counterforce nuclear attack, nationalism is less important from a military standpoint in a nuclear relationship."[73]

Using these two variants of the model, Posen analyzes the outbreak of conflict between the Serbs and the Croats on the one hand and the lack of conflict between Russia and Ukraine on the other. Posen's work is of singular importance because it provides a dynamic model linking causal inputs from the external environment (in his case, inputs affecting state or group security) with the outbreak of intense nationalism among and aggressive behavior by states or groups emerging from the wreckage of empires or states. At the same time, however, Posen's work does not really explain intense conflict among ethnic groups as a result of security dilemmas in those situations where the ideal state monopolizing the use of violence does not exist, but yet state authority has not completely collapsed, a condition perhaps prevailing in such states as Afghanistan, Tajikistan, and Iraq.

To understand ethnic conflict as a result of security dilemmas in these *halfway-house states*—which fall in between *ideal states* with no ethnic problems because the state monopolizes the use of violence and guarantees security and fairness to all ethnic groups within the state, and *collapsed states* where no state authority exists and where groups must protect their own security by shoring up their group cohesiveness, using worst case analyses, and by pressing home any military advantages that might exist—we turn to the analysis provided by Stephen Saideman.

According to Saideman, in those states that are between ideal and collapsed types, political or state authority "may be biased towards or against particular ethnicities, so competition is waged among different ethnic groups for control of the state."[74]

Because the state could be an ethnic group's greatest ally or greatest adversary due to the resources it possesses, competition between ethnic groups for capturing state power will result, and in this kind of political environment, an ethnic group will typically come to believe that if it fails to capture state power, then someone else will, which will put the group at the mercy of the state. This, as Saideman suggests, is at the core of the security dilemma of ethnic groups within existing states located between ideal and collapsed types. As he notes:

> If the state cannot protect the interests of all ethnic groups, then each group will seek to control the state, decreasing the security of other groups and decreasing the ability of the state to provide security for any group. Consequently, many of the dynamics present in international politics emerge domestically. For instance, each group will consider their interests and actions to be limited and benign while those of other groups are seen as irreconcilably hostile.[75]

Saideman goes on to correlate ethnic insecurity with ethnic politics because the preference of constituents and therefore the preferences and strategies of politicians are shaped by their perceived sense of security. The actions of politicians are important because they determine the ethnic security environment of the state:

> If politicians take radical stands favoring some ethnic groups at the expense of others, the security climate will deteriorate. On the other hand, if politicians downplay ethnic identities, building multiethnic constituencies and developing civic or other non-ethnic ideologies, then ethnic groups will feel more secure.[76]

The interaction of these two processes—ethnic insecurity and ethnic politics—determines ethnic political outcomes. If insecurity among ethnic groups is high and if politicians opt for ethnic oriented policies (as they may do under pressure from their supporters), intense ethnic conflict may occur.[77]

The End of Bipolar Superpower Rivalry and Its Effect on Ethnic Conflicts

It is generally believed that during the cold war, bipolar politics between the superpowers managed to suppress ethnic conflicts. One reason was that superpower confrontation through support of rival proxy ethnic groups was inherently dangerous. Generally, superpowers stayed out of internal ethnic conflicts unless the costs and risks of the intervention were perceived to be reasonably low.[78] Another reason why superpowers were able to suppress ethnic conflict was because of the structure of the global bipolar alliance system. Each superpower maintained firm control over its allies. The priorities and behavior of domestic political actors in client states were overshadowed by considerations of superpower competition. With the cold war's end, instability is the most palpable fear in many parts of the world. Thus in the Middle East, South and Central Asia, Africa, and parts of Europe, various types of internal conflicts and instability reemerged.

A case in point is Afghanistan. The de facto partition of Afghanistan into semiau-tonomous territories was a major cause for instability in the south, southwest, and central Asian regions.[79] Since the collapse of the Soviet-backed government and of the Soviet Union itself, regional states such as Pakistan, Saudi Arabia, and Iran have sought to expand their influence in Afghanistan and the region by exploiting divisions within the country. The potential for a wider, more intense conflict is enormous because "Iran has egged on the minorities, even though the bulk of these are not Shias, in the hope of advancing Iranian influence in Afghanistan against the fundamentalist Pashtun *mujahideen* who are supported by Pakistan and Saudi Arabia."[80] Furthermore, instability in Afghanistan has acted as a breeding ground for radical Islamic groups and Afghan guerrillas trained in insurgency warfare to engage in joint operations with insurgent groups in neighboring states such as India.[81]

Afghanistan, therefore, quickly became a much larger and newer version of Lebanon. Before the Taliban (Muslim seminarians) takeover in 1997, it was not only a matter of a weak government that could not assert its authority over the profusion of fighting forces in the country. As a collapsed state, it provided conditions for the coun-try to become a key crossroads for drug traffickers, illicit-arms dealers, and regional insurgents. The evolution of Afghanistan as a training ground for Islamic fundamen-talist forces (with Iran's involvement uncomfortably reminiscent of Revolutionary Guard activity in Lebanon) is also of concern to its neighbors. With the end of Soviet occupation in Afghanistan in 1989, Islamic "volunteers" who had once fought along-side the Afghan *mujahideen* returned to their home countries. Subsequently, Western and Arab governments alike suspected that thousands of Muslim militants operating against established governments in Algeria, Egypt, Yemen, and other Muslim coun-tries were veterans of the Afghan war who still used the country as a base.[82]

Central Asian politics also exemplifies the problems associated with the fall of communism and the end of the cold war. An upsurge in Islamic sentiments and rivalry between foreign powers for influence was apparent in Uzbekistan and Tajikistan. In the former, Saudi Arabia helped finance the construction of more than 600 mosques in the Fergana Valley alone. In neighboring Farsi- (Persian-) speaking Tajikistan, Iran invested large sums to support Islamic insurgents fighting the central government in a protracted civil war. The turmoil in Afghanistan could also overspill to Central Asia. Although states such as Uzbekistan, Tajikistan, and Turkmenistan would prefer north-ern Afghanistan to be governed by their own respective ethnic kinfolk rather than Pashtun fundamentalists, the *mujahideen* use this to invoke the specter of a greater Uzbekistan or a greater Tajikistan that would threaten to carve up Afghanistan. In turn, as Erlanger reports, the potential for a Tajik–Uzbek crisis is great.[83]

The emergence of new independent Muslim states in Central Asia has intro-duced an unpredictable new dynamic into the region. These new states temporarily distracted Iran as it competed with Turkey and other Muslim states for influence. But should the Soviet-drawn artificial boundaries prove unable to prevent transna-tional interethnic strife, the turmoil could rapidly spread beyond Afghanistan into Pakistan, a home to many of the same ethnic groups. Conflict in Central Asia could destabilize all of Muslim Asia and increase the power of fundamentalist forces in the Muslim world. Should Islamic fundamentalists score gains in this area, the demonstration effect could boost the efforts of fundamentalists in Algeria, Egypt, Saudi Arabia, and elsewhere.

The Link Between Arms Trading, Drug Trafficking, and Ethnic Conflict

The enormous proliferation of weapons across the globe has had a powerful effect on ethnonationalists and secessionists. Their military capabilities have been augmented and they may feel ready to challenge the power of existing states. The easy availability of weapons also provides ethnic separatists with a degree of freedom that they never enjoyed before. One source for weapons is found in the vestiges of certain cold war conflicts such as Afghanistan: At the height of the Afghan war, Americans and Soviets poured in huge quantities of highly sophisticated weapons. When the Soviet–American confrontation ended, sophisticated weapons, such as Stinger anti-aircraft missiles supplied to the Afghan rebels in the 1980s by the United States, were transshipped to rogue states such as Iran and to various terrorist and insurgent groups in the region.

The emergence of Russia, China, and North Korea as willing suppliers of weapons to developing states (the United States remains the world's largest arms supplier), and through them to insurgents and terrorists, is another reason for widespread availability. The need for hard currency became a major incentive for Russia to sell arms. Under Yeltsin, Russia has sold new weapons and technology to Kuwait, Iran, Syria, and China among others, and it has become a major international arms supplier.[84] In turn, China has sold M–11 missiles and missile technology to Iran and Pakistan in violation of the Missile Technology Control Regime (MTCR).[85] North Korea also reportedly sold the Nodong I and II missiles to Iran.

Further contributing to the global proliferation of weapons is covert trade in sophisticated conventional weapons, ranging from tanks and aircraft to missile parts. The global covert arms trade, estimated between $1 and 2 billion to $5 to 10 billion annually, makes it easier for states to acquire the technology and hardware necessary for making nuclear, advanced conventional, and chemical and biological weapons. In Michael Klare's words, it has produced a "deadly convergence" where certain third-world powers have acquired the capability to conduct the type of military operations that previously only the superpowers could carry out.[86] Closely connected to the covert trade of weapons are drug-trafficking networks linked to terrorist and insurgent activities. The threat from terrorists and insurgents has increased due to the easy availability of weapons and the use of drug trafficking to finance their activities.

One should not discount the importance of drug trafficking as a source of financial and military power to insurgent groups. As Said and Simmons argue, a noticeable trend in world politics is that more and more ethnic groups are resorting to "illicit trafficking in contraband in order to finance guerrilla activities or to maintain their bases of political and cultural sovereignty within a state."[87] Similarly, Jayawardhana has shown that Sri Lankan Tamil separatist groups, such as the Liberation Tigers of Tamil Eelam (LTTE), have peddled drugs (LTTE apparently worked for the Colombian drug lords) to raise money for their military campaigns and for their arms procurements.[88] Ethnic separatists and other internal dissident groups operating in such countries as

Thailand, Laos, Burma, Turkey, and Afghanistan are closely involved in the covert trade in contraband and narcotics. More than 80 percent of the drug traffic in Myanmar is controlled by ethnic and other separatist groups in the country such as the Shan, Karen, and Kachin rebels. Moreover, joining this trade in recent years are a number of ethnic and tribal insurgent groups operating in the Indian northeast, such as Nagas, Kukis, Mizos, Manipuris, and the Assamese, and in the Chittagong Hill Tracts (CHT) region of Bangladesh.[89] In Southwest Asia, the largest supplier of drugs is Afghanistan. It is believed that more than 70 percent of Afghan heroin arrives in the West through India.[90] Apart from nomadic tribes, ethnic and insurgent groups involved in this trade include the Ghilzai, the Pathans, the Baluchis, the Shinwaris, the Tajiks, the Hazaras, and the Turkmen. Afridi and Pathan mafia groups in Pakistan are also believed to be couriers of Afghan drugs.[91]

Apart from the interplay of insurgencies and drug traffickers in both the Golden Triangle—Myanmar, Thailand, and Cambodia—and the Golden Crescent—Iran, Afghanistan, and Pakistan—the long anarchy that prevailed in Lebanon brought the drugs-for-guns cycle directly into the heart of the Middle East. Lebanon's position as a producer and refiner of opium, hashish, heroin, and cocaine and a major transit route for Asian opium and heroin enabled its ethnoreligious-based militias to use the drug trade to finance their operations and acquire arms.[92] With the rise in Palestinian militancy and the increased activities of the Shia fundamentalist Hizbollah, two more significant players entered this circle. With an independent source of finances provided by the drug trade, the various militias in Lebanon continue to destabilize Lebanon, Israel, and Syria. The drug trade's tentacles in Lebanon may even prove to be a threat to the Arab–Israeli peace process as a whole.[93]

CONCLUSION

In this chapter, we have demonstrated the various ways that ethnic conflicts at the national level can carry over to international politics and also how developments that occur at the international level can influence ethnic politics at the national level. For the most part, ethnonationalism exerts a destructive influence on the world system, though we should recall that an international normative regime unsympathetic to secessionist claims, however morally justified they may be, can try the patience of the most liberal-minded ethnonationalist movement. The next chapter focuses on how the international system—both transnational organizations and state actors—can contribute to resolving ethnic conflict.

DISCUSSION QUESTIONS

1. What is meant by the internationalization of ethnic conflict? Through what different processes can such internationalization occur?
2. Why is partisan external support so crucial for most ethnonationalists? Why is it so difficult to obtain?

3. What is meant by the *security dilemma*? Under what circumstances can it lead to intense ethnic conflict?
4. There is growing evidence that many ethnic groups use drug trafficking to fund their politico-military operations. Do you think that the guns-for-drugs nexus provides ethnonationalists today with a greater operational advantage and flexibility? What are the costs of using the guns-for-drugs nexus for ethnonationalists?
5. In what ways has the end of the cold war affected ethnic conflicts across the globe? Do you believe in the argument that the end of the cold war simply lifted the lid on ancient ethnic hatreds in many societies?

NOTES

1. George Modelski, "The International Relations of Internal War," in James N. Rosenau, ed., *International Aspects of Civil Strife*. (Princeton, NJ: Princeton University Press, 1964), pp. 14–15.
2. Judy S. Bertelsen, "An Introduction to the Study of Nonstate Nations in International Politics," in Bertelsen, ed., *Nonstate Nations in International Politics: Comparative System Analyses*. (New York: Praeger, 1977), p. 3.
3. David Carment and Patrick James, eds., *The International Politics of Ethnic Conflict*. (Pittsburgh: University of Pittsburgh Press, 1997).
4. Myron Weiner, "Peoples and States In a New Ethnic Order?" *Third World Quarterly*, 13, 2, 1992, p. 320.
5. Alexis Heraclides, *The Self-determination of Minorities in International Politics*. (London: Frank Cass, 1991), p. 37.
6. Bertelsen, "An Introduction to the Study of Nonstate Nations in International Politics," p. 3.
7. Heraclides, *The Self-determination of Minorities in International Politics*, p. 41.
8. *Ibid.*, p. 42.
9. *Ibid.*, pp. 43–45.
10. *Ibid.*, p. 37.
11. See S. Bailey, "The U.N. and the Termination of Armed Conflict—1946–64." *International Affairs*, 58, 3, 1982, p. 469.
12. John F. Stack, Jr., "Ethnic Groups as Emerging Transnational Actors," in Stack, Jr., ed., *Ethnic Identities in a Transnational World*. (Westport, CT: Greenwood Press, 1981), p. 28.
13. See E. Marlin and E. Azar, "The Costs of Protracted Social Conflict in the Middle East: The Case of Lebanon," in G. Ben-Dor and D. R. Dewith, eds., *Conflict Management in the Middle East*. (Lexington: Lexington Books, 1981); and Stephen Ryan, *Ethnic Conflict and International Relations*. (Aldershot, Dartmouth, 1990).
14. Cynthia H. Enloe, "Multinational Corporations in the Making and Unmaking of Ethnic Groups," in Ronald M. Grand and E. Spenser Wellhofer, eds., *Ethno-Nationalism, Multinational Corporations, and the Modern State*. (Denver, CO: Graduate School of International Studies Monograph Series on World Affairs, University of Denver, 1979), p. 27.
15. *Ibid.*, pp. 21–22.
16. See Astri Suhrke and Lela Garner Noble, "Spread or Containment?" in Suhrke and Noble, eds., *Ethnic Conflict and International Relations*. (New York: Praeger, 1977), pp. 226–230.
17. Heraclides, *The Self-determination of Minorities in International Politics*, p. 52.
18. *Ibid.*

19. Frederick L. Shiels, "Introduction," in Shiels, ed., *Ethnic Separatism and World Politics.* (Lanham, MD: University Press of America, 1984), p. 11.
20. Ryan, *Ethnic Conflict and International Relations,* p. xvi.
21. See Judy S. Bertelsen, "The Nonstate Nation in International Politics: Some Observations," in Bertelsen, ed., *Nonstate Nations in International Politics,* p. 252.
22. See Sanjoy Hazarika, "Afghans Joining Rebels in Kashmir." *The New York Times,* August 24, 1993; Ahmed Rashid, "No Longer Welcome" and "Pulls and Pressures: President's Peace Offer Marred by Ethnic Violence." *Far Eastern Economic Review,* April 2, 1992, p. 18; Shiraz Sidhva, "Days of Despair." *Sunday,* June 16–22, 1991, p. 22.
23. Ryan, *Ethnic Conflict and International Relations,* p. xvi.
24. Heraclides, *The Self-determination of Minorities in International Politics,* p. 52.
25. Ted Robert Gurr and Barbara Harff, *Ethnic Conflict in World Politics.* (Boulder, CO: Westview Press, 1994), pp. 85–86.
26. Ryan, *Ethnic Conflict and International Relations,* p. 36.
27. See Alexis Heraclides, "Secessionist Minorities and External Involvement." *International Organization,* 44, 3, Summer 1990, pp. 371–372.
28. See Astri Suhrke and Lela Garner Noble, "Introduction," in Suhrke and Noble, eds., *Ethnic Conflict and International Relations,* pp. 17–18.
29. Heraclides, "Secessionist Minorities and External Involvement," p. 372.
30. See Richard Little, *Intervention: External Involvement in Civil Wars.* (London: Martin Robertson, 1975), p. 9.
31. Heraclides, "Secessionist Minorities and External Involvement," p. 369.
32. Abdul A. Said and Luiz R. Simmons, "The Ethnic Factor in World Politics," in Said and Simmons, eds., *Ethnicity in an International Context.* (New Brunswick, NJ: Transaction Books, 1976), p. 29.
33. Heraclides, "Secessionist Minorities and External Involvement," p. 373.
34. *Ibid.*
35. For details, see *Ibid.,* pp. 372–376.
36. *Ibid.,* pp. 352–353.
37. *Ibid.,* p. 353.
38. See Karl W. Deutsch, "External Involvement in Internal War," in Harry Eckstein, ed., *Internal War: Problems and Approaches,* (New York: The Free Press of Glencoe, 1964), pp. 104–106.
39. Heraclides, "Secessionist Minorities and External Involvement," p. 353.
40. See Jane Perlez, "Croatian Serbs Blame Belgrade for Their Rout." *The New York Times,* August 11, 1995, pp. 1, 2, and "Demonstration in Belgrade." *The New York Times,* August 10, 1995, p. 4.
41. Heraclides, "Secessionist Minorities and External Involvement," pp. 353–355.
42. Weiner, "Peoples and States in a New Ethnic Order," p. 326.
43. See Lucian W. Pye, "The Roots of Insurgency and the Commencement of Rebellions," in Eckstein, ed., *Internal War,* p. 170.
44. Bertelsen, "An Introduction to the Study of Nonstate Nations in International Politics," p. 4.
45. Bertelsen, "The Nonstate Nation in International Politics," p. 252.
46. *Ibid.*
47. F.S. Northedge and M.D. Donelan, *International Disputes: The Political Aspects.* (London: Europa, 1971), p. 131.
48. For an argument on the effectiveness of terrorism for ethnonationalists, see Andrew J. Pierre, "The Politics of International Terrorism." *Orben,* 19, 4, Winter 1976, p. 1252.
49. Bertelsen, "The Nonstate Nation in International Politics" p. 251.

50. Said and Simmons, "The Ethnic Factor in World Politics," p. 30.
51. Weiner, "Peoples and States In a New Ethnic Order?" p. 321.
52. *Ibid.*
53. Stack, "Ethnic Groups as Emerging Transnational Actors," p. 21.
54. Walker Connor, "Nation-Building or Nation-Destroying?" *World Politics,* 24, 3, April 1972, p. 352.
55. Stack, "Ethnic Groups as Emerging Transnational Actors," p. 21.
56. Pierre, "The Politics of International Terrorism," p. 1253. Here quoted from *Ibid.*
57. *Ibid.*
58. For details of specific cases, see Walter Laqueur, *Terrorism.* (Boston, MA: Little, Brown, 1977), p. 194; Walter Jayawardhana, "Guns For Drugs." *Sunday,* November 4–10, 1990, p. 84; Shireen T. Hunter, *Iran and the World.* (Bloomington, IN: Indiana University Press, 1990), pp. 123–127; Tabitha Petran, *The Struggle Over Lebanon.* (New York: Monthly Review Books, 1987), pp. 374–375; Barry Rubin, *Revolution Until Victory: The Politics and History of the PLO.* (Cambridge, MA: Harvard University Press, 1994), p. 203.
59. Stack, "Ethnic Groups as Emerging Transnational Actors," p. 25.
60. Myron Weiner, "The Macedonian Syndrome: An Historical Model of International Relations and Political Development." *World Politics,* 23, 4, July 1971, p. 673.
61. *Ibid.,* p. 674.
62. *Ibid.,* pp. 673–674.
63. *Ibid.,* p. 674.
64. *Ibid.,* pp. 276–277.
65. *Ibid.,* pp. 676–677.
66. *Ibid.,* p. 678.
67. I. William Zartman, "Introduction: Posing the Problem of State Collapse," in Zartman, ed., *Collapsed States: The Disintegration and Restoration of Legitimate Authority.* (Boulder, CO: Lynne Rienner, 1995), p. 1.
68. Barry R. Posen, "The Security Dilemma and Ethnic Conflict." *Survival,* 35, 1, Spring 1993.
69. *Ibid.,* pp. 27–29.
70. *Ibid.,* pp. 29–31.
71. *Ibid.,* pp. 31–34.
72. *Ibid.,* pp. 34–35.
73. *Ibid.,* p. 32.
74. Stephen M. Saideman, "The Dual Dynamics of Disintegration: Ethnic Politics and Security Dilemmas in Eastern Europe." *Nationalism and Ethnic Politics,* 2, 1, Spring 1996, pp. 22–23.
75. *Ibid.,* p. 23.
76. *Ibid.,* p. 25.
77. *Ibid.,* pp. 25–26.
78. Shiels, *Ethnic Separatism and World Politics,* p. 11.
79. For details of the political turmoil in Afghanistan, see Salamat Ali, "Uneasy Truce." *Far Eastern Economic Review,* September 17, 1992, p. 30, and "Pound of Flesh." *Far Eastern Economic Review,* August 6, 1992; Jayanta Bhattacharya, "Killing Fields." Sunday, September 13–19, 1992, pp. 52–53; Edward A. Gargan, "Afghanistan, Always Riven, Is Breaking Into Ethnic Parts." *The New York Times,* January 17, 1993; "Leaders of Afghan Factions Seem Closer to Peace," *The New York Times,* March 4, 1993.
80. Rashid, "Pulls and Pressures: President's Peace Offer Marred By Ethnic Violence," p. 18.
81. P.S. Suryanarayana, "Afghan Support to Pak. in the Event of War." *The Hindu,* International Edition, October 15, 1994, p. 3.

82. Mahmud Abohalima and Sheikh Omar Abdel Rehman, chief suspects in the World Trade Center bombing, were known to have had ties with Afghan rebels. See Chris Hedges, "Many Islamic Militants Trained in Afghan War." *The New York Times,* March 28, 1993.

83. The origins of the Tajik-Uzbek conflict go back to 1925 when Stalin dismembered Turkestan and the People's Republics of Bukhara and Khorezm to create the republics of Tajikistan and Uzbekistan. Khozhent, an ethnically Uzbek city, was placed in Tajikistan whereas Samarkand and Bukhara, two prominently Tajik cities, were incorporated into Uzbekistan. With the disintegration of the Soviet Union, some radical Tajik nationalists have demanded the return of Bukhara and Samarkand from Uzbekistan, increasing tensions between these two states. See Steven Erlanger, "Tamarlane's Land Trembles: Bloodshed at Gates." *The New York Times,* February 15, 1993.

84. Russia recently agreed to sell 18 MiG-21 fighter aircraft to Malaysia. This sale marks a major breakthrough by Russia in the ASEAN weapons market. Syria purchased antisubmarine helicopters, BMP-2 armored vehicles, and 300 T-72 tanks from Russia in 1994. Syria is interested in acquiring MiG-31 fighter aircraft, Su-27s, and multiple rocket launchers from Russia. Kuwait has agreed to purchase BMP-2 infantry vehicles and Smerch rocket systems from Russia. Iran also recently purchased a second Kilo-class submarine, 10 Su-24 aircraft, and 150 BMP armored vehicles from Russia. There are reports of additional weapons deals in the pipeline. China is expected to receive 72 Su-27 fighter aircraft and S-300 surface-to-air missiles from Russia. Moreover, it has been reported that China will manufacture MiG-31 fighters under license. See Dov Zakheim, "Russia Resumes Old Business Habit." *Defense News,* August 29, 1994, p. 31.

85. Steven A. Holmes, "China Denies Violating Pact by Selling Arms To Pakistan." *The New York Times,* July 26, 1993.

86. "The Covert Arms Trade." *The Economist,* February 12, 1994, p. 21.

87. Said and Simmons, "The Ethnic Factor in World Politics," p. 30.

88. Jayawardhana, "Guns for Drugs," p. 82.

89. For details, see Bertil Lintner, "The Indo-Burmese Frontier: A Legacy of Violence." *Jane's Intelligence Review,* 6, 1, January 1, 1994.

90. See David Pugliese, "Private Armies Threaten Established Borders." *Defense News,* April 4, 1994, p. 12; and Jayawardhana, "Guns for Drugs," p. 84.

91. Said and Simmons, "The Ethnic Factor in World Politics," p. 32.

92. Richard Clutterbuck, *Terrorism and Guerrilla Warfare: Forecasts and Remedies.* (London: Routledge, 1990), p. 157.

93. See Clutterbuck, *Terrorism and Guerrilla Warfare,* pp. 103–104; and Rachel Ehrenfeld, *Narco-Terrorism.* (New York: Basic Books, 1990), pp. 52–73.

chapter 4

Resolving Ethnic Conflicts Through International Third-Party Action

WHY RESOLVING ETHNIC CONFLICTS IS IMPORTANT

The resurgence of ethnic conflict, as we noted earlier, has confronted the international community with difficult normative as well practical challenges. The biggest normative challenge is to devise criteria for accepting or rejecting ethnic communities' claims to sovereign statehood. The ever-growing literature on this subject proves that there is little international consensus on this issue. More important, perhaps, from a practical standpoint is that not every ethnic group's claim to sovereign statehood can or should be satisfied. The persistence of ethnic conflicts has also confronted the international community with certain unacceptable consequences associated with such conflicts, whether they be ethno- or narcoterrorism, humanitarian crises, refugee flows, and the threat of wider systemic wars due to interventions and counterinterventions by outside states in these conflicts. For the sake of international security, peace, and stability, therefore, the international community must find ways to resolve such conflicts either peacefully or, if needed, through the use of force.[1]

In this chapter, we focus on ethnic conflict resolution through the involvement of international third parties in the conflict. More specifically, we stress two interrelated points connected with the role of international third parties vis-à-vis ethnic conflict resolution. First, we analyze conceptually the various objectives an international third party may pursue in attempting to resolve an ethnic conflict and the criteria needed for success in each of these different roles. Second, we discuss the international actors who have played or are more likely to play a third-party role in ethnic conflict resolution and the resulting consequences.

ETHNIC CONFLICT RESOLUTION BY INTERNATIONAL THIRD PARTIES

There are three basic methods of resolving disputes. First, disputants may resolve a conflict by recourse to violence. The inevitable consequence of doing so—armed conflict—may ultimately settle the dispute when one side secures a military victory. The character of this method of dispute resolution is harsh and brutal—precisely what the international community seeks to avoid in ethnic conflict situations. Second, and diametrically opposite to the first, disputants may settle their differences through peaceful bargaining and negotiation on their own initiative. Although such peaceful methods are most favored by the international community, in the case of ethnic conflicts, which are usually regarded as zero-sum by the adversaries, the disputing parties usually fail to resolve their differences peacefully on their own initiatives. The limitations of the first two approaches have raised the importance of the third method—the involvement of international third parties—especially in situations of protracted and complex ethnic conflict where the disputants have exhausted their own attempts at compromise.[2]

Dispute resolution through third-party action can be defined as "the intervention into a dispute of a person or an agency whose purpose it is to act as an instrument for bringing about a peaceful settlement to that dispute, while creating structures whereby the foundations of a lasting settlement can be laid."[3] To that extent, an international third party can pursue any of three useful objectives in ethnic conflicts—peacekeeping, peacemaking, and peacebuilding.

Peacekeeping

When severe ethnic conflicts break out, the international community's first priority is likely to be to put an immediate stop to the fighting so that a peaceful context (however unstable) may be created for holding talks between the disputants and also to provide humanitarian relief to civilian populations who are the victims of such violence. Toward this end, an international third party may undertake *peacekeeping* operations in the conflict. Peacekeeping operations involve the physical interjection of outside military forces between the forces of disputants to keep them apart and thereby halt the fighting.[4] The target of peacekeeping operations is thus the "soldiers" or "warriors" of the disputing sides, and its aim is to curb their bellicose behavior, thereby creating a peaceful context for political negotiations and relief operations.

The conventional wisdom articulated by the enormous scholarly literature on international peacekeeping is that to be effective, peacekeeping operations by international third parties must fulfill three requirements. First, all parties to the dispute must give their prior consent to the peacekeeping operations by the international third party. Second, international peacekeepers must be impartial when dealing with the adversaries.[5] Finally, the use of force in peacekeeping operations must be limited, and peacekeepers may only use the minimum amount of force needed for self-defense.

The failure of peacekeeping operations by such international third parties as the United Nations to halt spiraling violence in recent cases of ethnic conflicts, such as in

Bosnia, Somalia, and Rwanda, has generated tremendous skepticism about the effectiveness of limited and impartial peacekeeping operations by international third parties. Richard Betts, for instance, was quick to point out that limited and impartial peacekeeping operations by international third parties sometimes succeeded in the past not because they were undertaken to halt the violence between adversaries who were willing to fight on, but because they were undertaken to monitor ceasefires worked out and accepted by the adversaries themselves prior to the interjection of the peacekeepers. But in those situations where no prior ceasefire or peace agreement was worked out and accepted by the adversaries, limited and impartial peacekeeping operations by international third parties failed to halt the hostilities; it would again fail today because it is a "destructive misconception" to believe that limited and impartial peacekeeping operations by international third parties can keep peace where none exists. The fundamental issue in a war (especially in ethnic conflict) is almost always "Who rules when the fighting stops?" Wars do not begin unless both parties in a dispute prefer to fight than concede, and as a corollary, wars do not end "until both sides agree who will control whatever is in dispute."[6] It is, therefore, a mistake to assume that peacekeeping intervention along with the offer of good offices will by themselves influence the belligerents to recognize the advantages of peaceful negotiation.[7]

Instead, Betts has suggested that it is better to undertake international "peace enforcement" operations in those situations of ethnic conflict where the belligerents have yet to be convinced that they have little more to gain by fighting.[8] International peace enforcement operations can be carried out in one of two ways. On the one hand, it could be a limited operation in terms of the use of force, provided it is not impartial. In other words, an international peace enforcer carrying out a limited military operation must choose sides in the conflict. The peace enforcer can then tilt the military balance in favor of one side in the conflict, thereby helping it to win and end the conflict. On the other hand, an international peace enforcement operation can be carried out impartially, provided it is not undertaken on a limited scale in terms of the use of force. In other words, an impartial international peace enforcer must deploy overwhelming military force in the conflict and thus gain total control of the situation. Only in this way can the peace enforcer have the power to impose and enforce a peace settlement on belligerents who are unwilling to give up fighting. Anything short of this, Betts argues, would block peace "by doing enough to keep either belligerent from defeating the other, but not enough to make them stop trying."[9]

Peacemaking

In contrast to peacekeeping or peace enforcement, peacemaking operations by international third parties usually involve politico-diplomatic activity whose objective is to bring the leaders of the disputing parties closer to a political settlement achieved through peaceful negotiations. In other words, peacemaking requires international third parties to play the role of intermediary during the negotiation process between the adversaries; the role-playing is aimed at achieving a political settlement of the conflict. The role of the intermediary in the negotiation process is particularly important during intense ethnic conflict because once the fighting begins, the adversaries are likely to be "reluctant to continue consultations or come together in order to discuss their problem."[10]

An international third party can play the role of the intermediary in the negotiation process between the adversaries by employing such methods as arbitration, mediation, or facilitation. *Arbitration* refers to "binding, authoritative third-party intervention in which conflicting parties agree to hand the determination of a final settlement to outsiders."[11] Arbitration, therefore, is a legal or quasi-legal method of conflict resolution that works only if the disputants submit their respective claims for outside arbitration and agree to abide by the arbitrator's decision. It is most effective in those situations "where the conflict has a strictly legal character."[12] However, its effectiveness and utility in intense ethnic wars is likely to be limited.

Compared to arbitration, *mediation* by international third parties may offer greater hope for resolving violent and intense ethnic conflicts. International mediators can offer their "good offices" to the adversaries to initiate meaningful political dialogue. In this way, lines of communication between the adversaries can be opened and different ideas and information shared. International mediators can also help change each adversary's image of the other by helping each side understand better the other's position, concerns, and constraints. In this way, the mediator may be able to induce concessions from the adversaries by narrowing their differences. In addition, by suggesting face-saving compromises, stressing common interests between the adversaries outside the immediate conflict, offering alternative proposals for settlement, and "linking agreement on one set of issues to agreement on another set of issues" through the building of "coalitions of support for desired outcomes and against undesired outcomes," the mediator may be able to bring the adversaries closer to a settlement.[13] Finally, at the postagreement stage, the mediator can offer guarantees that the terms of the agreement will be honored and implemented by all sides to the dispute.[14]

To be effective as mediator, an international third party must possess leverage over the adversaries. Leverage may come from the fact that mediation is a three-sided process, like a triangle. Knowing that there is a possibility that the mediator may support the other side, adversaries may abandon their inflexible stance and become more supportive of the mediator's position, thus giving it substantial leverage.[15] Moreover, availability of resources (political, economic, military, informational, conceptual, tactical, and supervisory) may also increase the mediator's leverage and enhance its ability to induce concessions from the adversaries by alternately using the carrot- (rewards for compliance) and-stick (punishment for noncompliance) approach.[16] The mediator's own image, prestige, standing, and credibility may also determine the leverage it enjoys over the adversaries.[17]

It is also believed by some scholars that the effectiveness of a mediator depends on whether adversaries perceive the mediator as impartial. Because mediation is a voluntary process to secure the trust, confidence, and cooperation of the adversaries (without which mediation would be ineffective), a third party must be perceived as impartial.[18] The impartial image of a third-party mediator depends largely on the prestige and credibility it enjoys internationally, the motives for its involvement, and its ability to treat all sides in the dispute fairly and equally. Credibility and prestige are crucial because an important source of influence is "possession of resources (physical, financial, informational)" that can be used "as 'leverage' when dealing with tactical rigidities."[19] But if the third-party's credibility is perceived as dubious, then the use of such resources to force concessions will only result in the hardening of positions during negotiations. Similarly, a third party that gets involved because of its own self-interest and calculations of gain will fail to secure "positive attitudes" of the adversaries towards a peaceful settlement of the conflict. Furthermore, the failure of the third party to be fair toward, and supportive of, all the disputants may rob it of its impartial image.[20]

As with peacekeeping operations, not everyone agrees that international mediation in intense ethnic conflicts calls for the third party to be impartial. In fact, effective mediation, it is argued, inevitably requires the mediator to threaten the adversaries that their noncommitment toward the peace process will force the mediator to take sides in the conflict.[21] As Touval points out, adversaries will accept the peace "package" advocated by the mediator only if they come to believe either that the mediator can help them get a better deal than the one they can get themselves by fighting or that rejecting the mediator's offer will cause it to side with the enemy.[22] Second, some scholars point out that because mediation represents a form of multilateral bargaining, all the parties, including the mediator, pursue their own interests. Hence, mediators cannot by definition be impartial, although mediators may find that their and the disputants' interests are best served by encouraging a fair and equitable settlement. Those who believe in this line of reasoning argue that the only qualification needed of an international mediator is its "acceptability" to the disputants.[23] Finally, some scholars suggest that the leverage of a mediator vis-à-vis the adversaries is at its maximum (the best moment for mediation to succeed) when the conflict is "ripe"—that is, when the conflict is at a stage of "hurting stalemate" where adversaries are exhausted and come to believe that little can be gained by escalating the conflict.[24] If this is so, then mediators may find it desirable to "induce ripeness [to a conflict] and contribute to the making of a 'hurting stalemate'" in order to "create a disposition among the disputants to settle the conflict."[25] But this would require the mediator to side with the weaker party, at least in the initial stages of the conflict, to create a military stalemate.

Another method of international third-party peacemaking is *facilitation* that differs from mediation in terms "of the assumptions on which it is based, its objectives, the participants, the identity of the third party, and the nature of the outcomes."[26] An assumption of the facilitation approach is that conflicts are the result of the suppression and denial of basic and inherent human needs for survival and development, such as security, identity, and recognition. From this it follows that the facilitation approach focuses more on human than institutional behavior. Facilitation, moreover, is cooperative, nonhierarchical, and noncoercive: "It does not include direct bargaining or negotiation, nor does the third party advocate or impose specific solutions."[27] Instead, the third party aims to "transform the situation from a 'conflict' that divides the parties into a 'problem' that they share and over which they need to cooperate if it is to be resolved."[28] In other words, by facilitating the interaction of the parties to the conflict and by provoking their creative thinking, the third party can play a constructive role in the process of finding a self-sustaining settlement. But that settlement can and must only come from the parties themselves because resolution of a conflict "means that a new set of relationships will eventually emerge which are self-sustaining and not dependent for their observance upon outside coercion or third parties. It is not a settlement imposed by a victor or a powerful third party, but rather a new set of relationships freely and knowledgeably arrived at by the parties themselves."[29]

Facilitation requires a third party to be knowledgeable about the various causes and theories of human behavior (especially violent behavior), human motivation and goals that influence human behavior, and the political value that human beings attach to their motivations, goals, status, and role. These are highly specialized qualifications; therefore a third party must be professionally qualified and experienced "to ensure that there is available to the parties all possible relevant information."[30] At the same time, it is preferable that the third party does not possess any specialized knowledge about the conflict and about the parties involved because, as Burton puts it, "the dispute or conflict is that of the parties. It is for them to define it, and to determine the issues, values and motivations that are relevant. An 'expert' is likely to know the answers before the parties have met!"[31]

Peacebuilding

A final role that an international third party can play in attempting to resolve ethnic conflicts is that of *peacebuilder*. Peacebuilding requires an international third party to undertake long-term socioeconomic and cultural activity directed mostly at the ordinary members of the disputing parties to change their negative image, perceptions, and attitudes toward the followers of the other side. Thus the main objective of peacebuilding is to implement "peaceful social change through socio-economic reconstruction and development."[32] An international third party can play this role either before conflict has erupted or in the postconflict years. If it has to play the peacebuilder role in the preconflict stage, then an international third party, perhaps acting on early warning signals of impending ethnic violence, may undertake certain socioeconomic and cultural activities to foster better understanding among hostile ethnic communities. On the other hand, postconflict peacebuilding activities may require economic reconstruction of war-ravaged societies and the reconciliation of ethnocultural communities. The important criteria for the success of peacebuilding perhaps are the financial resources at the third party's disposal and its patience and perseverance in what is bound to be a slow and ardous process.

Now that we have conceptually discussed the various ways that international third parties can attempt to resolve ethnic conflicts, let us assess the particular roles played by different international actors in resolving ethnic conflicts.

ETHNIC CONFLICT RESOLUTION BY THE UNITED NATIONS

It is generally assumed that the United Nations is ideally suited to play the role of a third-party reconciler of ethnic conflicts. Because of its impartial image as an international organization, the UN may be more readily acceptable to the adversaries as a third party. Second, UN intervention, by deinternationalizing a conflict—that is, preventing

TABLE 4.1   Resolving ethnic conflict through international third party action: techniques, qualities, targets, and objectives.

Techniques	Qualities	Targets	Objectives
Peacemaking	Impartiality, substantial leverage mediation, prior consent of adversaries not essential	Leaders	Induce or coerce the adversaries to sign a peace accord
Peacekeeping	Impartiality, limited use of force, prior consent of adversaries needed	Soldiers	Stop the violence
Peace Enforcement	Take sides if needed, massive use of force if needed to enforce peace accord, prior consent of adversaries not essential	Leaders/ soldiers	Coerce the adversaries to accept and implement a peace accord
Peace Building	Can be pre- and postconflict, policy coordination between various agencies essential	Masses	Foster mutual understanding between adversaries, reconstruction of war-torn societies, socioeconomic development

partisan intervention and counterintervention—may help prevent it from escalating.[33] Finally, the UN through its various bodies and agencies may be better suited to perform a whole range of tasks important for the successful de-escalation and resolution of the conflict. These tasks may include monitoring ceasefires and undertaking peacekeeping operations, arbitrating, mediating, or facilitating a negotiated peace agreement between the adversaries, providing humanitarian relief to the suffering populations, and undertaking pre- as well as postconflict peacebuilding measures.

In spite of these perceived advantages, the UN was not very active in resolving ethnic conflicts during the cold war period. It did not become involved in the war in Biafra or in the intercommunal clashes in Northern Ireland. It played only a token role in the India–Pakistan dispute over Kashmir and also during the secession of Bangladesh. The UN also has not been involved in Sri Lanka's brutal ethnic war, has failed to prevent ethnic clashes in Myanmar and Malaysia, did little to censure Indonesian atrocities in East Timor, and played no role in preventing the rise of ethnic passions in the former Soviet Union and Eastern Europe.

What factors can explain this dismal UN record when it comes to resolving ethnic conflicts? It is possible to argue first that the UN, contrary to its name, is an organization of independent states, and thus it is natural for the organization to take a pro-state stand in intrastate ethnic conflicts, which it has done repeatedly.[34] Moreover, because state sovereignty and nonintervention in a state's internal affairs are long-established international norms, the UN, under Article 2, Paragraph 7 of the charter, legally cannot intervene in intrastate ethnic conflicts unless the state concerned seeks UN intervention or a compelling case can be made to override the principles of state sovereignty and nonintervention.[35] But as we saw in the earlier chapters, states confronted with ethnosecessionism rarely seek international intervention in the fear that such intervention would legitimize the secessionists or restrict it from using force against the secessionists. International law also does not clearly define the conditions under which the international community could override the norms of state sovereignty and nonintervention in the domestic affairs of states. Finally, the UN's limited financial and military capabilities and constraints of cold war politics contributed to its inability to play an active role in resolving ethnic conflicts.[36]

But to be fair to the UN, it must be pointed out that in spite of these shortcomings the UN was not always a bystander in internal conflicts during the cold war period. As long as the major goal of the UN remained the maintenance of international peace and security, as enshrined in Article 1 of the charter, it had to be involved in some internal conflicts that threatened international peace, security, and human rights. Also, although the principle of self-determination under the charter was not meant to confer a right of separate statehood to ethnic groups, it still imposed an obligation on the UN not to ignore this principle's implications for ethnic conflicts. Further, some states did seek UN intervention in their internal conflicts, especially when they could not resolve these on their own.[37] Let us now assess the UN record in internal conflicts to judge how effective it has been as a peacekeeper, peacemaker, and peacebuilder.

The United Nations as a Peacekeeper

Evolution of UN Peacekeeping. Chapter VII of the UN charter provides the Security Council with powers to take action when breaches of peace or acts of aggression take place under the principle of *collective security.* Under Article 41, the Security Council may recommend to UN members any measure short of the use of force to be carried out against any one or more of the parties to the dispute. If these measures fail, then under Article 42 the Security Council may "take such action by air, sea and land forces as may be necessary to restore international peace and security." Articles 41 and 42 of the charter, therefore, provide the UN with the power to intervene in a conflict and to resort to coercive action in order to maintain global peace and security.

Yet, for the UN to undertake any action under the principle of *collective security,* the full agreement of the Security Council's five permanent members (the United States, Britain, France, Russia, and China) is an essential prerequisite because each has the power to veto any proposed action. Achieving unanimity among the five permanent members was difficult during the cold war period when the Security Council was ideologically split between the communist (the Soviet Union and China) and capitalist (the United States, Britain, and France) blocs. Consequently, the principle of *collective security,* as envisaged by the framers of the charter under Chapter VII, was never actually realized.

In this situation of paralysis, on Secretary General Dag Hammarskjöld's initiative, the UN devised the concept of *peacekeeping operations,* which went beyond the provisions of Chapter VI (dealing with the peaceful settlement of disputes) but did not resemble the military enforcement provisions of Chapter VII. As defined by the UN, the main aim of peacekeeping operations was to bring about a cessation of hostilities by interposing UN forces between the warring factions. Additionally, UN peacekeepers could perform other tasks (such as relief operations) as defined in their specific mandates. Thus peacekeeping is not specifically mentioned in the charter but "evolved as a noncoercive instrument of conflict control at a time when Cold War constraints prevented the Security Council from taking the more forceful steps permitted by the Charter."[38]

As defined by the UN, for peacekeeping operations to be conducted certain requirements had to be met. First, UN peacekeeping operations could only be undertaken if all parties to a dispute gave it their consent and continued cooperation. Second, UN peacekeepers were required to remain impartial toward all sides in a conflict at all times. Third, UN peacekeepers could only use the minimum amount of force required for self-defense and self-protection. Fourth, UN peacekeeping operations required a mandate from the Security Council under Chapter VI and its continued support throughout the duration of operations. Fifth, any changes to the peacekeeping mandate effected by the Security Council required the consent of all the disputants before it became applicable. Sixth, troops and personnel provided by member states for UN peacekeeping duties were to be under the exclusive control of the secretary general. Finally, UN peacekeeping operations were to be fully financed by the UN.

UN Peacekeeping Operations During the Cold War. Between 1948 and 1988, the UN undertook a number of peacekeeping operations. The record of these operations is mixed. Although the interjection of peacekeepers often provided brief periods of relief from war and suffering in some cases, the UN generally failed to turn these short-term gains into more lasting peace settlements. For example, in the Congo, crumbling state authority and the outbreak of conflict brought in UN peacekeepers in 1960. For the next three years, fighting continued in the country in spite of the presence of UN peacekeepers. In Cyprus, UN peacekeeping operations ended up hindering rather than facilitating a settlement by "reducing any sense of urgency for a political solution to the stalemate."[39] Similarly, in Lebanon, apart from some minor successes, UN peacekeepers failed to put an end to the festering conflict.

UN Peacekeeping Operations After the Cold War. The end of the cold war led to a dramatic expansion in the UN's peacekeeping duties. Since 1988, the UN has undertaken several new peacekeeping operations under three broad categories. The first included peacekeeping to control or manage unresolved conflict between states. As part of these traditional military-type operations, UN military observers helped monitor the cease-fire between Iran and Iraq from 1988 to 1991. UN military personnel also continue to monitor the demilitarized border between Iraq and

Kuwait. A second category included operations "to help implement negotiated settlements of long-standing conflicts, as in Namibia, Angola, Cambodia, El Salvador and Mozambique."[40] The third category comprised peacekeeping operations to bring intense ethnic conflicts, such as in Bosnia, under control.

The UN's expanding peacekeeping role in intrastate ethnic conflicts in the post–cold war period reflected the development of an international consensus regarding the conditions under which the norms of state sovereignty and nonintervention would no longer automatically prohibit the UN from intervening in domestic ethnic conflicts.[41] These conditions are threefold: (1) when domestic ethnic violence threatens to spill beyond international borders and threatens a wider conflict involving others not previously involved; (2) when ethnic violence results in massive civilian suffering and engenders refugee problems; and (3) when ethnic violence leads to crimes against humanity, including genocide, ethnic cleansing, repression, and forced expulsions.[42] Yet, contrary to rising expectations, the UN has failed to stop ethnic violence and prevent human rights abuses from Somalia to Sri Lanka. Consequently, its reputation has became tarnished because, ultimately, "it is the peace and security agenda that serves as the prism through which the UN is judged by the media and the public."[43]

Why Has the UN Not Lived Up to Expectations? Michael Mandelbaum believes that UN humanitarian intervention (the ostensible reason for undertaking peacekeeping operations in the post–bipolar period) has failed because such intervention invariably leads to political intervention—that is, "the task of alleviating suffering inevitably involves political consequences when suffering has political causes."[44] In particular, intervention in ethnic conflicts for purely humanitarian reasons calls for performing two political tasks: "guaranteeing the borders of countries under challenge, and constructing an apparatus of government in places where it is absent."[45] In Iraq and Bosnia, where ethnic groups (Shi'a and Serbs respectively) were trying to secede, the main goal of peacekeeping operations was to provide humanitarian relief and aid to civilians. But very quickly the UN became tangled in the web of local politics; this raised fundamental questions about whether the UN would help groups secede and how borders were to be drawn. The UN, in Mandelbaum's opinion, was clearly unprepared for such decisions.[46]

On the other hand, peacekeeping operations on humanitarian grounds in "failed states" such as Somalia and Haiti required the intervener to engage in state reconstruction, a task for which the UN was again unprepared.[47] Mandelbaum argues, therefore, that peacekeeping should obtain the backing of the international community but should be carried out by individual states—historically, the most successful agents of state building.[48] The exception to this rule was Cambodia where the United Nations Transitional Authority in Cambodia (UNTAC) was involved in policing the country, monitoring elections, and establishing a civilian administration. It is an open question whether the success of UNTAC could be replicated elsewhere.

Richard Falk puts the blame for the UN's ineffectiveness in restoring domestic peace and order on an anachronistic Security Council. The council's permanent membership, in Falk's opinion, no longer reflects the world power structure and the changes that have occurred in the relative power and wealth of states during the past few decades. Consequently, ascendent states have been reluctant to bestow the UN with substantial autonomy in matters relating to financing and enforcement—areas that are crucial to the UN's effectiveness. Furthermore, an obsolete Security Council results in the UN acting virtually as a foreign policy arm of its permanent members (particularly the United States). This has had serious repercussions on the ability of the UN to respond to aggression and threats to peace. In cases of domestic conflict perceived by the permanent members as affecting their national interests, they have preferred to pursue unilateral action based on the ancient concept of spheres of influence. This was evident in France's policy in Rwanda, the U.S. role in Haiti, and Russia's self-declared role as peacekeeper in its "near abroad."[49] By contrast, intractable conflicts that carry no immediate threat to the permanent members have been dumped on the UN without simultaneously providing it the capabilities necessary to take effective action.[50]

Paul Schroeder has offered a third explanation for the failure of the UN to punish violators of international law in the so-called New World Order (NWO). He suggests that the present trend in international politics (especially championed by those who believe in the formation of an NWO in light of the allied victory in the Gulf War) is to depict a confrontation emerging between states that allegedly break international law and those that supposedly uphold it. But it is a dangerous trend because when carried to its logical extreme, "the concept of the NWO as the collective enforcement of international law against transgressors" provokes resistance and violence on the part of lawbreakers in four distinct ways.

First, it makes international politics a zero-sum game and therefore violates a key assumption of the international system that "all essential actors should be preserved, because even an aggressive opponent, once curbed, has a necessary role to play."[51] Second, when the international community portrays the sanctions it imposes as law enforcement against violators, it impugns the honor of the accused party, thus giving it strong incentives to resist the sanctions (a government that cannot defend its honor can quickly lose power) and to mobilize domestic support against the international community.[52] This is what happened in the former Yugoslavia and Somalia. Third, in strategic terms the collective enforcement of international law against violators often causes the international community to pursue vague and undefinable goals. This may raise the stakes for the international community in terms of its prestige and credibility while the means of enforcement at its disposal remain limited. Thus disunity, defections, and juridical challenges to the legitimacy of international actions may quickly result within the international community.[53] Finally, the collective enforcement of international law against aggressors may create disputes among the coalition members over "sharing the costs and burdens of enforcement, and fears that enforcing the law will result in more suffering and damage than did the original alleged violation."[54] Schroeder thus concludes that the NWO, "so long as it is conceived as a collective effort to enforce compliance with international law or the will of the international community," as the UN has done, is unworkable and counterproductive.[55]

The Future of UN Peacekeeping.   Given these difficulties, how should the UN react if asked to enforce peace in situations of intense domestic conflict? Scholars are agreed that if the UN is called upon to perform peace enforcement functions, then limited and impartial military intervention undertaken with the consent of the adversaries (the traditional peacekeeping role) is unlikely to work. The UN must therefore redefine its traditional peacekeeping role to meet the new peace enforcement demands that are thrust on it—as indeed it did in sending an Implementation Force (IFOR) to Bosnia in late 1995.

A redefinition of the UN's peacekeeping role in internal conflicts will not be easy, however. Thomas Weiss, for instance, has warned that the UN must be prepared to face painful alternatives as a result of growing incongruity between available resources and increasing demand for intervention in internal wars with high civilian casualties, human rights violations, and other war crimes.[56] But what exactly are the UN's painful alternatives? Some are of the opinion that the UN should stay out of situations that call for peace enforcement through military means.[57] On the contrary, others point out that the UN has the moral duty to protect innocent civilians from slaughter and so must undertake military peace-enforcement operations in situations of conflict where ethnic cleansing, genocide, forced displacement, and other human rights abuses are occurring. But such military peace-enforcement operations should not be limited and impartial, nor should they be undertaken with the prior consent of the adversaries. In calling for UN peace enforcement operations, therefore, these critics envisage military operations that go beyond traditional peacekeeping.[58]

The United Nations as a Peacemaker

Charter Provisions on Peacemaking.   While the UN Charter does not explicitly mention the organization's peacemaking role in ethnic or other types of internal conflicts, under the provisions of Chapter VI the Security Council is empowered in situations that threaten international peace and security to call on all parties to settle their dispute by peaceful means and to recommend appropriate procedures and actual terms of a settlement. But it is up to the parties themselves, acting voluntarily, to resolve their dispute peacefully in the light of the UN's recommendation. The UN's traditional peacemaking role as understood from the charter is therefore closer to facilitation than mediation.

UN Peacemaking During the Cold War.   During the years of the cold war, the UN was caught in a dilemma. Although effective mediation was difficult to undertake as a result of the political division of the world and the virtual paralysis of the Security Council, at the same time the UN quickly realized that the permanent resolutions of conflicts can only be achieved through political negotiations; for that, leverage mediation was often required.

To overcome this dilemma, Secretary Dag Hammarskjöld introduced the concept of *preventive diplomacy.*[59] One common form preventive diplomacy took was the establishment of commissions of inquiry or observation units to examine the facts of a dispute. Such fact-finding activities included interrogation, observation, area surveys, and inspection, as well as the analysis and interpretation of these facts.[60] Generally, the office of the secretary general, often working under instructions from the General Assembly or the Security Council, supervised the commissions of inquiry, although these bodies could undertake their own investigative work. The UN could then make recommendations to the parties involved for a peaceful settlement. Another form of preventive diplomacy was the offer of "good offices" of the organization by the secretary general to disputants to hold political negotiations. In these negotiations, the UN often participated as a facilitator. A third way in which the UN practiced preventive diplomacy was to use the resources of the secretary general's office and the vast diplomatic network of the organization to establish behind-the-scenes meetings and contacts with various adversaries to win approval for peaceful settlements. Finally, the UN supervised elections, helped to draft constitutions, and provided early warnings of impending conflict.

To be sure, preventive diplomacy by the UN was a positive step forward, but when it came to resolving ethnic conflicts, the UN's peacemaking efforts were miniscule. Cold war restrictions aside, both the General Assembly and the Security Council were "inappropriate arenas for the settlement of ethnic conflict because they are composed of states and exclude ethnic groups that do not represent sovereign states."[61] Moreover, there was nothing in the charter that would allow the Security Council or the General Assembly to "relate to non-state agencies such as liberation movements, communal minorities, or political parties."[62] Ethnic groups, therefore, found it difficult to communicate their views to the UN unless they could find a state sponsor willing to raise their case, as Turkey did for the Turkish Cypriots in Cyprus and Arab states did for the Palestine Liberation Organization (PLO). But most ethnic groups did not have such state sponsors, which usually resulted in UN inaction.[63] The UN's lack of enforcement capability further undermined its effectiveness as a peacemaker, especially in cases where UN members passed resolutions in support of an ethnonationalist movement. Finally, the General Assembly and Security Council's style of operation—the passing of resolutions—undermined the UN's facilitating role in two distinct ways. For one, the tendency of UN members to outvote their opponents did little to encourage adversaries to negotiate on the issues that divided them.[64] Also at times closely worded resolutions, instead of providing the UN a general framework for pursuing a peace settlement, actually restricted the organization's room to maneuver.[65]

Has the UN Become a More Effective Peacemaker After the Cold War?   Between 1987 and 1991, the UN achieved a number of successes in settling outstanding conflicts. In 1988, the UN secretary general brokered the end of the Iran–Iraq war. The UN was also successful in affecting a peace agreement in El Salvador's civil war for which Secretary General Javier Pérez de Cuéllar received the Nobel Peace Prize for 1988. The accords that helped get the Soviet Union out of Afghanistan in 1989 were also constructed under UN auspices. The UN also shepherded Namibia, the last colonial country, to independence, was instrumental in securing the release of hostages in Lebanon, and worked out a political settlement in Cambodia.

These successes in peacemaking, argues Giandomenico Picco, are mainly attributable to the disassociation of the institution of the secretary general from use-of-force operations, unlike past UN practice.[66] Picco argues that "the functions of the institution of the Secretary General and the Security Council are complementary and work best when separated at the key dividing line involving the use of force."[67] To do otherwise—to associate the institution of the secretary general with UN military actions under Chapter VII of the charter—would have certain negative consequences, as the UN has come to experience.

First, military action under the secretary general would be ineffective considering the limited tools at his disposal and would ultimately undermine the credibility of the UN (and ultimately the credibility of the member states). Under the charter, the authority to use force is given to the Security Council. Even though the council is dominated by strong states, they are rarely willing to provide the secretary general with the resources (financial, military, and intelligence) needed to launch large-scale military actions. Consequently, "the Secretary General has managed use-of-force operations with tools better suited to Chapter VI peacekeeping ventures," and "This gap has led to questionable results in Somalia and Bosnia."[68]

Second, the involvement of the institution of the secretary general in UN actions involving the use of force "would undermine the Secretary General's impartial negotiating role, thus depriving the international community of a further instrument that it already possesses."[69] This impartial negotiating role of the secretary general is crucial if the UN is to play the role of the "good cop" during negotiations aimed at peacemaking, as opposed to the "bad cop" image that the Security Council would acquire in conducting use-of-force operations. Maintaining this distinction between good cop and bad cop is even more crucial if the secretary general is to hold high moral authority, often crucial to negotiations. This moral high ground would be lost if he ordered the use of lethal force as operations under Chapter VII would entail.[70]

Finally, compared to the Security Council, which represents the vested interests of its member states, the strength and effectiveness of the secretary general emanates from the office's high credibility and lack of vested interests. This standing could be damaged if the secretary general became closely identified with the use of force.[71]

Picco, therefore, strongly recommends that the tasks of the secretary general and the Security Council should be kept separate in the future if the UN is to become an effective peacemaker. The secretary general could more effectively play the role of a peacemaker and negotiator with help from skilled colleagues, special representatives, and a consistent approach. For its part, the Security Council could play a more effective role in the UN's use-of-force operations. It has the means, the ability, and a favorable political climate to define the *red lines of international conduct*—those activities of states or groups that are impermissible because they threaten international peace and security. Also, it can play this role even better by making its decision making more streamlined and its operations more predictable and consistent. Moreover, if needed, it can subcontract the use-of-force operations under Chapter VII "to a coalition of member states, as in the case of the war against Iraq, to a military alliance or a combination of alliances and other states."[72]

To be sure, not everyone is convinced that the UN has turned the corner in peacemaking because most of the structural limitations that restricted the organization's peacemaking efforts during the cold war era have carried over into the post–cold war period. Thus, Saadia Touval accounts for the UN's recent successes as peacemaker in terms of "the exhaustion of local parties and the unwillingness of external powers to continue supporting clients whose usefulness had expired with the Cold War."[73] As an example, Touval contends that Iran and Iraq accepted the UN-brokered cease-fire only after they had exhausted themselves by fighting for eight years. In Afghanistan and Cambodia, the Soviet Union and China were no longer interested in providing partisan support, thereby robbing local factions of the ability to continue the conflict. Similarly, in El Salvador the United States was interested in seeing an end to the conflict and, therefore, put pressure on the right-wing government to come to terms with the left-wing insurgency.

Therefore Touval cautions that these successes should not raise expectations about the UN's peacemaking capabilities. It still continues to suffer from inherent limitations that make it less effective in mediating complex international disputes or even *orphan conflicts*—those conflicts where no states are willing to mediate either because they have more pressing priorities or because they consider the conflict too risky and not directly affecting their interests.[74] The UN also lacks one of the principal criteria for effective mediation—leverage. It has neither its own military or economic resources, nor can it "harness the assets of international financial or trading institutions."[75] The UN can mediate only to the extent that its members (especially the permanent members of the Security Council) allow it to. The resources (material and diplomatic) needed by the UN for successful mediation also must come from the states, but while states have increasingly sought UN mediation in orphan conflicts, they have spared few resources to assure its success. Moreover, while the UN has a significant amount of legitimacy behind its actions, its credibility is "consistently eroded by its inability to formulate and pursue the kind of coherent policy essential to mediation."[76] The problem, as Touval sees it, lies with the UN's decision-making process that deprives the organization of dynamism and flexibility in pursuing mediation. Lack of credibility further decreases the leverage of the UN, hindering the bargaining process and diminishing the probability that the adversaries would accept the proposals put forward by the UN for settling the conflict. The erosion of credibility further hinders UN mediators from offering crucial "guarantees for implementing and observing an agreement."[77] For Touval, then, rather than becoming involved directly, the UN should encourage individual states to assume the responsibility for mediating conflicts in their region of influence.[78]

The United Nations as a Peacebuilder

The UN's Record as a Peacebuilder.   While the attention of most experts remains focused on the peacekeeping and peacemaking roles of the UN, a crucial function performed by the organization is the more long-term task of *peacebuilding*. Let us recall that peacebuilding requires changing the mutually antagonistic attitudes of ordinary people from each side of the conflict and initiating socioeconomic reconstruction to improve the lives of people shattered by war. These tasks can be performed in a variety of ways: (1) by undertaking economic development projects; (2) by providing education to ordinary people on different sides of the conflict to increase mutual understanding of each other's culture, belief, religion, practices, fears, priorities, and interests; (3) by pursuing superordinate goals—urgent goals that can only be achieved through cooperation between the conflicting sides—that cut across parochial interests; and (4) by implementing confidence-building measures between the conflicting parties.[79]

The UN charter underscores the importance of international cooperation in the economic and social spheres. Article 1, Paragraph 3 stipulates that a primary objective of the UN is to "achieve international cooperation in solving international problems of an economic, social, cultural, or humanitarian character." Further, Article 55 explicitly states that to create stability and well-being, which are necessary for peace, the UN shall promote:

> (a) higher standards of living, full employment, and conditions of economic and social progress and development; (b) solutions of international economic, social, health, and related problems; and international cultural and educational cooperation; and (c) universal respect for, and observance of, human rights and fundamental freedoms for all without distinctions as to race, sex, language, or religion.

Overall, the charter devotes two full chapters (IX and X) and a few other provisions towards these goals. Though not explicitly cited, some clearly fall within the realm of peacebuilding in ethnic disputes.

At the time the UN was established, it was assumed that specialized agencies of the UN would play a central role in peacebuilding activities. These included the Economic and Social Council (ECOSOC); the United Nations Educational, Scientific, and Cultural Organization (UNESCO); the International Labor Organization (ILO); the Food and Agricultural Organization (FAO); the International Bank for Reconstruction and Development (IBRD); the International Monetary Fund (IMF); and the World Health Organization (WHO).[80]

Disappointingly, these agencies have not always succeeded in building peace. Because it is not a supranational organization, the UN does not have the power to make decisions that are binding upon member states and their citizens, especially with respect to economic and social matters that fall within the domestic jurisdictions of states.[81] In cases of ethnic conflict, which would require working with governments and ethnic groups who may be politically and militarily opposed to each other, this task has proven to be even more difficult.[82]

Moreover, although the charter explicitly spells out the general principles and aims of the organization in social and economic matters, it does not provide any specific guidelines as to how these socioeconomic goals are to be achieved.[83] Consequently, the commitment of member states to pursue joint or separate action to achieve the aims of the charter in the socioeconomic sphere became a matter of good faith. In addition, the ECOSOC was composed of representatives of governments, often without the technical competence to tackle the large volume of complex questions that came before it. To obtain technical assistance, it created a number of functional subsidiary organs and commissions. For these to function efficiently, they should be staffed by experts chosen on the basis of personal qualifications, as the Dumbarton Oaks Proposals recommended. However, at the San Francisco Conference, this proposal was dropped in favor of having appointed representatives of member states who may or may not be experts in their fields. This undermined the effectiveness of the ECOSOC and the UN in undertaking economic and social tasks.[84]

Lack of coordination between the UN and the specialized agencies has hampered the organization's limited peacebuilding efforts. When it was created, there were wide variations in the membership of the UN and the specialized agencies. Although these have been greatly reduced, the specialized agencies remain different from the UN in terms of their composition, power, and voting procedures. Moreover, these specialized agencies, though a part of the UN system, have retained substantial autonomy. Coordinating the policies and operating practices of these various agencies has proved difficult for the UN, reducing its ability to engage in constructive and sustained socioeconomic development activities in conflict-torn areas.

Finally, the General Assembly's and ECOSOC's established procedure of passing resolutions and recommendations directed at member states and specialized agencies does not impose any legal obligation for them to take action. Members who disagree with a particular resolution are free to continue their dissent. Especially when the implementation of a resolution requires the support of crucial states—for example, asking states to contribute funds to the UN for undertaking economic development projects, such as road and school construction in strife-torn areas—the stance of the United States and other wealthy states is crucial. Furthermore, while the reports, studies, and surveys published by the UN and its specialized agencies serve the important purpose of providing information and drawing attention to important questions, the contributions of these studies "to the actual achievement of useful results are likely to be overemphasized."[85]

In spite of these obstacles, the UN and its specialized agencies have done some useful peacebuilding work in cases of ethnic and intercommunal conflicts. For example, in divided Cyprus, the Nicosia Master Plan (a project of the United Nations Development Program, UNDP) has developed better understanding between, and found solutions to common socioeconomic problems of, the Greek Cypriot and Turkish Cypriot communities through collaborative efforts of technical specialists from both communities. The UNESCO also initiated projects aimed at economic development and enhancement of mutual understanding between adversaries in Sri Lanka's ethnic conflict. The UN High Commissioner for Refugees (UNHCR) has done admirable work in Cyprus, Nicaragua, Cambodia, Somalia, Bosnia, and Rwanda.

UN Peacebuilding Under Post–Bipolarity.   With the resurgence of ethnic and other forms of violent internal conflicts in a post–bipolar world, increasing demands are being made on the UN to undertake peacebuilding activities either to prevent the outbreak of conflict or to reconstruct states torn by violent conflict. Secretary

General Boutros-Ghali stressed that political stability and security without sustained and durable economic and social development could be achieved because the root causes of political strife and military conflict are often the deterioration in economic and social conditions. He recommended that the UN adopt the concept of *postconflict peace building* not only in cases of international conflict but of internal conflicts as well.[86]

Postconflict peace building was best illustrated in El Salvador where a UN-sponsored peace agreement was signed in January 1992. After the signing, the UN disarmed the disputants and began "to play a central role in ensuring that far-reaching political, social, and institutional reforms agreed to in the negotiations were carried out to prevent the recurrence of violence."[87] But the UN peacebuilding experience in El Salvador exposed the problem of coordination in implementing diverse policies involving multiple actors in complex situations. The peace accord called for the creation of a National Civil Police that would remain separate and distinct from the armed forces, and it also envisaged land grants to the former guerrillas in exchange for their arms. From the UN's perspective, implementing these two proposals was critical for the return to normal civil life in the country. But the proposed reforms entailed high financial costs that were difficult to meet due to a drastic fall in the price of coffee (50 percent of El Salvador's export earnings come from coffee) after 1989. The lack of commitment on the part of foreign countries to help meet peace agreement requirements and, most important, the inability of the Cristiani government in El Salvador to increase the level of domestic financing to pay for these projects—itself constrained by the economic stabilization program put in place by the IMF—contributed to only partial realization of the peace plan.[88] UN and IMF peacebuilding policies were at cross-purposes, therefore. For de Soto and del Castillo, it was "as if a patient lay on the operating table with the left and right sides of his body separated by a curtain and unrelated surgery being performed on each side."[89]

To avoid this type of surgery in the future, the authors made three recommendations. First, international organizations should allow greater transparency between actions of different institutions and agencies through periodic and systematic exchange of information. This would provide the UN with "a unique source of early warning of potential clashes between different agencies" that in turn might "pave the way for action to enhance coordination."[90]

Second, international organizations must integrate their goals and activities to assist peacebuilding efforts under the overall supervision of the UN. For this purpose the long-dormant Liaison Committee—established in 1961 to include the UN secretary general, the president of the World Bank, and the heads of the UN Technical Assistance Board and the UN Special Fund, both predecessors of the UNDP and whose aim was to review peacebuilding by various international organizations and integrate them into a common set of goals—should be reactivated. Finally, "flexibility in the application of rules of financial institutions or adjustment of such rules when UN preventive diplomacy, peacemaking, or post-conflict peacebuilding so requires" is a must.[91] By establishing a closer link between the UN and the Bretton Woods institutions, it would introduce the concept of rewards into peacebuilding activities.

Concessional financing, for example, could be linked to compliance with peace agreement provisions. In this way, conditionality would serve peace along with pure economic objectives. In addition, flexibility would also prove helpful in carrying out unconventional institutional reforms in the host country, such as the creation of the National Civil Police in El Salvador. International lending institutions are reluctant to fund such projects, but if a degree of flexibility was allowed to permeate their operations, they might be pursuaded to reconsider their decisions on such projects.[92]

In making these proposals, de Soto and del Castillo recommend that the UN be able to draw upon and utilize the expertise and resources of the various international institutions engaged in peacebuilding activities. To make these bold changes, political will on the part of the major players is needed. The post–bipolar environment might offer greater incentives for such exercise of will.

United Nations' shortcomings in resolving ethnic conflicts have raised the question of whether other international players stand a better chance in settling ethnic and other types of internal conflicts in the post–cold war period. Let us now examine the third-party role that can be played (or are played) by three other types of international actors—states, regional organizations, international nongovernmental organizations—in ethnic conflict resolution.

STATES AS THIRD PARTIES IN ETHNIC CONFLICT RESOLUTION

Intervention by states in ethnic and other types of internal conflicts presents a dilemma for the international community. On the one hand, critics point to the long-established international norms of sovereignty and nonintervention and argue that intervention by a state in the affairs of another, even if for the ostensibly benign act of settling a conflict, violates these principles of international conduct and is akin to "an international version of assault or burglary."[93] Therefore, state intervention, even for conflict settlement, is impermissible. On the other side are those who argue that, in spite of the international norms of sovereignty and nonintervention, powerful states' involvement in the affairs of the weak has been a consistent feature of international politics. Because it cannot be wished away, it should be utilized in constructive ways to contain or settle conflicts. It is this second view that we consider here.

Major Powers and Ethnic Conflict Resolution

It is often argued that major powers have a special responsibility to help resolve ethnic conflicts because of these powers' enhanced capabilities and global roles and interests. This, of course, does not mean that every ethnic conflict would attract major power intervention, but that in their respective spheres of interests, major powers could play the leading role in settling or containing ethnic and other types of conflict.

For a third party to be an effective peacekeeper or peacemaker in ethnic conflicts, quick reaction to a threat to peace is often decisive. Unfortunately, international organizations such as the UN often remain paralyzed for months in conflict situations while its members debate various policy options. By contrast, major powers, due to vital interests in their spheres of influence, are unlikely to remain passive for very long in the face of threats in their regions.

As we have seen, successful third-party peacemaking depends on the resources, capabilities, and resolve of the third party. In these respects, major powers have an advantage over international organizations to make the intervention more effective. Whether acting unilaterally or in tandem with others, they are better suited to carry out military actions compared to international organizations. The UN does not have a standing army, nor does it have the resources to carry out large-scale military operations often required to keep peace in some of today's brutal and intense ethnic conflicts. Major powers have both and will use them to keep peace if the conflict affects their vital interests. In the post–cold war environment, European powers such as Britain, France, Russia, and increasingly Germany (forbidden by its constitution to engage in military action abroad) have demonstrated their resolve to intervene in conflict situations.

Critics have pointed out that because states—in particular major powers or superpowers—intervene in a conflict situation primarily to exploit the conflict for their own gains, such intervention—instead of containing or settling the conflict—may actually lead to conflict escalation by inviting counterintervention. A second critique is that exploitative intervention, by lacking legitimacy and impartiality, will not be credible enough to produce conflict settlement through peaceful negotiations. Fearing the intentions of the third party, adversaries would be disinclined to compromise.

Addressing the first criticism, it can be argued that during the cold war a major reason why the United States and the Soviet Union were able to contain ethnic and intrastate conflict within their respective spheres of influence was their tacit understanding that neither side would overtly intervene in the other's sphere of influence. Covert intervention was not ruled out but, if caught, the side trying to upset the status quo generally retreated without a showdown (the Soviet withdrawal during the Cuban Missile Crisis of 1962 was a good illustration). The mutual acceptance of these "rules of the game" meant that each superpower had virtually unlimited powers to make unilateral decisions within its region. Both the United States and the Soviet Union regularly intervened in their backyards (Latin America for the United States and Eastern Europe for the Soviet Union) to suppress conflict. The end of the cold war and the global disengagement of the major powers has not led to an abandoning of the idea of regional spheres of influence. The West has tacitly accepted a prominent Russian role in policing its "near abroad." Western European states have taken the lead in managing European crises such as Bosnia. China and Japan are also increasingly seeking to manage domestic conflict in their regions. The United States has not lost sight of domestic conflict in its traditional sphere, Latin America, as evidenced in the effort to resolve the dispute in Mexico's Chiapas state.

Regarding the second charge of exploitative intervention, the lessons of peace enforcement in Bosnia and Somalia make clear that impartial and limited interventions may be more counterproductive than partisan aggressive ones. Hopkins has noted that the possibility of great power intervention in ethnic conflicts may encourage ethnonationalists to search for "domestic solutions" to their grievances because such intervention may prove detrimental to their interests. Due to the cold war alliance structure, superpowers helped enhance the coercive capabilities of states that were their allies and ignored their repressive policies toward ethnic minorities. Thus, the United States supported the Pakistani and Indonesian governments in their repression of the Bengalis in East Pakistan and the Muslims in East Timor.[94] It also supported Turkey in its conflict with the Kurds. The Soviet Union, too, helped the government of Ethiopia in its fight with separatists in Eritrea and Tigre. It also provided support to Iraq in its conflict with the Kurds. These one-sided, pro-statist policies of the super-powers often "inhibited ethnic community members from committing resources to the assertion of rights or to demands for a separate political entity."[95] On the other hand, states (especially weaker ones) that were dependent on superpower support for resolving their internal problems risked becoming totally penetrated by an external power unless they could find a negotiated solution to their internal problems.

Peacebuilding is a costly and complex process requiring the simultaneous performance of different tasks at different levels of operation. Considering the limitations of the UN and its specialized agencies and the disinclination of major powers to make money available for peace-related projects in remote conflicts, it may be more realistic to ask major powers to undertake peacebuilding exclusively in their own regions. Such a division of labor would provide much needed relief to an already overburdened UN.

Ethnic Conflict Resolution by Third-World Regional Powers

In a more multilateral world, some scholars have argued that third-world regional powers should take the lead in settling ethnic and other types of internal conflicts in their regions. As Chester Crocker points out, "If nobody else gets involved in conflict resolution in regions around the world, you can be pretty sure that regional hegemons will."[96] Crocker is also skeptical that in a period of post–bipolarity, increasingly cooperative relationships between the great powers can diminish the importance of third-world regional powers as third-party reconcilers of regional ethnic conflicts because, in his opinion, solutions and settlements of regional conflicts are ultimately reached by regional powers.[97]

What factors explain the growing assertiveness of certain third-world states in their respective regions? Using Modelski's and Riggs's classification of states in the contemporary world, third-world states such as India, Brazil, Egypt, Nigeria, Turkey, Argentina, Thailand, Indonesia, and Malaysia can be classified as advanced "transitional" states.[98] While not as developed and powerful as states of the developed world, they possess greater power capabilities compared to their regional neighbors. Because a state's foreign policy behavior is a function of its power capability, an advanced transitional state may have an expanded foreign policy capability.[99] Therefore, at least in regional affairs, these states may be attracted to play the role of regional cop, especially when the major powers show little interest.

Self-interest could also motivate regional powers to play the role of third-party reconciler of regional ethnic conflicts. Bandyopadhyaya argues that advanced transitional states are particularly keen to use foreign policy to foster national development, for which regional stability is an important prerequisite.[100] Thus, the outbreak of ethnic conflict in a neighboring country may be perceived by a regional power as destabilizing and harmful to its interests. Such states, therefore, cannot remain indifferent toward the conflict, nor can they assume that the adversaries will be able to settle their differences without outside help.

Protection of ethnic kin in neighboring states may also motivate a regional power to intervene in ethnic conflicts. States, as we saw in the previous chapter, may have both affective and instrumental reasons for supporting their ethnic kin—especially when they are a persecuted minority—in neighboring countries. Regional powers may be tempted to provide partisan support to their co-nationals, but a policy of diffusion and encouragement may at times be deemed too risky, especially if the possibility of "conflict transformation" through counter-intervention is high. At such times, a regional power may decide to follow a policy of reconciliation toward the conflict as a compromise option.

Other instrumental factors, such as security and geopolitical considerations as well as pressures of domestic and international politics, may also influence a regional power to intervene in a neighboring ethnic conflict with the aim of reconciling the adversaries. For instance, the desire to prevent a regional rival from exploiting a conflict close to its borders (thereby posing a security threat) may motivate a regional power to intervene to find a solution quickly. A regional power may favor a negotiated settlement of a neighboring state's ethnic conflict to stem the flow of refugees, which almost always puts an enormous socioeconomic burden on the receiving state. Sometimes, the fear of a contagion effect may motivate a regional power to seek a quick end to ethnic violence in a neighboring state. Pressure exerted by the international community may also induce a regional power to play the role of a third-party reconciler in regional ethnic conflicts. Such pressure may be brought by the UN to avert a humanitarian disaster, or it may be brought by a major power if it is engaged elsewhere.

While it is clear that regional powers have strong incentives to become involved in regional ethnic conflicts as third-party reconcilers, what is not clear is whether these states possess the qualities needed to be effective in such a role. If we accept the view of Ryan, then we have to conclude that intervention of regional powers in regional ethnic conflicts as third-party reconcilers ends up transforming them into more complex and protracted ones, less amenable to resolution.[101]

There are reasons to expect such an outcome. If a regional power intervenes in a neighboring ethnic conflict for purely instrumental reasons, it may come to see the conflict "as something to be exploited rather than resolved."[102] In that case, the primary concern of the regional power would be to promote its own interests rather than to help adversaries overcome their mutual antagonism and suspicion and find a negotiated political solution. The regional power may begin to demonstrate lack of sensitivity toward the issues in dispute, to start taking sides, and even to introduce new issues and priorities, thereby complicating the conflict. The failure of the Indian peacekeeping mission in Sri Lanka furnishes a good example.

If, on the other hand, a regional power intervenes primarily for affective reasons, such intervention may be seen as biased, leading to loss of legitimacy and credibility of the intervener. The regional power will fail to secure the compliance of all the disputants for a negotiated political settlement. This in turn may lengthen the conflict. The only way biased intervention may succeed in bringing an end to conflict is if the force introduced by the third party is great enough to ensure the outright victory of one side.[103] A good example is the Indian military intervention on behalf of Bengali secessionists in Pakistan in 1971; such events are rare, however.

Finally, the capabilities of regional powers in the third world are inadequate for any major peacebuilding operations, a task best left for international organizations operating in close association with major powers. The role of regional powers is to help with the implementation of various peacebuilding projects.

REGIONAL ORGANIZATIONS AS THIRD PARTIES IN ETHNIC CONFLICT RESOLUTION

The involvement of regional organizations as third-party reconcilers of ethnic conflict is not a new phenomenon. During the cold war period, two kinds of regional organizations played active roles in diffusing tension in crisis situations. First, regional organizations representing specific geographic regions often took an active part in maintaining peace in case of conflicts within that region. Second, regional organizations making up political blocs or alliances took an active part in diffusing subsystem or intrabloc crises.[104] In the first category of interventions were those undertaken by the Organization of American States (OAS) in a number of Latin American conflicts; the peacekeeping operations undertaken by the Arab League in Lebanon in the mid–1970s, ostensibly to encourage Syrian disengagement from the conflict; and intervention by the Organization of African Unity (OAU) in a number of internal conflicts such as in the Congo, Chad, and Western Sahara, as well as in conflicts between such states as Morocco and Algeria, and Ethiopia and Somalia. In the second category were North Atlantic Treaty Organization (NATO) efforts to deal with the Cyprus crisis so as to defuse the tense relations between two bloc members, Greece and Turkey. The Political Committee of the Warsaw Treaty Organization (WTO) also sought to prevent friction between bloc members, such as between Hungary and Romania over Transylvania.

Regional organizations possess certain characteristics that allow them to play the role of a third-party conflict manager effectively. While some regional organizations are little more than forums for their members and lack the independence needed to become an effective third party, actions undertaken under the auspices of regional organizations are often more highly valued than state action. Regional organizations tend to acquire an image of impartiality that make them more acceptable to the adversaries. Young notes that the "parties responsible for shaping the actions in question [that is, conflict management or resolution] are likely to be the same whether the regional organization acts or not but the promulgation of actions through a regional structure sometimes makes a real difference in terms of a factor such as subjective impartiality."[105]

During the cold war, regional organizations "tended to exhibit a strong 'external orientation' and to concern themselves with the security of their area vis-à-vis outside threats rather than with the processes of interaction among their members."[106] As a result they were usually not considered to be salient third-party reconcilers of intra-regional disputes. To a large extent, this was a function of bipolar politics, although notable exceptions existed: the OAS and the OAU played important third-party roles in intraregional conflicts. In the post–bipolar environment, however, with the growth in the popularity of multilateral approaches toward peace and security, regional organiza-tions have demonstrated more willingness to become active in intraregional conflicts.

For instance, the European Union (EU) and the Organization on Security and Cooperation in Europe (OSCE) have been active in regional crisis management and resolution, while the Council of Europe has sought to enforce state compliance with minority and linguistic rights to avert future conflicts. The EU and the NATO were at the forefront of international action in Bosnia. The OSCE sent fact-finding and rappor-teur missions to the Balkans to support the sanctions and humanitarian measures taken by the UN, EU, and NATO. Moreover, OSCE missions designed to provide early warn-ing of the spill-over of the hostilities in Bosnia into the nearby regions of Serbia, Montenegro, Kosovo, and Macedonia were undertaken in 1992 and continued until mid–1993. The OSCE also sent missions to Hungary, Bulgaria, Romania, Ukraine, and Albania to monitor sanctions compliance. Furthermore, under OSCE auspices, interna-tional efforts were made to solve the conflict in Nagorno-Karabakh—an Armenian enclave in Azerbaijan. The OSCE was active in the former Soviet Union, undertaking limited peacebuilding missions in Moldova and Estonia to promote better understand-ing between communities in these states. It established a mission in Latvia to monitor issues related to the Russian minority. The OSCE also sent peacekeepers to other areas of the former Soviet Union where local wars had broken out. We discuss this in Chapter 5. In Africa, the OAU was engaged in Angola, Mozambique, and Somalia. In Southeast Asia, the Association of Southeast Asian Nations (ASEAN) has emerged as a powerful actor in fostering cooperation between regional states.

Given the increased role of regional organizations and the difficulties faced by the UN in maintaining peace and security across the globe, some experts have sug-gested that it would be better for the UN to delegate future peacekeeping, peacemak-ing, and peacebuilding operations to regional organizations, provided they accept the UN secretary general's overall command of these operations. For instance, as Bosnia has demonstrated (see Chapter 9), peacekeeping and peace enforcement operations in Europe may be better performed by NATO forces than by a UN one. This idea envis-ages NATO as a military arm of the UN. The idea especially appealed to those who believed that the end of the cold war and the loss of a common enemy eroded much of NATO's earlier purpose as a defensive military alliance against the Soviet Union. So these critics suggested modifications to NATO's size, troop strength, and mission to reflect the new environment of peace and to enable its members to extract a financial dividend from that peace. The idea also appealed to those who advocated the creation of a permanent UN military force but were aware of the practical difficulties involved. For this group, NATO forces acting as the military arm of an active UN were the next best alternative. The concept of NATO as the military arm of the UN for peacekeeping and peace enforcement tasks may work provided its role is confined to the European theater of operations. Moreover, as the experience of Bosnia demonstrated, NATO operations may prove ineffective for peace enforcement if the international community itself lacks a clear military strategy and a proper chain of command.

Another alternative to NATO in Europe is the Western European Union (WEU), formed by the Brussels Treaty of 1948 after the dissolution of the wartime Western Union (WU). During the cold war years, the WEU was made a part of the NATO defense system, but with the ascendency of NATO as the dominant security structure of the Western alliance, it gradually lost most of its original relevance, power, and influence. The revival of the WEU started in the mid–1980s. In 1987, many European powers, concerned that the United States and the Soviet Union were conducting bilateral nuclear disarmament talks and then imposing the outcomes on Europe, demonstrated a desire to strengthen the WEU to bring about greater European integration in social, economic, and security matters. As the WEU grew in importance after 1989, its position relative to NATO became blurred and it may have acquired certain advantages over NATO. Unlike NATO, the WEU is a European organization that previously represented European security concerns and interests within NATO, so it may be more effective as a peacekeeper and peace enforcer in European conflicts. The WEU may also have greater freedom of maneuver than NATO in defense matters outside of the European theater, as was evident during the Gulf War when the WEU—not NATO—deployed European forces from all three services in the gulf.

Other regional organizations may be more suited to play the roles of peacemaker and peacebuilder rather than peacekeeper or peace enforcer. As the failure of the OAU peacekeeping operations in Chad demonstrated, regional political organizations, when asked to keep peace, often face the same kinds of problems as the UN. Ryan maintained that the OAU peacekeeping mission in Chad failed mainly because of the disinclination of regional states to contribute troops, the lack of adequate financial resources, the disinclination of the adversaries to seek a negotiated political settlement (the force went in without a cease-fire agreement being signed by the adversaries beforehand), and the continued support that was being provided by some members of the OAU to one or other of the parties to the dispute.[107] Similar problems have at one time or another undermined the effectiveness of peacekeeping operations undertaken by the UN. Regional political organizations, therefore, may be more effective as peacemakers because this involves less financial cost and because these organizations usually have high stakes in, and better knowledge about, intraregional conflicts. Local mediators may also have personal contacts with key leaders of the disputing parties that may prove useful at the negotiating table. Similarly, regional economic organizations may be able to play effective peacebuilding roles both in the pre- and postconflict phases.

INTERNATIONAL NONGOVERNMENTAL ORGANIZATIONS AS THIRD PARTIES IN ETHNIC CONFLICT RESOLUTION

International nongovernmental organizations (INGOs) have made significant contributions as third parties in conflict situations. A case in point is the International Committee of the Red Cross, which has provided invaluable service in a number of conflicts dating back to the early years of the cold war. For instance, during the Algerian war of the 1950s and the Hungarian crisis of 1956, the Red Cross was able to provide medical services and humanitarian relief to combatants and civilians.[108] More recently, the Red Cross has been involved in a number of conflicts—Cambodia, Afghanistan, Somalia, Bosnia, and Rwanda to name a few. Similarly, Amnesty International has played an important role in highlighting abuses of human rights in various regions of the world. One has also seen humanitarian services rendered by Doctors Without Frontiers.

How effective are international nongovernmental organizations in containing or resolving conflict? International nongovernmental organizations cannot be very effective as peacekeepers or peace enforcers because they lack too many of the important physical resources needed for such operations. On the other hand, their real strength lies in their impartial image, freedom of operations, and unique ability to rise above the political struggles. In this way, INGOs have the potential to be effective peacemakers.

Still, one must be aware of certain deficiencies of INGOs that can inhibit them from effectively playing this role. INGOs may not possess substantial powers of leverage over the adversaries. Mediators need to earn the respect of the adversaries by offering innovative suggestions, ideas, and frameworks for a political solution. INGOs may not always have full information, first-class diplomatic skills, and an authoritative image. As Young points out, the "lack of such qualities as saliance and respect, coupled with typically low scores in such areas as relevant information and diplomatic skill, severely limits the interventionary roles which nongovernmental organizations might undertake successfully."[109] These deficiencies may further limit INGOs from performing various service roles "such as inspection and supervision, which are useful in maintaining rules during a crisis or in implementing agreed-upon termination arrangements."[110]

Humanitarian assistance together with preventive and postconflict peacebuilding are areas where INGOs can and do play positive roles. Because of the resurgence of violent conflicts in the post–bipolar world and also because of the increasing demand being made on the international community to "do something" to avert humanitarian disasters, the perception of the international community regarding the usefulness of INGOs in such operations is changing. A clear sign of this change came in 1988 when the UN General Assembly passed a resolution upholding the principle of intervention within a sovereign state by international nongovernmental organizations on humanitarian grounds, such as systematic violations of human rights, persecution and genocide of ethnoreligious minorities by state machineries, and the need to deliver humanitarian aid urgently. In adopting this principle, the UN recognized that force may be used if necessary to help and support the work of INGOs in these circumstances.

A special task for the international community in the future will be preventive and postconflict peacebuilding. The lead role rightfully belongs to the UN but the UN will need all the help that it can get. In this respect, a historic opportunity is present today to create an interactive mechanism among the UN, regional associations and agencies, and international nongovernmental organizations with global reach and operations. Specifically, INGOs could play a constructive role in implementing, monitoring, and overseeing a range of UN peacebuilding operations. Because they are active in the field, INGOs could also serve as early warning mechanisms for the UN and the international community by providing information on potential or actual violations of peace agreements, problems of project implementation or coordination, the failure of disputants to respect human rights, and so on. This would not only help the international community to better coordinate peacebuilding activities, but also to pinpoint regions where preventive diplomacy, peacekeeping, and peace enforcement activities must be directed or redirected.

CONCLUSION

In this chapter, we have conceptually analyzed the role of international third parties in ethnic conflict resolution. We have also surveyed the various international actors that may be drawn into domestic ethnonationalist disputes and suggested types of actors and the roles seemingly best suited to resolve such conflicts. We recognize that these actors, the roles they play, and the modes of operation they pursue may be redefined in the course of the conflict. Almost by definition, each ethnic conflict is idiosyncratic and different in important ways from others. A dynamic perspective that describes the evolution of a conflict has many advantages over a static, snapshot approach. The case studies in Part II provide such a dynamic perspective.

DISCUSSION QUESTIONS

1. Why is resolving ethnic conflicts so important? What roles can the international community play in this regard?
2. What are the essential differences between peacekeeping and peace enforcement? Do you feel that traditional international peacekeeping in ethnic conflicts should be abandoned in favor of international peace enforcement?
3. In your assessment, has the United Nations succeeded or failed as an international third party in resolving ethnic conflicts? Are other international actors more able to play this role in the future?
4. What is preventive diplomacy? Can it be an effective strategy for preventing future ethnic conflicts?
5. Most scholars argue that the most difficult aspect of ethnic conflict resolution by international third parties is both pre- and postconflict peacebuilding. Why is this so?

NOTES

1. Jacob Bercovitch, "Third Parties in Conflict Management: The Structure and Conditions of Effective Mediation in International Relations." *International Journal,* 40, 4, Autumn 1985, p. 736.
2. *Ibid.,* pp. 737–738.

3. Michael Harbottle, "The Strategy of Third Party Interventions in Conflict Resolution." *International Journal,* 35, 1, Winter 1979–1980, p. 120.
4. Ibid., pp. 120–121.
5. *Impartiality*—not taking sides—is not the same as *neutrality*—having no effect on the outcome—because the very presence of a third party changes the nature and structure of the dispute. See Bercovitch, "Third Parties in Conflict Management," p. 739, fn. 5.
6. Richard K. Betts, "The Delusion of Impartial Intervention." *Foreign Affairs,* 73, 6, November/December 1994, p. 21.
7. *Ibid.,* pp. 21–22.
8. *Ibid.,* p. 20.
9. *Ibid.,* p. 21.
10. John W. Burton, "The Procedures of Conflict Resolution," in Edward E. Azar and John W. Burton, eds., *International Conflict Resolution,* (Boulder, CO: Lynne Rienner, 1986), p. 100.
11. Mark Hoffman, "Third-Party Mediation and Conflict Resolution in the Post–Cold War World," in John Baylis and N.J. Rengger, eds., *Dilemmas of World Politics: International Issues in a Changing World.* (Oxford: Clarendon Press, 1992), p. 264.
12. *Ibid.*
13. *Ibid.,* pp. 268–269.
14. Saadia Touval, "Why the U.N. Fails." *Foreign Affairs,* 73, 5, September/October 1994, p. 51.
15. *Ibid.*
16. On this point, see Oran Young, *The Intermediaries: Third Parties in International Crises.* (Princeton, NJ: Princeton University Press, 1976).
17. Bercovitch, "Third Parties in Conflict Management," p. 749.
18. *Ibid.,* p. 749.
19. *Ibid.*
20. Burton, "The Procedures of Conflict Resolution," p. 105.
21. See D.G. Pruitt, *Negotiation Behavior.* (New York: Academic Press, 1981); S. Touval, ed., *The Peace Brokers: Mediators in the Arab-Israeli Conflict 1948–1979.* (Princeton, NJ: Princeton University Press, 1982); S. Touval and I.W. Zartman, "Introduction: Mediation in Theory," in Touval and Zartman, eds., *International Mediation in Theory and Practice.* (Washington, DC: Westview Press for the SAIS, 1985).
22. Touval, "Why the U.N. Fails," p. 47.
23. Hoffman, "Third-Party Mediation and Conflict-Resolution in the Post–Cold War World," p. 268.
24. See D.G. Pruitt and J.Z. Rubin, *Social Conflict: Escalation, Stalemate and Settlement.* (New York: Random House, 1986); and Touval, "Why the U.N. Fails," p. 51.
25. Touval, "Why the U.N. Fails," p. 51.
26. Hoffman, "Third-Party Mediation and Conflict Resolution in the Post–Cold War World," p. 270.
27. *Ibid.,* p. 271.
28. *Ibid.,* p. 272.
29. A.J.R. Groom, "Problem Solving and International Relations," in E. Azar and J.W. Burton, eds., *International Conflict Resolution.* (Brighton: Wheatsheaf, 1986), p. 86.
30. Burton, "The Procedures of Conflict Resolution," p. 105.
31. *Ibid.*
32. Harbottle, "The Strategy of Third Party Interventions in Conflict Resolution," p. 121.
33. Stephen Ryan, *Ethnic Conflict and International Relations,* (Aldershot: Dartmouth, 1990), p. 42, 176.

34. Frederick L. Shiels, "Introduction," in Shiels, ed., *Ethnic Separatism and World Politics.* (Lanham, MD: University Press of America, 1984), p. 10.

35. Milton J. Esman and Shibley Telhami, "Introduction," in Esman and Telhami, eds., *International Organizations and Ethnic Conflict.* (Ithaca, NY: Cornell University Press, 1995), pp. 9–10. For an excellent analysis of the norm of "collective non-intervention" under the charter, see Ann Van Wynen Thomas and A.J. Thomas, Jr., *Non-Intervention: The Law and Its Import in the Americas.* (Dallas: Southern Methodist University Press, 1956), Chapter 7.

36. Raymond E. Hopkins, "Anomie, System Reform, and Challenges to the UN System," in Esman and Telhami, eds., *International Organizations and Ethnic Conflict,* p. 89.

37. Ryan, *Ethnic Conflict and International Relations,* pp. 120–121.

38. See Boutros Boutros-Ghali, "Empowering the United Nations." *Foreign Affairs,* 72, 5, Winter 1992/1993, p. 89; and Jack Donnelly, "The Past, the Present, and the Future Prospects," in Esman and Telhami, eds., *International Organizations and Ethnic Conflict,* p. 59.

39. W. Andy Knight and Mari Yamashita, "The United Nations' Contribution to International Peace and Security," in David Dewitt, David Haglund, and John Kirton, eds., *Building a New Global Order: Emerging Trends in International Security.* (Toronto: Oxford University Press, 1993), p. 300.

40. Boutros-Ghali, "Empowering the United Nations," p. 89.

41. Two developments promoted this consensus. First, the end of bipolar ideological rivalry eliminated the main reason for the norm of nonintervention—that is, the prevention of conflict among superpowers each trying to impose its own model of legitimacy on other states—and created a broad agreement as to what the appropriate domestic system within states should be. The Gulf War demonstrated this when the UN General Assembly adopted a resolution demanding that Saddam Hussein's regime stop the repression of Iraq's own citizens. Second, the widespread endorsement of human rights as an international norm encouraged humanitarian intervention by the international community to alleviate the suffering of those whose rights were violated by their own governments, by rival groups or nations, or by other states. See Michael Mandelbaum, "The Reluctance to Intervene in Foreign Country Problems." *Foreign Policy,* 95, June 22, 1994, pp. 13–14.

42. See Esman and Telhami, "Introduction," p. 12.

43. Richard Falk, "Appraising the U.N. at 50: The Looming Challenge." *Journal of International Affairs,* 48, 2, Winter 1995, p. 625.

44. Mandelbaum, "The Reluctance to Intervene in Foreign Country Problems," p. 4.

45. *Ibid.,* p. 5.

46. *Ibid.,* pp. 4–5.

47. *Ibid.,* p. 11.

48. *Ibid.,* p. 10.

49. Falk, "Appraising the U.N. at 50," pp. 630–631, f.n. 10.

50. *Ibid.,* pp. 637–638, 642–643.

51. Paul W. Schroeder, "The New World Order: A Historical Perspective." *The Washington Quarterly,* 17, 2, Spring 1994, p. 29.

52. *Ibid.*

53. *Ibid.*

54. *Ibid.*

55. *Ibid.*

56. Thomas G. Weiss, "Intervention: Whither the United Nations?" *The Washington Quarterly,* 17, 1, Winter 1994, pp. 123–124.

57. See Mandelbaum, "The Reluctance to Intervene in Foreign Country Problems;" Falk, "Appraising the U.N. at 50;" Weiss, "Intervention."
58. See Betts, "The Delusion of Impartial Intervention;" Boutros-Ghali, "Empowering the U.N."
59. See Inis Claude, *Swords into Plowshares: The Problem and Progress of International Organization.* 4th ed. (New York: Random House, 1984), p. 312.
60. Knight and Yamashita, "The United Nations' Contribution to International Peace and Security," p. 301.
61. Ryan, *Ethnic Conflict and International Relations,* p. 143.
62. Sydney D. Bailey, "The U.N. and the Termination of Armed Conflict—1946–64." *International Affairs,* 58, 3, 1982, p. 469.
63. *Ibid.*
64. See Claude, *Swords into Plowshares,* p. 179.
65. Sydney D. Bailey, *How Wars End: The United Nations and the Termination of Armed Conflict, 1946–1964.* (Oxford: Clarendon Press, 1982), vol. 1, p. 168.
66. The only instance in this period where force was used by the United Nations was in the Gulf War. However, in that conflict the UN Security Council empowered the U.S.-led military coalition to take action against Iraq, and the secretary general's office was kept outside these actions in a de facto fashion.
67. Giandomenico Picco, "The U.N. and the Use of Force: Leave the Secretary General Out of It." *Foreign Affairs,* 73, 5, September/October 1994, p. 15.
68. *Ibid.*
69. *Ibid.*
70. *Ibid.,* p. 18.
71. *Ibid.,* p. 16.
72. *Ibid.*
73. Touval, "Why the U.N. Fails," p. 44.
74. *Ibid.,* pp. 45–46.
75. *Ibid.,* p. 52.
76. *Ibid.*
77. *Ibid.,* p. 54.
78. *Ibid.,* pp. 45–46.
79. Ryan, *Ethnic Conflict and International Relations,* pp. 61–76.
80. Under the charter, the central organ responsible for discharging the duties of the UN in the social and economic sphere is the General Assembly. This was a concession to the smaller states in return for their reluctant acceptance of the prominance given to the Security Council and the major powers in matters of peace and security. However, being a large and cumbersome body, it was anticipated that the General Assembly would have difficulty in discharging these functions. So the framers of the UN charter created the Economic and Social Council (ECOSOC)—a subsidiary organ of the General Assembly—to undertake more specialized tasks to realize this goal of the UN. The ECOSOC consists of eighteen members elected by the General Assembly and its powers are enunciated under Chapter X of the charter.
81. Leland M. Goodrich, *The United Nations.* (New York: Thomas Y. Crowell, 1959), p. 268.
82. Ryan, *Ethnic Conflict and International Relations,* p. 147.
83. Goodrich, *The United Nations,* p. 267.
84. *Ibid.,* p. 272.
85. *Ibid.,* p. 281.
86. Boutros-Ghali, "Empowering the United Nations," pp. 101–102.

87. Alvaro de Soto and Graciana del Castillo, "Obstacles to Peacebuilding: United Nations." *Foreign Policy,* 94, Spring 1994, p. 70.
88. *Ibid.,* p. 71.
89. *Ibid.,* p. 74.
90. *Ibid.,* p. 79.
91. *Ibid.*
92. *Ibid.,* pp. 80–81.
93. Mandelbaum, "The Reluctance to Intervene in Foreign Country Problems," p. 13.
94. For a good description of U.S. policy toward East Pakistan and East Timor, see Seymour M. Hersh, *The Price of Power: Kissinger in the Nixon White House.* (New York: Summit Books, 1983), pp. 444–464; and N. Chomsky, *Radical Priorities.* Edited by C.P. Otero. (Montreal: Black Rose, 1984).
95. Hopkins, "Anomie, System Reform, and Challenges to the U.N. System," p. 86.
96. "Resolving Conflict in the Post–Cold War Third World: The Role of Superpowers." *In Brief . . . .* (Washington, DC: United States Institute of Peace). May 29, 1991, no page number.
97. *Ibid.*
98. For details of Riggs's and Modelski's study, see F.W. Riggs, "International Relations as a Prismatic System," and George Modelski, "Agraria and Industria: Two Models of the International System," in Klaus Knorr and Sydney Verba, ed., *The International System: Theoretical Essays.* (Princeton, NJ: Princeton University Press, 1961).
99. See Jayantanuja Bandyopadhyaya, *The Making of India's Foreign Policy.* (New Delhi: Allied Publishers, 1979), p. 16.
100. *Ibid.*
101. Ryan, *Ethnic Conflict and International Relations,* p. 37.
102. *Ibid.*
103. *Ibid.*
104. Young, *The Intermediaries,* p. 105.
105. *Ibid.,* p. 106.
106. *Ibid.*
107. Ryan, *Ethnic Conflict and International Relations,* pp. 130–131.
108. Young, *The Intermediaries,* p. 108.
109. *Ibid.,* pp. 109–110.
110. *Ibid.,* p. 110.

PART II

Case Studies

Nationalism and the Collapse of an Empire: The Soviet Union, Russia, and Chechnya

In Part I, we explored the meanings of nationalism and ethnic conflict and we considered the international dimensions of the two phenomena. In Part II, we apply the analysis of the domestic and international aspects of ethnic conflicts to specific cases. We organize the analysis of each case into four sections: why ethnic conflict occurred; how the international system reacted; why the conflict was or was not internationalized; and the extent to which external parties sought to intervene or not.

In addition, each of the chapters in Part II considers a distinct theme related to ethnic conflict. In this chapter, we ask how the collapse of an empire can provide an opportunity structure for the emergence of self-determination movements. In Chapter 6, we focus on the theme of constitutional secessionionism as a form of ethnic conflict. By contrast, Chapter 7 is concerned with a violent case of secession and its impact on the forms that third-party intervention took. Finally, Chapter 8 examines the international conditions that allowed an ethnic conflict to be resolved in favor of the breakaway group.

THE BREAKDOWN OF EMPIRES

Does the collapse of an empire fan ethnic conflicts because of the power vacuum that is left in its wake? Is there a ripple effect by which one large nation's nationalism is mimicked by smaller nations? The case we study to answer these questions is the dismantling of the Soviet empire. The unholy alliance between Russian nationalism and the nationalisms of other peoples of the USSR—Balts, Ukrainians, Armenians—helped put an end to the communist imperium in 1991. It led to a phenomenon that has been dubbed "matrioshka nationalism:" Like the brightly painted Russian wooden doll that contains constantly smaller dolls within it, the resurgence of Russian nationalism in the 1990s spawned "lower order" nationalisms and, with them, ethnic conflicts. The clearest example of this is seen in Chechnya's fierce struggle for independence from Russia.

It is surprising to discover that in the literature on the rise and fall of empires, nationalism is rarely identified as a pivotal factor; historians and political scientists theorizing about the nature and fate of empires have looked to other explanations. One understanding of empire was that it was primarily shaped by the economic needs of a great power. British political historian John Strachey developed a simple chronology of empires in history: "(i) the original, servile, empires based upon slave labor, (ii) the mercantile empires based upon the plundering sort of commerce which we have described . . . in the case of the East India Company's eighteenth-century empire in India, and (iii) the fully developed capitalist empires."[1] The latter developed "a distribution of income and other characteristics which leave their directing classes little choice but to attempt the conquest, colonization and exploitation of as much of the world as they can get hold of."[2] Strachey recognized that shortly after World War II even the latter type of empire had become unprofitable and obsolete.

Influential twentieth-century theories describing how empires were formed and imperialism engendered included those of John Hobson in his *Imperialism* (1902) and Vladimir Lenin in his *Imperialism: the Highest Stage of Capitalism* (1917). Political scientist Michael Doyle regarded Hobson and Lenin as examples of the "metrocentric theory" of empire, where it was essential "to look within the dominant metropoles and examine the internal drive to external expansion."[3] This "domestic structures" approach stood in contrast to systemic theory, which "combines an account of motives with a portrait of opportunities and arrives at a determinate result."[4] Realists in international relations such as Hans Morgenthau could be included in this category. Doyle also referred to pericentric theory, the primary focus of which was on a second actor other than the metropole.

We can also use this framework to explain how the *collapse* of empires can be metrocentric, systemic, or pericentric. In his magisterial *Decline and Fall of the Roman Empire,* eighteenth-century scholar Edward Gibbon offered a nuanced social explanation for the decay of Rome during its 1300-year history. He favored a primarily metrocentric explanation, though he acknowledged that systemic features, such as disparity of power and states' struggles for survival, also were influential. The avarice and materialism of both Romans and peoples ruled by Rome weakened the human fiber of society. But Gibbon identified as "the most potent and forcible cause of destruction, the domestic hostilities of the Romans themselves."[5]

Although describing not empires but great powers, Paul Kennedy singled out imperial overstretch as a cause of decline. He employed the notion not in some vague way as gobbling up more than what could be digested but in quantifiable terms:

> the fact remains that all of the major shifts in the world's *military-power* balances have followed alterations in the *productive* balances; and further, that the

rising and falling of the various empires and states in the international system has been confirmed by the outcomes of the major Great Power wars, where victory has always gone to the side with the greatest material resources.[6]

A country's industrial base was crucial, therefore, in helping it attain great power status. Pursuing a metrocentric explanation, Kennedy also contended that a disequilibrium between productive capacity and widening great-power commitments would lead to its military weakening and hasten its decline:

> The history of the rise and later fall of the leading countries in the Great Power system since the advance of western Europe in the sixteenth century—that is, of nations such as Spain, the Netherlands, France, the British Empire, and currently the United States—shows a very significant correlation *over the longer term* between productive and revenue-raising capacities on the one hand and military strength on the other.[7]

In focusing on twentieth-century empires, Doyle was inclined to stress a multicausal explanation of their rise and fall: "The course of modern empire has been determined by changes in the character of the international environment, in the domestic society of the metropole, and in the development of social change and the balance of collaboration in the peripheries."[8] The latter pericentric framework is particularly well suited to the study of anticolonial and secessionist types of ethnic conflicts arising after the collapse of an empire.

WHY DID ETHNIC CONFLICT OCCUR?

Soviet Imperialism and Great Russian Nationalism

The end of the Soviet Union raised a number of historical controversies concerning the nature of the communist system that Lenin had constructed. Three controversies are particularly relevant to the relationship between Soviet power and Russian nationalism. First, there has been considerable debate about whether the Soviet Union represented a mere variation of long-standing Russian imperialism or, to accept a succession of Soviet leaders at their word, marked a departure from the imperial idea and a shift toward internationalism.

A second historical controversy is whether the Soviet period was characterized by a sustained effort at the russification of non–Russian peoples (symbolized by the notion of *sliyanie,* or merger of cultural groups), or whether Soviet federalism provided for significant cultural space for more than 100 national groups.

A third controversy is whether, despite the existence of an elaborate police state, non–Russians opposed the Soviet state or they were so repressed that a nationalist explosion could only occur when the Soviet center lost its ability to rule.

We can shed light on all three issues by examining the character of the Soviet political system. There are important similiarities and differences between the former Soviet empire and other empires.[9] The imperial quest, evidenced in the conquest and acquisition of new territories, is a defining characteristic of all empires. Expansion of Soviet power into Transcaucasia in the early 1920s and into Central Asia in the late 1920s—even though indigenous socialist forces had already gained considerable power—testified to Soviet leaders' concern with ensuring Russian rather than mere communist control in peripheral lands. Hugh Seton-Watson caustically pointed out how "The arguments of Soviet historians that the conquest of Central Asia by the Tsars was objectively progressive are essentially a Marxist-Leninist version of the arguments of Kipling."[10] Also, as in the case of most imperial conquests, Seton-Watson was correct to emphasize how "The journey to 'socialism' of the Soviet type is a one-way trip: there is no return ticket."[11]

There were some notable differences between the Soviet model of empire and other ones. Seton-Watson noted two points:

> The first is that the non–Russian peoples of the Russian Empire were very much more advanced in their general level of civilisation than the peoples of the British colonies in Africa, and even than those of India. The second is that the proportion of the metropolitan to the colonial peoples was quite different. The proportion of Russians to all non–Russians was about 1:1, and of Russians to Central Asian Moslems about 5:1, whereas the proportion of British to Asian and African colonial subjects was about 1:10.[12]

The Soviet empire was unique in ways other than the use of the ideology of socialist internationalism to justify Russian conquest and domination.

We come to the important question: Did Soviet interests coincide or conflict with the agenda of Russian nationalism? Some historians contend that Lenin became the founder of a new Russian dynasty disguised as national bolshevism. In this role, Lenin was effectively a promoter of Russian national interests. But those concerned about the *sang pur* of Russia's leaders point to Lenin's impure origins (a maternal grandfather had been Jewish) and to Jews such as Trotsky, Sverdlov, Kamenev, and Zinovyev among the early bolshevik leaders.

Neo–Stalinists claim that it was the Georgian native who engaged in Russian empire building.[13] The ultimate proof of Stalin's nationalist credentials was the fact that many non–Russian groups had been forcibly annexed (Baltic peoples), exiled (Tatars, Chechens), starved (Ukrainians), targeted for purges (Jews), or simply denied any semblance of political autonomy (the various federal republics). In the Stalin era and especially during World War II, grand Russian historical figures such as Ivan the Terrible, Alexander Nevsky, and Dimitri Donskoi (hero of the battle of Kulikovo in 1380) were romanticized as builders of a greater Russia. All of this constitutes compelling evidence that Stalin was the first communist representative of Russian nationalism.

If Soviet leaders were simply disguised Russian empire builders, they failed to russify conquered peoples. This is a characteristic the Soviet empire shares with the Ottoman or Habsburg empires that also did not force the imperial language on subject peoples. The results of russification were poor in 1920, in 1950, in 1970, and in 1990. In a book published in 1952 in the period of high Stalinism, East European historian Roman Smal-Stocki polemicized:

A convincing proof of the invincible national oppositions against Soviet Moscow and of their strength lies in the fact that the Russian Communist Party faced in 1950 practically the same problems as in the late 20's. In Europe the "orientation to the West" of the non–Russian nationalities; in Asia Pan-Islamism, Pan-Turkism and Pan-Afghanism, offer encouragement to the national independence movements of the non–Russian peoples.[14]

Studies of language learning among non–Russians showed that two decades later little progress had been recorded in making non–Slavic peoples proficient in Russian. Russians living outside their own republic were also invariably not bilingual. They were under no pressure to learn the local language, indicating the privileged status they enjoyed uniformly across the USSR. The need for *parity bilingualism,* whereby Russians living outside the Russian republic (Russia was one of fifteen republics within the Soviet federative system) would learn the local language, was evident then as it is still today.[15] More significant distortions were reflected in data pointing to the overrepresentation of Russians in political, economic, and military leadership positions.

But if the USSR was a Russian empire in disguise, there were features about it that were unsatisfactory to more ardent Russian nationalists. During the Gorbachev years, Russian nationalism seemed to be directed primarily against the ossified Soviet structure rather than against the non–Russian peoples. Thus in the glasnost period, key communist publications backed Gorbachev's reforms seeking to decentralize power.[16] A leading representative of moderate Russian nationalism was medieval literary scholar D.S. Likhachev. On close terms with Raisa Gorbachev, he defended Russia's national heritage from Soviet degradation. Moreover, he represented a current in Russian nationalism that did not seek aggrandizement at the expense of other nations. As historian Simon Dixon noted, "Likhachev represents that part of the nationalist spectrum least inclined to denigrate other nations, consciously opposing (inoffensive) patriotism to (aggressive) nationalism."[17]

But another current, Russian ultranationalism, lamented the failure of Soviet policy to russify minority peoples. It was this orientation that sowed the seeds of ethnic conflict. Its adherents were unhappy with the state of interethnic relations prevailing in the USSR. Supposedly a multinational state, little cross-ethnic bonding took place naturally. Conservative Russian nationalists sought to exclude non–Russians from the Russian polity altogether. The ultranationalist critique of Soviet power was then that it had failed to bring about integration of the many nations living in the USSR.

Official Soviet nationality policy proclaimed the goal of forging a *sovietskii narod*—a Soviet nation—that would allow all nationalities to retain their formal cultural identities while injecting a socialist content and value-system into them. But this policy failed to integrate not only the titular peoples (those nations after whom Soviet republics were named) such as Lithuanians, Georgians, and Uzbeks but also with second-order titulars (minorities within the Russian republic itself): Tatars, Chuvash, Bashkirs, and Mari in the Middle Volga region; Chechens, Balkars, and Karachai (all deported peoples) in the north Caucuses; and Yakuts, Buryats, and Tuvans in Siberia.

Some writers have argued that the failures of the policy of assimilation were due to the nature of Soviet federalism itself. Gregory Gleason suggested that:

> Soviet national federalism has not produced a mobilizational conduit for political loyalties, shifting them first from ethnic group to republic, then from republic to the union, then from union to the larger internationalist community of man. On the contrary, Soviet national federalism has resulted in divided loyalties. In precisely this way, Soviet federalism has become an instrument by which ethnic identities are reinforced, aspirations for collective ethnic advancement are encouraged, and the visions of minority national futures are legitimized.[18]

A real policy of russification would have denied even restricted autonomy to national minorities. But it is difficult to accept this reasoning given that autonomy hardly existed in fact: "Any American town has a larger measure of independence and self-government than a Soviet republic."[19] Russian nationalists had little reason to complain about too much decentralization of power in the former USSR.

Furthermore, when the Soviet center sought to assimilate nontitular nations such as Jews, Crimean Tatars, Lithuanian Poles, or Volga Germans, evidence of linguistic russification was clear-cut. In a number of cases, Soviet leaders used proxies to push for assimilation of smaller peoples, such as Yakuts, exerting assimilationist pressure on other minority peoples in Siberia. Russification was one of a number of forms of dominance pursued by Soviet rulers, then, to keep nationality groups in check. The Soviet central authorities succeeded when they bullied the weak. These were the conditions that engendered ethnic conflict between Russians and others when the Soviet Union disintegrated.

Democratization as a Source of Ethnic Conflict

The Russian nationalism emerging in the Gorbachev period, from 1985 to 1991, seemed to take a more inclusionary form, encouraging other nations to assert themselves too. In Gorbachev's first years in power the agenda of reform—perestroika and glasnost—overshadowed all other issues including, incredulously, the concerns of the 45 percent of the Soviet population that was not Russian. The large-scale institutional changes envisaged by the new Communist Party leader were unprecedented in the seventy-year history of the Soviet Union. Preoccupied with reforming the Soviet system, Gorbachev overlooked the nationalist challenges being organized against the Soviet system. More understandably, he failed to perceive a threat to the Soviet system posed by its dominant nationality, the Russians. The probability that a powerful Russian nationalist movement would emerge, that it would be led by a high-ranking Soviet apparatchik (Yeltsin), and that it would then create a duplicate set of political institutions (foreign ministry, interior ministry) in Moscow, in the shadows of the Kremlin walls where Soviet institutions were housed, remained a far-fetched scenario at the beginning of the 1990s.

The unintended consequence of Gorbachev's liberalization policies was also unimaginable. As historian John Dunlop starkly put it: "Presumably the last thing that Mikhail Gorbachev wanted to accomplish when he took power in 1985 was to prepare the emergence of an independent Russian state."[20]

During the next five years, the issue of nationalism came to dominate politics in the USSR. A special Central Committee Plenum on nationalities policy was held in September 1989 and sought to remake the Soviet federation by investing republics with real political and economic responsibilities. The reinvigorated form of Soviet federalism advocated by Gorbachev ended up being stillborn. Parallel structures for an independent Russian state, created step-by-step by Russian President Yeltsin during 1990–1991, overwhelmed the petrified Soviet system. Thus, devolution of power only reinforced emerging centrifugal tendencies.

In December 1989, the Lithuanian Communist Party seceded from the federal Communist Party of the Soviet Union (CPSU) and in March 1990 the Lithuanian parliament declared Lithuania's independence from the USSR. The following month the Supreme Soviet, or federal parliament, countered with a law requiring a waiting period of up to five years before a republic could secede. In April 1991 a new union treaty was drafted and several months later submitted to the Soviet population for approval. While it was approved in those areas where it was held, six Soviet republics refused to conduct the referendum on their territory, rendering the result moot.

The nationalist surge was visible elsewhere. It mobilized large numbers of citizens, brought new leaders to power, and occasionally produced violent encounters with Soviet security forces. In July 1991, a month after being elected president of the Russian republic, Yeltsin announced that he was prepared to recognize the independence of the three Baltic states. When Gorbachev's Soviet Union followed suit in September 1991 in the aftermath of the failed coup to reestablish Soviet authoritarianism, it provided further evidence that the USSR's days were numbered.

The remaining twelve republics of the USSR—most of which had already issued declarations of sovereignty—now considered the full independence option. The Almaty accords, signed in the capital of Kazakhstan on December 21, 1991, created an eleven-member (Georgia did not participate) Commonwealth of Independent States (CIS). It recognized Russia as the successor to the USSR in the UN Security Council and other international organizations. When the military formally pledged allegiance to Yeltsin as commander-in-chief and Gorbachev handed over nuclear codes to him that same week, all that remained was for the Russian flag of the tsars to be raised over the Kremlin on Christmas day.

The Conflict of Identities

Scholars east and west have been divided as to the causes of the nationalities explosion that brought down the USSR. One explanation was to attribute the systemic crisis to mistakes committed earlier in the Soviet period. One-time Gorbachev advisor Fyodor Burlatsky implored observers to "look at the intense national feelings and hatreds that are erupting around the country. All these problems were created by the authoritarian past."[21] Political dissident Len Karpinsky noted: "We ourselves created this danger by trampling these republics, disregarding their national interests, culture, and language. Our central authorities planted the roots of the emotional explosion of national sentiment we are now witnessing."[22]

These views largely ignored the deep-rooted identities and attachments being awakened in many peoples of the USSR. Explanations for Soviet collapse could not be focused solely on the Soviet center, then, but much Western literature shared a similar perspective. A major study of the nationalities question by Bohdan Nahaylo and Victor Swoboda concentrated "on the relationship between the Russians and the non–Russians."[23] The central thesis of *Soviet Disunion* was that Russian domination exercised through the Soviet state was responsible for nationalist unrest. Timothy Colton, too, discounted the importance of grass-roots nationalism in overthrowing the communist empire. In *After the Soviet Union,* he wrote:

> In sum, the Soviet Union's end was crafted, not by representatives of the state in concert with a political opposition and private groups, but by public officials alone, working for the most part behind closed doors. The compact reached was one *among governments,* meaning by this time the cooperating republic governments. Nongovernmental players were not welcome at the table and were informed of what had been decided only after the fact.[24]

By contrast, in her incisive study of Latvia's road to independence, Rasma Karklins provided a more nuanced analysis of the self-reinforcing processes that led to the creation of new states. She described three principal types of ethnopolitical identities: the ethnic community proper, the territorial state, and the political regime.

> Although many theorists ask what economic, social, or other factors promote or assuage ethnic assertiveness, few examine the links between types of political regimes and types of ethnic politics. The Soviet experience suggests that regime type is crucial to whether nations want to identify with an established multinational state or seek to form new states.[25]

The author emphasized the multicausal character of the assault on the Soviet system. The struggle was over regime change and it, in turn, impacted ethnopolitics. She asked: "Does it matter whether a multinational state—be it the former USSR or another state—is ruled autocratically or democratically, and if so how? Moreover, once a transition to democracy starts, does multiethnicity play a constructive or destructive role, and under what conditions?"[26] For her, a democracy could not be reconciled with an ethnic control system. As a corollary, empowerment of ethnic communities went hand in hand with empowerment of democratic forces.

The linkage between democratic and nationalist projects is clear from Karklins's analysis. German political scientist Claus Offe also highlighted the "ethnification of the politics of transition" (his focus was on Eastern Europe).[27] Yeltsin's first term as president exemplified how fusing democratic and nationalist objectives was good politics in the transition phase, but it became perilous politics subsequently when more committed democrats and more determined nationalists each accused Yeltsin of betraying their cause, producing greater internal strife in Russia.

Regime identity was an especially significant factor in the rise of separatist movements throughout the Soviet Union. The rejection of an identity based on the

USSR brought democrats from many countries together and encouraged them to assist each other's efforts to find new political and ethnic identies. Karklins concluded that, above all, "The changing self-definition of Russians was crucial for the collapse of the USSR. During the late 1980s more and more Russians rejected a Soviet identity and opted for the self-rule of people and peoples."[28] This was because "For most Russian democrats and some traditionalists, any territorial state larger than the RSFSR became discredited due to links to Communist Soviet identity."[29] Mark Beissinger echoed this point: "The construction of a modern Russian identity could occur only on the basis of the deconstruction of the symbiosis between Russian and Soviet imperial identities."[30] Roman Szporluk even traced Russia's crisis of identity back to the time of Lenin's seizure of power in 1917:

> Precisely because Russia itself had not yet resolved the key issues of its modern identity when the Bolsheviks won—the relations between state and society, between nation and empire—the same issues reemerged as Soviet power was disintegrating. In a real sense, among the post–Soviet nations facing the problem of nation and state building, the Russians are in a particularly difficult situation. They were used to being "the leading nation" in the USSR, but they were also an object of manipulation and a victim of political manipulation—their identity made and remade by the party.[31]

A key assumption made by Russia's nascent democratic movement of the late 1980s was that a nation oppressing others could not be free itself. Russian democrats came to believe that the separatist claims of non–Russian nations had to be treated as part of the broad movement toward participatory democracy. But by the mid–1990s, much of the idealism of the democratic movement had dissipated. Further, when separatist movements in Russia proper arose, even democrats supported their suppression. Inadvertently, democrats had created conditions for the emergence of ethnic conflict.

Nationalist Mobilization in Post–Soviet Russia

Walter Laqueur has described the momentous impact on the Russian psyche of the collapse of the USSR: "Three centuries of Russian history were undone in a few days in August 1991 as the result of the weakness of the center."[32] There could be no question, in his view, that the calamity of losing many Russian-ruled territories when the Soviet Union passed out of existence would eventually produce a reaction in Russian society: "The breakup of the Soviet Union is the central event bound to shape the course of Russian nationalism and of Russian politics, as far ahead as one can see. It could be compared with the impact of the Treaty of Versailles (1919) on postwar Germany and with the loss of North Africa for French politics in the 1950s and 1960s."[33]

Whether Russia's own independence from the USSR has served as adequate compensation for loss of imperium remains an open question. Russian independence was achieved through the combination of Yeltsin's deft leadership and wider political mobilization, witnessed in the euphoria of defeating coup forces in August 1991. But more deep-seated, enduring factors ensured that the combination of pressure from below and opportunism from above became the immediate catalyst for independence.

The theory of reactive ethnicity can help explain why Russian nationalist mobilization occurred. It points to the infiltration of a peripheral, subnational area by members of the dominant cultural group. A "cultural division of labor" results in the region, thereby fomenting an ethnic backlash. Russia was the dominant nation in the USSR and not in its periphery, but we should draw attention to the perception shared by many Russians that it was their country that had been infiltrated by other nations— from the Soviet Muslim republics, the peoples of the Caucasus, the indigenous groups of the Far East. Russians concluded that there were now too many non–Russians in a Russian-dominated state. As a result, reactive ethnicity was palpable in Moscow, Leningrad, and above all in Russian provincial towns.

Furthermore, lands considered historically Russian such as the Crimea—indeed, most of Ukraine—the northern part of Kazakhstan, and much of the Caucasus, were also viewed by Russian nationalists as having been infiltrated and stolen by other nations. On the streets of Almaty (Kazakhstan), Kiev (Ukraine), Chisinau (Moldova), Simferopol (Crimea), and Kazan (Tatarstan), a Russian backlash against the titular nationality had become perceptible. The 25-million members of the Russian diaspora stranded outside Russia in 1991 felt that they had become a lower stratum of people in traditional Russian lands. Reactive ethnicity could operate even among a dominant nation feeling it was losing its dominance.

Russian ethnic mobilization can also be explained by the ethnic competition perspective. Under conditions of competition, "Ethnic political mobilization is sparked when ethnic groups (dominant and subordinate) are forced to compete with each other for the same rewards and resources."[34] Of former constituent republics of the USSR, only Ukraine was in a position to challenge Russian dominance. But competition for centrally allocated resources can be viewed in relational as well as absolute terms. The problem of inequity was raised by Russian nationalists when small or backward states were perceived to be receiving more than their fair share of resources. Russian nationalists invoked the predatory behavior of many non–Russians. "Why do Estonians and Latvians, Armenians and Georgians enjoy higher standards of living than we do?" was a question asked more frequently. It was the *kto kovo* question—who is taking advantage of whom? Many Russians came to believe that they were forced to compete for dwindling resources with smaller, undeserving nations, and one writer traced Soviet economic stagnation to "the system of patronage inherent in the affirmative action programs which, in turn, led to the rise of regionally and/or ethnically based criminal networks that operated at the expense of the official economy."[35] Perceptions of unequal competition, therefore, helped fuel the nationalist tide within Russia. In turn, it led to ethnic countermobilization by many non–Russian peoples.

James Rosenau has argued that most societies would soon use performance criteria to evaluate their governments. He believed that if this happened, patriotism and nationalism would decline and "Unabashed assertions of sovereign rights will diminish in frequency and intensity as adequate proof and appropriate performance become increasingly salient as criteria of national conduct."[36] Unfortunately, there is little evidence that performance criteria have served to stabilize the political situation in Russia and its shaky neighbors. In fact, adopting performance criteria when the performance is poor may actually exacerbate parochial or nationalist sentiments. Security specialist Jack Snyder has asserted that

> The failure of some post–Soviet states to provide economic security may also galvanize nationalist reactions. This would be especially dangerous in Russia, where economic nationalists are politically allied with nationalists calling for the forceful protection of co-ethnics whose security is seen to be at risk in neighboring states. An economic depression sweeping nationalists into office might, therefore, change not only Russian economic policy, but also foreign and military policy."[37]

The Core Ideas of Russian Nationalism

The Russian federation, often viewed as isomorphic with Soviet power, launched its independence struggle when it concluded that the results of sovietization policies had served to undermine rather than strengthen the status of Russians. However, it would be wrong to deduce from the swiftness with which independence was achieved that Russian nationists comprised an ideologically united group.

Dunlop has described the different currents in Russian nationalism from the early perestroika period on.[38] These included liberal nationalists who renounced Russia's authoritarian past while taking pride in its cultural achievements. Centrist nationalists were modern-day Slavophiles, cautious about Westernization but avoiding outright xenophobia. By the early 1990s, nationalists with more authoritarian platforms competed with democratic ones. These included the nationalist right, sometimes called the National Bolsheviks, who manipulated Leninism to achieve nationalist aims. But authoritarian, anticommunist nationalists emerged as well. The best known of these was the controversial new leader of the ultraright, Vladimir Zhirinovsky (see the next section). A Russian nationalist who did not fit into any one of these categories was Aleksandr Solzhenitsyn, a Nobel prize laureate in literature.

A longtime critic of the harm that the USSR was said to have inflicted on Russia, Solzhenitsyn not only attacked the nihilism of communist ideology but also praised the fundamental goodness of traditional Russian life: its spirituality, its innocence, the village. He also advanced damning criticism of Western civilization—its materialism, veniality, and misguided notion of political democracy that produced feebleness and naivete.[39]

For Solzhenitsyn, Russia is not defined by some imperial mission; indeed, the West was mistaken to equate Russia with the Soviet Union. "The word 'Russia' has become soiled and tattered through careless use; it is invoked freely in all sorts of inappropriate contexts. Thus, when the monsterlike USSR was lunging for chunks of Asia and Africa, the reaction the world over was: 'Russia, the Russians . . . .'"[40] Stressing the overriding importance of regaining inner spirituality, Solzhenitsyn made clear what choice post–Soviet Russia had before it: "The time has come for an uncompromising *choice* between an empire of which we ourselves are the primary victims and the spiritual and physical salvation of our own people."[41]

Russian nationalist empire builders were disappointed by Solzhenitsyn's views, but as an indication of how quickly politics changed in the early 1990s, his reservations about statehood for Kazaks, Ukrainians, and Belarusians came in for harsh criticism by nationalists in these countries when they attained independence in 1992. Solzhenitsyn held out hope that a union of Slav peoples could be formed among Russia, Ukraine, and Belarus. He drew a distinction between *Rus* and *Russian*. The first corresponded to the usage in the Russian language of *russkiǐ*, referring exclusively to ethnic Great Russians. The second referred to the more inclusive notion of *rossiiskii* (an older term was *rossiianin*) that subsumed ethnic Russians and related ethnic groups.[42]

> And so, after subtracting these twelve republics, there will remain nothing but an entity that might be called Rus, as it was designated in olden times (the word "Russian" had for centuries embraced Little Russians [Ukrainians], Great Russians, and Belorussians), or else "Russia," a name used since the eighteenth century, or—for an accurate reflection of the new circumstances— the "Russian [Rossiiskii] Union."[43]

Solzhenitsyn's imperial vision was at most limited to a voluntary union of the three Slav republics and of incorporation of parts of northern Kazakhstan where Russians had lived for centuries. By nationalist standards, it was a moderate rather than maximizing position.

Regarding the new minorities in independent Russia—Chechens, Tatars, Siberian peoples—the author patronizingly claimed that they needed to remain within Russia more than Russia needed to have them in the federation. Accordingly, Solzhenitsyn did not consider a multicultural Russia as necessarily good: "Even after all the separations, our state will inevitably remain a multicultural one, despite the fact that this is not a goal we wish to pursue."[44]

Solzhenitsyn's writings had less influence on nationalist circles in the chaotic conditions prevailing in independent Russia in the 1990s than in the authoritarian framework of Soviet rule. But his views were representative of the inner contradiction many nationalists confronted:

> it is paradoxical that so many of the Russians who wish to see her borders expand should be unwilling to face the consequences of living in a multinational state. Instead, they have been dismayed to see recreated—even in the "truncated" Russian Federation—what from their point of view were the worst features of the USSR.[45]

Russian Nationalists Resurgent

Solzhenitsyn represents a benign side of Russian nationalism. There are darker forces on the nationalist right that exert influence in Russian politics. Historian Walter Laqueur identified a variety of such forces. First were the monarchists, themselves divided between constitutional and autocratic tendencies. Some monarchists urge tolerance toward minorities while ensuring Russian domination; others adopt an exclusionary view of political rights. The most extreme right-wing monarchists were organized into *Zemshchina,* an antidemocratic group opposed to rights for minorities and religions other than Russian Orthodoxy. Supporting the nineteenth-century Romanov slogan of "Autocracy, Orthodoxy, Nationality," this group understood the relationship of the people to the ruler as one of subservience. But this view also showed the weakness of the monarchist movement because Russians holding antidemocratic sentiments and a desire for rule by strength were more likely to support a military dictator rather than a new tsar(ina).

Another right-wing movement in Russian society is the Cossacks. Romanticized in Russian literature as horsed guards of the steppe protecting Russia's borders and conquering new lands (such as Siberia), they were originally a mobile people coming from different ethnic backgrounds: Tatar, Turkic, Ukrainian. In the nineteenth century, Cossacks sometimes attacked minorities (such as the Poles) and carried out pogroms of the Jews. Not surprisingly, because of their identification with tsarist rule, they suffered persecution in the Soviet period.

A Cossack revival began in the anarchic conditions of the early 1990s. They demanded rehabilitation and sought to reaffirm an identity lost to sedentary, demographic, and territorial processes. They lobbied the defense ministry to permit them to become border guards again, so Cossack units were subsequently legalized by Yeltsin. In the Caucasus, especially Chechnya and Abkhazia (a breakaway region of Georgia), they played a pivotal role in supporting pro–Russian forces and destabilizing their opponents.

One of the first Russian right-wing groups to emerge in the Soviet period was *Pamyat* (often translated as "Memorial"). Initially it was an innocuous-sounding, loosely organized group in Moscow and Leningrad committed to the restoration of historic monuments. Its vague platform allowed Pamyat to curry the favor of well-known Russian poets, novelists, and filmmakers, and even Yeltsin attended one of its gatherings. Though nationalist, it was not hostile to the Communist Party and sought to attract its more nationalist members.

In the Gorbachev years Pamyat was outflanked on the right by noisier, more outrageous groups like that of Zhirinovsky. The candidates Pamyat supported all lost in the 1989–1990 elections, it was kept out of nationalist initiatives such as the July 1991 "Message to the People," and it was too weak to play a part in the coup attempt staged the following month. As Laqueur wrote, "Seen in historical perspective the role of Pamyat was that of a precursor; it was the first in a field that later on became crowded."[46]

Russian nationalism is also found within the Orthodox church, revived at the end of the Soviet period. Laqueur made the psychological point how "Most clergymen feel more at home with the nationalists than with the liberals. The nationalists will not constantly remind them of their past collaboration with the Communist regime and demand purges in their leadership."[47] Right-wing nationalists were initially attracted to the church as the quintessentially Russian national institution, but many became disillusioned, having no regard for the "Jewish" Old Testament, for mystic "theologians" like Berdyayev, Bulgakov, or Florensky, or for spiritual redemption in the afterlife.

Lacqueur also examined the nationalist political establishment. *Soyuz,* together with *Interfront,* began as antiseparatist movements in the Baltic republics and republics of the western Soviet Union. In 1990 Soyuz constituted itself as a parliamentary faction and comprised the largest grouping in the Supreme Soviet with more than 500 deputies. For many Russians, however, because of its resolve to save the USSR, Soyuz became indistinguishable from the Communist Party establishment and was unable to tap the nationalist constituency.

A similar public image—without the parliamentary base of support of Soyuz—plagued Nina Andreyeva's *Edinstvo* party. She had first become known in March 1988 for an anti–Gorbachev manifesto published in a Leningrad newspaper, but the former schoolteacher could not subsequently parlay her notoriety.

In March 1990 a more obscure figure established another seemingly fringe party, but one year later Zhirinovsky, head of the misnamed Liberal Democratic Party, obtained nearly six million votes—"as many as all the people in Switzerland" in his words—in the first democratic elections to the Russian presidency held in June 1991. In September 1991 his vice-presidential candidate, entrepreneur Andrei Zavidia, purchased the large-circulation newspaper *Sovetskaya Rossiya* and thus gave Zhirinovsky even more exposure. Liberal Democrats were among the three strongest parties in the state Duma following the elections of December 1993 and December 1995. Zhirinovsky's populism, drinking, fistfights, outrageous statements (insults to women, to Islamic peoples, to Jews—though himself of Jewish background), connections with heavy-metal rock bands, and "soundbite" persona gave the ultranationalist right a strength it could not hope to have on the basis of a political platform alone.

Zhirinovsky has been described as a character out of Dostoyevsky and as a "holy fool" (*yurodivye*) regularly reappearing in Russia's history. "Holy fools embrace self-humiliation and self-abasement, then get up from the dirt and present themselves to the world in their revealed spiritual beauty and power."[48] Zhirinovsky scandalized many people with his obscenities while charming them with stories of his youth as an unhappy child—"the smallest and the weakest, underfed, ugly, badly dressed, and often without shoes. . . . This ugly duckling grows up to be an equally ugly gander. . . . In videos, Zhirinovsky, displaying a hairy beer belly, drinks vodka and gesticulates exaggeratedly."[49]

Not unexpectedly, much of the respectable nationalist Right disowned Zhirinovsky because his pronouncements—exposing the Baltic peoples to radiation, comparing Poland's foreign policy to a prostitute servicing differenˇ clients, regaining Alaska, impregnating women to boost Russia's population—invited ridicule. One observer noted that "In Pamyat circles . . . Zhirinovsky is quite beyond the pale but not because of his extremism; on the contrary, he is seen as a dubious cheat, a traitor, the agent of a global conspiracy against the rebirth of Russia."[50]

Zhirinovsky's popularity appeared to peak with the 1993 Duma elections and his subsequent decline—he finished far behind the leading vote getters in the 1996 presidential election—was in part due to the more nationalist line appropriated by Yeltsin himself—and not just by Yeltsin: Former vice-president Alexander Rutskoi, head of a political alignment called "Power" (*Derzhava*), openly called for Russia's return to imperial status, while Lebed, former head of the Russian army in Moldova and a leader of the Russian Communities' movement, became the rallying point for military and security officials demanding the rebuilding of Russia's lost empire.

In his study of the extreme Right in Russia's twentieth-century politics, Laqueur identified the Russian proneness to extremism. He acknowledged that "Nationalism can still be a powerful force for the mobilization of dissatisfied and disadvantaged elements"[51] but he added:

> There is the time-honored Russian tendency toward radicalism and extremism, toward pursuing an idea or ideal relentlessly, well beyond the confines of good sense. The Russians did take socialism, a political doctrine that elsewhere led to social democracy and the welfare state, and turned it into a nightmare. There is the danger that nationalism, an explosive force at the best of times, might fare similarly, fueled by hatred and selfishness and pursued at the expense of all other values, and become yet another monster.[52]

Our account of contemporary Russian nationalism's sources would be incomplete without reference to the growth of right-wing street violence in Russian cities. Fascist groups made up of skinheads have organized around people like Alexander Barkashov and have beaten up citizens from the "near abroad" (the former Soviet republics), students, and businesspeople. These groups are not a political movement but anarchic or criminal phenomena, but like the brownshirts in interwar Germany, they may pose a special threat should ultranationalist organizations decide to make use of them for furthering their own political agendas.

Russia's New Minorities

At the time of Soviet collapse, concerted efforts were undertaken by minority peoples within Russia to liberate themselves from rule by Moscow. Disturbances in Yakutia and the north Caucasus were among the first to demonstrate minorities' dissatisfaction at still being ruled by the Kremlin, whether it was inhabited by a communist or a democrat. The seven million Tatars, scattered throughout Russia and now its largest minority group, also became restless. The center of the Russian Federation seemed as remote from Tatars and Yakuts as before. During 1990–1991 most of the republics within Russia declared state sovereignty. These "sovereignty games" were intended to consolidate local rulers' positions as well as enhance the status of their republic within Russia. The leaders of these republics also thought that they might be allowed to join the CIS as members in the future. In rare cases, sovereignty declarations were intended for an international audience. Thus, addressing the Islamic world, Tatarstan asserted that it was the northernmost Muslim state in existence.[53] The rhetoric of sovereignty was largely instrumental, therefore. As we see below, Chechnya alone took the sovereignty game literally.

After 1991 the new minorities in Russia hoped for a fresh start in interethnic relations.[54] Some of them had distinct identities (Chuvash, Mari); others were sizeable

(Bashkirs, Mordovians); others counted on outside support for their cause (Chechens, Ossetians); others still possessed significant natural resources (Yakuts). The success of what might be termed the "first round" of self-determination movements in the former USSR had a demonstration effect on the new minorities, a number of which considered themselves equally worthy of international recognition and full statehood. As Dunlop observed:

> Just as Yeltsin's idealistic vision of a future confederation [the Commonwealth of Independent States] had been rudely rebuffed by the other union republics, so did his model of a harmonious Russian federation encounter suspicion and outright rejection on the part of certain minority peoples of the Russian Republic, as well as by some ethnic Russians who began to push for full independence of their regions from Moscow. If Estonia could be fully independent, then why not, they argued, Tatarstan, Chechnya, or the Russian Far East?[55]

It was Chechen president Dzhokhar Dudayev's drive for independence that led to the worst case of ethnic conflict in the Russian federation. It culminated in a Russian military invasion in late November 1994, indiscriminate use of Russian air power against military and civilian targets alike, incidents of hostage taking by Chechen fighters in southern Russia in 1995, and efforts by Yeltsin to set up a Chechen puppet government that exacerbated the conflict. The struggle had all the appearances of a classic confrontation between the subnationalism of an upstart nation and the imperial nationalism of a humiliated great nation.

Russian nationalism alone, however, does not explain Yeltsin's decision to carry out military intervention in Chechnya. Strategic considerations, national interests, and his own power calculations are important factors as well. The fact that acknowledged Russian nationalists such as General Alexander Lebed—who served for a time in 1996 as the president's national security adviser—and General Alexander Rutskoi—who was Russian vice-president until his involvement in 1993 in the parliamentary standoff with the president—condemned military intervention is evidence that there were alternative conceptions of how Russia could remain a great power. For example, why not show Russia's contempt for the backward Chechen gangster state by unilaterally expelling it from the Russian federation? Let us examine more closely the Chechen nationalist challenge, the Russian response, and the international reaction.

Russia and Chechnya

In late 1991, as the USSR was disintegrating, Chechen leader Dudayev joined with Soviet republics such as Ukraine and neighboring Georgia in proclaiming his nation's independence. Even though Gorbachev was still Soviet president, it was Yeltsin who, as president of Russia, had to tackle the problem of secession in his own country. Initially Yeltsin made a feeble attempt to impose martial law and, when that did not work, he purused a policy of benign neglect of the region until 1994. This three-year interlude gave Chechen forces the time to stockpile an enormous quantity of weapons, most purchased in shady deals with the Russian military itself. Russian involvement

Chechnya

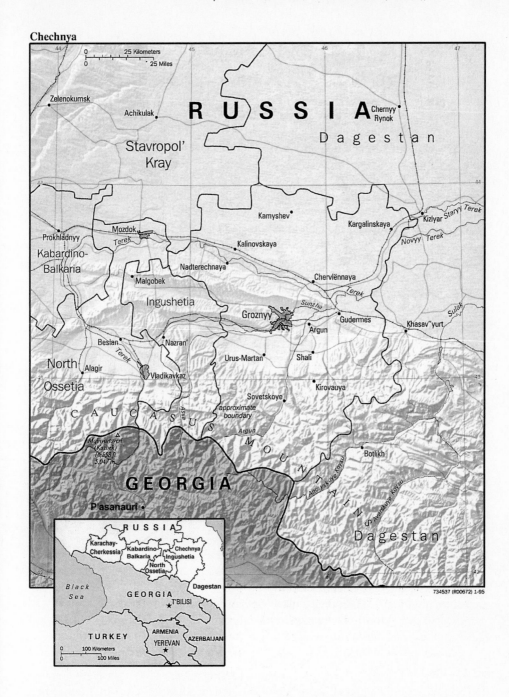

in Chechen politics in this period was insidious. In May 1994 a car bomb narrowly missed killing Dudayev, and in August 1995 the Russians organized a Chechen movement opposed to secession that launched an unsuccessful military campaign on Dudayev's forces.

Yeltsin's decision finally to invade Chechnya has been explained in many ways unrelated to ethnic conflict: the need to keep the Russian federation together; to demonstrate Russia's resolve; to show that the Russian military remained a cohesive fighting body; to create conditions for a declaration of a state of emergency that would allow Yeltsin to postpone the 1996 presidential elections; to distract attention from hyperinflation, unemployment, poverty, and general economic decline; to combat organized crime in the region; to maintain Russian control over the trans-Chechnya oil pipeline running from Baku on the Caspian Sea to Novorossiisk on the Black Sea, rendering superfluous pipeline projects that would run through Turkey or Iran; to sabotage an $8 billion oil contract between nearby Azerbaijan and a consortium of multinational oil companies that Russia questioned in terms of who had jurisdiction over the Caspian Sea shelf; to prevent the unification of Moslem peoples of the north Caucases into a confederation of mountain peoples (as had happened in the early 1920s) that would be dominated by Chechen leaders in Grozny; to indicate that a "war party" in the Russian government, made up of military, security, and industrial leaders, was now in charge of Russia's national security policy.

All of these reasons help explain Russian intervention, but it is also evident that most of these calculations backfired during the Chechen campaign. Yeltsin's popularity was eroded, the military fell into disarray, decision making proved chaotic and disunified, Chechen society became more nationalistic and militarized than before, other minorities (as in neighboring Ingushetia) found even less appeal in remaining within a federation threatened with renewed authoritarianism, relations with the West were set back, and the probability of an expanded NATO role in Central European states increased. Furthermore, by deploying a large military force in Chechnya to defeat the rebels, Russia stood in violation of the Conventional Forces in Europe (CFE) Treaty limiting the massing of troops in a particular region.

Above all, however, it was the assumption that military intervention would produce a speedy victory for the Russians that caused Yeltsin to authorize the attack. From the beginning, Russian political and military leaders underestimated the strength and determination of the irregular Chechen forces. As one Russian journalist noted:

> In attacking Grozny on November 26, 1994 with Russian tanks, supported by pro-Moscow Chechen infantry, the Russian government hoped to achieve victory in one day. After that, then-minister of defense Pavel Grachev said that Chechnya could be subdued in two hours by one airborne regiment. When they sent troops into Chechnya in December 1994, the Russian authorities planned to take the Chechen capital and the "bandit formations' main strong points" in a month, and conclude all military actions in two months.[56]

The war in Chechnya reversed a trend of settling disputes over autonomy between the central government and the regions through peaceful means. In March 1992 Tatarstan, together with Chechnya, were the only two republics that refused to sign the Russian Federation treaty. However, after walking out of the Russian Constitutional Assembly in June 1993, Yeltsin and Tatarstan leader Mintimir Shaimiev signed an accord in February 1994 granting that nation considerable autonomy. Tatarstan secured sovereignty over its oil and other natural resources and obtained recognition for its self-proclaimed constitution and presidency, republican citizenship laws, and special rights for military service on the territory of Tatarstan. During the next months Russia concluded similar treaties with the republics of Bashkortostan and Kabardino-Balkaria (the latter next door to Chechnya).

The full-scale invasion of Chechnya demonstrated that Yeltsin had abandoned his earlier policy of encouraging minority nationalities to demand as much political autonomy from the center as they could manage. Until then, he was aware of the destructive dynamics of *interactive ethnonationalism.* A notion used by Shantha Hennayake to study Sri Lanka (see Chapter 7), it refers to how majority nationalism is the principal cause triggering minority ethnic nationalism.[57] Accordingly, exclusionary policies toward minorities are invariably counterproductive and inclusionary ones efficacious.

Pressured by Russian empire savers who were either nationalists or communists, and now himself secure in power, Yeltsin stopped pursuing inclusive, accommodative policies toward minority nations. In contrast to the 1994 agreements granting far-reaching territorial autonomy to three republics in Russia, he now approved scorched-earth policies: on Grozny in 1995 and on Pervomaiskoye—a Russian village where Chechen rebels and their Russian hostages were shelled—in 1996. His inconsistency on nationalities issues was reflected in the succession of advisers appointed to counsel him on the subject. That he reluctantly accepted the conditions for an end to the war negotiated by Lebed and then promptly fired him further illustrated how much agonizing Yeltsin, other leaders, and indeed all Russian society, had endured in dealing with Chechen ethnosecessionism.

Chechen Ethnosecessionism

We have suggested that Russian nationalism cannot by itself be held accountable for the fierce war fought in Chechnya between 1994 and 1996. The basis for the conflict was Chechnya's ethnosecessionism. Its armed struggle against Russia in the nineteenth century, its unilateral declaration of independence in late 1991, and its highly charged form of nationalism in the wake of Soviet collapse explain the confrontation with Moscow. Dudayev, a former Soviet air force general, was elected to the presidency by a council of clan elders to create an independent state of Ichkeria (the preferred Chechen name for the country). The council passed over the candidature of Ruslan Khasbulatov, a Chechen leader who helped organize the October 1993 parliamentary insurrection against Yeltsin. Though better qualified than Dudayev, Khasbulatov adhered to a federalist variant of Chechen nationalism that would keep the republic inside the Russian Federation.

The mutual animosity between Dudayev and Yeltsin exacerbated the confrontation, but the Chechen leader was far from the gangster depicted in the Russian media. In Dudayev's view, the war in Chechnya "demonstrated to the world what the Russian leadership is capable of, and what direction it is headed in." He imputed the cause of war to "the rapid nationalist shift in Russia's leadership" and called for UN intervention because the war was neither an internal Russian nor regional Caucasus problem but a human rights tragedy. He appealed for international recognition of Chechnya while insisting that "we must run our own affairs, which we have done since the collapse of the USSR."[58]

Instead of a short victorious war, Russian forces were extended even after their initial capture of Grozny and after the technologically sophisticated assassination of Dudayev in April 1996 (reports say that he was making a prearranged call to an international mediator in a remote part of Chechnya when a Russian military jet suddenly appeared overhead and launched a laser-guided missile at Dudayev). Chechen fighters slipped into the southern Russian towns of Budennovsk and, later, Kizlyar to take hostages. Even so, as late as July 1996 no one seriously believed that the Russian army could be defeated militarily. There were other reasons for ending the war. Much of Russian society, exposed to graphic television coverage of the carnage in Chechnya, became opposed to the war effort. Russia may have lost as many as 10,000 armed services personnel in combat, and polls showed that Russian citizens wanted to cut their losses, even if it meant admitting defeat. Russian leaders, notably Lebed, concluded that it was not worth fighting to keep Chechnya in the federation. They did not believe that Chechnya's independence would necessarily produce a domino effect felt throughout the country: "The centrifugal forces unleashed by the collapse of the Soviet Union have dissipated. The republics and states on Russia's fringes are seeking the security of closer ties with the center, not the freedom of more distant ones."[59]

The war in Chechnya ended suddenly. In August 1996 rebel Chechen forces retook Grozny in a surprise attack. The pro–Russian puppet government of Doku Zavgayev and some Russian politicians as well charged that the city was deliberately surrendered to the rebels. This claim was supported by some evidence. Two weeks before the loss of the capital, federal checkpoints guarding the western approach to the city were removed, allowing an advance group of rebels to inflitrate the city. Most of Grozny's residents were aware of the planned raid: "People talked about it in the Grozny markets, on the streets, in the barracks, and in their apartments."[60] Russian special services also knew in advance that separatist forces were planning an operation on Grozny. When the attack came, however, there was no resistance, and Chechen forces moved freely through the city in the first hours after its capture. Spokespeople for the Russian military command explained the inaction by claiming they intended to "entice the enemy into a trap" (they assumed that the rebels would send all their forces into Grozny). But this seemed a threadbare excuse in the eyes of those who saw either a conspiracy behind the city's return to the separatists or, more plausibly, remarkably inept Russian military conduct of the war from start to finish. With the debacle in Chechnya, coupled with cuts in defense spending, the Russian army was in such a state of demoralization that finding an honorable way to leave Chechnya seemed to Lebed to be the only alternative.

To be sure, Russian troops made several attempts to take back Grozny. But the rebels had dug in and a few Russian units took heavy casualties. The Russian commander in the field, General Pulikovsky, presented the separatists with one last ultimatum to surrender or face an all-out artillery barrage, but the war effectively ended when Security Council head Lebed countermanded Pulikovsky's order. Russian troops were forbidden to retake Grozny, the continued presence of the Russian army in Chechnya lost all meaning, and federal troops began to pull back.

On August 31 at Khasavyurt, the impulsive Lebed candidly announced: "The war is over. That's it. Finished. We're sick of fighting." Acting largely on his own, without the prior approval of Yeltsin or Prime Minister Viktor Chernomyrdin, Lebed signed an armistice agreement with then Chechen Chief of State Aslan Maskhadov (he became premier shortly after). By the terms of the accord, Russian troops were to withdraw. By the end of January 1997, all of the more than 30,000 troops had left. The agreement also foresaw a referendum in Chechnya on independence in five years' time. For Russian optimists, it represented a return to the status quo ante. For Chechen leaders, it was a five-year process of reconstructing the economy and building the infrastructure for an independent state.

When Yeltsin fired Lebed six weeks after signing the accords, doubts arose as to whether the peace in Chechnya would hold. A Yeltsin loyalist, Ivan Rybkin, became Security Council secretary and envoy to Chechnya and, on his first visit, pledged to honor the accords. Shortly thereafter Boris Berezovsky, banker and media mogul, was named deputy secretary. Chechen leaders were reassured by both appointments and even saw Berezovsky as a potential investor in the republic. Chechen Premier Maskhadov scheduled presidential elections in January 1997, which he won, and Russia promised recognition if Chechnya was demilitarized. Even hard-line Russian Interior Minister Anatoly Kulikov, who had called the accords treason and Chechen leaders bandits, met with them in October 1996. Some of these moves suggested that Russia was slowly coming around to accepting Chechnya's independence as a fait accompli. But with a five-year interval in which to persuade the Chechens of the advantages of staying in the Russian Federation, Moscow also began to offer concessions, such as declaring all of Chechnya a free economic zone on the model of Hong Kong. As is often the case, it is after the war is ended that the struggle for influence between competing groups begins.

INTERNATIONAL REACTION

What were, a short time earlier, the internal affairs of the USSR became transformed in the 1990s into foreign policy questions as fifteen new countries gained recognition from the international community. According to Barry Posen, the breakdown of an empire and the accompanying disappearance of a hegemonic power has traditionally produced anarchy in the international system:

> In areas such as the former Soviet Union and Yugoslavia, "sovereigns" have disappeared. They leave in their wake a host of groups—ethnic, religious, cultural—of greater or lesser cohesion. These groups must pay attention to the first thing that states have historically addressed—the problem of security—even though many of these groups still lack many of the attributes of statehood.[61]

While fifteen new states embarked on the task of enhancing their security interests, it was those of Russia, the fallen hegemon, that were of greatest concern to the international community. As the long-standing anchor of order and stability in Eurasia, and as a nuclear superpower still, ensuring Russia's sense of security was of great importance to all major and regional powers in the international system.

What was the role of the United States, the Soviet Union's long-standing superpower adversary, during the process of Soviet disintegration and the emergence of Russia as an independent state? In September 1991 U.S. Secretary of State James Baker toured many of the Soviet republics and announced five principles supported by the United States that should govern future relations in the region: (1) a peaceful process leading to self-determination of Soviet peoples; (2) respect for existing internal and external borders; (3) support for democracy and the rule of law; (4) protection for human rights; and (5) respect for international law and treaty obligations. In December, following the referendum vote in Ukraine in favor of independence, presidential spokesman Marlin Fitzwater included as a further political test of the new states the expectation they would establish free market economies and assume a fair share of the Soviet Union's debt.[62] While the popular nationalist movements that had mobilized throughout Soviet space had many sources, the road to statehood by the republics was to be determined by established international rules and norms, with the United States playing an important role as adjudicator.

A distinctive phenomenon of the post–Soviet political landscape is, as we have seen in this chapter, the presence of new minority groups in newly independent states. The single most important new minority is the Russian diaspora, located in the Baltic states, the new European states (Belarus, Moldova, Ukraine), throughout the Caucasus, and in northern Kazakhstan. The issue of Russia's security has been interpreted by most political leaders of Russia as being synonymous with Russians' security, whether they live in the federation or outside of it.

Not surprisingly the West, in particular the United States, was apprehensive about Russia's reaction to recognition of a country such as Ukraine, whose history was so intertwined with Russia and where so many ethnic Russians lived. As a result, American recognition of the independence of Soviet republics was slow. To be sure, the United States had long maintained that the Baltic states were forcibly incorporated into the USSR by Stalin, and so it was aware that it was not surprising Russia when it recognized them, but that was not the case in other lands ruled for centuries by Russia.

The West was doubly apprehensive, therefore, about Russia's reaction to any attempt to lend support to independence struggles within the federation. Whether it was Chechnya and Tatarstan in Russia, Abkhazia and Adzharia in Georgia, Trans-Dniester and Gaugazia in Moldova, or Crimea in Ukraine, virtually all states in the international system abided by the principle that this second round of ethnosecessionist disputes was an internal affair of the new states. Although, in the case of Chechnya, there was mild rebuke by Western states of Russia's violation of human rights in its conduct of the war, there was no reference to Russia's violation of the group rights of the Chechen people. The international response to Chechen ethnosecessionism was, therefore, one of feigned indifference. The practical consequences of such a response was that the battlefield would determine the winner of the struggle, and the West, like Russia's leaders, did not imagine that Russia might suffer a military defeat.

The regional reaction to the Chechen conflict is also important to consider. Meeting in the Ingushetia capital of Nazran in September 1996, the leaders of eight republics and the regions of the north Caucasus endorsed the Khasavyurt accords, though they expressed concern about the domino effect on the region if Chechnya did secede from Russia. In particular, if Chechnya became an independent state, the issue of how to draw new international borders would become controversial. The problem was that Chechnya's borders were repeatedly redrawn in the Soviet period. First, Stalin merged Chechens and Ingush into a single territory in 1934. Then in 1944, he deported the Chechens and created different administrative units in the Caucasus. Finally in the mid–1950s, after Stalin's death, Chechens returned to their homeland and to new borders.

Three of Chechnya's borders are contentious. First, Chechnya's leaders claim a larger territory that extends beyond the present western border with Ingushetia. The claim is based on Chechnya's territory before the 1934 merger with the Ingush. Leaders of the two republics have agreed to defer the issue. Second, Chechnya makes irredentist claims on parts of Dagestan to the east. The Khasavyurt district on the border is inhabited primarily by Chechens. In addition, the Aukhovsky district was Chechen-settled until the 1944 expulsions, and Chechnya might challenge the Laks' right to live there. Third, the northern border with Stavropol Krai in Russia itself is in dispute, too. Many Russians spill over from Stavropol and live in Chechnya's northern area. Many pro-Zavgayev supporters fled to the historically pro–Russian Nadterechny district after escaping from Grozny. They are prepared to stop any attempt by Grozny to establish control over Nadterechny. While their exact numbers and the source of their arms supply are not officially known, it is evident that they have the backing of Russian federal authorities. What are today's regional territorial disputes may become international border conflicts in the future.

NONINTERNATIONALIZATION OF THE CHECHEN CONFLICT

Spillover of ethnic conflict into the international arena can occur in any of four ways. First, ethnic conflict and the resulting instability in a region may tempt outside parties to intervene. Let us recall Stephen Ryan's typology of reasons why states become involved in an ethnic conflict in another country: They may have affective links to one of the parties, these links ranging from ethnic solidarity with another state's minority to irredentist claims on the other state. But no other ethnic groups existed that had affective ties to the Chechens, so third-party intervention on these grounds was ruled out. For Ryan, "Rarely . . . will affective concerns prompt action without fears relating to security and loss of geopolitical advantage."[63] Accordingly, intervention based on instrumental concerns involves a state's pursuit of its own national interests, which include the interrelated issues of national security, balance of power, and geopolitics. Only Russia had important instrumental reasons to intervene in its breakaway republic.

Some Russian nationalists saw the Chechen debacle as marking the first stage of
Russia's collapse and, therefore, supported military intervention. In 1970, Soviet dissident Andrei Amalrik published a seminal book called *Will the Soviet Union Survive
Until 1984?* Although it presented a scathing critique of the Soviet system, it also contained an oblique attack, recognized by few readers at that time, on Russian empire
builders. Amalrik wrote: "I have no doubt that this great Eastern Slav empire . . . has
entered the last decades of its existence. Just as the adoption of Christianity postponed
the fall of the Roman Empire but did not prevent its inevitable end, so Marxist doctrine has delayed the break-up of the Russian Empire—the third Rome—but it does
not possess the power to prevent it."[64] Thus, Amalrik anticipated not only the breakup
of the USSR as a result of nationalist movements like those in Russia, Ukraine, and
the Baltic states, but also the rise of centrifugal forces within Russia organized by
non–Russians, like the Chechens.

With the breakup of the USSR, many areas of opportunity presented themselves
to regional states. Turkey, Iran, and a Pathan-ruled Afghanistan have been lured into
the politics of Central Asia, but none has become involved in the Caucasus. This is not
to disregard the importance of a resurgent transnational religious force that is becoming politicized and making an impact on the region, Islam.

There are four million Muslims in the north Caucasus and another fifteen million
in the Russian Federation. Although most mosques and *medrese* ("seminaries") were
shut down in the Soviet period and religious persecution pursued, Muslims of the
north Caucasus, especially those living in mountainous areas, continued to adhere to
Islamic brotherhoods, or Sufism. The collapse of Soviet power provided an opportunity for the "re-Islamicization" of the region as people searched for a new identity.
While one possible identity was ethnically crosscutting, stressing the common bonds
found in the *Ummah* ("Muslim community"), another type of reidentification was
based on ethnoreligious fusion, where to be Chechen was to be Muslim and the two
were inseparable. This latter type of identification inhibited the spread throughout the
north Caucasus of the belief that the Russian–Chechen war was fundamentally a clash
of Christianity and Islam.

In the war with Russia, Islam became the fundamental ideology of the Chechen
resistance. Rebels declared a jihad ("holy war") and attacked Russian positions shouting *Allahu akbar!* ("God is great"), and the cry was repeated as residents of Grozny
greeted the victorious forces entering the city in August 1996. But it should be pointed
out that when Dudayev declared an Islamic state in 1991, it had little appeal to the
Chechen population, partly because of some successes in the Soviet period in fashioning a secular, atheistic way of life here and partly because Islam came late to
Chechnya—in the nineteenth century, compared to southern Dagestan where it was
introduced by the Arabs in the seventh century. Dudayev himself did not set out to
politicize the Muslim faith and repeated how "Russia forced us into Islam."

When the war began, Islam gained many new supporters in Chechnya. Islam was
what distinguished them from the Russians, it had already served as the ideological
adversary of Russian Marxism and now of Russian Orthodoxy, and it imposed itself

upon Chechens because of the logic of resistance. During the war, largely ceremonial Shariat courts (those based on the teachings of the Koran) operated in rebel-controlled territory. Shortly after the capture of Grozny, Ichkeria leader Zelimkhan Yandarbiev announced that a new legal code, based on the Shariat, would replace the Russian criminal code. It is still difficult to say, however, whether Islamic law is an expedient for enforcing order in Chechnya or whether it is an indication of the growing power of Islam in Chechnya and throughout the north Caucasus.

In late 1996 some Chechen leaders acknowledged that Islamic solidarity in the war with Russia had led to the recruitment of dozens of fighters from Saudi Arabia and other gulf states. The number was low, especially when compared to the thousands of fighters—many of them professional and well equipped—from the Islamic world who took part on the Bosnian Muslims' side in the war with Serbia. It is surprising that the depiction, by both sides, of the Russian–Chechen struggle in terms of Christianity against Islam was received so skeptically by the wider religious communities.

Considering the military victory of David over Goliath, it seems counterintuitive that third-party intervention was all but nonexistent in Chechnya. More typical of third-party intervention in ethnic conflicts in former Soviet space have been Russia's efforts at "mediating" conflicts in Tajikistan, Georgia, and Moldova. Frequently perceived by international actors as manifestations of Russian neoimperialism, the most egregious case of self-serving Russian intervention was in the civil war in Georgia in 1994. The Russian military swung the balance of power to the government side (headed by former Soviet Foreign Minister Eduard Shevardnadze) and, in no time, Georgia became the last of the Soviet republics (excluding the Baltic ones) to join the CIS. This organization seemed poised to provide Russia with the institutional framework and international legitimacy needed for it to regain dominance. CIS agreements allow Russia, for example, to oversee border posts and defend common air space. Russia's use of the CIS blurs the dividing line between third-party instrumental intervention and international mediation and peacemaking.

In the case of Chechnya, no countries existed in the Caucasus that could profit from siding with the separatists. Although Georgia was a contiguous state with Chechnya, transportation and communication links through the mountainous border area were very limited. Moreover, Georgia had already proved no match for Russian-supported secessionist movements in Abkhazia and Adzharia. An opportunity structure existed in Chechnya to weaken Russia, but there were no states able or willing to take advantage of it.

A second way ethnic conflict can be internationalized is that of an ethnic group that is spread over more than one state but is a majority in none. Ethnic strife arising in one state is likely to spill over to another. Chechnya's bid for independence had a demonstration effect on other republics in the Caucasus (notably, Ingushetia and Dagestan). As we noted above, area borders did not coincide with ethnic divisions, and overspill of conflict from one republic to another was possible. But this did not represent internationalization of conflict, only greater domestic instability for Russia.

A third way ethnic conflict is internationalized is where a dominant group in one state is separated from co-nationals that are a minority in another state. Chechens had no co-nationals in any other country (they were present in great numbers in Moscow) and only some ethnic kin in neighboring republics.

A fourth way that ethnic disputes are internationalized is through resort to terrorism. In 1996 Chechen leader Dudayev threatened to spread political terrorism to Western Europe if it continued to ignore Russia's military intervention in the republic. A threat was also made to set off a nuclear device in Moscow; as evidence of their ability to do so, Chechens left some radioactive material in a Moscow park. It is remarkable that ethnopolitical violence has been limited to the clash of armies and militias and has not involved terrorist acts. The massive inventory of the former Red Army, combined with the Russian military's desperate need for hard currency, have facilitated arms transfers to disaffected ethnic groups including the Chechens. When Abhazian separatists shot down Georgian fighter jets with sophisticated ground-to-air heat-seeking missiles in 1993, it was clear evidence of the proliferation of conventional high-tech weaponry. The fear remains that ethnic conflict in the post–Soviet landscape can be internationalized through terrorist methods.

We should note that for Chechen leaders, as for other separatist ones, the conflict with Russia was fundamentally an international one. Referring to Latvia, Karklins made the point that "Some ethnic conflicts are internationalized; in Latvia an international conflict has been 'ethnicized.'"[65] Chechens perceived Russian military intervention in a self-proclaimed independent state as a war between two countries. It was the Kremlin that depicted the conflict in ethnic terms, as a majority group fighting a rebellious minority one.

In summary, the international system—in contrast to the states of the near abroad—has tended to overlook neoimperialist tendencies emerging within Russia. International actors—the Organization (previously Conference) on Security and Cooperation in Europe (OSCE), the IMF, and the Council of Europe—have occasionally chided Russia for human rights violations, believing that the best way to civilize the country is through its incorporation in Western structures. Because of the balance of power in the region and their own security dilemmas, regional actors, such as the Central European states seeking NATO membership, have avoided involvement in Russia's ethnic conflicts (though Poland allowed Chechens to establish an information bureau in the country). Ethnic conflicts in Russia have not become internationalized, then, but the reasons for this may provide more grounds for pessimism than optimism.

THIRD-PARTY MEDIATION IN CHECHNYA

Is third-party mediation in an ethnic conflict likely to be successful, or can it fuel conflict between warring parties? As a general rule, third-party conflict management undertaken by a regional actor tends to escalate rather than reduce conflict, rendering it more complex and intractable.[66] But as Jacob Bercovitch observed, the crucial factor determining "whether a conflict relationship is expressed through acts of violence and hostility, or whether it produces a more fruitful form of interaction [is] the way it is managed." Conflict management efforts need to devise "a range of mechanisms to limit the destructive effects of a conflict and increase its potential benefits."[67] This role is increasingly falling upon the OSCE, a European UN consisting of more than fifty states. The main instrument of the OSCE in dealing with ethnic conflicts is the Office of High Commissioner on National Minorities, a body of specialists headed by Max van der Stoel.

Shortly after the USSR's collapse, when wars over sovereignty and borders seemed imminent, the OSCE established peacekeeping operations in three former Soviet republics: Georgia (3000 peacekeepers in Abkhazia), Moldova (5000 peacekeepers in the Trans-Dniester Republic), and Tajikistan (where most of the 20,000 non–Tajik troops were Russian). The major objectives of the missions were to negotiate peaceful settlement to conflicts, to promote respect for human rights, and to help build democratic institutions and a legal order. Let us review the results of these operations.

In July 1994 the UN Security Council supported CIS deployment of peacekeeping troops in the breakaway Georgian region of Abkhazia. Under Chapter VIII of the UN charter, member states are enjoined to make every effort to settle local disputes peacefully through regional arrangements. For the first time, the UN sanctioned a CIS-organized peacekeeping force. The troops sent to Abkhazia were Russian, and the danger arose, as we mentioned earlier, that Russia would use its peacekeeping operations to regain control over the new states using the CIS as cover. International organizations such as the UN and OCSE seemed to contribute to this possibility. Russian diplomats countered that in Abkhazia, Russia was acting at the request and with the consent of the parties to the conflicts. Subsequently, perhaps because of the OSCE umbrella under which it was operating, Russia discouraged Abkhazian separatists from seeking international recognition.

The OSCE presence in Moldova succeeded in preventing armed conflict between the Russian and Romanian parts of the country. But as in Tajikistan where the Russian army was engaged in a war to prop up the Tajik government in the face of rebel attacks, the OSCE in Moldova seemed powerless to do anything about Russian interference. A tripartite armistice control commission had been established, consisting of Russia, the Russian-backed Trans-Dniester republic, and Moldova. When an OSCE mission attempted in fall 1996 to carry out an inspection of military sites in Trans-Dniester that were suspected sites for production and storage of Grad missiles, the Russian majority on the armistice commission vetoed the mission. As elsewhere in the Russian sphere of influence, the OSCE was hamstrung in carrying out impartial mediation efforts.

In December 1994 the OSCE approved deployment of a peacekeeping force in Nagorno-Karabakh, an Armenian enclave in Azerbaijan where fighting had been taking place since Gorbachev's first years in power. Troops here were also predominantly Russian. Combined with the Tajik operation approved by the OSCE and others resulting from bilateral agreements (with Belarus) or by unilateral decisions (as in Moldova), Russia had about 100,000 troops based in other CIS countries by 1995.

Following Russian military intervention in Chechnya in late 1994, the OCSE established a permanent mission in Grozny. Its delegation, calling itself the "Assistance Group," set itself up as a facilitator between the warring sides, but Russian leaders did not trust the OSCE because of the contacts its officials had with the Dudayev group. Moreover, its monitoring of human rights was often obstructed by Russian officials. In turn the Chechens were upset that the OSCE called separatist forces "rebels" and did not recognize Chechen independence. An interesting point is how the OSCE machinery itself gave the impression of having two tracks on the Chechnya conflict. Because it is part of the international state system, the OSCE itself seemed to lean toward a policy of keeping Russia intact. The high commissioner's team, by contrast, appeared naturally more disposed toward minority rights and was willing to entertain solutions to the conflict that included secession, but such a distinction seems of mere scholastic importance because international mediation of the conflict was never given a chance to succeed.

CONCLUSION

Nationalism was both cause and effect of the collapse of the Soviet empire. The realization of one nation's historic goal can contribute to the breakup of an empire; equally important is that it has a demonstration effect on other nations who are not treated as legal successors to the empire. These generally smaller nations may feel that dominant-subordinate relations are being reproduced in a new form, but international actors are rarely prepared to give support to "second-round" nationalists in their struggle against central authority. The international normative regime discourages tampering with the state system, even one only recently expanded as a result of the breakup of an empire.

DISCUSSION QUESTIONS

1. What are the main causes given by historians for the collapse of empires? Has nationalist assertion on the part of subjected peoples represented an important factor?
2. Was the Soviet Union a Russian empire in disguise? Did it successfully russify non–Russian peoples? Were the interests of Russia promoted by the Soviet system of government?
3. In what ways was nationalist assertion linked to the democratic movement in the former Soviet republics? Describe the connection between regime identity and national identity in these republics.
4. Describe the different forms that Russian nationalism has taken in the 1990s. Which forms are a threat to Russia's fledgling democratic system? To Russia's minorities? Which types are compatible with Western liberalism?
5. What were the reasons for Russian military intervention in Chechnya? How was the conflict ethnicized? To what extent was it also internationalized? What factors gave Chechens a renewed sense of national identity?
6. Describe international reaction to the 1994–1996 war in Chechnya. Did the Chechens receive outside help? Were third parties involved in peacemaking?

NOTES

1. John Strachey, *The End of Empire.* (New York: Frederick Praeger, 1966), p. 325.
2. *Ibid.,* p. 340.
3. Michael W. Doyle, *Empires.* (Ithaca, NY: Cornell University Press, 1986), p. 123.
4. *Ibid.,* p. 125.
5. Edward Gibbon, *The History of the Decline and Fall of the Roman Empire,* Vol III. David Womersley, ed. (New York: Allen Lane, 1994), Chapter LXXI, p. 1073.
6. Paul Kennedy, *The Rise and Fall of the Great Powers: Economic Change and Military Conflict From 1500 to 2000.* (New York: Random House, 1987), p. 439.
7. *Ibid.,* p. xvi.
8. Doyle, *Empires,* p. 353.
9. For one comparison, see Richard L. Rudolph and David F. Good, eds., *Nationalism and Empire: The Habsburg Monarchy and the Soviet Union.* (New York: St. Martin's Press, 1992).
10. Hugh Seton-Watson, *The New Imperialism.* (Totowa, NJ: Rowman and Littlefield, 1971), p. 135.
11. *Ibid.,* p. 133.
12. *Ibid.,* p. 131.
13. Walter Laqueur, *Black Hundred: The Rise of the Extreme Right in Russia.* (New York: Harper Perrenial, 1994), pp. 156–157.
14. Roman Smal-Stocki, *The Nationality Problem of the Soviet Union and Russian Communist Imperialism.* (Milwaukee, WI: Bruce Publishing Company, 1952), p. 260.
15. Rasma Karklins, *Ethnopolitics and Transition to Democracy: The Collapse of the USSR and Latvia.* (Washington, DC: Woodrow Wilson Center Press, 1994), p. 152.
16. They included two journals of the prestigious Writers' Union of the Russian republic, *Nash Sovremennik* and *Moskva,* as well as the Komsomol (Young Communist) newspaper *Molodaya Gvardiya.*
17. Simon Dixon, "The Russians: The Dominant Nationality," in Graham Smith, ed., *The Nationalities Question in the Soviet Union.* (London: Longman, 1991), p. 28.
18. Gregory Gleason, *Federalism and Nationalism: The Struggle for Republican Rights in the USSR.* (Boulder, CO: Westview Press, 1990), p. 135.
19. Stephan Kux, "Soviet Federalism." *Problems of Communism,* March–April 1990, p. 1.
20. John Dunlop, *The Rise of Russia and the Fall of the Soviet Empire.* (Princeton, NJ: Princeton University Press, 1993), p. 3.
21. Fyodor Burlatsky, in Stephen F. Cohen and Katrina vanden Heuvel, eds., *Voices of Glasnost.* (New York: W.W. Norton, 1989), p. 195.
22. Lev Karpinsky, in *Ibid.,* p. 303.
23. Bohdan Nahaylo and Victor Swoboda, *Soviet Disunion.* (New York: Free Press, 1990), p. xii.
24. Timothy J. Colton, "Politics," in Colton and Robert Legvold, *After the Soviet Union: From Empire to Nations.* (New York: W.W. Norton, 1992), p. 21.
25. Karklins, *Ethnopolitics and Transition to Democracy,* p. 9.
26. *Ibid.*
27. Claus Offe, "Ethnic Politics in East European Transitions." Paper for conference on European Nationalisms, Tulane University, April 1994, p. 2.
28. Karklins, *Ethnopolitics and Transition to Democracy,* p. xviii.
29. *Ibid.,* p. 48.

30. Mark B. Beissinger, "Elites and Ethnic Identities in Soviet and Post-Soviet Politics," in Alexander J. Motyl, ed., *The Post-Soviet Nations: Perspectives on the Demise of the USSR.* (New York: Columbia University Press, 1992), p. 150.

31. Roman Szporluk, "Introduction: Statehood and Nation Building in Post-Soviet Space," in Szporluk, ed., *National Identity and Ethnicity in Russia and the New States of Eurasia.* (Armonk, NY: M.E. Sharpe, 1994), p. 6.

32. Laqueur, *Black Hundred: The Rise of the Extreme Right in Russia,* p. x.

33. *Ibid.,* p. 276.

34. Charles Ragin, *The Comparative Method.* (Berkeley: University of California Press, 1987), p. 136. Examples of the ethnic competition approach include Michael Hannan, "The Dynamics of Ethnic Boundaries in Modern States," in Hannan and John Meyer, eds., *National Development and the World System.* (Chicago: University of Chicago Press, 1979), pp. 253–277; Francois Nielsen, "Toward a Theory of Ethnic Solidarity in Modern Societies." *American Sociological Review,* 50, 1985, pp. 133–149. The resource mobilization view is described in Charles Tilly's magisterial *From Mobilization to Revolution.* (Reading, MA: Addison-Wesley, 1978).

35. Kurt Nesby Hansen, "Continuity within Soviet Nationality Policy: Prospects for Change in the Post-Soviet Era," in Miron Rezun, ed., *Nationalism and the Breakup of an Empire: Russia and its Periphery.* (Westport, CT: Praeger, 1992), p. 15.

36. James N. Rosenau, *Turbulence in World Politics.* (Princeton, NJ: Princeton University Press, 1990), pp. 435–436.

37. Jack Snyder, "Nationalism and the Crisis of the Post-Soviet State," in Michael E. Brown, ed., *Ethnic Conflict and International Security,* (Princeton, NJ: Princeton University Press, 1993), pp. 95–96.

38. John Dunlop, "The Contemporary Russian Nationalist Spectrum." *Radio Liberty Research Bulletin,* December 19, 1988, pp. 1–10.

39. Aleksandr Solzhenitsyn, *Warning to the West.* (New York: Farrar, Straus and Giroux, 1979).

40. Aleksandr Solzhenitsyn, *Rebuilding Russia: Reflections and Tentative Proposals.* (New York: Farrar, Straus and Giroux, 1991), pp. 5–6.

41. *Ibid.,* p. 11.

42. The distinction approximates that in the case of the United Kingdom between *English* and *British.*

43. Solzhenitsyn, *Rebuilding Russia,* p. 9.

44. *Ibid.,* p. 19.

45. Dixon, "The Russians and the Russian Question," p. 61.

46. Laqueur, *Black Hundred: The Rise of the Extreme Right in Russia,* p. 221.

47. *Ibid.,* p. 243.

48. Mark Yoffe, "Vladimir Zhirinovsky, the Unholy Fool." *Current History,* October 1994, p. 326.

49. *Ibid.*

50. Graham Frazer and George Lancelle, *Absolute Zhirinovsky: A Transparent View of the Distinguished Russian Statesman.* (New York: Penguin Books, 1994), p. xxxii.

51. Laqueur, *Black Hundred: The Rise of the Extreme Right in Russia,* p. xi.

52. *Ibid.*

53. See John W. Slocum, "Sovereignty Games in the Russian Federation." Paper prepared for the ISA-West Annual Meeting, October 20, 1995, University of Colorado, Boulder.

54. Regions of Russia also demanded more devolution of powers from Moscow. Some demanded the same powers as the ethnically determined republics and in a few separatist tendencies even emerged. Because they are not ethnically driven, we do not consider such movements here.

55. Dunlop, *The Rise of Russia and the Fall of the Soviet Empire,* p. 63.
56. Maria Eismont, "Uncertain Steps Towards Peace in Chechnya." *Prism,* The Jamestown Foundation Monthly on the Post–Soviet States, (Vol. II, September 1996), Part 2.
57. Shanta K. Hennayake, "Interactive Ethnonationalism: An Alternative Explanation of Minority Ethnonationalism." *Political Geography,* 11, 6, November 1992, pp. 526–549.
58. Cited in *Jamestown Monitor Special Report,* January 22, 1996.
59. "Yeltsin's Vietnam?" *The Economist,* February 10–16, 1996, p. 52.
60. Maria Eismont, "Uncertain Steps Towards Peace in Chechnya."
61. Barry R. Posen, "The Security Dilemma and Ethnic Conflict," in Michael E. Brown, ed., *Ethnic Conflict and International Security.* (Princeton, NJ: Princeton University Press, 1993), p. 104.
62. Reported by James P. Nichol, *Diplomacy in the Former Soviet Republics.* (Westport, CT: Greenwood Press, 1995), pp. 61, 97–98.
63. *Ibid.,* p. 36.
64. Andrei Amalrik, *Will the Soviet Union Survive Until 1984?* (New York: Harper and Row, 1970), p. 65.
65. Karklins, *Ethnopolitics and Transition to Democracy,* p. 133.
66. For evidence, see David Carment and Patrick James, eds., *The International Politics of Ethnic Conflict: Theory and Evidence.* (Pittsburgh: University of Pittsburgh Press, 1997).
67. Jacob Bercovitch, "Third Parties in Conflict Management: The Structure and Conditions of Effective Mediation in International Relations." *International Journal,* 40, 4, Autumn 1985, pp. 736–737.

chapter 6

Constitutional Separatist Movements: Canada and Quebec Nationalism

INTRODUCTION

Why is it that some separatist movements produce violent confrontations between dominant and minority groups and others do not? What are the factors that can lead to the successful secession of a nation disenchanted with an existing political system? What are the conditions—domestic and international—that usually mitigate against successful secession? These are the issues we explore in this chapter.

There is probably no greater a contrast between constitutional and coercive efforts to attain sovereignty in the 1990s than the respective cases of Canada and Yugoslavia.[1] Indeed, some scholars would challenge the essential "comparability" of the two cases. Cultural differences between North America and the Balkans, divergent historical paths leading from the Westminster model of democracy and that of socialism, the relative newness of the Canadian confederation contrasted with the "ancient curses" that have set Balkan peoples against each other for a long time, and differing stages of social and economic development can explain the respective peaceful and violent approaches to challenging a flawed federal system of government. Although the wars of Yugoslav succession have received widespread attention from policy makers, scholars, and the general public, the constitutional impasse in Canada was, for many people, a one-night drama—when the results of the Quebec referendum on sovereignty, held in October 1995, showed how close Canada was to fracturing.

Yet, the legal, constitutional road to independence may pose a greater threat to the integrity of states than simmering ethnic wars. Especially in established Western liberal democracies, such as Canada, Great Britain, Belgium, Spain, and Italy, an ethnosecessionist movement that can prove at the ballot box that it has the support of a substantial majority of the population will have an impeccable case for proceeding with separation. As an example of this possible scenario, in this chapter we consider the evolution of nationalism in Quebec and its near-success in 1995 in obtaining majority support for separation from English Canada. In Quebec, as in Yugoslavia, Czechoslovakia, the USSR, and Ethiopia, separatist movements emerged from the failure to construct enduring, crosscutting identities based on a federal system. Only in Canada and Czechoslovakia have ethnosecessionist challenges been entirely peaceful. Although in Czechoslovakia it was elite consensus that produced the split of the federation into two separate states in 1993, in Canada it will be an electoral verdict that will determine the country's future. We consider the type of response, therefore, that democratic, federal states make to a centrifugal challenge. For although many are attracted to cultural explanations for why nationalism becomes or does not become violent in particular states, it is at least as important to examine the institutionalized interaction between central authorities and the prospective breakaway state to discover why ethnosecessionsm can be peaceful and still hope for success.

WHY HAS ETHNIC CONFLICT OCCURRED? SOURCES OF QUEBEC NATIONALISM

Quebec nationalism and the sovereignty movement it engendered in the 1970s and after is based on the historical grievance, territorial rights, and cultural defense claims. Indeed, the majority of those opposed to Quebec secession does not question the assertion that the French constituted the first founding nation of the country. But Canadian federalists—those opposed to the breakup of the country and, therefore, to Quebec's separation—do challenge the argument that French speakers were historically not treated as equals in Canada.

The European involvement in Canada officially begins in 1534, when Jacques Cartier landed in the Gaspé Peninsula and claimed the land for the king of France. The first settlement was established by Samuel de Champlain in 1608 but French colonization proceeded slowly. In 1666 the nonnative population was barely 3500. In the aftermath of wars between France and England, the former's position in the New World weakened. By the Treaty of Utrecht in 1713, New France (as Canada was called at the time) lost Acadia (parts of today's New Brunswick and Nova Scotia), Newfoundland, and territory around Hudson Bay to the British.

British Colonization

More important than the Treaty of Utrecht to establishing English domination in North America was massive English-speaking colonization of the New World, overwhelming the few French settlers. At about the time of the battle on the Plains of

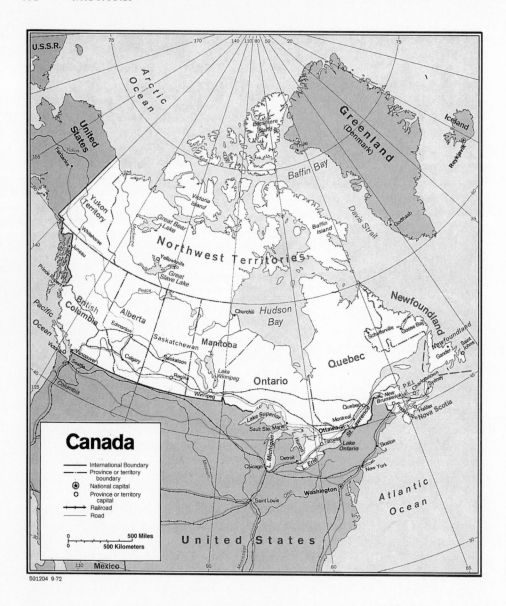

Canada

— International Boundary
--- Province or territory boundary
⊛ National capital
○ Province or territory capital
�꜔╌╌ Railroad
— Road

| 0 | | 500 Miles |
| 0 | | 500 Kilometers |

501204 9-72

Abraham in 1759, 65,000 French settlers faced one million English colonists. To worsen the odds for the French, the British sent the Royal Navy to North America while the government in Paris was largely indifferent to the fate of its possessions. Inevitably, British forces led by General Wolfe defeated the French army commanded by General Montcalm on the plains overlooking Quebec City. As with other nations' historic defeats—the loss of the Alamo to Santa Ana's army in 1836, the defeat of the Serbs by Turkish armies on Kosovo field in 1389, or the heroic but unsuccessful battle waged by Zulu warriors against the British in Ulundi in 1879—"the conquest" became etched in the minds of generations of French Canadians, or *Canadiens*—an earlier term for what are today the *Québécois,* the native French speakers of Quebec.

From being colonizer, then, New France found itself in the nineteenth century becoming the victim of colonization. To be sure, British colonization policy was neither consistent nor ruthless. The 1774 Quebec Act reinstated the borders of New France, while British governors strengthened the power of the large French landholders, or *seigneurs,* and of the ecclesiastical hierarchy, seeing in them allies against a possible popular democratic revolution as was breaking out in the Thirteen Colonies. The Constitutional Act of 1791 divided the British colony in North America into two provinces, Upper (Ontario) and Lower (Quebec) Canada, each with a governor and legislative assembly.

These postconquest institutional arrangements were meaningful enough to have English and French communities join forces—together with Native American tribes both within and outside Canada—in beating back an American invasion in 1812. The War of 1812 was the first clear manifestation of an emerging Canadian nationalism and it was based, as it has been ever since, on a common unwillingness among those living above the forty-ninth parallel—a long stretch of the Canadian–U.S. border—to become American. James Madison's boast that the conquest of Canada was "a mere matter of marching" thus helped stimulate the growth of a distinct Canadian identity.

After the common effort to stop invading American armies, rivalry began to develop between the dominant English merchant class of Lower Canada, living almost exclusively in Montreal, and the French population scattered throughout the rest of Quebec. A French nationalist movement, the *Patriotes,* emerged and in 1837 staged a revolt in Montreal. The rebellion was crushed by British forces and political oppression of the Canadiens followed.

Of special symbolic importance to the historical grievance claim made by contemporary Quebec nationalists is the "Report on the Affairs of British North America," written by newly appointed British Governor General Lord Durham and published in 1839. Seeking to avoid a repeat of the 1837 rebellion, he put forward both the idea of responsible government for all of Canada and the forced assimilation of French speakers into English culture. To achieve these twin goals, he recommended a legislative union of Upper and Lower Canada that would have erased the political autonomy and identity of French Canada. Lord Durham resigned after five months as governor general and his report was never implemented, but the insidious character of his recommendations was not lost on French Canadians thereafter.

Confederation

The political uncertainty caused by the Durham report, combined with severe economic recession in Lower Canada, compelled 500,000 French Canadians to emigrate to the United States, mostly to New England states, between 1840 and 1900. Some moved to the Canadian west and established small French-speaking communities, as in Manitoba, but French settlement in the western territories was discouraged by English Canadian leaders. The threat to the survival of French Canadian culture was never as great as it was in the mid-nineteenth century. In response, a small nationalist movement demanded full independence for Lower Canada, but progressive liberal French Canadian leaders were persuaded to join talks about creating a new federal union. A renewed threat from the United States, seemingly intent on punishing British North America for England's sympathy toward the South during the United States Civil War, made negotiations to form a Canadian union urgent.

Building on a proposal to create a union of the Maritime Provinces, both Upper and Lower Canada entered discussions, held in Charlottetown, Prince Edward Island. After much debate, especially over federal-provincial power sharing, a compromise was arrived at. A confederation of Canada was created—a sovereign state having the status of a British dominion—on July 1, 1867. The British North America Act (BNA Act) of that year enumerated the powers of the federal government and those of the provinces. Even though Canada was officially a confederation, suggesting that the provinces enjoyed far-reaching autonomy, in practice the new country was a federation, its central, or federal, government in Ottawa holding sweeping powers. For more than a century since then, most provinces but especially Quebec (the successor to Lower Canada) have demanded that greater decentralization of power take place. Related to this questioning of the original terms of confederation is the contention, often heard from Quebec sovereigntists, that Canada was pieced together without popular approval, as through a plebiscite, ever having been solicited.

The constitutional procedures that led to the act of confederation has shaped the political process ever since. Demands for greater powers for the provinces are regularly made at meetings of the premiers of the ten provinces.[2] Just as Canada was constructed through constitutional means, Quebec nationalists seek to deconstruct it through constitutional procedures.

Economic Stagnation

From 1867 up to World War I, Ontario, like much of the United States, experienced a sustained industrial boom. Quebec, as well as the Maritime Provinces, were not major beneficiaries of this rapid economic growth.[3] French Canadian society remained largely agrarian, and the all-powerful Catholic clergy wished to keep it this way. The strategy of *survivance* (survival) of French Canadian culture was shaped by the church, but it had its own institutional interests in this: it wished to retain its monopoly over education, welfare, and other social services rather than to share it with governmental institutions. French Canadians were encouraged to have large families as part of the strategy of *survivance*. Francophones in Quebec had a high birthrate in the first half of the twentieth century, leading historians to write of *la revanche des berceaux*—the revenge of the cradles. But if demographic growth helped keep a culture alive, it did nothing to empower it.

Furthermore, the integration of more and more immigrants from Europe into anglophone society produced a worsening ratio between French and English speakers. The growth of Montreal as an economic center was, simultaneously, the growth of a powerful English community isolated from the rest of francophone Quebec. Up to the late 1960s, socio-occupational mobility in Quebec was only possible through integration into the English-speaking milieu. To make matters worse for the French fact in Canada, francophone communities located elsewhere in Canada—in Manitoba, Saskatchewan, and even in neighboring Ontario—were increasingly deprived of French language education. These violations of the rights of French speakers to an education in their own language were subsequently recognized in belated Supreme Court decisions rendered in 1979 and 1988. Symbolizing the repression of the French fact in the rest of Canada was the fate of Louis Riel. Agitating on behalf of native communities in Manitoba—he himself was Métis—part French, part Indian—Riel organized a rebellion. While English participants in the so-called North West Rebellion were freed, Riel was accused of high treason, a charge originating in a rarely used British medieval law. Riel was found guilty and hanged in 1885, demonstrating to francophones the religious (Riel was Catholic) and racial bigotry prevalent in English Canada.

If in this period French Canadians did not fight persecution, it was in part at least their own fault. McGill University philosopher Charles Taylor has described "the old nationalism" evidenced in French Canadian attitudes during that period:

> The old nationalism was defensive; it was oriented around the defense of a way of life that was held already to exist but was in danger of being, if not submerged, at least undermined by the more robust North American culture alongside which it lived. It was meant to defend a civilization based on a set of values, mainly the religious values of a certain interpretation of Roman Catholicism and the linguistic values of the ancestral language. It was feared that these values would ultimately lose out to the North American values of material progress, of wider communication, of the cult of achievement.[4]

Conscription Crises

The sense of backwardness, of persecution, and of forming a society under siege was exacerbated by the call to arms issued by the Canadian government on two occasions early in the twentieth century. From 1899 to 1902, Britain was at war with Dutch Calvinist settlers in South Africa, who had proclaimed two free states. Urged on by British empire builder Cecil Rhodes, the Canadian government agreed to send troops to help the British defeat this minority. For many French Canadians, however, the Boer War not only did not involve Canadian interests, but it was also setting an ominous precedent: launching an attack on a minority that sought political autonomy. They were aware that Quebec, even with its limited provincial autonomy, could become the next target, as through a second Durham report.

For somewhat different reasons, French Canadians balked at fighting in World War I. British participation in the war constitutionally forced its dominions (sovereign states that did not have powers in foreign policy matters) to go to war, too. Contending that they could not identify with king and country when these were British, French-Canadian leaders organized an anticonscription movement. In 1932, by the Statute of Westminster, Canada was given control over its foreign policy but not fully. When Britain declared war on Germany in 1939, Canada again was at war, too, not in the role of an ally, such as the United States or the Soviet Union were to become, but directly on behalf of the British government. Another anticonscription movement, bolstered by more general pacifist sentiments in Quebec society, welled up in the province.

Disputed Borders

A territorial dispute also brought into question whether the treatment of Quebec within Canada was fair. In 1927 the Judicial Committee of the British Privy Council awarded Labrador, a vast territory situated on the Canadian mainland, to Newfoundland—then still a British colony (it became a Canadian province in 1949). New France had first obtained the territory by statute in 1774. For a brief period between 1809 and 1825, it was annexed by Newfoundland, but in 1825 it was restored to Lower Canada. The Judicial Committee's ruling was based on a 1763 commission giving Newfoundland jurisdiction over "the coasts of Labrador." The British lords considered that "coast" did not mean a 1-mile-wide strip of land along the seashore but, instead, a more remote watershed line that in places extended 200 miles from the shore. Quebec was not even permitted representation in this legal dispute between Canada and Newfoundland but clearly was the main victim. The manner in which the territorial award was made worried Quebec nationalists more than anything. Neither Quebecers nor Newfoundlanders lived in any great numbers in Labrador. Consequently, the catalyst of so many ethnosecessionist conflicts—claims of rival ethnic groups to the same territory—was nonexistent. The problem was a procedural one.

Major social and economic changes took place in Quebec during the interwar period. The proportion of Quebec's production accounted for by the industrial sector fell from 37 percent in 1920 to 10 percent in 1941. By contrast, manufacturing increased from 38 percent to 64 percent in these years. At the same time, the balance of power between federal and provincial governments—determined by the 1867 BNA Act—shifted even more to the central government. Not only Quebec was opposed to the historical revisionism that claimed that Canada was always designed to be a centralized state.

The interwar period produced the intellectual father of the Quebec sovereignty idea, Abbé Lionel-Adolphe Groulx. Groulx was drawn to the notion of an autonomous French–Canadian, or "Laurentian" state. It seemed the best form of defense of francophone culture and language and, of course, the Catholic religion in the increasingly Anglo-Saxon Protestant-dominated world of business.[5] After World War II, power in Quebec was concentrated in the hands of a conservative, proclerical, and generally corrupt government. At the same time the composition of Quebec society was radically transformed by enormous postwar immigration. Most immigrants spoke no English or French and, upon arriving in Quebec, were faced with the choice of learning one language or the other. The majority did not perceive Quebec to be a distinct society within Canada and most assumed that it was as natural to opt for English in Quebec as elsewhere in North America. In making this choice, immigrants were encouraged by the disinterest that francophone authorities displayed.[6] It was a second wave of European immigration in the late 1950s, numerically headed by Italians, that lay the groundwork for a nationalist backlash.

The Quiet Revolution

A so-called Quiet Revolution began in Quebec in 1960 when the Quebec Liberal Party (QLP) led by Jean Lesage was elected to power. Influenced in part by the existence of francophobe Canadian Prime Minister John Diefenbaker, who came from rural Saskatchewan, by the spread of French-language television, and even by the 1959 Cuban revolution that brought a nationalist and anti-imperialist, Fidel Castro, to power, the Quiet Revolution involved both accelerated institutional and societal change. Quebec began to close the gap with the rest of Canada in institution building.

By the terms of the BNA Act, education was to be a provincial responsibility. In Quebec, educational policy had been in the hands of the *Comité Catholique,* a non-governmental institution linked to the church. As one of his first reform measures, Prime Minister Lesage created a department of education to formulate policy; very quickly he also set up a department for cultural affairs. The Quebec government began to expand its provision of social services, while an Economic Development Council was established to map out economic strategy. The government also nationalized the profitable hydroelectricity industry, successfully negotiated new taxation powers from Ottawa, and by the late 1960s had arrived at an agreement with the central government allowing Quebec to opt out of certain federally administered social programs.[7]

Well before nationalists took power in Quebec, Lesage had initiated the policy of establishing Quebec diplomatic missions abroad, with the opening of the *Maison du Québec* in Paris in 1961. The employment opportunities created for francophones by these many institutional changes inspired greater self-confidence and ambition. The coming of age of a French Canadian middle class, conscious of itself both as a class and as a distinct nation, took place during this decade. In a few years, nationalist political organizations were established, culminating in the creation of the *Parti Québécois* (PQ, or *Péquiste*) in 1968. Interpreting these events, one writer argued that rising expectations rather than economic adversity gave rise to nationalism: "The surge of nationalism and collective self-confidence in the 1960s, including the rapid growth of the *Parti Québécois* and the enthusiasm it prompted among Francophone youth, appeared to be the product of optimistic expectations in an environment of economic expansion and global decolonization, rather than a response to specific threats or grievances."[8]

Equally important developments affecting Quebec nationalism were taking place at the federal level. The 1965 report of the Royal Commission on Bilingualism and Biculturalism (known as B & B) recognized the threat that French Canadians felt to their culture and language. In 1968 Canada had a new prime minister, Pierre Elliot Trudeau, a highly educated, cosmopolitan Montrealer, who embarked on reforming the federal government in the spirit of the B & B report. The 1969 Official Languages Act declared French and English to be coequal official languages, requiring that all federal services be available in each, at the client's choosing. The number of ministerial posts and civil service positions staffed by native French speakers increased dramatically beginning in the early years of Trudeau's long reign (1968–1979, 1980–1984).

Trudeau's vision of a united country functioning smoothly in two languages was put to the test in 1970 when a terrorist cell, calling itself *Front de Libération du Québec* (FLQ), kidnapped a British diplomat and murdered a profederal Quebec government minister. The impulsive Canadian prime minister overreacted: he swiftly invoked the War Measures Act—in practice, martial law—and the Canadian army was sent onto the streets of Montreal to project federal power. Leading French intellectual and cultural figures with nationalist leanings were rounded up and interned. While the handful of terrorists eventually released their British hostage in return for safe passage to Cuba (two decades later they made an almost triumphant return home), the impact of Trudeau's harsh response to the October crisis was to alienate permanently most of Quebec from the Montreal-born leader. The 1970 events were the only case of nationalist violence in modern Quebec history.

Quebecers expressed their nationalist sentiments through the ballot box in November 1976 when they elected the PQ to power. Under its charismatic leader René Levesque, economic expansion was promoted successfully and Quebec transformed into a dynamic, secular, technologically advanced society leaving behind its agrarian, clerical past. Levesque also secured French language and culture through the enactment of the Charter of the French Language, or Bill 101. It transformed French into the language of work, business, and education in the province, rather than a language spoken only at home or in the tavern. In practice, Quebec had little choice but to become a unilingual state: only by making French the sole language to be used in schools, corporations, the professions, and public signs could it hope to survive the remorseless pressures of creeping anglicization. Levesque pointed precisely to the greater sense of cultural security resulting from the enactment of the French Language Charter as the reason why Quebecers, by a margin of 60 to 40 percent (52 to 48 percent among francophone Quebecers) turned down a referendum on independence in 1980. The continued personal popularity of Levesque and his pragmatic nationalism was demonstrated by the PQ's reelection in 1981 on a platform that set aside the sovereignty issue.

Taylor has depicted this new nationalism as not defensive, as in the past. Rather,

> Its aim was not to defend the traditional way of life but to build a modern French society on this continent. In its pure form, practically the only value it had in common with the old was the French language itself. The rest of what has been defined as the French-Canadian tradition was seen in a very negative light. The modern nationalists were often anticlerical, if not unbelievers, and in any case the traditional conception of Catholicism in this society was anathema to them.[9]

Taylor added the important point that "Independence could be the symbol even if not always the actual goal of the new nationalism because, in the era of decolonization, it represented the awakening of underdeveloped societies that were determined to take control of their own history and in doing so to wrest it from both foreign domination and the dead hand of millenial tradition."[10] In this new society, the priest and the historian would be displaced by the businessperson and the technocrat. By 1995, however, it was clear that sovereignty was in fact the goal of many Quebecers, not just of symbolic value.

Quebec's Exclusion from the Canadian Constitution

In April 1982 Canadian Prime Minister Trudeau, encouraged by the referendum defeat, fulfilled his vision of centralized federalism by patriating the Canadian constitution. Until then, all laws passed by the Canadian parliament had to receive royal assent—a formality, to be sure, but refreshing memories of Canada's past status as a British dominion.

At the provincial premiers' meeting held in November 1981 in Ottawa that hammered out a patriation formula, Quebec leader Levesque was left out of the all-night negotiations in which the other nine provincial premiers participated. According to Trudeau, "Levesque left himself out," but, as far as the Quebec leader was concerned, he had been "tricked by Trudeau" on that "day of anger and shame."[11] Not only did the new constitution end the process of obtaining royal assent for Canadian legislation, but it also weakened provincial powers—something both major parties in Quebec—the nationalist PQ and the profederalist QLP—opposed. Not only was Quebec not a signatory to the original agreement, but it also never approved the constitution and, therefore, felt not bound by it for the next fifteen years. Thus, the unintended consequence of Trudeau's new constitution was to trigger a simmering constitutional crisis that still remains unresolved today.

The impasse has revolved over the issue of asymmetry. The Pepin-Robarts commission (officially termed the Federal Task Force on Canadian Unity) set up by Trudeau had recommended in 1979 that all provinces should enjoy augmented, equal powers, but that only Quebec should be permitted to exercise all of them. Such a political solution to a legal matter demonstrated the centrality of building in asymmetrical arrangements that could accommodate Quebec within the new constitution. But the Canadian prime minister was unsupportive. "Trudeau's image was of French-speaking Canadians as individuals without the collective dimensions of identification with *la nation canadienne-française*."[12] In their turn, Quebec leaders from across the political spectrum concurred that the new Canadian constitution, especially if it limited the power of the Quebec National Assembly to legislate on language issues, would confirm the province's minority status within confederation.

It would be simplistic to attribute the rebirth of Quebec nationalism solely to the constitutional crisis or to Trudeau's centralizing policies. In economic terms, while Quebec had recorded impressive *absolute* gains throughout the 1970s, it also suffered *relative* losses compared to Ontario, Alberta, and British Columbia. Toronto became corporate headquarters for many Canadian and foreign-owned businesses, easily overshadowing what had been until not long ago Canada's largest metropolis, Montreal. As a lone center of corporate finance activity in the province, by the early 1990s Montreal became the city with the highest unemployment rate nationwide. Militant *syndicats* (trade unions) were a discouragement for outside investment, while "The Canadian business establishment sealed the fate of Pierre Trudeau's brand of federalism by refusing to integrate French-speaking persons in the upper reaches of management and in head-office operations."[13]

The Failure to Bring Quebec Back In

The deadlock on the constitutional crisis seemed to be broken when a new Canadian prime minister was elected in 1984. The Progressive Conservative Party, led by another Quebec native, Brian Mulroney, won the federal elections with the largest majority in Canadian history and put an end to the long rule of Trudeau's Liberals. Traditionally the Conservatives were more open to decentralization of power to provincial governments. Mulroney, speaking the colloquial French of most Quebecers rather than the intellectual variant that Trudeau had polished in his elitist education, was personally more sympathetic to Quebec's desire for greater political autonomy within a decentralized federal system. He declared that he wanted to integrate Quebec into the constitution "with honor and enthusiasm."

Another election result seemed to improve the chances further of a deal bringing Quebec into the constitutional fold. In 1985, after nearly a decade in power, the PQ was defeated in Quebec elections by the provincial Liberals headed by a pragmatic economist, Robert Bourassa. As Quebec prime minister between 1970 and 1976, Bourassa had introduced legislation giving priority to the French language but, as a Harvard-trained economist, he had given priority to a strategy of economic growth for the province and was less concerned with cultural issues.

For a period of eight years, the opportunity for reaching an agreement on a renewed Canadian federalism appeared ripe. Mulroney won another federal election in 1988 and served as Canadian prime minister from 1984 to 1993. Bourassa won reelection in 1989 and was therefore Quebec prime minister from 1985 to 1994. But the most that the decentralizing Canadian prime minister and the profederalist Quebec prime minister could produce in the period their terms overlapped was the so-called Meech Lake Accord.

Agreed upon in April 1987 by Mulroney, Bourassa, and the nine other provincial premiers, it provided for Quebec's accession to the Canadian constitution in return for concessions on five principal Quebec demands: constitutional recognition of Quebec as a distinct society, a constitutional veto for the province, three of nine judges on the Supreme Court, the right to opt out of future federal programs, and shared immigration powers. Bourassa spoke of these demands as the minimum any Quebec prime minister would ever be able to put forward.

The problem with the agreement was, once again, a procedural one. In accordance with his ideal of centralized government, the amending formula for the Canadian constitution enacted by Trudeau required unanimity among all ten provinces. In 1990 the two provincial governments of Manitoba and Newfoundland, for idiosyncratic reasons of their own, refused to approve the Meech Lake Accord. This effort to incorporate Quebec into the constitutional order had failed.

Predictably, the failure of the Meech Lake Accord led Quebec to a resurgence in nationalist sentiment. An opinion poll conducted in November 1990 found that 62 percent of all respondents and 75 percent of francophone ones expressed support for Quebec sovereignty.[14] Jonathan Lemco described the mood of growing self-confidence in Quebec society:

> Quebec's emergence as a confident nation has been the result of various factors, including a more politically sophisticated population, a militant trade union movement, a more enterprising business class, better educated state elites, examples of successful nationalist movements elsewhere, perceived slights or injustices committed by officials in the rest of Canada and best exemplified by the failure of the Meech Lake Accord, ambitious politicians with their own political motives, and a sense that francophone and non–francophone goals are incompatible."[15]

After the defeat of Meech Lake, Bourassa blustered in a June 1990 speech that "The Quebec government will not return to the constitutional negotiating table," that "If we have been moderate, it is because we wanted to succeed," and that Quebec was "free and capable of taking responsibility for its destiny and development."[16] But he was satisfied to limit post–Meech Lake protest to a temporary boycott of federal-provincial meetings rather than holding a referendum on sovereignty that, he feared, would pass. Bourassa's own PLQ shifted to the sovereignty option, evidenced in the recommendations of a party committee (called the Allaire report for its chair, Jean Allaire) to demand twenty-two powers for Quebec. If Quebec did not obtain such new powers, the Liberals, too, would seek sovereignty within a confederal framework.

Bourassa was aware of the rapid growth of support for sovereignty in Quebec society and sought to postpone any clearcut decision on Quebec's future within Canada. In August 1992 he rejoined talks with other premiers, and they led to a new proposal incorporating the substance of Meech Lake, called the Charlottetown accord. But the "constitutional moment" had passed, and in English Canada too a mood not to compromise with Quebec had taken hold. In a referendum held across Canada in October 1992, the Charlottetown formula was defeated in six provinces. While English provinces generally turned down the constitutional compromise because it gave in to Quebec "blackmail," the 56 percent of Quebecers who opposed the accord did so primarily because it did not provide Quebec with sufficient new powers. Faring poorly at the polls, in 1993 both Bourassa and Mulroney resigned as leaders of their parties.

The Growth of the Sovereignty Movement

In July 1990 a Mulroney associate, Lucien Bouchard, broke away from the Conservative cabinet and established the *Bloc Québécois* (BQ), a sister party of the PQ that contested federal elections on the platform of Quebec sovereignty. In the October 1993 national elections, the Liberals led by former Trudeau deputy Jean Chrétien (also a native of Quebec) returned to power in place of the scandal-plagued

Conservatives. But the strongest showing in Quebec was recorded by the BQ, which captured fifty-four of the seventy-five federal ridings in the province. The BQ, seeking the breakup of Canada, became the official opposition party in the Canadian House of Commons.

To be sure, support for the BQ was not based exclusively on its sovereignty platform. An opinion poll carried out during the 1993 election found that 44 percent of BQ supporters wanted the party to concentrate on job creation in Quebec. Only 3 percent said it should focus on achieving Quebec independence.[17] The popularity of the BQ was also, to a great extent, a function of the public's perception that it could strengthen the Quebec economy.

Within a year of Chrétien's victory, the PQ had won a comfortable majority of seats in the Quebec provincial election. Close examination of the result found that the PQ edged out the PLQ in the popular vote by the slimmest of margins, 44.7 percent to 44.3 percent, but making good on the PQ promise made in the campaign, upon taking office in September 1994 new Prime Minister Jacques Parizeau promised a referendum on sovereignty during his term in office.

The PQ's National Executive Council explained the rationale for sovereignty: "The Canadian federal system is a major obstacle to the pursuit of the goals of both societies. Quebec and English Canada are caught in a constitutional trap that prevents both of them from enjoying the benefits of their sovereignty and adopting strategies to meet the most important challenges of our time. Canada is at an impasse, and it is clearly in the interest of both partners to get out of this impasse as quickly as possible."[18]

The wording of the referendum question would be crucial to eliciting support. Reference to independence would limit supporters to the 25 percent of hard-line unconditional *indépendentistes* in the province. Coupling Quebec sovereignty with continued economic association with Canada would expand the support base. A disagreement arose between sovereignty party leaders. Whereas Parizeau, representing the *pur et dur* ("purist and hard-line") wing of the PQ, wanted a "hard" question addressing independence, BQ chief Bouchard preferred a "softer" question stressing continued association with Canada. Another problem for *indépendentistes* was that for a sovereignty referendum to succeed, at least 61 percent of francophones would have to be in favor because English speakers and immigrant groups would vote heavily against the proposal. For Quebec's bargaining position vis-à-vis Ottawa to be strong, at least 60 percent of all voters would have to support sovereignty, thereby requiring 77 percent support among French speakers.

On October 30, 1995, Quebecers went to the polls to give a yes or no to the question: "Do you agree that Quebec should become sovereign, after having made a formal offer to Canada for a new economic and political partnership, within the scope of the bill respecting the future of Quebec and of the agreement signed on June 12, 1995?" The bill in question, introduced in the Quebec legislature on September 7, 1995, provided for drafting a new Quebec constitution and clarified the territory, citizenship, and currency status that a sovereign Quebec would have. The agreement cited in the referendum question was one concluded on June 12, 1995, by the three major prosovereignty movements: the PQ, BQ, and the *Action*

Démocratique du Québec, a third party—in addition to the Quebec Liberals—represented in the Quebec National Assembly.

The result was closer than the complacent federal forces had imagined: only 50.6 percent of voters opposed the question and 49.4 percent supported it. Slightly more than 60 percent of francophones opted for the sovereignty option, while the overwhelming majority of English speakers and members of Quebec's ethnic groups rejected it. Bouchard's greater personal popularity had placed him in the role as leader of the "yes" campaign and, together with the "softer" question, gave sovereigntists hope that they would win the referendum. Public opinion polling just before the vote, done on behalf of the "yes" campaign, showed that the "yes" side was poised to win, and Prime Minister Parizeau prerecorded a victory speech in which he referred to Quebec joining the family of nations.

The close result was, therefore, a shock to both sides. The federalists had been slow to react to the surge of support for sovereignty, had no one to counter Bouchard's charisma, and were badly divided as to tactics. The sovereigntists had seen victory slip away as massive "unity rallies" in Montreal—the core of opposition to sovereignty—were staged. Well-intentioned pledges by sovereigntists to guarantee employment in the Quebec public service to Quebecers who presently worked for federal agencies backfired. Civil servants of the Quebec government felt they would lose out. In predominantly francophone Quebec City, therefore, a surprising number of voters opposed sovereignty.

But for Parizeau, conceding defeat in the referendum, the loss was attributable to two sources: ethnic groups and big money (the large corporations operating in Quebec). Even though true, his divisive speech was the opportunity that his opponents had been waiting for. On the day after the referendum Parizeau, under pressure, announced his resignation. Following a leadership convention a few months later, the PQ elected Bouchard as its new head.

In the first six months after the referendum, the rhetoric between sovereigntists and federalists was heated. Both sides accused the other of vote rigging, and indeed voting irregularities were uncovered. There were references to both a unilateral declaration of Quebec independence and the partition of Quebec if the province left Canada. The logic used was that if Quebec could break up Canada without seeking the consent of the rest of Canada, so Quebec could be partitioned based on the failure of various regions (above all, the island of Montreal and the Cree territories in northern Quebec) to give their consent. By the end of 1996, however, Prime Minister Bouchard was forced to concentrate on the problem of rising unemployment in Quebec, not sovereignty, even as the rest of Canada was experiencing an economic boom. Bouchard talked less about holding another referendum on sovereignty or a snap election, began to participate in federal–provincial premiers' meetings that his predecessor had boycotted, and noted public opinion polls showing that support for sovereignty had fallen to as low as 40 percent. At an economic summit of corporate and union leaders held a year after the referendum, angry students, health workers, and other disaffected groups gathered before the meeting site, smashed windows, and burned an effigy of Bouchard. For his part, Canadian Prime Minister Chrétien had passed a bill in the parliament giving parliamentary (though not constitutional) recognition to Quebec as a distinct society. His government's popularity assured him of reelection in 1997. Nevertheless, so long as discussions about meaningful restructuring of the federal system giving Quebec asymmetrical status were avoided, the Quebec sovereigntist movement had every reason to hope for a "yes" majority at the next referendum, likely to be held by the end of the century.

WHY PEACEFUL SECESSION IS RARE

In his study of the consequences of a successful Quebec separation from the Rest of Canada (ROC), political scientist Robert Young explored the theory of peaceful secessions. He argued that the outcomes of secessions are path dependent; that is, they depend on the process through which it occurs. The secession outcome is contingent on historical events, the procedure of separation, the antecedent institutional structures, and the nature of the transition moment. That is why so far in this chapter we have been describing the path dependence of the Quebec sovereignty movement.

As in the case of most secessionist movements, so in Quebec's case "The legal issues are fundamentally contestable."[19] A referendum on sovereignty, even if supported by a large majority of voters, would not by itself suffice as a constitutional instrument of secession. Some English Canadian leaders have argued that only a Canada wide referendum on Quebec separation could have legal force. To be sure, a vote by Quebec's National Assembly in favor of sovereignty might initiate a constitutional process terminating in appropriate amendments to Canada's constitutional acts, making clear that they no longer applied to Quebec. Given the difficulties of amending the Canadian constitution, however, such a process could only be pursued alongside political negotiations between Quebec and the ROC.

Economic studies of Quebec secession usually distinguish between the immediate impact of the transition to sovereignty and Quebec's long-term prospects as an independent state. In both cases, the province's resource endowment and industrial base are a constant, but the short-term impact would be negative for both Canada and Quebec due to transaction costs (such as institutional restructuring), fiscal costs (increased tax burdens), and uncertainty (affecting currency markets, investment, and migration). Estimates of Quebec's budget deficit in the first year of independence have ranged from $10 billion to $22 billion.[20] Young contrasted two economic scenarios of successful secession:

> In the optimistic view, a cohesive, flexible Quebec, with a loyal business class and state policies tailored to its needs, outward looking and with access to markets assured through international trade regimes, would fare better than it currently does. In the pessimistic view, either Quebec would fail to gain adequate access to international markets, or its sociocultural endowment would fail to produce economic growth, or the effects of the transition to sovereignty would hobble its long-run prospects.[21]

Young was drawn to the obvious conclusion that "studies of the transition to Quebec sovereignty show that the economic stakes could be very high, the legal arguments are indeterminate, and the outcome of the transition would depend on the politics of the event."[22]

So as to contextualize Quebec's bid for separation, the same author examined the comparative politics of peaceful secession.[23] He noted that few cases existed, limited in the twentieth century to Norway's secession from Sweden in 1905 and Singapore's from Malaysia in 1965. In these cases secession events happened abruptly, negotiations involved few political participants, they centered on a few significant provisions, agreements were accomplished constitutionally, and foreign powers played an important role.[24] Young was aware of the more recent cases of separatism in the USSR and of Czechoslovakia, but he judged these cases to involve the complete disintegration of a "predecessor state" into separate parts rather than one unit (prospective "secessor state") seeking to break away.

Czechoslovakia's "velvet divorce" was the product of increasing political polarization within the federation. "This is a process of growing mutual hostility between two communities, accompanied by a sense among members of each that their interests are distinct and can only be met through separation."[25] Thus, whereas in June 1990 only 5 percent of Czechs and 8 percent of Slovaks favored dividing the country into two separate states, by October 1992 56 percent of Czechs in Bohemia and 43 percent in Moravia, and 37 percent of Slovaks thought separation was necessary. Young made the broader point, applicable to the Canada–Quebec case, that "how polarization took place in Czechoslovakia is a reminder that political competition is not restricted by the rules of the game: politicians will try to shift public opinion and even to reshape society for their own advantage."[26] This is why the anti-Quebec rhetoric of Reform Party Leader Preston Manning, whose strength lies in Alberta and British Columbia, carries the potential for polarization.

Successful Quebec secession would also be the result of contingent circumstances. Milton Esman referred to a political opportunity structure within which ethnic movements operate. It "furnishes incentives, limitations, permissible boundaries, potentials, and risks that inform the behavior of ethnic entrepreneurs and activists and influence the expectations of their constituents. It enables and facilitates certain actions, constrains and proscribes others."[27] Esman identified two principal dimensions to the political opportunity structure:

(a) the rules and practices that enable or limit the ability of the ethnic movement and its component organizations to mobilize, to propagandize, and to assert claims for access, participation, redress, or benefits; and (b) the propensity of the political establishment to consider such claims as legitimate and subject to possible accommodation.[28]

Esman contrasted three cases of ethnic mobilization with different processual features. In Northern Ireland, Catholic groups had the opportunity to mobilize but could not obtain recognition from the political leaders for the legitimacy of their grievances. In South Africa, the absence of established rules and practices and of an accommodation-oriented regime did not permit mobilization, so, according to Esman, violent or revolutionary strategies were adopted by ethnic groups. By contrast, in Canada both dimensions were positive, thereby encouraging Quebec nationalists to rely on constitutionally oriented methods. Their legal strategy is an outcome of a political opportunity structure that is both open and accommodative.

We should remember that nationalism often has a momentum and direction of its own. The authors of a political science text on Quebec observed how Quebec nationalism's "evolution began with the Church, moved to the State, and now is expressed by individual francophones in the market economy. Nationalism is a permanent fixture of Quebec political culture."[29] There has been a parallel change in this nationalism's ideological content, too: "Gradually, nationalism evolved from this insular, collectivist perspective—rooted in a deep-seated conservatism—to a confident, functional, statist orientation, to, finally, an entrepreneurial, materialistic individualism rooted in economic liberalism."[30]

To some degree, the growth and modernization of Quebec nationalism has been a function of the ambiguity of Canadian nationalism. For Taylor,

> the search for identity seems to be at odds in Canada with the search for national unity; for our country is very diverse—not only in the obvious sense, that there are two major languages and cultures, or in the 'mosaic' sense, that there are people from many different backgrounds, but in the geographical and historical sense. . . . Many of Canada's constituent groups or regions have a strong sense of identity. The case hardly has to be made for French Canada, but it can easily be made for the Maritimes, Newfoundland, British Columbia—to mention only indisputable areas of strong feeling.[31]

Yet, the most important fault line in Canada remains language and ethnolinguistic identity. Taylor argued how "For English Canadians, who are acutely aware of the diversity of the country, of the tenuous and indefinable nature of what holds it together, the question of unity is paramount. For any part of Canadian society to demonstrate that it prizes its part over the whole smacks of treason."[32] He added that "If French Canadians must learn to understand the English anxiety about unity, English Canadians must learn that the identification with *la nation canadienne-française* is not at all the antechamber to separatism."[33] By the second half of the 1990s the learning process that Taylor emphasized no longer seemed important to many in Canada.

INTERNATIONAL REACTION

When the results of the 1995 referendum became known outside Canada, two diametrically opposed and entirely predictable reactions were perceptible. The first was that of fellow states in the international community: They expressed relief that the Canadian federation had survived a stiff democratic challenge and that the country's unity had received majority backing in a province still excluded from the constitutional framework. In particular, liberal democracies such as the United States and Britain, both of which wished to maintain the appearance that they were neutral in the dispute and were not interfering in Canada's internal affairs, were pleased that the referendum maintained the status quo.

Most other states in the international system also endorsed the result. Canada's image in the world had been nearly without blemish (other than for its seal hunting), and it had often been rated by a United Nations commission as the country having the best quality of life in the world. In addition, many states had significant diaspora populations in Canada: Italy, Portugal, Sweden, Poland, Iran, India, the Philippines. Like most of the immigrants settling in Canada, leaders of these states could not understand the historical and cultural basis for Quebec's dispute with English Canada. Because Canada claimed to be a multicultural state, most natives of these other countries understandably concluded that there was no essential political difference between being a Chinese Canadian or a French Canadian. If other ethnic groups in Canada did not demand autonomy, the logic went, why should the French? The question that English Canadians first posed shortly after the Quiet Revolution—What do Quebecers want?—now had international resonance.

By contrast, nations that themselves sought greater political independence from centralized states were heartened by the closeness of the Quebec referendum result. Nationalist leaders in Scotland, Catalonia, northern Italy, and elsewhere were reassured that democratic procedures could work to their advantage. Another consideration was that ethnosecession had been stigmatized by the wars taking place in Bosnia, Chechnya, and Sri Lanka. The Quebec verdict, even though it had failed by a small margin to endorse sovereignty, had illustrated the compatability between national assertion and liberal democracy.

The U.S. view of the eventuality of Quebec sovereignty has been benign. According to Jonathan Lemco,

> the United States has long maintained that an independent Quebec would be a viable country and a good neighbor. It acknowledges that Quebec would likely support all of Canada's existing defense and economic commitments and remain a staunch supporter of American policies in a broad sense. The most pertinent reason for U.S. opposition to Quebec's sovereignty, then, has less to do with Quebec per se and more to do with the fractionalization of Canada that could result.[34]

To be sure, for a long time U.S. officials have been careful not to make commitments to a future independent Quebec. A two-track policy was illustrated by President George Bush in March 1991 when he stated that the United States had no desire to interfere in domestic Canadian politics, but he quickly added, "We are very, very happy with a united Canada."[35] During President Bill Clinton's visit to Canada in early 1995, protocol required that he meet with the official opposition leader, who was the BQ's Bouchard. Some members of parliament criticized Clinton for going ahead with the meeting, and the brief gathering was cordial (we should point out that Bouchard's wife is an American). But true to form, Clinton then made a speech in the House of Commons that included the exhortation: "*Vive le Canada.*" He thereby antagonized, in turn, Quebec nationalists seeking to leave confederation.

Lemco has stressed that the U.S. two-track policy is contingent on other important factors: "If the threat of sovereignty were somehow to have devastating economic implications or strategic costs for the United States, then American officials would undoubtedly rethink their position."[36] It might not even take a security threat but simply the complexity of including Quebec in reconfigured institutions to persuade the United States to dampen Quebec hopes for membership in international organizations. Thus Lemco concluded that "it is not outside the realm of possibility that the United States, faced with difficult issues such as how to incorporate Quebec into NORAD [North American Air Defence Command] and how to retain friendly political relations with Canada as a whole (including access to its natural resources), would choose not to include Quebec in the free trade agreement."[37] Indeed, this was what seemed to have happened when, late in the referendum campaign when the "no" side feared defeat, U.S. Secretary of State Warren Christopher praised the excellent relationship between his country and Canada and then warned that there would be no guarantees of the same advantages for Quebec as currently existed between Ottawa and Washington if Canada was reorganized.[38]

Arguably the most influential international reaction having a direct bearing on Quebec's future is that of foreign investors. We have noted that many Canadian and multinational corporations pulled their operations out of Quebec, wholly or in part, in the 1970s and 1980s. Corporations largely sided with the "no" campaign in the 1995 referendum, and they urged Bouchard after that to eliminate political uncertainty by agreeing not to hold another referendum for the forseeable future. During a visit to Japan in 1996, Bouchard was told by a major entrepreneur that Japanese businessmen would be saddened by the breakup of Canada, and that it was not a good idea to make Japanese businessmen sad. But the calculus of Quebec sovereigntist leaders is just the opposite: an independent Quebec would provide better investment opportunities than one wrapped up in red tape coming from Ottawa. Quebec forms an important part of the North American economy and its economic activity is regulated not only by the Canadian government but by more general trade agreements. We study the internationalization of Quebec's economic policies in the following section.

CAN A CONSTITUTIONALLY BASED DISPUTE BE INTERNATIONALIZED?

The role of France in encouraging Quebec separatism has been exaggerated. Other than President Charles de Gaulle's famous cry from Montreal City Hall in 1967, "*Vive le Québec Libre,*" successive French leaders have done nothing to give the appearance of helping break up Canada. To be sure, the return of a Gaullist to the Élysée palace in 1996 provided some reasons to believe that French policy on Quebec might change. President Jacques Chirac made clear before the referendum that France would recognize Quebec independence if it originated in a constitutional process and was produced by a democratic verdict. In May 1997, former PQ Leader Parizeau claimed that Giscard d'Estaing, French president in the 1970s, had encouraged him in 1995 to issue a unilateral declaration of independence following a referendum victory. But for pragmatic considerations alone, France was aware that its support for the Quebec sovereigntist movement would likely prove counterproductive: Not only would opponents of sovereignty have a new argument to make about outside interference, but French Quebecers have also long objected to what they perceive is a condescending attitude by France to their former colony. There is no major Quebec nationalist leader whose priority is closer ties to the French-speaking world.

Not surprisingly, the key international actor in the Quebec issue is the United States. Although American interest in Canada generally and Quebec in particular is limited, specialized U.S. governmental agencies have considered what spillover, if any, there would be on the United States of Quebec separation. According to Quebec journalist Jean-François Lisée, beginning in the 1970s the U.S. State Department regularly studied the options it would have if Quebec seceded, but these consisted of academic studies, and the State Department did not engage in any diplomacy that could be interpreted as interfering in Canada's internal affairs.[39]

The international dimensions of the Canada–Quebec dispute were more clearly seen in the economic rather than political relations with the United States. Both the Canadian and Quebec economies were closely integrated with the United States one. Alfred Hero, a specialist on economic relations between the United States and Quebec, highlighted Quebec's growing economic dependence: Whereas in 1978 about 73 percent of Quebec's material (or tangible) exports went south, by 1995, with the implementation of most of the North American Free Trade Agreement's (NAFTA) articles, the proportion rose to 84 percent. Forty-five percent of Quebec imports originated in the United States and, surprisingly, this one Canadian province represented the seventh-largest export market in the world for the United States. Furthermore, Quebec's trade balance per capita with the United States was more positive than even Japan's.[40] All political parties in Quebec, then, whether federalist or sovereigntist, supported the NAFTA agreement when it was finalized by the Mulroney government in Ottawa.

Gaining admission into NAFTA would be the top foreign policy priority of an independent Quebec, according to Hero and other Quebec experts. The new state would also seek membership in the North Atlantic Treaty Organization (NATO), the Organization of American States (OAS), the North American Air Defense Agreement (NORAD), and *La Francophonie* (a community of French-speaking nations roughly modeled on, but much less integrated than the British Commonwealth). From 1994 onward, the PQ government lobbied Washington for U.S. support for NAFTA membership should Quebec separate; however, the NAFTA agreement provides charter members with a veto power over admission of applicants. If there was enough rancor following the breakup of the country, it was conceivable that the ROC would prevent breakaway Quebec from joining the free trade agreement. But this threat was most effective when used as leverage to keep Quebec in confederation.

If Quebec established a separate state, doubts exist about the ROC's ability to survive together, the resulting uncertainty of which would become a serious concern to U.S. foreign-policy makers. Before he became prime minister, Chrétien contended that Quebec independence would be an invitation for the ROC to join the United States. There are few "annexationists" in U.S. politics today, the most notable being Republican Patrick Buchanan. The United States is aware that the Canadian provinces most anxious to join the United States would likely be the "poorhouse" provinces of the Maritimes. Economically endowed provinces such as Ontario and Alberta would probably be least enthusiastic, while British Columbia's militant union movement and long-serving labor-oriented New Democratic Party governments would make it very radical by U.S. standards.[41]

Canada's ability to survive Quebec's withdrawal can be gauged in terms of economic data. While Quebec accounted for 25 percent of Canada's population and 23 percent of its GNP in the early 1990s, it had only a 17 percent share in Canadian exports. More important, about 80 percent of interprovincial trade in Canada takes place between Quebec and Ontario. Quebec's economy was more dependent on trade with Ontario—more than 40 percent of its cross-Canada trade was with its western neighbor—than Ontario was dependent on Quebec.[42] The economic costs of Quebec leaving Canada would be borne proportionally more by Quebec, and Canada's economy would not be devastated. Indeed, Canadian entrepreneur Conrad Black has written that "A Canada no longer subject to Quebec's endless threats of secession . . . would be a steadily more important G–7 country. It would fully occupy the political role available to one of the world's ten or twelve most important countries."[43]

The international dimension to the Quebec sovereignty issue is circumscribed, therefore. There is, to date, little threat perception by the United States, by other countries, or by international organizations. To some provincial leaders in Canada, especially heads of the Reform Party in the western provinces, rather than making this region vulnerable to U.S. expansion, Quebec secession might prove to be a positive-sum game. These provinces could "piggyback" on Quebec and gain increased powers for themselves from Ottawa. But in the political climate following the close referendum vote, both international and local actors were taking stock in the possibility of some future breakup of Canada.

WHAT CAN EXTERNAL PARTIES DO ABOUT THE CONFLICT IN CANADA?

Because the issue of Quebec sovereignty has been path dependent and consistent with established democratic procedures prevailing in Canada, international organizations have been superfluous to the domestic process of mediation. Canada's membership in such institutions as the UN, NATO, and the G–7 (Group of Seven highly industrialized nations) may make them the first to attempt mediation should the crisis get out of hand, but only the outbreak and protraction of violence would produce such an attempt.

The only conceivable third-party mediation outside of an IGO would be by the United States. We have highlighted the guarded American approach to the Canada–Quebec dispute. Two additional factors would make the United States circumspect about becoming involved. Its experience in mediating conflicts not only in Bosnia but also Northern Ireland has taught American leaders that good-faith peacemaking efforts are fraught with dangers, the most serious one being that it is difficult to withdraw once involvement has occurred. The case of Bosnia is clearcut: the withdrawal of peacekeepers that separate warring sides can lead to a renewed explosion of violence. More subtle is the trap the United States became ensnared in in Northern Ireland. American pressure helped bring about the Anglo–Irish agreement of November 1985 dealing with the future of Northern Ireland, but the breakdown of the peace process and the end of the IRA's cease-fire a decade later had the effect of making it still difficult for the United States to disengage from peacemaking. "Indeed, by underlining the need for a political settlement to underpin the peace, the course of events has further enhanced the American role in the process, with all the parties in Northern Ireland seeking to influence both American opinion generally and the Clinton administration in particular, on the next steps and on the shape of an overall settlement."[44]

A second factor inhibiting any type of U.S. involvement in the Canada–Quebec dispute is the proximity of the country in crisis. The United States is likely to be doubly hesistant to become involved in mediating internal disputes in neighboring states—whether in Canada's constitutional impasse with Quebec or Mexico's dispute with the Zapatista movement—because latent anti–American sentiment could be mobilized by one of the parties. Good-faith mediation that produces an unsatisfactory outcome for one of the parties could lead to political complications for the United States.

Canada has a long history of sending troops to carry out peacekeeping missions in various parts of the world. For many specialists on Canada, it is unimaginable that the federal government will not be able eventually to reach a solution to a problem at home: how to accommodate Quebecers' desire for asymmetrical status. But should it not succeed, it still remains improbable that external mediation would be used to fashion an outcome that would transcend domestic stalemate.

DISCUSSION QUESTIONS

1. What are the historical grievances advanced by Quebec nationalists to justify separation from English Canada? Are these more important than arguments emphasizing Quebec's cultural and linguistic development?
2. In what way has Canada's political culture, stressing constitutional procedures for resolving disputes, affected the nature and methods of the Quebec sovereignty movement? In what way does Quebec's political culture, shaped by democratic and more egalitarian values, influence the sovereignty movement?
3. Which external parties have stakes in Canada's possible breakup? What role, if any, have they played in the dispute between Quebec and Ottawa? Would that role change if a majority of Quebecers voted for sovereignty?
4. What are the major characteristics of peaceful secession? Why is it so rare? Would Quebec's peaceful secession from Canada have a demonstration effect on national minorities living in other Western liberal democracies?
5. Using Quebec as an example, how does global economic interdependence affect secessionism? Does it offer an opportunity structure for smaller nations to conduct their own economic affairs, or does economic interdependence leave the future of smaller nations in the hands of large international actors?

NOTES

1. For an argument about the commonalities, see Mihailo Crnobrnja, "Could It Happen Here?" *The Gazette* (Montreal), October 29, 1996, p. B3.
2. See Richard Simeon, *Federal-Provincial Diplomacy: The Making of Recent Policy in Canada.* (Toronto: University of Toronto Press, 1977).

3. For an excellent introduction, see Paul-André Linteau, René Durocher, Jean-Claude Robert, *Quebec: A History 1867–1929.* (Toronto: Lorimer, 1983).

4. Charles Taylor, *Reconciling the Solitudes: Essays on Canadian Federalism and Nationalism.* (Montreal: McGill-Queen's University Press, 1993), p. 5.

5. See Paul-André Linteau, René Durocher, Jean-Claude Robert, *Quebec Since 1930.* (Toronto: Lorimer, 1991).

6. On language of education for immigrants, see Donat Taddeo and Raymond Taras, *Le débat linguistique au Québec.* (Montreal: Les Presses de l'Université de Montréal, 1986).

7. See Claude Morin, *Quebec Versus Ottawa: The Struggle for Self-Government 1960–72.* (Toronto: University of Toronto Press, 1976).

8. Milton J. Esman, *Ethnic Politics.* (Ithaca, NY: Cornell University Press, 1994), p. 164.

9. Taylor, *Reconciling the Solitudes,* pp. 5–6.

10. *Ibid.,* p. 6.

11. Pierre Elliot Trudeau, *Memoirs.* (Toronto: McClelland and Stewart, 1994), pp. 325–326.

12. Taylor, *Reconciling the Solitudes,* p. 34.

13. Dominique Clift, *Quebec Nationalism in Crisis.* (Montreal: McGill-Queen's University Press, 1982), p. 142.

14. On the evolution of sovereigntist support in Quebec in the period 1962–1994, see Jonathan Lemco, *Turmoil in the Peaceable Kingdom: The Quebec Sovereignty Movement and Its Implications for Canada and the United States.* (Toronto: University of Toronto Press, 1994), p. 75. Also, Jean-François Lisée, *The Trickster: Robert Bourassa and Quebecers 1990–1992.* (Toronto: Lorimer, 1994), p. 360.

15. Lemco, *Turmoil in the Peaceable Kingdom,* p. xiii.

16. Lisée, *The Trickster,* pp. 16–17.

17. Lemco, *Turmoil in the Peaceable Kingdom,* p. 54.

18. National Executive Council of the *Parti Québécois, Quebec in a New World: The PQ's Plan for Sovereignty.* (Toronto: Lorimer, 1994), p. 6.

19. Robert A. Young, *The Secession of Quebec and the Future of Canada.* (Montreal: McGill-Queen's University Press, 1995), p. 104.

20. Lemco, *Turmoil in the Peaceable Kingdom,* p. 135.

21. Young, *The Secession of Quebec and the Future of Canada,* pp. 94–95.

22. *Ibid.,* p. 127.

23. Robert A. Young, "How do Peaceful Secessions Happen?" *Canadian Journal of Political Science,* 27, 4, December 1994, pp. 773–792.

24. Young, *The Secession of Quebec and the Future of Canada,* pp. 127–144.

25. *Ibid.,* pp. 147–148.

26. *Ibid.,* p. 292.

27. Esman, *Ethnic Politics,* p. 31.

28. *Ibid.,* pp. 31–32.

29. Guy Lachapelle, Gerald Bernier, Daniel Salee, and Luc Bernier, *The Quebec Democracy: Structures, Processes and Policies.* (Toronto: McGraw-Hill Ryerson, 1993), p. 70. We are grateful to Guy Lachapelle (Concordia University, Montreal) for comments on this chapter.

30. Lachapelle et al, *The Quebec Democracy,* p. 70.

31. Taylor, *Reconciling the Solitudes,* p. 26.

32. *Ibid.,* p. 31.

33. *Ibid.,* p. 32.

34. Lemco, *Turmoil in the Peaceable Kingdom,* pp. 149–150.

35. Quoted in Keith G. Banting, "If Quebec Separates: Restructuring North America," in R. Kent Weaver, ed., *The Collapse of Canada?* (Washington, DC: Brookings Institution, 1992), p. 176.
36. Lemco, *Turmoil in the Peacable Kingdom,* p. 147.
37. *Ibid.,* p. 156.
38. See the special issue on "The 1995 Quebec Referendum: An American View," in *American Review of Canadian Studies,* 25, 4, Winter 1995.
39. Jean-Francois Lisée, *In the Eye of the Eagle.* (Toronto: HarperCollins, 1990).
40. See Alfred O. Hero, Jr., and Louis Balthazar, *Contemporary Quebec and the United States, 1960–1985.* (Lanham, MD: University Press of America, 1988). Also, Hero and Marcel Daneau, eds., *Problems and Opportunities in U.S.-Quebec Relations.* (Boulder, CO: Westview Press, 1984).
41. See Lansing Lamont, *Breakup: The Coming End of Canada and the Stakes for America.* (Toronto: Key Porter Books, 1995).
42. Lemco, *Turmoil in the Peacable Kingdom,* pp. 92–95.
43. Conrad Black, "Canada's Continuing Identity Crisis," *Foreign Affairs.* 74, 2, March/April 1995, pp. 114–115.
44. Adrian Guelke, "The United States, Irish Americans, and the Northern Ireland Peace Process," *International Affairs,* 72, 3, July 1996, p. 535.

chapter 7

Protracted Ethnic Wars: The Tamil–Sinhalese Conflict in Sri Lanka

INTRODUCTION

In this chapter, we move away from Europe and North America to focus on ethnic conflict in Asia. The case we chose to study—the Tamil–Sinhalese conflict in Sri Lanka—is different from our first two case studies in several respects. First, the ethnic conflict in Sri Lanka is a classic case of protracted ethnic war whose roots go deep in the history of Sri Lanka. Second, as we can expect, protracted ethnic wars are more likely to acquire an international character, as evidenced by events occurring in Sri Lanka. Finally, protracted ethnic wars are difficult to resolve through international third-party action, again proven by the failure of India's resolution attempt in Sri Lanka. The overall point that we wish to convey is that protracted ethnic wars are in a real sense *dirty wars*—they are deep rooted, highly internationalized, fought ruthlessly with enormous human suffering, and difficult to resolve.

But before we begin our narrative of the ethnic war in Sri Lanka, we would like to touch briefly on another secessionist conflict in South Asia: This is the story of the birth of Bangladesh. Although ethnosecessionist movements have been quite frequent in South Asia, there has been no more momentous an event having an enduring impact upon South Asian secessionists (elsewhere too for that matter) than Bangladesh's secession from Pakistan in 1971. The "message" of Bangladesh was unique in two respects: First, the secession of Bangladesh was the only case of *successful* secession by an ethnic group during the long cold war period; second, Bangladesh was also one of those rare cases where secessionists were able to attract direct military intervention by their partisan external supporter. As we have discussed earlier, most secessionist movements end in *failure* because they fail to attract *direct military intervention* by their partisan external supporters. Bangladesh's "demonstration effect" on future South Asian secessionists was therefore significant. As our discussion later in this chapter will show, the Sri Lankan Tamils' decision to opt for secession in the mid–1970s was partly based on the calculation that by doing so they might be able to induce India to carry out another Bangladesh-type operation to create a separate Tamil state in Sri Lanka.

THE PRECEDENT OF BANGLADESH'S SECESSION

Genesis of the Bangladesh Crisis

The birth of Bangladesh in 1971 marked the culmination of a very long period of nationalist struggle by the Bengali people.[1] Nationalist feelings were not new to Bengalis. Ever since the formation of Pakistan in 1947, Bengali political demands centered around achieving the greatest possible degree of regional autonomy, reflecting mainly their sociocultural and ethnic distinctiveness from the rest of Pakistan; their linguistic, economic, administrative, and political exploitation at the Pakistan government's hands, dominated by ethnic groups from the West Wing; and their geographical separation from Pakistan's power seat—the center of Pakistan's political power, the West Wing, was separated from the East Wing by 1200 miles of Indian territory.[2] The process reached its peak with the Bengali demand that except for matters of defense, communication, and foreign affairs, all other powers should belong to the provinces. In spite of repeated Pakistani government rebuffs, the Bengalis stuck to their demand for regional autonomy.

The crystallization of Bengali ethnonationalism into a secessionist movement geared to the creation of an independent Bangladesh occurred in early 1971 as a result of two main developments. First, under the promise made by General Yahya Khan's military government that political power will be handed over to civilian authorities, national assembly elections were held in Pakistan in 1970. In this election, the Awami League, a predominantly Bengali political party led by the charismatic Sheikh Mujibur Rehman (popularly known as Mujib), emerged with a clear majority. Immediately, the Yahya Khan regime reneged on its promise and refused to allow the Awami League to form the national government. Even then, Sheikh Mujibur Rehman did not call for secession; instead, he continued to negotiate with the Yahya regime in the hope that the military would not crush the aspirations of the Bengali people, who formed a majority of Pakistan's total population (approximately 54 percent).[3] As this political deadlock continued after the elections, another sinister development occurred: The Yahya regime imprisoned Mujib and decided to crush forcibly the Bengalis' aspirations to form Pakistan's government. In early 1971, the Yahya regime let loose the Pakistani military in East Pakistan. Mujib and the Awami League, therefore, had no other options but to call for secession.[4]

Internationalization of the Bengali Secessionist Movement

From a very early stage, the Bengali secessionist movement became highly internationalized. Once the Pakistani military crackdown in the East Wing started and full-blown secession resulted, neighboring India was immediately affected. As the carnage went on, New Delhi had to accept an enormous refugee burden from East Pakistan (some estimates put it at around six million). From early 1971, therefore, India embarked on a policy of diffusion and encouragement of the Bengali secessionists that occurred at two levels. First, New Delhi's diplomatic initiatives focused the international community's attention on the atrocities being committed by the Pakistani army in East Pakistan and on the economic and social hardships being faced by India as a result. Then, from the middle of 1971, New Delhi unleashed a diplomatic campaign to garner support for a possible Indian military campaign in East Pakistan. Second, India started to provide the Bengali secessionists with covert material aid so that they could offer armed resistance to the rampaging Pakistani army in East Pakistan. India further helped organize and train irregular Bengali forces known as the Mukti Bahini (Freedom Force). By late 1971, however, it seemed that in spite of India's best efforts, the Mukti Bahini would be no match for the professional Pakistani military. Covert intervention, therefore, turned to overt military intervention with the Indian military invasion of East Pakistan in December 1971. In the ensuing India–Pakistan war, India emerged victorious and the state of Bangladesh was created. Thus the direct Indian military intervention in late 1971 on behalf of the Bengalis was the decisive factor behind the secessionist movement's success. Such instances of direct military intervention by a foreign state on behalf of secessionists are rare in international politics, so the Indian military intervention in Bangladesh is singular in its importance.

India's decision to pursue a policy of diffusion and encouragement toward the Bengali secessionist movement in East Pakistan and ultimately to intervene militarily was based on a combination of affective and instrumental motives: First, the affective ties that existed between the Bengalis in East Pakistan and those in the neighboring Indian province of West Bengal generated much sympathy in West Bengal for the plight of fellow Bengalis in East Pakistan, which New Delhi could not ignore; second, the refugee influx that the army crackdown caused in East Pakistan presented India with a major humanitarian crisis that it could not tackle but also could not accept; third, India was also concerned that the instability in East Pakistan could have an adverse effect on the internal security of West Bengal, given the rise of radical politics in the state at the time; finally, India wanted to use the crisis in East Pakistan to dismember Pakistan, its main enemy.

Although India's intervention in East Pakistan was overwhelming, other states, too, became involved in different ways and at different levels. For instance, concerned by the news that India might take advantage of its ally Pakistan's vulnerability, the United States involved itself in the crisis as a supporter of the Yahya regime. In this role, President Nixon's National Security Adviser Henry Kissinger visited New Delhi in 1971 to warn the Indian government that severe consequences would follow if it invaded East Pakistan. At the same time, to silence such critics in Congress as Senator

Edward Kennedy, the Nixon administration authorized millions of dollars of relief aid to India earmarked for the starving and sick Bengali refugees and urged the Yahya regime to return power to East Pakistani civilians.[5]

Another state that supported the Yahya regime was Communist China, which happened to be a close ally of Pakistan and a bitter enemy of India. In 1962, India had lost a border war with China, and Sino–Indian relations hit an all-time low after that year. On the other hand, Pakistan's relations with China had improved significantly after the Sino–Pakistan boundary agreement of 1963. Pakistan was also instrumental in reconciling China and the United States in 1971. Thus during Kissinger's visit to China in July 1971, Chinese Premier Zhou Enlai had made it clear that China would not remain indifferent if India and Pakistan came to blows over East Pakistan.[6]

United Nations involvement, while minimal, was clearly directed against Pakistan. Due to India's presentation of the case for Bengali secession, both Britain and France abstained on crucial United Nations resolutions on East Pakistan. Further, both states called for a political solution in East Pakistan based on the results of the 1970 elections, a position that India adhered to. Britain also suspended all developmental aid to Pakistan but continued to provide arms and relief aid to India. The communist world also came out in support of India and along with the Soviet Union voted against Pakistan in the United Nations. Other third-world states in the UN also showed solidarity with the Bengali people.

India's biggest diplomatic victory, however, came in August 1971 with the signing of the Indo–Soviet Treaty of Peace and Friendship. The twenty-year treaty, which was announced on August 9, 1971, had actually been discussed two years earlier, but at that time India had hesitated to sign it for fear of antagonizing the United States. Now, confronted with the crisis in East Pakistan that showed no signs of abating and animosity demonstrated by the United States and China toward India, Indira Gandhi decided to link India to the Soviet Union formally in case hostilities broke out with Pakistan.

The Road to War

With the signing of the Indo–Soviet Treaty of Peace and Friendship, the Soviet Union strongly committed itself to India's side. India, therefore, had less reason to fear a joint American–Chinese move on behalf of Pakistan in case war broke out. By late 1971, the rationale for launching a preemptive war on Pakistan seemed sound to New Delhi. It had become quite clear that the Mukti Bahini was no match for the professional Pakistani army, which continued to massacre the Bengali people, thus generating more refugees in India. New Delhi was clearly economically overstretched. A return to normalcy and the repatriation of the refugees provided a perfect moral cover for direct military action.[7] The prolongation of the secessionist conflict was also seen by New Delhi as harmful for the postsecession political interests of the pro–India Awami League. The Awami League had waited until the last second to declare independence as its goal, hoping that a political compromise would be possible with the Yahya regime. This had not made the Awami League very popular among the

Bengalis, who were faced with the Pakistani army crackdown. The Indian government, thus, calculated that any prolongation of the war would lead to a fragmentation within the ranks of the secessionists and an erosion of the pro–India Awami League's authority.

Despite these reasons to start a military showdown with Pakistan in October, New Delhi again demonstrated restraint at the urging of the Soviet Union. In November 1971, Indira Gandhi visited Washington to apprise the Nixon administration of India's position and of its difficulty in caring for the Bengali refugees in India. Washington, instead of showing sympathy, rebuked India, leading Indira Gandhi to declare: "We have acted with patience, forbearance and restraint. But we cannot sit idly if the edifice of our political stability and economic well-being is threatened."[8]

Ironically, the Bangladesh war was not initiated by India but Pakistan. On December 3, 1971, Yahya Khan ordered the Pakistani Air Force to launch a surprise air attack on eight Indian airfields in the north and west.[9] On December 4, India formally declared war on Pakistan and launched its military offensive in the east. Then on December 6, India officially recognized the People's Republic of Bangladesh. Within the next two weeks, the war in East Pakistan came to an end with the total defeat of Pakistan and the creation of Bangladesh. India captured around 90,000 Pakistani POWs and substantial weapons.

During the war, the much-trumpeted Chinese support for Pakistan did not come. The United States had sent a warship from its Pacific Seventh Fleet into the Bay of Bengal. The U.S. warship, however, turned back and accepted the Indian victory as a fait accompli when the Soviet Union threatened to send a warship of its own into the Bay of Bengal. During this war, Kashmir saw limited Indo–Pakistan fighting.

India's role was the decisive factor behind the success of the Bengali secessionist movement in East Pakistan. India's diplomatic campaign to publicize internationally the atrocities on the Bengalis in East Pakistan and plight of the Bengali refugees in India helped to obtain widespread international condemnation of Pakistan and sympathy for the "justness" of the Bengalis' desire to secede. The international visibility and acceptability of the Bengali secessionists was thus greatly enhanced, something that few secessionists can boast of. While India's covert support did not help the secessionists greatly, it bought valuable time for India to prepare for a direct military confrontation with Pakistan. The Indian military invasion, however, was decisive as it was overwhelming. It not only liberated Bangladesh and put a stop to the suffering of the Bengali people, but it also prevented a serious rupture within the ranks of the secessionists by preventing the prolongation of the secessionist struggle.

WHY DID ETHNIC CONFLICT OCCUR IN SRI LANKA?

Historically, the Sinhalese–Tamil relationship in Sri Lanka included both traditional rivalry and peaceful coexistence between the two groups.[10] But in the past three decades, conflict between the Sinhalese and the Tamils has reached such proportions that it has undermined national unity and has all but destroyed the political integration of Sri Lanka. The ethnic conflict in Sri Lanka is the outcome of fundamental demographic, sociocultural, religious, linguistic, economic, and political issues that have foundations in the island's history. Until Sri Lanka became independent of British rule, these issues, while being present in society, remained in check because neither of the two communities had the political power and muscle to resolve them in their own favor. But independence from British rule in 1948 provided the numerical Sinhalese majority with the political power and determination to resolve these issues in a way that favored the Sinhalese community at the expense of the minorities, especially the Tamils.

The Issue of Original Inhabitancy and Traditional Homeland

Legends, religious teachings, and some historical accounts contained in the *Pali Chronicles,* the *Dipavamsa,* and the *Mahavamsa* (composed by *bhikkhus* or Buddhist clergy between the fourth and sixth centuries A.D.) suggest that the Sinhalese were the first civilized people to settle on the island, long before the Veddhas[11] and the South Indian Dravidians[12] appeared on the scene.

The *Mahavamsa,* written in the fifth century A.D., traces the origin of the Sinhalese people to the year 543 B.C.[13] According to mythical legends in the *Mahavamsa,* Vijaya, a crown prince, was banished by his father from the city of Sinhapura in Bengal. He landed at Tambapanni on the northwest coast of Sri Lanka with a group of 700 men under the protection of Lord Buddha. It is claimed by *bhikkhus* that Lord Buddha attained nirvana (died) in India the very same day that Vijaya landed on the island and that he supposedly prayed to God to guard Vijaya, his followers, and the island of Sri Lanka so that his religion could be established there.

Many Sinhalese historians, such as K.M. de Silva, argue that this myth of religious–ethnic destiny was deliberately contrived by the Buddhist clergy in order to propagate the theme that the Sinhalese people, as descendants of Vijaya, are destined by divine will to protect and foster the Buddhist religion in Sri Lanka.[14] In any case, upon his arrival, Vijaya quickly gained control of the island by marrying Kuveni, the queen of the nonhuman Yaksha people.

As the story goes on in the *Mahavamsa,* after a few years Vijaya banished Kuveni along with his son and daughter into the forest. Manogaran points out in this context that "This story of the banishment of his family was deliberately contrived [by the Buddhist clergy] to imply that Vijaya and his men did not propagate the Sinhalese race with nonhuman Yaksha women."[15] Thereafter, Vijaya married the daughter of the Pandyan king of Madura in South India, and his men married Pandyan women of high caste.[16] So as it is contended by the Buddhist clergy, the Aryan settlers maintained their separate identity and propagated the Sinhala race.

The *Mahavamsa* also claims that the Veddhas were not the original people of Sri Lanka but were propagated by Vijaya's Yaksha son and daughter in the island's isolated parts. Manogaran argues in this context that "the Veddha connection to Vijaya is emphasized [by the Buddhist clergy] to insure that the Sinhalese are considered the original inhabitants of the island and that no ethnic links are established between the aboriginal tribes of Sri Lanka and those of South India of the pre–Dravidian period."[17]

The Sinhalese claim of being the original inhabitants of the island has been challenged by many historians. Some have claimed that Tamil-speaking Dravidians were very likely on the island at the time of the Sinhalese arrival. For instance, Wijesekera believes that the physical characteristics of the Veddhas resulted from the successive fusion of Mediterranean, Australoid, and Negrito racial groups in South India; this suggests that they were not the aboriginal people of Sri Lanka but had migrated from South India in prehistoric times. While accepting the mythical link between Vijaya and the origin of the Sinhalese race, Wijesekera notes that this purity of race could not be preserved in the course of time.[18] On his part, Rasanayagam has argued that the Yakshas and Nagas, who are referred to in the *Mahavamsa* as nonhumans, were actually the aboriginal tribes of India and Sri Lanka. He cites the Indian epics of *Mahabharata* and *Ramayana* to suggest that the Yakshas and Nagas were actually Tamil-speaking people who worshiped the Cobra (Naga) and the Demon (Yaksha) respectively in the prehistoric period.[19] Ponnampalam, taking a similar view, points out that the *Mahavamsa* misrepresents the Tamil Nagas and Yakshas as nonhumans. He refers to the accounts in the *Ramayana* in which the Naga kingdoms were conquered by Ravana, the Tamil Yaksha king of Sri Lanka. This leads him to suggest that the Tamils were already on the island when the Sinhalese arrived.[20] Another hypothesis is that the origin of the Dravidian group of languages can be traced to the formerly widespread Megalithic culture that existed in peninsular India and Sri Lanka prior to 700 B.C. As proof, advocates of this view claim that the Yakshas and Nagas were the ancestors of Tamil-speaking Dravidians who belonged to an earlier colony of settlers that migrated from South India to Sri Lanka and established the Yaksha kingdom described in the *Mahavamsa*.[21]

Because of the different claims made by the Sinhalese and the Sri Lankan Tamils, it cannot be said with absolute certainty which community was the first to set foot on the island. The Sinhalese claim is essentially based on grand myths, whereas the Sri Lankan Tamil claim is not substantiated by any solid evidence. In any case, the fact remains that Sri Lanka was a relatively peaceful multiethnic society from the early days of its recorded history in which "there was a distinct Dravidian element which could not alter the basic Aryan or North Indian character of the population."[22]

The ethnic harmony was shattered by the fifth century A.D. when the rulers of South India's three most powerful Tamil kingdoms—the Pandyan, the Pallava, and the Chola—subjected the island to repeated invasions. Under these invasions from South India, the Sinhalese kingdom in the northern part of Sri Lanka finally collapsed in the thirteenth century A.D., and the Sinhalese people started to drift south to the Wet Zone.[23] With the collapse of this northern Sinhalese kingdom, the island was divided into three distinct sectors. The northern part (the area between Jaffna and Anuradhapura up to the Jaffna Peninsula) formed the Jaffna Kingdom, occupied by Tamil settlers and ruled by the King of Jaffna.[24] The coastal area of the southwest came under the Kingdom of Kotte. The central hill country became the Kandyan Kingdom.

Large-scale settlement by Tamils in northern Sri Lanka followed after the establishment of the Jaffna Kingdom. Within the next couple of centuries, this northern part as well as large portions of the Batticaloa and Trincomalee districts of eastern Sri Lanka were almost entirely populated by Tamils. It was in the Kingdom of Jaffna that the Sri Lankan Tamils developed their own collective ethnopolitical identity, distinct not only from the Sinhalese but also from the Tamils of South India.[25] Arasaratnam points out that the Sri Lankan Tamils never identified themselves politically with the Tamils of South India and that their South Indian heritage operated only as a source of historical inspiration.[26] It is not surprising, therefore, that the Sri Lankan Tamils should think of the island's northern and eastern parts as their most important possession, a traditional homeland where they could "underline their attribute of nationality and distinctiveness from, and, non-assimilability by, the Sinhalese."[27]

In the present climate of ethnic tension and violence, the original-inhabitancy issue has been the most difficult to resolve. On the one hand, the Sri Lankan Tamils' demand for political autonomy in their traditional homeland (later changed to the demand for a separate state) is ultimately based on their claim to being the first people to settle on the island and to having a long history of separate existence from the other Sinhalese kingdoms prior to British rule. They believe, therefore, that they have the natural right to claim this territory as their own. The Sinhalese community, on the other hand, claims to be the first on the island and therefore denies any Sri Lankan Tamil claims in this regard. Historically, it has regarded the Sri Lankan Tamils as invaders who caused the destruction of Sinhalese kingdoms in the northern areas—the very same region that the Sri Lankan Tamils claim to be their traditional homeland. The Sinhalese have, therefore, refused to accept the view that the Sri Lankan Tamils may have a legitimate claim to this territory; so, they have rejected the Sri Lankan Tamils' demand for an independent state. The failure to resolve this issue to both communities' satisfaction has been catastrophic for the political stability of Sri Lanka.

Cultural and Religious Issues

Cultural and religious issues have also played a crucial role in destroying ethnic and racial harmony in Sri Lanka. Both the Sinhalese majority and the Sri Lankan Tamil minority of contemporary Sri Lanka assert their respective identities on the basis of language, religion, ancestral territory, and cultural attributes. The Sinhalese are overwhelmingly Buddhist despite some conversions to Christianity in the colonial period, consider themselves to be descendants of the fair-skinned Aryan people of North India, and trace their religious origin to Lord Buddha himself. The fact that they adhered to Buddhism even after it had declined in India during ancient times and continue to do so now emphasizes their desire for distinctiveness from the non–Sinhalese Hindus.

On the other hand, the darker-skinned Sri Lankan Tamils of South Indian origin are largely Hindus, but as Bruce Matthews contends, the identity of the Sri Lankan Tamils does not have any specific religious or Hindu dimensions. He also argues that, historically, the Sri Lankan Tamils never expressed any fear about the Sinhalese people's desire to revive Buddhism because they considered it an integral part of Hinduism, expounding the same themes on life and religion.[28]

The Sinhalese–Buddhist clergy, however, always attempted to convince generations of Sinhalese that their race was chosen by Lord Buddha to establish a

Sinhalese–Buddhist society in Sri Lanka.[29] Faced with Tamil invasions from South India, Sinhalese rulers and Buddhist clergy became apprehensive about the Buddhist plight should Sri Lanka come under the control of Dravidian Hindu kingdoms: Because Buddhism was the Sinhalese kingdoms' official religion, the Sinhalese–Buddhist clergy feared that political domination by Dravidian rulers would deprive them of the power they traditionally wielded over Sinhalese rulers.[30] Therefore, they tried to gather support from the Sinhalese people to defend their kingdom and religion by appealing to their religious and racial sentiments—they consistently expounded the theme that the Sinhalese were destined by divine will to defend their state and religion from incursions by non–Sinhalese and non–Buddhist Tamils. The impact of the Buddhist clergy on the people and the rulers was so profound that Buddhism became the state religion and a powerful instrument in shaping the Sinhalese people's outlook.

Later, the Buddhist clergy also influenced Sinhalese national consciousness "by deliberately exaggerating historical events dealing with Sinhalese–Tamil conflict."[31] They blamed the Tamils for the disintegration and collapse of the ancient Sinhalese–Buddhist kingdom of northern Sri Lanka and for the Sinhalese people's forced migration from the Dry Zone to the Wet Zone in the thirteenth century.[32] Legends and myths have also advocated the view that Sinhalese society faced the constant danger of being destroyed or polluted by the Dravidian Hindu civilization and that heroic efforts were taken by past Sinhalese rulers to curb Tamil invasions.[33] Such legends have had a tremendous impact on the Sinhalese national consciousness and to a large extent "accounts for the negative way some Sinhalese have reacted to Tamil demands for regional autonomy for the northern and eastern areas of the country, which the Tamils consider to be their traditional homeland."[34]

The Issue of Language

Language probably is the most important single attribute delimiting both the Tamil and the Sinhalese communities. Both communities are essentially linguistic groups;[35] within each community, language acts as a source of emotional identification; "the connection between the speakers of the language and the members of the community is extremely close."[36] This strong sense of linguistic identity and its uniqueness and distinctiveness from neighboring peoples has characterized the Sinhalese for many centuries. The Sinhalese language, belonging to the Aryan family of languages and spoken only by the Sinhalese in Sri Lanka, also "has been a major factor in creating and maintaining the Sinhalese view of themselves as a unique people."[37] On their part, the Sri Lankan Tamils, being ethnically and religiously similar to South India's Dravidian Hindu people, speak the same language as that area's Tamil people. However, in Sri Lanka, the Sri Lankan Tamils are not the only ones to use the Tamil language: A major portion of the Indian Tamil community and the Muslim (Moors) community in Sri Lanka also speak the Tamil language.

The language issue emerged as the most explosive and divisive issue in ethnic relations in Sri Lanka after independence, but the roots of the language controversy lay in Western colonial rule.[38] Sri Lanka has experienced three colonial masters in its history—the Portuguese, the Dutch, and the British. Under Portuguese and Dutch rule, administrative functions were generally carried out in the island's languages; only for record keeping and some central government tasks was the language of the colonial power used. The language of government became a crucial issue only during British rule "both because the British Imperial Policy regarding languages differed and because after the late nineteenth century the state became of much greater importance to the [Sinhalese]."[39]

From the commencement of British rule in Sri Lanka at the end of the eighteenth century, the country was, in practice, governed in English. The local people's demand for English education rose quickly as it was realized that knowledge of English was essential for public services employment. The task of providing English education fell on the government. For administrative purposes also, the British colonial government required local people well versed in the English language to fill the positions of government clerks. But the task of providing English education presented enormous difficulties for the colonial administration, and therefore by 1885, the government changed its education policy; thereafter, the emphasis was on vernacular education and the task of providing English education was largely given over to Christian missionaries.[40]

As a result of the new education policy, the division between the English-educated and the vernacular-educated local people increased and formed a formidable class hierarchy.[41] English-educated persons enjoyed positions of wealth, prestige, and power. Moreover, students educated in English found it relatively easier to secure government jobs, while the vernacular-educated mostly worked as cultivators, laborers, village traders, and service workers.[42] This created substantial anger and frustrations among the vernacular-educated masses.

The disenchantment of the vernacular-educated masses came openly to the surface once universal suffrage was adopted and political control passed into Sinhalese hands. Gradually, a demand arose for *swabhasha,* or the people's "own language," to be the language of government.[43] Closely associated with this demand were demands for equality of opportunity, particularly in public service appointments. From its inception, the *Swabhasha* movement was largely a Sinhalese movement. The Sri Lankan Tamils had very little to gain by changing the official language. For one, the establishment of Christian missionary schools in the northern part of the island made English education available to a large number of Sri Lankan Tamils, who promptly took advantage of the opportunity. Second, because of this advantage they had over the Sinhalese, who were suspicious of Christian missionaries and therefore more reluctant to pursue English education, the Sri Lankan Tamils came to dominate the professions and the public service.[44] Finally, the Sri Lankan Tamils were not divided by a language barrier to the same extent as were the Sinhalese; consequently, the social discontents that led to the *Swabhasha* movement in the south were less pronounced in the Tamil areas of the north.[45]

Although the *Swabhasha* movement grew mainly as a contest between the use of *swabhasha* and English as official language, the nature of the demand was transformed after independence into insistence on Sinhalese as the sole official language. The controversy, therefore, shifted from "the question of *swabhasha* or English to that of both Sinhalese and Tamil or Sinhalese only."[46] The official-language issue thus became the most contentious issue between the two communities. To the Sinhalese, the issue came to symbolize "their aspirations to retrieve their ancestral heritage and reassert their position and prerogatives as the majority, which they felt were denied them under colonial rule."[47] To the Sri Lankan Tamils, on the other hand, the official-language issue came to symbolize the Sinhalese majority's dreaded domination that could threaten Tamil existence as a separate group.[48]

Economic Issues

The official-language issue assumed a greater importance for ethnic relations in the postindependence period in Sri Lanka because of the close connection between language and the island's economy. After the British took over the island's administration from the Dutch, they established a centralized form of government in 1833, thereby abolishing the separate system of administration for low-country Sinhalese, hill-country Kandyan–Sinhalese, and Sri Lankan Tamils.[49] This was mainly done to prevent the division of the country along ethnic lines, but the outcome of this British policy was twofold: first, it created a centralized form of government and brought the Sinhalese and the Sri Lankan Tamils into direct contact with each other after centuries; second, for British commercial purposes, the Wet Zone was developed more rapidly than the Dry Zone.[50] Consequently, large numbers of Sri Lankan Tamils migrated out of the Dry Zone, and "the Sinhalese-dominated Wet Zone became the focus of competition between Sinhalese and Tamils for employment."[51]

Initially, such competition did not destroy the ethnic harmony between the two communities, but friction gradually grew as it became apparent to the Sinhalese community that in this competition for employment the Sri Lankan Tamils had the upper hand—by virtue of their proficiency in the English language, they had acquired a disproportionate representation in the public services and the professions compared to their community's actual size.[52] Sinhalese backlash was, therefore, natural because they resented the fact that the Sri Lankan Tamils, though a minority community, had a higher income and a greater share of the employment market than that of the majority Sinhalese.[53]

Another aspect of the economic problem concerned the status of a substantial number of Indian Tamils who were brought by the British from South India in the 1830s to work in the British-owned coffee, tea, and rubber plantations, located primarily in the Kandyan Hills.[54] The Indian Tamils (who together with the Muslims constitute about 6 percent of the total population) were considered by the Sinhalese to be foreigners who had no abiding interest in the country, yet were prepared to work for low wages on the plantations. The Sinhalese also feared that the Indian Tamils and the Muslims (who speak the same Tamil language as Sri Lankan Tamils), together with the Sri Lankan Tamils, would dominate the national economy and pose a challenge to the survival of the Sinhalese race, religion, and civilization. It was not surprising, therefore, that after independence, Sinhalese politicians took advantage of this fear to achieve their own political ambitions. Added to this was the resurgence of Sinhalese nationalism, to which the Buddhist clergy gave a religious bent. The ethnic problem, thus, became not only complex but also extremely volatile.

The Political Fallout

The fallout of all these differences and fears played out on the political front. Sinhalese politicians realized very early on that greater Sinhalese participation in the political process was the only way to change matters to their advantage. Communal representation in the Legislative Council had hitherto been the vehicle through which the various communities participated in the political process; since the 1920s,

Sinhalese politicians demanded that this communal representation be replaced by some form of territorial representation that would be reflective of the majority Sinhalese community's size relative to that of the other minority communities.[55] Being anxious for self-government, the Sri Lankan Tamils, at this stage, were willing to accept a Sinhalese majority in the Legislative Council provided that the Ceylon National Congress (CNC) "actively supported the proposal for the reservation of a special seat for the Tamils residing in the Western Province."[56] When no such support came from the CNC, suspicion developed that Sinhalese politicians were willing to sacrifice Tamil interests, a suspicion further reinforced when the CNC came under the 1920s Buddhist Revivalist Movement's influence. The Sri Lankan Tamils therefore sought to convince the Donoughmore Commission, which was charged with recommending constitutional reforms, to retain communal representation.

In this effort, the Tamil community failed, and the objective of Sinhalese politicians to secure territorial representation was achieved in 1931.[57] The implications of this development for interethnic relations were obvious: Because the Sinhalese constituted more than two thirds of the island's population, with the introduction of universal suffrage, an overwhelming number of territorial constituencies was bound to contain a majority of Sinhalese voters. With such political advances, the Sinhalese majority would be able to assert its strength politically. The minorities, especially the Sri Lankan Tamils, therefore demanded that any constitutional reform must incorporate safeguards for minority interests. For this purpose, Ponnambalam, a state-council Tamil representative from the Jaffna constituency, suggested to the Soulbury Commission, which arrived in Sri Lanka in 1944 to draft a constitution for an independent Sri Lanka, a 50:50 formula—that is, 50 percent of the seats in the parliament of independent Sri Lanka for the Sinhalese and the remaining 50 percent for the Sri Lankan Tamils and other minorities, such as the Muslims and the Burghers. This proposal was rejected. Instead, the Soulbury Commission incorporated a provision in the constitution that prohibited the parliament of independent Sri Lanka from enacting laws prejudicial to minority interests. Except for this limitation, which could be overcome by constitutional amendment, the Soulbury Constitution did not provide any other safeguards for the minorities. This constitution was adopted and Sri Lanka became independent in 1948.[58] The ground was thus prepared for the emergence of ethnic conflict in postindependent Sri Lanka.

The first sign of trouble came when, contrary to assurances made by Prime Minister D.S. Senanayake that no harm would come to the minorities,[59] the United National Party (UNP) government passed the Ceylon Citizenship Act of 1948 and the Indian and Pakistani Residents (Citizenship) Act of 1949. These two pieces of legislation and the Parliamentary Elections (Amendment) Act of 1949, designed to deny voting rights to the Tamils of Indian origin, laid down strict requirements and documentation for eligibility for Sri Lankan citizenship, and only the Indian Tamils were called on to prove their claims of citizenship. Because few could do so, a vast majority of Indian Tamils became stateless.[60] But these acts had a major effect on the Sri Lankan Tamils, too, by reducing their parliamentary capacity to defend their legitimate rights as citizens. For instance, when the Indian Tamils lost their voting rights, "the parliamentary strength of the Sinhalese was increased from 67 percent in 1947 to 73 percent in 1952."[61]

Thereafter, successive Sinhalese-dominated governments in Sri Lanka utilized this parliamentary strength to implement measures that reduced the minorities, particularly the Sri Lankan Tamils, to an inferior status. In this effort, the governments of Sri Lanka were greatly influenced by the resurgence of extremist Sinhalese–Buddhist nationalism after independence. As Senewiratne points out, one main reason why communal relations deteriorated was that Sinhalese politicians "adopted an increasingly anti–Tamil stance as a means of getting the majority Sinhalese–Buddhists onside in an effort to get into (and remain) in power."[62] Thus despite repeated assurances to the minorities that their rights would be protected, successive Sri Lankan governments enacted such discriminatory legislation as the Official Language Act of 1956[63] and adopted such discriminatory policies as the policy of "standardization,"[64] as well as state-aided programs of colonization of Tamil areas by Sinhalese peasants.[65] Even at the societal level, persecution of minorities continued, often with tacit governmental approval. In the process, constitutional safeguards of minorities' rights were flagrantly violated.

The Drift Toward Tamil Militancy

Faced with such grim prospects, it was only natural for the Sri Lankan Tamils to resort to agitation, strikes, demonstrations, and civil disobedience movements to "protect their community from domination and possible assimilation by the large Sinhalese majority."[66] It was not, however, until the mid–1970s that the nature of Tamil agitation acquired its present-day secessionist dimension. Until the early 1970s, Tamil demands were concerned primarily with protecting their cultural, linguistic, economic, educational, and political rights through the decentralization of political power that could lead to some sort of regional autonomy for Tamil areas. Tamil leaders came to believe that without regional autonomy, protection and promotion of their civil rights and the improvement of economic conditions in their traditional homeland would not be possible. No demand had been made for a separate state for the Tamils, but in the mid–1970s, the nature of Tamil agitation and demands underwent a major qualitative change when "serious calls for a separate Tamil state were made by leading political figures and organizations."[67] To achieve this goal, Sri Lankan Tamil groups were ready to engage in guerrilla operations.

One primary reason for the rise of Tamil militancy and the demand for secession was the failure of negotiations between the Sinhalese and Tamil political leaders. Over the years, moderate Tamil leaders tried to secure concessions from Sinhalese-dominated governments through negotiations. All such attempts at negotiations failed, mostly because of Buddhist clergy activities and those of other Sinhalese extremists who portrayed any concessions that Sinhalese leaders were prepared to make as a sell-out to the Sri Lankan Tamils.[68] Second, Sri Lankan Tamil youths were encouraged by the successful secession of East Pakistan in 1971 and the creation of the new state of Bangladesh. It is plausible that India's support of the Bengali secessionist aspiration in East Pakistan raised the hopes of Tamil youths that similar support would be forthcoming in their nationalist struggle. Finally, the immediate precipitating factors behind the rise of militancy were threefold: first, a new constitution was adopted by Sri Lanka in

1972 that did not contain any provisions for a federal setup of political power and that reiterated the preeminent status of Sinhalese as the sole official language; second, the constitution bestowed a special status on Buddhism, which is the religion of the majority; and third, Sri Lankan Tamil youths were impatient with conventional methods of old guard politicians.[69]

The drift toward militancy on the part of Sri Lankan Tamil youths continued throughout the 1970s. It received a further impetus in 1978 when the ruling United National Party of J.R. Jayewardene introduced a new constitution, which was modeled on the Fifth French Republic. Introducing a presidential form of government with Jayewardene as the first executive president of Sri Lanka, the constitution provided certain important concessions to the minorities: First, it gave Tamil the status of a "national language," although Sinhalese remained the only "official" one; second, it introduced a new system of voting whereby minorities' votes would count in national politics;[70] a third concession was the creation of new district councils that gave the Sri Lankan Tamils considerable autonomy in Tamil-dominated areas. But all these provisions came to nothing because the ruling party was not serious in implementing them: The increased official use of Tamil did not come about, as the minorities had expected; district councils were not also given enough powers of autonomy; finally, parliamentary elections, in which the Sri Lankan Tamils could have played an important part, were declared unnecessary by the ruling party.[71] The Sri Lankan Tamils, therefore, became more alienated and frustrated with the central government, and militancy seemed to be the only option left.

Consequently, militancy gathered momentum and by the early 1980s a number of guerrilla organizations had cropped up. The largest and the most ferocious insurgent group was the Liberation Tigers of Tamil Eelam (LTTE) led by Velupillai Prabhakaran. Founded in 1972 as the Tamil New Tigers, the group changed its name to Liberation Tigers of Tamil Eelam in 1976, which coincided with the demand for a separate Tamil state to be called Eelam. The LTTE chose the tiger as its symbol, reflecting "not only the ferocity of that animal but a deliberate contrast with the lion (singha), which traditionally has been a symbol of the Sinhalese people and is depicted in the Sri Lankan flag."[72] In 1981, a faction of the LTTE led by Uma Maheswaran broke away from the parent organization to form the People's Liberation Organization of Tamil Eelam (PLOTE). A host of other groups also emerged in the early 1980s. Chief among these were the Tamil Eelam Liberation Organization (TELO) led by Sri Sabaratnam; the Eelam People's Revolutionary Liberation Front (EPRLF) led by K. Padmanabha; the Tamil Eelam Liberation Army; the Tamil Eelam Army; and the Eelam Revolutionary Organization of Students (EROS) led by V. Balakumar.[73]

In terms of ideology and strategy, there were significant differences among these groups. The LTTE, though ideologically and rhetorically Marxist, seemed to have as its goal "the creation of an independent Tamil state, irrespective of ideology," and in pursuance of this objective it "seemed more wedded to direct and violent action than formation of principles on which the independent state would operate."[74] The PLOTE, on its part, "claimed to represent a purer form of Marxist orthodoxy."[75] The EROS, on the other hand, was said "to prefer acts of economic sabotage."[76] Collectively, these groups posed a serious threat to Sri Lanka's territorial integrity and national security. At frequent intervals, these groups also worked at cross-purposes based on their different ideological orientations. Violence, thus, erupted not only between the Tamil militant groups and the Sinhalese forces, but also among the Tamil militant groups.

The Escalation of Ethnic Violence in the 1980s

In the initial years of Tamil militancy, the acts of violence and terrorism were mainly in the nature of assassinations of government personnel and robberies. By the 1980s, however, militancy "escalated from isolated attacks on policemen and Tamil politicians who cooperated with the government to organized attacks on [Sinhalese] military units."[77] The events that transformed the intensity of the Tamil militancy in Sri Lanka were the brutal anti–Tamil riots that swept Colombo and other towns in July 1983; in these, state machinery and resources were used for the first time by senior government personnel in a concerted effort directed against the lives and properties of a minority ethnic group.[78] In the aftermath of the anti–Tamil riots, the LTTE and the other guerrilla organizations intensified their attacks on the government forces, which brought harsh retaliation against the Tamil population of Jaffna. These harsh reprisals "forced the great majority of Sri Lankan Tamils, whatever their point of view on the goals or methods of the guerrillas, into the arms of the extremists."[79]

The 1983 anti–Tamil riots and their aftermath also signaled the growing marginalization of the moderate Tamil United Liberation Front (TULF) from mainstream Tamil politics in Sri Lanka. The TULF had supported the United National Party (UNP) of President Jayewardene in the 1977 elections against the promise that if it came to power, the UNP would look into the Tamil issue sympathetically.[80] The TULF had accepted the government-sponsored District Development Committee (DDC) proposals thereafter, in 1982; these only weakened the TULF by causing a major split within the party and by distancing it from the militant movement.[81] The TULF was totally shattered after July 1983 when Sri Lankan Tamils lost "all trust and faith in those wielding power to implement what has been agreed upon."[82] Full-blown secessionist war ensued in Sri Lanka after July 1983.

INTERNATIONAL REACTION TOWARD SRI LANKA'S ETHNIC WAR

As ethnic war in Sri Lanka broke out in full force after the 1983 riots, international reaction was sharp. One of the states directly affected by Sri Lanka's ethnic conflict was neighboring India, which contained more than 80 million Tamils in the southern province of Tamil Nadu; they were naturally sympathetic toward fellow Tamils in Sri Lanka. Until the early 1980s, India's policy toward Sri Lanka's ethnic turmoil was characterized by neutrality and nonintervention. In pursuing such a policy, the framework that was strictly adhered to by New Delhi was to remain noncommittal over issues of domestic concern to Sri Lanka and to allay Sinhalese fear of an Indian intervention. But faced with a growing insurgency movement in the island–nation only 30 miles from India's southern border, New Delhi began to take the view that the protection and promotion of India's national interest required an immediate deescalation of the conflict and the commencement of a peace process aimed toward the ultimate resolution of the dispute. From the Indian perspective, the resolution of the conflict demanded the incorporation of two objectives—the unity of Sri Lanka had to be protected and, at the same time, the Sri Lankan Tamils' demands had to be accommodated. New Delhi, therefore, made it clear that only a political solution incorporating these two objectives would be acceptable.

In adopting such a stance, New Delhi could not ignore the upsurge of sympathy that Tamils in India felt for fellow Tamils in Sri Lanka. To do so would have appeared insensitive and potentially dangerous for the internal security of Tamil Nadu.[83] At the same time, the Indian government could not endorse the Sri Lankan Tamils' demand for Eelam in Sri Lanka, while at the same time rejecting secessionist demands at home such as in the Punjab and in Assam.

Other states generally followed India's line toward the ethnic war in Sri Lanka. Through India's diplomatic support, the Sri Lankan Tamil political parties were able to reach a wide global audience with accounts of systematic Sinhalese discrimination against their community. This helped the Sri Lankan Tamils to earn substantial international goodwill because a major segment of world public opinion regarded the Sri Lankan government's policy toward the Tamil minority on the island as grossly violating human rights. Western countries were therefore sympathetic toward the plight of the Sri Lankan Tamils. Britain, for instance, offered prominent Sri Lankan Tamil politicians asylum and allowed Tamil guerrilla groups such as the LTTE to open public relations offices in Britain. Canada also took a sympathetic stand and allowed many Sri Lankan Tamils who fled the island to escape the war to settle in Canada. But most important, due to India's sustained diplomatic campaigns on behalf of the Tamils, both the United States and the Soviet Union accepted India's concern for the Sri Lankan Tamils as legitimate and professed full faith in its ability to effect a successful resolution of the conflict. Thus when President Jayewardene visited the United States in June 1984 to seek U.S. support for the Sri Lankan government's position on the ethnic issue and also to obtain military assistance, Washington declined to provide such help. In doing so, Washington implicitly recognized that the management of the Sri Lankan conflict "should be left to the . . . region's predominant power, India, and there was also a general appreciation of India's mediation."[84] Similarly, the Soviet Union also refused to involve itself in Sri Lanka's conflict, leaving the field open to India.

INTERNATIONAL COVERT INVOLVEMENT IN SRI LANKA

With the rise of Tamil militancy and an escalation of conflict in Sri Lanka after 1983, the Sri Lankan government actively started to seek military help from abroad to tackle the Tamil insurgency. In this context, Kadian claims that British, Rhodesian, Israeli, and South African mercenaries were hired by the Sri Lankan government through a private security company called Keeny Meeny Services, which was based in the Channel Islands and reportedly had links with the British government.[85] Assistance was also sought by the Sri Lankan government from Israel, with which Sri Lanka had severed diplomatic relations in 1970. However, responding to Sri Lanka's call, Israel set up an interests section in the U.S. Embassy in Colombo and the Mossad, the external intelligence agency of Israel, and Shin Beth, which dealt with counterinsurgency, became active in Sri Lanka in the training of government forces in counterinsurgency operations.[86] Sri Lankan forces also received arms and military training from Pakistan.[87] On a state visit to Sri Lanka, President Zia-ul Haq pledged Pakistan's full support "for Sri Lanka's war against terrorism" and "called upon the neighbors and friends of Sri Lanka to give maximum support to preserve its unity and integrity."[88] China, South Africa, Singapore, and Malaysia also supplied arms to Sri Lanka.[89]

By 1984, the existence of Sri Lankan Tamil guerrilla training camps in India was also an open secret. These training camps were mostly in the Ramanathapuram district in southern Tamil Nadu. The Tamil guerrilla training camps in India were under the aegis of the Research and Analysis Wing (RAW) of the Cabinet Secretariat—therefore, directly under the Indian prime minister's office.[90] RAW's interest in Sri Lanka's ethnic conflict started in the late 1970s because of three major developments—the election of the pro–West and anti–India Jayewardene as prime minister in 1977, increased American interest in the strategic Trincomalee harbor in eastern Sri Lanka as a forward base for its Rapid Deployment Force, and the rising Tamil insurgency on the island. RAW's interest was particularly aroused when reports came of Colombo's granting of oil storage facilities to U.S. companies in the port of Trincomalee.[91]

The first Tamil group to be trained by RAW was the Tamil Eelam Liberation Organization (TELO), which in 1983 did not have any organizational basis and was a small group of merely six men, all of whom were in Tamil Nadu. RAW chose the TELO primarily because it consisted of criminal elements. Politically unsophisticated, the TELO had no goals or ideology and so was the perfect private army for RAW. But later on, RAW provided major military training to the three largest Sri Lankan Tamil militant groups—the LTTE, the PLOTE, and the EROS. All three groups reportedly had contacts with the Palestine Liberation Organization (PLO); in fact, even after Indian assistance and training, these groups continued to maintain their Middle East connections for training and tactics.

Initially, the RAW training was quite basic. However, the growth in the number of militants and the increased participation of various guerrilla groups led to more sophisticated training in different parts of India, one such training institution being Chakrata in Uttar Pradesh. Training was provided in fieldcraft, tactics, map reading, and jungle and guerrilla warfare, and in sophisticated weapons systems such as light and medium machine guns, automatic rifles, pistols, and rocket-propelled grenades. Regular Indian Army personnel also taught the use of bombs, laying of mines, and the establishment of telecommunications.[92]

OTHER INTERNATIONAL ASPECTS OF SRI LANKA'S ETHNIC CONFLICT

One way that intrastate ethnic conflicts become internationalized, as we alluded to in Chapter 3, is through the flow of refugees. This aspect of internal ethnic wars assumes a greater importance and significance as the duration and intensity of a war increases. The entrenchment of Tamil militancy in Sri Lanka in the 1980s intensified the conflict;

as a result of it, substantial numbers of refugees (mostly Tamils) fled the war zones in the north and crossed over into Tamil Nadu in India. These refugees brought with them stories of Sinhalese atrocities against the Tamil people of Sri Lanka and helped fuel local sentiment in Tamil Nadu. The government of India was thus confronted with not only a huge economic burden of taking care of these refugees but also with increasing political pressure from Tamil parties in India to take action in Sri Lanka.

The 1983 anti–Tamil riots in Sri Lanka added fuel to the fire. As reports of Tamil massacres on the island reached India, the situation in Tamil Nadu became volatile. The ruling All India Anna Dravida Munnetra Kazhagam (AIADMK) government in Tamil Nadu came under pressure from the people, as well as from the opposition Dravida Munnetra Kazhagam (DMK), to take up the issue with the central government. Even within the AIADMK, great sympathy existed for the plight of the Sri Lankan Tamils. The state's chief minister M.G. Ramachandran therefore requested the Indian government to take action in Sri Lanka to save Tamil lives and to raise the issue in the UN.[93] The opposition DMK was even more outspoken. DMK President M. Karunanidhi observed that there was no reason why India, which had supported the Palestinian and several African liberation movements not to mention the liberation of Bangladesh, could not support the Sri Lankan Tamils' demand for separation. In a statement, he pointed out that unless Indian forces were sent to Sri Lanka, there was no hope for the Tamils there.[94] He, therefore, called for a Cyprus-type solution in Sri Lanka "in order to prevent the extermination of the Tamil race."[95]

The Indian government, as already mentioned, was not in a position to ignore these pleas for action. Moreover, New Delhi was aware that the Tamil political parties in Tamil Nadu were actively providing financial and material assistance to the various Sri Lankan guerrilla groups. But because New Delhi could not endorse the demand for Eelam, it "rejected the Eelam demand as well as the demand for military action against Sri Lanka, but . . . refrained from dislodging the [Sri Lankan] Tamil militants from Tamil Nadu since such action would have further inflamed the tempers of the local Tamils."[96] Foreign Minister Narasimha Rao, therefore, found it necessary to reaffirm that "in voicing its well meaning concern over the happenings in Sri Lanka, India was not in any way supporting the separatist demand of the Tamil extremists or condoning acts of terrorism."[97] At the same time, Prime Minister Indira Gandhi pointed out that India could not remain indifferent toward the ethnic conflict in Sri Lanka as people of Indian origin were being affected there.[98]

RESOLUTION ATTEMPT: INTERNATIONAL THIRD-PARTY ACTION IN SRI LANKA

India became involved in Sri Lanka's ethnic conflict as an international third party interested in conflict resolution from the mid–1980s mainly because such a role was the perfect "compromise option" between the two extremes of supporting Eelam and doing nothing. To prepare for this role, New Delhi enunciated in the immediate aftermath of the July 1983 ethnic riots in Sri Lanka the "Indian Doctrine of Regional Security."[99] This clarified the position that if a South Asian state requires external assistance to deal with serious internal conflict, it should seek help from within the region, including from India, and that the "Exclusion of India in such circumstances will be considered an anti–Indian move."[100] India's self-declared role of South Asia's "police officer" was largely welcomed by the international community. For instance, the Manchester *Guardian* in an editorial pointed out that India could play a "beneficial" and "delicate" role in Sri Lanka's ethnic conflict by persuading the Tamil parties and the Sri Lankan government to abandon their hard-line approach toward each other.[101]

In August 1983, Prime Minister Indira Gandhi announced that President Jayewardene of Sri Lanka had accepted India's offer of good offices and agreed to have a broad-based conference with the Sri Lankan Tamil community's leaders to work out a political settlement to the ethnic problem. Gandhi also mentioned that President Jayewardene had agreed not to confine the discussions to his earlier five-point offer[102] on India's recommendation that such outdated proposals would not meet the aspirations of the Sri Lankan Tamils, especially after the 1983 anti–Tamil riots.[103] This set the stage for intense diplomatic efforts to induce the various Sri Lankan Tamil as well as Sinhalese parties to come to the negotiating table. Indira Gandhi's personal envoy, G. Parthasarathy, was given the task of mediating between the Tamil groups and the Sri Lankan government toward working out a settlement.

The Parthasarathy Initiative and the All-Party Conference

What emerged from Parthasarathy's efforts came to be known as the Parthasarathy Formula. The key provision of this formula was "Annexure C," which envisaged elected regional councils in the northern and eastern provinces of Sri Lanka where Tamils formed the majority of the population. These councils would have jurisdiction over the subjects of law and order, social and economic development, and administration of justice and land policy. In addition, these councils would also have the power to levy taxes.[104]

An All-Party Conference (APC) was, therefore, called to discuss these proposals. All recognized political parties, including the TULF, and several Sinhala-Buddhist religious and nonpolitical organizations participated in a series of meetings throughout 1984, but the Parthasarathy Formula failed to resolve the conflict for a number of reasons. First, the major opposition party of Sri Lanka, the Sri Lanka Freedom Party (SLFP), withdrew from the APC. Second, the plan to create autonomous regional councils was opposed by all shades of Sinhalese-Buddhist opinion. They considered this to be a sellout to the Tamils and, therefore, exerted pressure on the ruling UNP and the SLFP to take a hard stand over the Tamil demand for regional autonomy and a reasonable measure of self-government. Third, President Jayewardene, sensing the Sinhalese mood, also withdrew his support for the Parthasarathy Formula. Instead, he proposed the creation of a second chamber in the national parliament that would "ensure" ethnic representation at the national level. He was deliberately vague about defining the powers of the proposed second chamber. This proposal was not acceptable to the TULF. Finally, because none of the Tamil militant groups were represented at the APC, it was doubtful whether any solution devised there could have brought an end to the conflict. In fact, before the first round of APC talks, the Tamil militant organizations and worldwide

Eelam Council members clearly said that they would put pressure on the TULF General Secretary A. Amrithalingam to boycott the talks. They pointed out that the offer made by the Sri Lankan government was unacceptable because a "point of no return" had been reached with the anti–Tamil riots of 1983. They also indicated that moderate leaders such as Amrithalingam had lost out to the hard liners and militants. As one Eelam Council member observed: "He can go for the talks on only one condition—to demarcate the boundary that would separate the Tamil State and Sri Lanka."[105]

The Thimpu Talks

The second major Indian diplomatic initiative did not come about until the middle of 1985. During this time, India faced a major tragedy at home when Indira Gandhi was assassinated by Sikh extremists and her son Rajiv Gandhi succeeded her as prime minister. Commenting on Rajiv Gandhi's approach to the ethnic conflict in Sri Lanka, Kodikara observes:

> He has, of course, adhered strictly to the principles enunciated by Indira Gandhi, of non-intervention in Sri Lanka's affairs, of supporting the unity and integrity of the island, and very unequivocally foreswearing any intention of invading Sri Lanka. At the same time, however, he has reiterated the conviction of his mother that no training camps for Sri Lankan guerrillas exist in South India, and he has repeatedly expressed concern over the influx of refugees from Sri Lanka.[106]

The Indian government, therefore, remained committed to the objective of a political solution to the ethnic conflict in Sri Lanka.

On the other hand, in Sri Lanka ethnic violence reached unprecedented levels after the Sri Lankan government announced plans to settle 3,000 Sinhalese families in the north and provide them with military training and weapons. The Sri Lankan government also undertook a massive program of weapons collection from all possible sources. President Jayewardene also toured China and several Western countries (including the United States and Britain) in an effort to build diplomatic support for the Sri Lankan government's position. The Tamils reacted by proposing a "government in exile" in Madras and by stepping up insurgent activities on the island. The success of the Tamil insurgents and the general mood of indifference displayed toward Sri Lanka in the Western capitals left Jayewardene with little choice but to turn again to New Delhi for help. He and Prime Minister Rajiv Gandhi met in New Delhi in June 1985 to discuss the Tamil problem; as a result, what appeared to be a workable compromise on a political settlement to the ethnic problem emerged. Bhutan's King Jigme Wangchuk's offer of his capital, Thimphu, was accepted as the neutral site for a more comprehensive conference between the representatives of the Sri Lankan government and the Tamil groups.

Two rounds of talks were held in Thimphu in July–August 1985. Under intense Indian pressure, five Tamil militant groups (the LTTE, TELO, EROS, TELA, and EPRLF) agreed to cooperate with one another and came to the negotiating table for the first time, united as Eelam National Liberation Front (ENLF). In addition, the PLOTE, the TULF, and the governments of India and Sri Lanka were represented at the talks.

In the first round of talks, the Sri Lankan delegation merely reiterated the proposals put forward before the aborted APC, but these were not acceptable to the Tamil groups. The Tamil delegation insisted that the following basic principles were cardinal for a settlement of the Tamil problem: recognition of the Tamils as a distinct nationality, recognition of their "traditional homeland," namely the northern and eastern province in Sri Lanka, recognition of the Tamils' right of self-determination, and granting of Sri Lankan citizenship to all Tamils on the island.[107] The Sri Lankan delegation argued that recognizing the above principles was tantamount to conceding Eelam. As a result, the talks fell through.

The December 19 Proposals

Following the failure of the Thimpu talks, both the Tamil guerrillas and the Sri Lankan forces sought a military solution in heavy fighting in the northern and eastern provinces. At the same time, internecine fighting broke out among the Tamil guerrilla organizations. The Sri Lankan government tried to take advantage of this situation by attempting to deal directly with the LTTE to sideline both India and the rest of the guerrilla groups. By this time the LTTE had clearly emerged as the most powerful group by eliminating most of their political rivals, and it unwaveringly kept to its goal of seeking Eelam by military means.

Sensing that the initiative was slipping out of its hands, India made a last-ditch effort in December 1986 to effect a negotiated settlement between the Tamil groups and the Sri Lankan government. Under Indian pressure, Jayewardene met Gandhi, the Tamil Nadu chief minister Ramachandran, and LTTE leader Prabhakaran in Bangalore. This meeting resulted in a document known as the December 19 Proposals,[108] under which Jayewardene "proposed the break-up of the present Eastern Province into three separate units representing Tamils, Sinhalese and Muslims."[109] In so doing, he rejected the traditional-homeland theory of the Tamils based on the merger of the northern and eastern provinces because the Sri Lankan government did not consider the eastern province to be a predominantly Tamil area and also because "such a merger would place in jeopardy both Sinhalese and Muslim groups within this region."[110] So, this proposal was not acceptable to the Tamils. Jayewardene did not care because he could "take comfort from the strengthening of his own forces and from the intense internecine warfare that engulfed the militant groups in 1986. In addition, his intelligence sources may have revealed that the number of trained guerrillas was vastly exaggerated."[111] Both sides therefore distanced themselves from the December 19 Proposals and the stage was once again set for the renewal of fighting as the year drew to a close.

The Indo–Sri Lankan Accord

With the beginning of 1987, intense fighting broke out in Sri Lanka between the Tamil guerrillas and the Sri Lankan forces. President Jayewardene, facing mounting pressure from hard-line Sinhalese, launched Operation Liberation Two in the Jaffna Peninsula with an aim to secure Vadamarachi, a LTTE stronghold.[112] Bombing of Jaffna was now started in earnest and a food and fuel embargo was imposed on the Jaffna peninsula.

The launching of Operation Liberation Two by the Sri Lankan government created a tremendous backlash in Tamil Nadu. Faced with intense pressure from the Tamil Nadu government that the Tamil cause had been sacrificed by New Delhi, the Indian government announced its intention to send relief supplies to the people of beleaguered and embattled Jaffna Peninsula. Despite warnings from Jayewardene that such an act by India would be considered an infringement of Sri Lankan sovereignty, India initially attempted to send the supplies by sea. When the Indian flotilla was intercepted and turned back by the Sri Lankan navy, 25 tons of food and other relief supplies were paradropped by Indian air force jets over Jaffna.

Amidst rumors of a possible Indian military intervention, a visibly shaken Jayewardene started to send feelers to India to work out a political solution to the conflict, and as a gesture of sincerity, the government of Sri Lanka terminated Operation Liberation Two and released a large number of Tamil detainees from prison. This set the stage for renewed Indian diplomatic efforts leading to the signing of the Indo–Sri Lankan Accord in July 1987.

From New Delhi's perspective, a deadlock in negotiations and the faith that Colombo and the Tamil militants placed on a decisive military solution was unacceptable. Because neither the Sinhalese nor the Sri Lankan Tamils seemed eager to move from their respective positions, India thought fit to work out a solution by itself and in classic peace-enforcement style to force both the parties to accept it. Considerable pressure was brought by New Delhi on both sides to accept the terms of the accord: India threatened Colombo with military intervention by paradropping food and relief supplies in Jaffna in open violation of Sri Lankan sovereignty; the Rajiv administration also used the carrot-and-stick policy to coerce the LTTE leader Prabhakaran to accept the Indo–Sri Lankan Accord.[113] In return for his approval, the chief Indian negotiator Hardeep Puri also offered Prabhakaran a package deal for the Sri Lankan Tamils—the recognition of Tamil as an official language, the merger of the northern and eastern provinces into a single unit as the Tamils had claimed, and the devolution of real authority to a newly constituted elected provincial council.[114] In spite of Indian assurances, Prabhakaran had serious reservations about the accord, but recognizing India's geostrategic interests in Sri Lanka, he decided not to oppose it.

Premdas and Samarasinghe argue that "The political faith of both Gandhi and Jayewardene weighed heavily in the making and timing of the Accord."[115] Jayewardene's UNP was facing elections for the presidency and parliament in 1988 and 1989 respectively; however, the UNP's prospects in the elections were not good considering that it had failed to resolve the Tamil problem and that the conflict had taken a heavy toll on the country's economy. The accord was, therefore, "expected to set the stage for a return to economic and political normalcy, an environment in which the UNP" felt "it could maximize its electoral prospects."[116] Moreover, Jayewardene, at the age of 82, had already expressed his intention to retire from politics at the end of his term in 1988. Therefore, he may not have wanted to leave office without resolving the ethnic problem.[117]

For Rajiv Gandhi, too, the imperatives of domestic politics were an important reason for signing the accord. He needed to solve the refugee problem in Tamil Nadu as well as to improve his image there considering that the national parliamentary elections were coming up in 1989. Moreover, his administration was besieged "by internal crises instigated by Sikh separatism, electoral defeats, and bribery scandals," and therefore his "international peacemaking role served to distract attention from his domestic difficulties."[118]

The accord also served to protect India's security interests. Through exchange of letters between the Indian prime minister and the Sri Lankan president, India sought and received three important guarantees from Sri Lanka. These included:

1. There will be an early understanding between the two countries about the employment of foreign military and intelligence personnel with a view to ensuring that such presence will not prejudice Indo–Sri Lankan relations;
2. The port of Trincomalee will not be made available for military use by any country in a manner prejudicial to India's interests, and India and Sri Lanka will jointly undertake the restoration and operation of the oil tank farm at Trincomalee; and
3. Any broadcasting facilities in Sri Lanka to foreign organizations will be reviewed to ensure that such facilities are not used for any military or intelligence purposes.[119]

Reciprocating the Sri Lankan gesture, India also provided a number of concessions to the Sinhalese in the accord. First, it recognized the unity, sovereignty and territorial integrity of Sri Lanka, thereby "eliminating Tamil claims for a sovereign state (Eelam) and averting the threat of an Indian invasion."[120] Second, India also recognized Sri Lanka as a "multi-ethnic and multi-lingual plural society" comprised of Sinhalese, Tamils, Muslims (Moors) and Burghers. Third, although India recognized that the northern and eastern provinces of Sri Lanka constituted "areas of historical habitation of Sri Lankan Tamil speaking peoples," the accord also recognized the territorial rights of other groups who have at all times lived in this territory. Fourth, the accord provided for the temporary merger of the northern and eastern provinces as a single administrative unit after the holding of elections to the provincial councils by December 1987. The permanency of this merger was to be determined by a referendum to be held no later than December 1988. Fifth, the accord provided for the cessation of hostilities, the surrender of arms by the Tamil militant groups, and the return of the Sri Lankan army to the barracks. It also provided for a general amnesty to all political detainees and the repeal of the Prevention of Terrorism Act and other emergency laws. Finally, India agreed to be the guarantor of the implementation of the accord and promised to provide military assistance as and when requested by Colombo in order to implement the provisions of the agreement.[121]

Tamil–Sinhalese Reactions to the Indo–Sri Lankan Accord

The Indo–Sri Lankan Accord came as a big disappointment for both the Sri Lankan Tamils and the Sinhalese. Although it repeatedly emphasized the territorial integrity of

Sri Lanka, it did not, in return, guarantee the most important rights sought by the Tamils–the meaningful devolution of authority bordering on autonomy for the Tamils and their protection from the Sri Lankan military. In addition, although India was supposedly acting on behalf of the Sri Lankan Tamils, none of their representatives were cosignatories to the accord. Hard-line Sinhalese politicians and some segments within the Sri Lankan military also had reservations about the accord. Two incidents dramatized this problem. First, when the accord was being signed at the presidential palace in Colombo, Prime Minister Premadasa of Sri Lanka, a confirmed hard liner, and six of his cabinet colleagues were conspicuous by their absence, indicating important opposition within the Sri Lankan cabinet toward the accord. Second, on July 30, 1987 (the day Gandhi was to return to India after signing the accord), a naval guard of honor was readied for his inspection at Colombo airport. During the inspection of the guard of honor, a Sri Lankan naval rating stepped forward and hit Gandhi in the back with the butt of his rifle. The rating was immediately apprehended.[122] Although an isolated incident, it nevertheless reflected the deep resentment against India in some segments of the Sri Lankan military.

Implementation of the Indo–Sri Lankan Accord

Given the reservations of the Sri Lankan Tamil and also the Sinhalese populations, the Indo–Sri Lankan Accord was a nonstarter from the beginning. Yet, it committed an Indian Peacekeeping Force (IPKF) in this conflict for the first time under Clause 6 of the Annexure to the Indo–Sri Lankan Agreement, which stated that "The President of Sri Lanka and the Prime Minister of India also agree that in terms of paragraph 2.14 and paragraph 2.16 (c) of the Agreement an Indian peacekeeping contingent may be invited by the President of Sri Lanka to guarantee and enforce the cessation of hostilities if so required." However, there was little in the accord about the specific role of the peacekeeping force. On July 30, 1987 (one day after the Accord was signed), came the orders for the IPKF to move into Sri Lanka. Initially, the IPKF comprised 8,000 troops. Because no fighting was anticipated, the maxim of concentration of force was ignored. For the same reason, heavy weaponry was left behind in India.

Within a few months after its induction, the IPKF became bogged down in Sri Lanka. On August 4, 1987, LTTE leader Prabhakaran returned to Jaffna from India and addressed a huge rally in which he rejected the Indo–Sri Lankan Accord. Prabhakaran provided three main reasons for rejecting the accord. First, he pointed out that the accord did not address the problems of the Sri Lankan Tamils but was concerned primarily with Indo–Sri Lankan relations. Second, the accord called for disarming the Sri Lankan Tamils without first guaranteeing their safety and protection from Sri Lankan military forces. Finally, Prabhakaran argued that the accord could not guarantee that the Sri Lanka government would fulfill the promises it made in the accord.[123] The LTTE, therefore, refused to cooperate with the IPKF by failing to surrender arms, suggesting that it was preparing for war. The Sri Lankan government, on the other hand, continued to colonize traditional Tamil areas by settling non–Tamils there. The LTTE countered such moves by attacking and killing Sinhalese civilians who had been settled in Tamil areas.

In such a charged atmosphere, decision makers in New Delhi made major mistakes on two crucial issues that had important consequences for the IPKF. The first concerned Thileepan's "fast unto death."[124] On September 15, 1987, Thileepan went on a "fast unto death" to seek redress for Tamil grievances. He consolidated the LTTE concerns into five demands—release of all political prisoners held under antiterrorist laws, end of Sinhalese colonization of Tamil areas, disarming of Sri Lankan home guards and other paramilitary forces, closure of all army and police camps in Tamil areas, and the setting up of the Interim Administrative Council.[125] The Indian government ridiculed Thileepan's "fast unto death" and threatened the LTTE with dire consequences for violating the accord. At the same time, India did not criticise the Sri Lankan government for failing to keep its part of the accord, thereby further convincing the LTTE that India was more anxious to maintain cordiality with the Sri Lankan government rather than protect Tamil interests. Matters spun out of control with the death of Thileepan on September 25. Tamil mobs, enraged by the Indian indifference toward the Sri Lankan Tamils, attacked an IPKF camp at Manner. Indian troops were forced to fire, causing the death of one person. Naturally, therefore, the LTTE no longer viewed the IPKF as the saviour of the Sri Lankan Tamils.

The second issue concerned the suicides of Kumarappa and Pulendran, two of the LTTE's regional commanders. On October 3, 1987, a Sri Lankan naval patrol captured a Tamil motorboat returning from India. On board were seventeen heavily armed LTTE cadres, including Kumarappa and Pulendran. All seventeen were taken to the Palaly Air Base and detained there to be transported to Colombo. The IPKF received news of the capture and mounted a guard around the hangar to prevent the captives from being moved. The Sri Lankan government, on the other hand, insisted on shifting the captives to Colombo for questioning and added that the men had broken the accord by transporting arms and ammunition after the deadline for the weapons surrender had expired. The LTTE countered that the men were carrying weapons for their own safety and security and that the Sri Lankan Navy had breached the accord by intercepting the boat. Unsure of what to do, the IPKF sought advice from New Delhi. The Indian government backed Colombo, whereupon the IPKF guard was withdrawn from the air base. The Tigers threatened to commit suicide rather than go to Colombo, and on October 5 all seventeen swallowed the cyanide capsules they wore around their necks; twelve of them died immediately. The next day, October 6, Prabhakaran repudiated the cease-fire agreed upon during the signing of the accord and executed eight Sri Lankan soldiers held captive by the LTTE for the past six months. Two hundred Sinhalese civilians were also killed in brutal retaliation and another ten thousand rendered homeless. Under scathing criticism from the Sri Lankan government for failing to restrain the Tamil militants and protect civilian life and property, Prime Minister Gandhi had no other alternative but to order the IPKF to apprehend anyone carrying arms or who was involved in the massacre of civilians. The message was loud and clear—destroy the LTTE. As Kadian observes: "The peacekeepers were going to war."[126]

For the next two years—from November 1987 to December 1989—the IPKF was engaged in a war in Sri Lanka that it was incapable of winning for a variety of reasons. First, the IPKF's preparation for a large-scale military action in Sri Lanka was grossly inadequate: Evidently, for example, the IPKF lacked adequate military intelligence on the various Sri Lankan Tamil guerrilla groups. As a result, neither the IPKF nor the Indian intelligence agencies had any clear idea as to how much manpower was needed for the task at hand. At the time of its induction, the IPKF comprised only 8000 men; in the next two years, its strength was increased to more than 100,000 men, but even this number proved to be inadequate. Similarly, military strategic and tactical intelligence was severely lacking. Thus, the IPKF was often surprised to find how powerful an enemy the LTTE was, and this greatly raised IPKF losses.

Second, the success of any military operation against a modern-day guerrilla force depends to a great extent on the degree of support it receives from the local population. But by the time the orders came for the IPKF to engage the LTTE, it had clearly alienated not only the Tamil people but even the Sinhalese. The outcome was that the IPKF was not only fighting against the LTTE guerrillas but even against a bitter and hostile Tamil population.

Third, the IPKF had to function under tremendous tactical and logistical restrictions because the Indian government could not appear to be insensitive to Tamil sentiments at home by cracking down brutally on the LTTE. So the IPKF was prevented from using heavy weapons, tanks, and aircraft against the LTTE, which reduced its battlefield capabilities. Faced with a well-armed and ruthless adversary, the IPKF suffered heavy casualties both in terms of material and manpower.

Finally, the constant failure of the IPKF to wipe out the enemy affected the morale of the entire force. Units in the field were dejected due to the very high casualty rates. Officers in Sri Lanka were very critical of the military top brass for being insensitive to their problems. In turn, the military top brass criticized the Indian government for imposing restrictions on the IPKF that reduced its fighting capability. On their part, Indian government officials criticized the IPKF for failing to wipe out a handful of Tamil militants. The Sri Lankan government also never let an opportunity slip by to criticize the IPKF whenever its operations bogged down or failed. Such constant criticism and countercriticism affected the morale of the IPKF and undermined its image.

As the IPKF became bogged down in Sri Lanka, opposition to the accord gathered momentum. Interested in scoring political points against the ruling UNP government that had signed the accord, the opposition SLFP of Sirimavo Bandaranaike openly criticised the accord as violating Sri Lanka's sovereignty. More disturbing for the ruling UNP was the revival of Sinhalese militancy led by the Janatha Vimukthi Peramuna (JVP), or the People's Revolutionary Front, which was essentially anti–Indian and anti–accord. In this context, Kodikara observes:

> Since 1971 the JVP has followed a consistently anti–Indian line. It has consistently regarded India as an expansionist power, and it purports to have found evidence to confirm this claim in such instances as India's role in the Bangladesh crisis of 1971 and India's absorption of Sikkim in 1975.[127]

It is no surprise, therefore, that the JVP viewed the accord as undermining the sovereignty and independence of Sri Lanka. Hence, the JVP unleashed a reign of terror with assassinations and killings of ruling UNP members, whom they considered to be traitors to the Sinhalese cause, and with massacres of Tamil and Indian civilians as reprisals for the killings of Sinhalese civilians by the LTTE. In its campaign of terror, the JVP received support from the Buddhist monastic order and from opposition parties. Some of Jayewardene's UNP colleagues, who were opposed to the accord, may also have provided support in order to bring pressure on the Sri Lankan president to reject the accord and ask for the IPKF's withdrawal from Sri Lanka.

The Indo–Sri Lankan Accord, therefore, clearly failed to bring about a peaceful resolution of the ethnic conflict in Sri Lanka. The strong identification of the accord with the promotion of Indian interests and the manner in which it was implemented undermined the effectiveness of the IPKF. In this context, Bruce Matthews observes:

> Although by the beginning of 1988 over 500 Indian troops had given their lives in combat, few Sinhalese seemed prepared to accept that this was done to keep Sri Lanka intact. Likewise, the [Sri Lankan] Tamils for the most part responded vehemently against the Indian occupation because it thwarted their political aims and brought much hardship and suffering to the innocent. An important corollary to this was the steady increase of anarchy and terrorism in the south and the spectre of a government seemingly helpless to prevent it.[128]

The accord thus succeeded in bringing about an intensification and transformation of Sri Lanka's ethnic conflict; the conflict now was not only between the LTTE and the Sri Lankan/Indian forces but also within the Sinhalese community between the JVP and the government.[129] By the early 1990s, another angle was added to this complex conflict—that is, conflict between Sri Lankan Tamils and Muslims in the eastern province. The Tamil–Muslim clashes started when the LTTE began to massacre Muslim populations in the eastern province in an effort to draw away troops that were massing against LTTE forces in the northern Jaffna Peninsula and also to foment communal clashes to scuttle any attempts at political settlement. The LTTE's attacks inevitably produced backlash from the Muslims who organized themselves into a political party, the Sri Lanka Muslim Congress (SLMC), to counter the LTTE.[130] With the JVP menace in the south and increasing communal clashes in the east and north, Sri Lanka's ethnic conflict progressively became more complex and violent.

Why Did India's Resolution Attempt Fail In Sri Lanka?

India's failure to resolve Sri Lanka's ethnic conflict confirms our belief that regional powers are poor international third parties when it comes to resolving ethnic conflicts, especially protracted and intense ones, for a number of reasons. For one, regional powers are often distrusted by the warring parties. This could be seen in Sri Lanka where the Tamils and the Sinhalese not only did not trust each other but distrusted India as well. India's offer of good offices to resolve the ethnic conflict after openly providing partisan support to the Sri Lankan Tamils only helped to sharpen both sides' suspicions: India had its own vested interests in the matter and was hardly sincere in helping the parties find a fair solution because New Delhi had clearly laid down the parameters of what would be acceptable to it as a solution.

Second, as we have seen, distrust of the third party may hamper the peace process by failing to secure the adversaries' positive attitude toward a peace agreement. This was clearly evident in Sri Lanka. Throughout the long period of negotiations, it gradually became clear that the disputing parties agreed to talk to each other, not because they believed that such talks would resolve the dispute but simply because they were in no position to antagonize India. For Colombo, the perception of a threat of Indian military intervention and the failure to secure guarantees against such an event from other powers meant that it had no other options but to accept the Indian line. For the Sri Lankan Tamil groups, noncompliance with Indian wishes would have meant the loss of the protection and support that they were receiving from India. Therefore, while they took part in negotiations, they gradually hardened their positions.

Third, again as expected, regional powers in their haste to find a solution often fail to understand the basic nature of the dispute. Thus, the Indian government failed to recognize the single most important factor in its dealings with the Sri Lankan government and the LTTE, that is, the Sinhalese unwillingness to share power meaningfully with the Tamils and the LTTE's uncompromising demand for Eelam. Because neither the Sinhalese nor the Sri Lankan Tamils trusted each other, both sides were resolved not to compromise on their respective standpoints. The Sri Lankan Tamils had the experience of witnessing numerous Sinhalese promises to accommodate Tamil demands being broken in the past. They also had serious doubts about the willingness and ability of Colombo to control its pan–Sinhalese policies, given that such sentiments were deliberately used in the past to achieve political objectives. Therefore, the LTTE was determined in its advocacy of secession. On the other hand, for Colombo, meaningful negotiations were possible only after the renunciation of secession by Tamil militant groups. India's attempt to safeguard Tamil interests within a unified Sri Lanka was therefore bound to fail because it ignored the fact that vital interests were at stake for both the adversaries. For the Sinhalese, the country's unity, integrity, and sovereignty were at stake, whereas for the Tamils, the struggle was for national survival, possible only by creating a separate Eelam. Hence, both sides placed a greater faith in a decisive military showdown rather than in a negotiated settlement: they were merely buying time by talking to each other and the Indians while preparing for a military showdown.

Finally, the Indians also failed to appreciate properly the difficulty of committing the adversaries to the peace process, given their identity and characteristics. For instance, President Jayewardene's cabinet was faction ridden with prominent hard liners present in it; this undoubtedly reduced Jayewardene's own ability to offer concessions to the Tamils. Moreover, because of the close connection between religion and politics in Sinhalese society, it was likely that any concessions made by the Sri Lankan government to the Tamils (as India wanted) would have been vetoed by the Sinhalese–Buddhist clergy. Therefore, any negotiated settlement had little chance of being implemented by the Sinhalese. It is also doubtful whether a negotiated settlement would have been accepted by the Sri Lankan Tamils. By the mid–1980s, the Tamil nationalist movement had clearly passed from such moderate groups as the

TULF to such militant groups as the LTTE, which was steadfast in its demand for Eelam. Yet, India chose to deal with groups like the TULF because moderate groups were more likely to accept a peace agreement. It was not surprising, therefore, that the LTTE lost faith in the peace process and came to regard India and the moderate Tamil groups as traitors to the Tamil cause.

CHANGING INTERNATIONAL PERCEPTION OF SRI LANKA'S ETHNIC WAR: WITHDRAWAL OF THE IPKF AND ITS AFTERMATH

As the IPKF became bogged down in Sri Lanka, demands rose in India to "bring the boys back." Both the LTTE and the Sri Lankan government wanted the IPKF out, too. Prime Minister Vishwanath Pratap Singh (who had replaced Rajiv Gandhi in late 1989) was also in favor of an early and essentially unconditional withdrawal of the IPKF. After high-level talks in September 1989, a cease-fire between the IPKF and the LTTE was arranged, and the withdrawal of the IPKF was fixed for December 31, 1989. The last day of March 1990 was fixed as the date for the completion of the withdrawal. As the IPKF withdrew, the LTTE once again moved into the northern and eastern provinces, emphasizing the support and confidence that the Tigers enjoyed among the Tamil population. The intensity of the ethnic conflict in Sri Lanka also reached alarming proportions after the IPKF pulled out. One had the impression that neither the Sri Lankan government, now headed by hard liner Ranasinghe Premadasa, nor the LTTE were interested anymore in a political solution but believed only in an all-out military showdown to break the deadlock.

India's policy toward Tamil secessionism in Sri Lanka after the IPKF's withdrawal changed drastically. Fed up with the LTTE's refusal to accept the Indo–Sri Lankan Accord and for its continual secessionist campaign, New Delhi adopted a "hands off" approach toward Sri Lanka's secessionist conflict which, in effect, strengthened the Sri Lankan government's hand. The Indian government also stopped all tangible and intangible aid to the LTTE. Further, to check pro-Tamil sentiments at home, the DMK government in Tamil Nadu was dismissed on charges of secretly aiding the LTTE and the state placed under President's Rule. This enabled New Delhi to run the administration of Tamil Nadu directly and so prevent the state from being used as a sanctuary by the LTTE.

India's policy change toward the Tamil secessionist movement in Sri Lanka in the 1990s was the result of several developments. First, the repeated failure of the Indian-sponsored diplomatic initiatives drove home the point to New Delhi that the LTTE was not interested in a negotiated peace and that it used the numerous cease-fire agreements and diplomatic exchanges to buy time and to regroup to launch fresh military offensives against the Sri Lankan government. India therefore came to regard the LTTE as the main obstacle to peace in Sri Lanka.

The LTTE's repudiation of the Indo–Sri Lankan Peace Accord and its war against the IPKF also altered the public mood in India toward the LTTE. Opposition parties, while blaming the government for sending the IPKF to Sri Lanka in the first place, were united in their condemnation of the LTTE and its uncompromising demand for

Eelam. The Indian military had also developed strong resentment against the LTTE for its brutal attacks on Indian soldiers. The public sympathy that the LTTE had enjoyed in Tamil Nadu was also eroded when it committed a tactical blunder by assassinating former Prime Minister Rajiv Gandhi while he was on a preelection campaign tour in Tamil Nadu in 1991. After the Gandhi assassination, public opinion in India toward the LTTE became extremely hostile.

India also had little strategic reason to support the LTTE in the 1990s. By the Indo–Sri Lankan Accord of 1987, New Delhi had successfully addressed most of its security concerns vis-à-vis Sri Lanka. With the end of the cold war in the early 1990s, India had even less reason to feel threatened by the Sri Lankan government's policies. In the changed post–bipolar international milieu, both the United States and Russia gave tacit approval for India's stated desire to become the dominant regional power in South Asia and expressed their confidence in India's ability to manage regional conflicts. Moreover, with the declining strategic significance of Pakistan to the United States after the Soviet withdrawal from Afghanistan and the increasing worry about the spread of Islamic fundamentalism, the United States started to woo India. For instance, it promised India a prominent role in policing the sea-lanes from the Persian Gulf to the Straits of Malacca in conjunction with a U.S.-led international force, a proposal in which senior Indian naval brass quietly expressed interest.[131]

India's changing perception of the Tamil secessionist movement in general and the LTTE in particular strongly influenced wider international opinion. In the initial years of the Tamil militancy, India's diplomatic campaign on behalf of the Sri Lankan Tamils had brought them considerable international sympathy and prestige, thereby making it difficult for the Sri Lankan government to procure military and diplomatic support from the international community. Moreover, India's covert military support to Tamil guerrilla groups substantially increased their firepower and therefore their durability. But the loss of India's patronage after 1991 severely affected the LTTE's audibility and visibility in international circles as well as its durability as a secessionist force. For instance, in 1995, the Kumaratunga administration in Sri Lanka decided to seek a military showdown with the LTTE in an effort to capture the Jaffna Peninsula after Prabhakaran rejected the government's peace offer to the Tamils.[132] This Sri Lankan military offensive—Operation Riviresa (Sunrays)—found widespread international sympathy.[133] It was also rumored that the Rao administration provided support to the Kumaratunga government in an effort to catch Prabhakaran and bring him to trial for Rajiv Gandhi's assassination. With or without India's help, the Sri Lankan military scored a decisive victory by capturing Jaffna and forcing the LTTE to withdraw to the eastern part of the island.

The LTTE's military defeat found few mourners internationally, although the LTTE public relations office based in London tried hard to project the Sri Lankan military offensive as an attempted "genocide" of the Tamil race. The reasons for such international apathy are not hard to find. The LTTE is now widely regarded in international circles as a terrorist organization: in the face of military and diplomatic obstacles, the LTTE has carried out numerous terrorist attacks and political assassinations in Sri Lanka and India to remain in the international media limelight. Furthermore, it is now widely believed that the LTTE is heavily involved in the international narcotics trade as a means of raising money to fund its operations.[134] It has also indulged in smuggling of weapons and ammunition obtained from the international underground arms market. Moreover, the LTTE's attempts to forge links with insurgents groups operating in India, such as the People's War Group in Andhra Pradesh, has not endeared the organization to India. Consequently, the LTTE's international image today is that of a criminal organization.

Certain other developments have hurt the LTTE's image, too. For one, it is now widely believed that the Sri Lankan Tamil population desperately desires peace so that refugees can return to Sri Lanka and put their lives back together. Support for peace is also widespread among the Sinhalese population, who are tired of the war and want it to end so that resources can be used to rebuild the country's war-ravaged economy. Peace in Sri Lanka is also ardently desired by the international community. President Kumaratunga's 1995 peace initiative—considered by almost everyone as a just and fair offer—was therefore welcomed wholeheartedly by broad majorities within the Sri Lankan Tamil and Sinhalese populations, as well as by the international community. But the LTTE's rejection of Kumaratunga's peace offer has not only further damaged its reputation internationally but is also bound to affect Tamils in Sri Lanka adversely in the future. As General K. Sunderji, former chief of staff of the Indian army, pointed out, the LTTE's rejection of Kumaratunga's peace offer and its subsequent military defeat is bound to affect the Tamil people in Sri Lanka, who are "sick and tired of the war and would like an honorable peace with generously granted autonomy in the north and the east," because "the fall of Jaffna is bound to make the Sinhalese right wing, including the Buddhist clergy, believe that there is little requirement now for the grant of any autonomy to the Tamils."[135] The LTTE may have therefore hurt the interest of the very people who it is supposedly defending.

CONCLUSION

Sri Lanka is the classic example of a dirty, ruthless, and protracted ethnic conflict whose roots go deep in the island state's history. Moreover, as can be expected of such conflicts, it came to acquire an international character fairly quickly. Further, it proved the point that these types of ethnic wars are difficult to resolve through international third-party actions. Today, Sri Lanka stands at a crossroad: After years of nonstop violence, it has a golden opportunity to resolve the ethnic problem, and almost everyone—the Tamil community, the Sinhalese, and the wider international community—wishes it to succeed. At the same time, Sri Lanka is confronted with extreme chauvinists within the majority Sinhalese community and with a minority secessionist organization whose ruthlessness, resilience of purpose, and survival skills against all odds is unparalleled in the world. It will therefore require tremendous political vision and acumen on the part of Sinhalese and Tamil politicians alike and wholehearted support of the international community to resolve this conflict peacefully. The sooner that can be done, the better it will be for Sri Lanka and South Asia.

If we compare the secessionist struggles of the Sri Lankan Tamils with that of the Bengalis in East Pakistan, then two facts stand out. First, unlike the Bengalis, the Sri Lankan Tamil secessionists seem to have substantially lost the legitimacy that their movement once had internationally. In many ways, the blame for this lies with the LTTE and its modus operandi. Second, unlike the Bengalis, the disinclination of India to support the idea of Tamil Eelam wholeheartedly has, true to expectations, been a major factor behind the Sri Lankan Tamils' failure so far to achieve Eelam. This outcome should not come as a surprise to us. As most secessionist conflicts vividly demonstrate, partisan external support (or the lack of it) is usually the most crucial variable that determines success or failure.

DISCUSSION QUESTIONS

1. What are protracted ethnic wars? Why are they more prone to become internationalized? What effect do they have for international security?
2. Discuss the processes through which protracted ethnic wars may come to acquire the status of an international problem.
3. For many years, Sri Lanka was considered to be a model of stable multiethnic democracy. Why and how did it emerge as an example of a brutal and protracted ethnic war?
4. Discuss the reasons for the failure of India's conflict resolution attempts in Sri Lanka. What lessons can be learned about ethnic conflict resolution from India's failed attempt in Sri Lanka?
5. Many scholars have argued that in recent years the international acceptability and legitimacy of the Tamil secessionists in Sri Lanka has been greatly eroded. Do you agree or disagree with this assessment?

NOTES

1. In 1947, with the departure of the British, the Indian subcontinent was divided into two independent states, India and Pakistan, based on the Muslim League's Two-Nation theory. The Muslim League had argued that the Muslims in the subcontinent constituted a separate nation distinct from the Hindus and, therefore, should be given the right to form their separate state. The state of Pakistan that thus came into being in 1947 comprised two separate geographical units separated by about 1200 miles of Indian territory. The two separate units came to be known as East and West Pakistan. With the separation of the East Wing from the rest of the nation in 1971, the state of Bangladesh was created.
2. For details of constitutional developments in Pakistan and the political demands of the Bengalis, see Mitra Das, *From Nation to Nation: A Case Study of Bengali Independence.* (Columbia: South Asia Books, 1981), Chapters IV and V. For an account of the role of the Awami League in the political developments in East Pakistan, see M. Rashiduzzaman,

"The Awami League in the Political Development of Pakistan." *Asian Survey*, 10, 7, July 1970, pp. 574–587.

3. Donald L. Horowitz, *Ethnic Groups in Conflict*. (Berkeley and Los Angeles: University of California Press, 1985), p. 242.

4. For a fascinating account of the events leading to the Pakistani army's crackdown in East Pakistan, see Anthony Mascarenhas, *The Rape of Bangladesh*. (New Delhi: Vikas Publications, 1971).

5. For an excellent analysis of the Nixon administration's "tilted" policy toward Pakistan during the East Pakistan crisis of 1971, see Christopher Van Hollen, "The Tilt Policy Revisited: Nixon–Kissinger Geopolitics and South Asia." *Asian Survey*, 20, 4, April 1980, pp. 339–361.

6. See Seymour M. Hersh, *The Price of Power: Kissinger in the Nixon White House*. (New York: Summit Books, 1983), pp. 450–451.

7. See Zubeida Mustafa, "The USSR and the Indo–Pakistan War, 1971." *Pakistan Horizon*, 25, 1972, p. 46–47.

8. Indira Gandhi quoted by Alexis Heraclides, *The Self-determination of Minorities in International Politics*. (London: Frank Cass, 1991), p. 157.

9. Hersh, *The Price of Power*, p. 457.

10. The island of Sri Lanka is the home of two major ethnic groups, the *Sinhalese* (who are in a majority) and the *Sri Lankan Tamils* (the principal minority group). Other minority groups include the *Muslims* (called *Moors*), the *Burghers* (people of mixed European blood), and the *Indian Tamils* (migrants brought to Sri Lanka by the British colonial administrations from South India to work in the plantation industry).

11. Veddhas are the descendants of the aboriginal tribes of ancient Sri Lanka. Their numbers have been greatly reduced over the years as many of them have been absorbed in the Sinhalese race. The remaining Veddhas continue to rely on hunting for their food and live under extreme, primitive conditions in the forests of eastern Sri Lanka.

12. The Dravidians are dark-skinned, largely Hindu people of south India.

13. For details, see W. Geiger, trans., *The Mahavamsa or the Great Chronicle of Ceylon*. (London: Oxford University Press, 1912).

14. For details, see K.M. de Silva, *History of Sri Lanka*. (Berkeley: University of California Press, 1981), pp. 3–4.

15. Chelvadurai Manogaran, *Ethnic Conflict and Reconciliation in Sri Lanka*, (Honolulu: University of Hawaii Press, 1987), p. 20.

16. Contrary to historical claims that the Dravidians were in the Indus Valley at the time of the Aryan arrival and that they were driven to the south by the new settlers, historians C.W. Nicholas and S. Paranavitana argue that the Pandyan people were not Dravidian Tamils, but Aryan Pandus of epic fame who occupied Central and South India during this period. They also argue that the Pandyan, Chola, and Chera dynasties ruled South India before the arrival of the Dravidians. The Dravidians merely adopted the names of these pre-Dravidian dynasties at a later date. See C.W. Nicholas and S. Paranavitana, *A Concise History of Ceylon*. (Colombo: Ceylon University Press, 1961), p. 58. Here taken from *Ibid*.

17. *Ibid.*, pp. 20–21.

18. N. D. Wijesekera, *The People of Ceylon*. (Colombo: M.D. Gunasena, 1965), pp. 57–58.

19. For an in-depth account of the ancient Nagas and the origins of Tamil settlements in Sri Lanka, see C. Rasanayagam, *Ancient Jaffna*. (Madras: Everymans Publisher, 1926).

20. S. Ponnampalam, *Sri Lanka: The National Question and the Tamil Liberation Struggle*. (London: Zed Books, 1983), pp. 16–20.

21. See de Silva, *History of Sri Lanka,* pp. 12–13.
22. K. M. de Silva, ed., *Sri Lanka: A Survey.* (London: C. Hurst, 1977), pp. 37–38. In this multiethnic society there was physical mixing and cultural contact between the two main ethnic groups that led to cultural and religious harmony. For instance, some Sri Lankan Tamil rulers were patrons of Buddhism, while Hindu deities were worshiped by the Buddhist Sinhalese.
23. The island of Sri Lanka is divided into a Wet Zone and a Dry Zone, based on the regional distribution of annual precipitation. The Wet Zone corresponds to the southwestern coastal plain and western portion of the central highlands where large quantities of moisture are delivered by the southwest monsoon. The Dry Zone, which covers the rest of the island, receives between 1,000 to 1,800 millimeters of annual rainfall from the often unreliable northeast monsoon and cyclonic storms during the months of November and December.
24. There is no consensus as to the exact date of the establishment of the Jaffna Kingdom, although both Sinhalese and Tamil historians agree that the Jaffna Kingdom was certainly in existence by A.D. 1325.
25. See S. Arasaratnam, *Ceylon.* (Englewood Cliffs, NJ: Prentice-Hall, 1964), pp. 98–116.
26. For details of the development of a distinct Sri Lankan Tamil identity, see S. Arasaratnam, "Nationalism in Sri Lanka and the Tamils," in Michael Roberts, ed., *Collective Identities, Nationalism, and Protest in Modern Sri Lanka.* (Colombo: Marga Institute, 1979).
27. *Ibid.,* p. 509.
28. Bruce Matthews, "The Situation in Jaffna—And How it Came About." *The Round Table,* 290, April 1984, pp. 188–204.
29. Legends and myths indicate that Buddha found the island to be an ideal place to establish a Buddhist society. In one such account in the *Pali Chronicles,* it is suggested that Buddha himself had asked Sakka, the king of gods and the protector of Buddha's doctrine, to protect Vijaya, the founder of the Sinhalese race, to establish the Sinhalese–Buddhist nation of Sri Lanka.
30. Shelton Kodikara argues that a close connection had always existed between the Sinhalese state and Buddhist religion. By virtue of this close association the Buddhist clergy wielded tremendous power and prestige in the state. Sinhalese rulers also were eager to maintain close relationships with the Buddhist clergy and to support Buddhism to receive the overwhelming support of the people. The Sinhalese king, therefore, became the defender of the Buddhist religion and it came to be looked upon as the king's special duty to uphold the religion and its institutions. See Shelton U. Kodikara, "Communalism and Political Modernization in Ceylon." *Modern Ceylon Studies,* 4, 3, January 1970, pp. 94–114.
31. Manogaran, *Ethnic Conflict and Reconciliation in Sri Lanka,* p. 24.
32. Manogaran offers alternative reasons for the Sinhalese migration from the Dry Zone to the Wet Zone in the thirteenth century. He points out that this drift was caused by a multitude of factors such as invasions from India, civil war and internal dissension, natural disasters, decline in the fertility of the soil, silting of reservoirs and canals, lack of administrative control to organize labor to maintain irrigation facilities, and a malaria epidemic of major consequences. See *Ibid.,* p. 81.
33. The *Mahavamsa* describes an epic battle in 101 B.C. between the Sinhala king Dutthagamani and Tamil king Elara. In this battle, Dutthagamani killed Elara in single combat and seized his capital, Anuradhapura. Tamil genocide followed and King Dutthagamani was advised by Buddhist monks that because the Tamils were non–Buddhists, they were subhuman and killing them was no sin. For details of this

and similar legends, see Geiger, trans., *The Mahavamsa or The Great Chronicle of Ceylon,* p. 175.

34. Manogaran, *Ethnic Conflict and Reconciliation in Sri Lanka,* p. 2.

35. It is significant that for both the Tamil and Sinhalese communities, the language and the people are identified by the same name.

36. Robert Kearney, *Communalism and Language in the Politics of Ceylon.* (Durham, NC: Duke University Press, 1967), p. 16.

37. *Ibid.,* p. 8.

38. *Ibid.,* p. 52.

39. *Ibid.*

40. For details of the British colonial government's education policy in Sri Lanka, see H.A. Wyndham, *Native Education.* (London: Oxford University Press, 1933).

41. Kearney, *Communalism and Language in the Politics of Ceylon,* p. 56–57.

42. *Ibid.*

43. *Ibid.,* p. 59.

44. The Buddhist Revivalist Movement in Sri Lanka of the nineteenth century was directed against foreign rule and Western influence. Therefore, the establishment of Christian schools in the Wet Zone (inhabited mostly by the Sinhalese) did not receive the same patronage from the Sinhalese as they received from the Tamils in the Dry Zone. For details, see Manogaran, *Ethnic Conflict and Reconciliation in Sri Lanka,* p. 118.

45. Kearney, *Communalism and Language in the Politics of Ceylon,* pp. 66–67.

46. *Ibid.,* p. 68.

47. *Ibid.,* p. 16.

48. *Ibid.*

49. At the beginning of the sixteenth century, Sri Lanka was divided into three kingdoms— the Sri Lankan Tamils lived in their traditional homeland in the northern and eastern provinces as a distinct nationality, the Sinhalese kingdom of the south, and the Kandyan–Sinhalese kingdom of the central hill country. This division was maintained by the Portuguese and the Dutch, and they administered the three states separately.

50. Manogaran, *Ethnic Conflict and Reconciliation in Sri Lanka,* p. 85.

51. This Tamil migration from the Dry Zone, their traditional homeland, to the Wet Zone for employment purposes was occasioned by a number of factors such as overpopulation, increasing landlessness, agrarian problems (such as small size of holdings, large size of peasant families, fluctuating and unreliable income, high cost of farming, lack of adequate credit), ecological constraints (such as lack of water, lack of rainfall, and the nature of the land—sandy and alkaline and consisting of rocky waste), and the lack of development caused by the British neglect of the area. For details, see *Ibid.,* pp. 116–117.

52. This disproportionate Sri Lankan Tamil representation in the public services and the professions is reflected in the 1953 Census that revealed that the Sri Lankan Tamils constituted only 12.8 percent of the total population whereas the Sinhalese were 79.2 percent of the total population. However, this 12.8 percent of the Sri Lankan Tamils dominated various government jobs and professions in the following manner: 30 percent—Ceylon Administrative Service; 50 percent—Clerical Services (including postal, railway, hospitals, customs); 60 percent—Professions (engineers, doctors, lecturers); 40 percent—Armed Forces; and 40 percent—Labor Forces. 1953 Census data obtained from Rajesh Kadian, *India's Sri Lanka Fiasco: Peacekeepers at War.* (New Delhi: Vision Books, 1990), p. 57.

53. Manogaran argues that although English-educated Tamils took advantage of their education to secure jobs and promotions, it does not suggest that the Tamils were appointed to

high positions in the public service even if they were less qualified than Sinhalese applicants for the jobs. Manogaran, *Ethnic Conflict and Reconciliation in Sri Lanka,* p. 118.

54. This was done because the Sri Lankan Tamils and the Sinhalese were alike in rejecting plantation labor as a way of life. The Sinhalese peasants in particular, were reluctant to give up their casual schedule of rice cultivation for the low-paid and strictly regulated work on the plantations. The Sri Lankan Tamils, on their part, utilized their proficiency in the English language and sought jobs in the public service and the professions.

55. Arasaratnam, "Nationalism in Sri Lanka and the Tamils," p. 502.

56. Manogaran, *Ethnic Conflict and Reconciliation in Sri Lanka,* p. 32.

57. The Donoughmore Constitution of 1931 abolished communal electorates and granted franchise to all adults over 21 years of age. Under this constitution, members of the newly formed State Council were to be elected through a territorial system, and for that purpose the country was divided into electorates based on area and population. In the State Council, the internal administration of Sri Lanka was to be carried out under the direction of the locally elected ministers and the powers reserved to the governor were to be handled by the British officers of state.

58. This constitution remained in force until 1972, when the United Front coalition government of Mrs. Bandaranaike introduced a new constitution that replaced the post of governor general by a president. The name of the country was also changed from Ceylon to Sri Lanka. In 1978, the UNP government of Mr. Jayewardene introduced another constitution that created a presidential form of government with Prime Minister Jayewardene becoming the first executive president of Sri Lanka for a six-year term.

59. D.S. Senanayake was the first prime minister of Sri Lanka. He assured the minorities that his governing United National Party (UNP) would protect their rights and interests. Such an assurance convinced G.G. Ponnambalam and a majority of his Tamil Congress to cross the floor and join the UNP in 1948. Only S.J.V. Chelvanayakam and few of his followers, who later organized the Tamil Federal Party (FP), remained in opposition.

60. Under the Citizenship Act of 1948, Indian Tamils could no longer become citizens of Sri Lanka by virtue of their birth on the island and had to prove three or more generations of paternal ancestry to become citizens by descent. It was virtually impossible for most Indian Tamils to provide such proof. As a result they were made stateless. Similarly, the Indian and Pakistani Residents (Citizenship) Act of 1949 and the Ceylon Parliamentary Elections Amendment Act of 1949 also disenfranchised most of the Indian Tamils who had participated in the country's general elections since 1931. The total outcome of all three acts was that about 975,000 Indian Tamils were rendered stateless.

61. Manogaran, *Ethnic Conflict and Reconciliation in Sri Lanka,* p. 40.

62. Brian Senewiratne, "The Problems of Sri Lanka," in Kalim Bahabur, ed., *South Asia in Transition: Conflicts and Tensions.* (New Delhi: Patriot Publishers, 1986), p. 237.

63. In the initial years after independence, the Sri Lankan government's position regarding official language was to recognize both the Sinhalese and Tamil languages as official language of Sri Lanka. When the Sri Lanka Freedom Party (SLFP) under S.W.R.D. Bandaranaike won the 1956 elections on a "Sinhala Only" platform, things changed for the worse. One of the first major acts of Bandaranaike's government was to pass the Official Language Act of 1956, by which the two-language policy was abandoned and Sinhalese was made the sole official language of Sri Lanka. The act granted no concessions to the Sri Lankan Tamils, the national minority, with regard to the use of the Tamil language for education, employment, and administrative purposes. The Sri Lankan Tamils resorted to protest. Faced with such mounting ethnic tension, the government passed the Tamil Language Act of 1958 to provide for the "reasonable use" of Tamil in

education, administration, and public service examinations in the northern and eastern provinces. The implementation of the act was, however, minimal.

64. This plan was devised in order to squeeze the Tamils out of higher education. Under this plan, for admission purposes in higher educational institutions, the marks obtained by Tamil students were "weighted" downward against marks obtained by Sinhalese students.

65. Because the Tamils have always claimed the northern and eastern provinces to be their traditional homeland based on the fact that they constitute a numerical majority in these areas, the Sinhalese-dominated governments of independent Sri Lanka started this deliberate policy of colonization of these areas by settling large numbers of Sinhalese families in the northern and eastern provinces. The purpose behind this policy was twofold: in the first place, by changing the population ratio between Tamils and Sinhalese in these areas, the Sri Lankan government sought to eliminate any legitimate claims the Tamils might have over these areas; and second, a changed population ratio would have been beneficial to the Sinhalese politicians during elections. Because election results reflected a clear polarization of politics (Sinhalese parties and Tamil parties won clear victories in their respective areas), a changed population ratio would have given the Sinhalese a greater control of traditional Tamil areas.

66. Robert N. Kearney, "Ethnic Conflict and the Tamil Separatist Movement in Sri Lanka." *Asian Survey,* 25, 9, September 1985, p. 902.

67. *Ibid.,* p. 903.

68. Senewiratne, "The Problems of Sri Lanka," p. 237.

69. Kearney, "Ethnic Conflict and the Tamil Separatist Movement in Sri Lanka," p. 905.

70. Under the 1978 constitution, the president was to be elected by direct popular vote. Therefore a candidate sympathetic to the minorities could hope to win by combining minority votes with a large minority of Sinhalese votes. Parliament was to be elected by proportional representation. Hence, Sinhalese parties now needed to form alliances with minority parties in order to form governments.

71. James Manor, "Sri Lanka: Explaining the Disaster." *The World Today,* November 1983, p. 452.

72. Library of Congress. Department of the Army. *Area Handbook Series. Sri Lanka: A Country Study.* (Washington DC: Government Printing Office, 1990), p. 204.

73. Ibid., pp. 205, 224.

74. Ibid., p. 204.

75. Ibid., pp. 223–224.

76. Ibid., p. 205.

77. Kearney, "Ethnic Conflict and the Tamil Separatist Movement in Sri Lanka," p. 906.

78. For an excellent account of the 1983 anti–Tamil riots in Sri Lanka and the role played by government agencies and personnel, see James Manor, "Sri Lanka: Explaining the Disaster." *The World Today,* November 1983, pp. 450–459. Manor argues that there were two distinct factions in President Jayewardene's cabinet—one faction was led by Prime Minister Ranasinghe Premadasa and the other by Cyril Matthew. The Matthew faction, concerned about its own prospects in the succession struggle that could follow after the death of the aging Jayewardene, used the anti–Tamil riots not only to undermine the stability of the Jayewardene government but also to weaken the Tamil support base of its main rival, Prime Minister Premadasa and his faction.

79. *Area Handbook Series. Sri Lanka: A Country Study*, p. 207.

80. S.D. Muni, "Sri Lanka's Ethnic Crisis," in Kalim Bahadur, ed., *South Asia in Transition: Conflicts and Tensions.* (New Delhi: Patriot Publishers, 1986), p. 279.

81. Karthigesu Sivathamby, "The Sri Lankan Tamil Question: Socio-Economic and Ideological Issues." *Bulletin of Peace Proposals,* 18, 4, 1987, pp. 628, 631.

82. *Ibid.*, p. 634.
83. One main reason why New Delhi could not be insensitive to the Tamil sentiments at home was because of the fear of provoking a secessionist demand for *Dravidastan* in Tamil Nadu. The Tamil desire for separatism in India has deep roots, and in the 1960s the Dravida Kazhagam (DK) movement had struggled to create a separate Tamil nation in the Indian mainland. While the DK movement had started as a movement against the imposition of Hindi as the national language by the Nehru government, it soon turned into a movement protesting the domination of the North over the South. In this struggle the DK had received support from the Sri Lankan Federal Party, whose leader S.J.V. Chelvanayakam had found a great parallel between the struggle of the Tamils in India against the imposition of Hindi and the resistance of the Sri Lankan Tamils to the Sinhalese in Sri Lanka. New Delhi, therefore, feared that if it remained unresponsive to popular sentiments in Tamil Nadu, the Tamil ethnic issue might acquire a transnational dimension, thus creating a serious security problem for India. See Urmila Phadnis, "India and Sri Lanka," in Bimal Prasad, ed., *India's Foreign Policy: Studies in Continuity and Change.* (New Delhi: Vikas, 1979), p. 206; and Salamat Ali, "The Dravidian Factor." *Far Eastern Economic Review,* February 4, 1988, p. 20.
84. P. Venkateshwar Rao, "Ethnic Conflict in Sri Lanka: India's Role and Perception." *Asian Survey,* 28, 4, April 1988, p. 425.
85. Kadian, *India's Sri Lanka Fiasco,* p. 67.
86. For an interesting account of the Israeli involvement in the ethnic conflict in Sri Lanka, see Victor Ostrovsky and Claire Hoy, *By Way of Deception.* (New York: St. Martin's Press, 1990), pp. 67–69 and 127–131. Ostrovsky and Hoy argue that the Israelis were training both the Tamil guerrillas and the Sri Lankan security forces at the same time. Also see P. Seneviratne, "The Mossad Factor in Government Repression," in Bahadur, ed., *South Asia in Transition,* pp. 288–294.
87. Rao, "Ethnic Conflict in Sri Lanka," p. 425.
88. *Ibid.*
89. *Ibid.*
90. RAW is India's foreign intelligence agency.
91. The Sri Lankan Government wanted to lease its oil storage facilities at the port of Trincomalee to a Florida-based firm, the Coastal Corporation. India viewed this arrangement as serious for its security as it could provide formal access to the U.S. Navy to the area. This Indian reaction was not without some basis because the draft agreement between Colombo and Coastal Corporation, which leaked out, reportedly provided for the exclusive use of 5 out of 99 tankers by the U.S. Navy. Simultaneously, a Pentagon map showed Trincomalee as a center catering to the needs of U.S. forces. Reaction in India, therefore, was sharp. Sri Lanka, failing to allay India's fears that the deal had no military strings attached, viewed the Indian reaction as interference in Sri Lanka's affairs. Colombo, however, had to back down under Indian pressure and the deal with Coastal Corporation was given up. Instead global tenders were floated with the object of leasing the storage facilities to the highest bidder. See *The Hindu,* May 21, 1983.
92. For details of the Indian covert involvement and the role played by RAW in the training of Tamil guerrillas, see Kadian, *India's Sri Lanka Fiasco,* pp. 98–109.
93. *The Times of India,* July 27, 1983.
94. *The Statesman,* July 30, 1983.
95. *The Times of India,* July 31, 1983.
96. Rao, "Ethnic Conflict in Sri Lanka," p. 424.
97. *The Hindu,* July 28, 1983.

98. *The Hindustan Times,* July 24, 1983.

99. This term has been coined by foreign policy analyst Bhabani Sengupta. For details, see *India Today,* August 31, 1983, pp. 14–15.

100. Robert L. Hardgrave, Jr., *India Under Pressure: Prospects for Political Stability.* (Boulder, CO: Westview, 1984), p. 167.

101. *The Guardian,* August 1, 1983.

102. President Jayewardene's earlier five-point offer included (1) the full implementation of the laws relating to the district development councils, (2) use of Tamil as provided for in the present (1978) Sri Lankan Constitution as a national language, (3) the initiation of a dialogue on amnesty on the condition that violence would be given up by the Tamil militant groups, (4) the discontinuance of the active role of the army in Jaffna on the cessation of terrorist violence, and (5) the repeal of the draconian Prevention of Terrorism Act.

103. *The Hindu,* August 13, 1983.

104. Kadian, *India's Sri Lanka Fiasco,* p. 92.

105. *The Hindustan Times,* August 14, 1983.

106. Shelton U. Kodikara, "International Dimensions of Ethnic Conflict in Sri Lanka: Involvement of India and Non-State Actors." *Bulletin of Peace Proposals,* 18, 4, 1987, p. 646.

107. Kadian, *India's Sri Lanka Fiasco,* pp. 93–94.

108. *Ibid.,* p. 96.

109. Kodikara, "International Dimensions of Ethnic Conflict in Sri Lanka," p. 647.

110. *Ibid.*

111. Kadian, *India's Sri Lanka Fiasco,* pp. 96–97.

112. "Operation Liberation One" was launched against the Tamils in 1985.

113. Kadian recounts that before the accord was signed, Prabhakaran was flown to New Delhi for talks with the Rajiv administration. He was virtually kept as a prisoner in Room 518 at New Delhi's Ashok Hotel until he gave his acquiescence to the accord. The Indian government also offered 5 million rupees to the LTTE, the assurance that the LTTE would enjoy a majority in the proposed Interim Administrative Council in the temporarily merged northern and eastern province, and the promise to provide one billion rupees in economic assistance for the rehabilitation of the Jaffna peninsula, in exchange for his support to the accord. For details, see Kadian, *India's Sri Lanka Fiasco,* pp. 24–25.

114. *Ibid.,* pp. 11–12.

115. Ralph R. Premdas and S.W.R. de A. Samarasinghe, "Sri Lanka's Ethnic Conflict: The Indo–Lanka Peace Accord." *Asian Survey,* 28, 6, June 1988, p. 684.

116. *Ibid.,* p. 685.

117. *Ibid.*

118. *Ibid.*

119. Kumar Rupesinghe, "Ethnic Conflicts in South Asia: The Case of Sri Lanka and the Indian Peace-keeping Force (IPKF)." *Journal of Peace Research,* 25, 4, 1988, p. 346.

120. Premdas and Samarasinghe, "Sri Lanka's Ethnic Conflict," p. 678.

121. Rupesinghe, "Ethnic Conflicts in South Asia," p. 346.

122. Immediately after the withdrawal of the IPKF from Sri Lanka in 1991, the rating was prematurely released by the Premadasa government.

123. Kadian, *India's Sri Lanka Fiasco,* pp. 25–26.

124. Twenty-three-year-old Thileepan was the chief of the LTTE's political wing in Jaffna.

125. Kadian, *India's Sri Lanka Fiasco,* pp. 30–31.

126. *Ibid.,* p. 34.

127. Shelton U. Kodikara, "The Continuing Crisis in Sri Lanka: The JVP, the Indian Troops, and Tamil Politics." *Asian Survey,* 29, 7, July 1989, p. 717.

128. Bruce Matthews, "Sri Lanka in 1988: Seeds of the Accord." *Asian Survey,* 29, 2, February 1989, p. 229.
129. Kumar Rupesinghe, "Sri Lanka: Peacekeeping and Peace Building." *Bulletin of Peace Proposals,* 20, 3, 1989, p. 348–349.
130. See Manik de Silva, "Communal Bloodbath." *Far Eastern Economic Review,* 30 August 1990, p. 19.
131. *India Today,* February 28, 1991, p. 18.
132. For details of President Kumaratunga's latest peace proposal to the LTTE, see Howard B. Schaffer, "Sri Lanka in 1995: A Difficult and Disappointing Year." *Asian Survey,* 36, 2, February 1996, pp. 216–223.
133. For details of this latest military offensive by the Sri Lankan government, see Nirupama Subramanian, "Fight to the Finish." *India Today,* November 30, 1995, pp. 38–43.
134. See Walter Jayawardhana, "Guns for Drugs." *Sunday,* November 4, 1990, p. 82.
135. K. Sunderji, "Sri Lanka's Chance for Peace." *India Today,* November 30, 1995, p. 44.

chapter 8

Weak States and Ethnic Conflict: Secessionism and State Collapse In Africa

INTRODUCTION

The majority of ethnosecessionist movements in the world today can be found in the developing world, particularly on the vast continents of Africa and Asia. The multitude of communal groups living there, combined with the artificial nature of state borders set by the European colonial powers, have furnished hothouse conditions for the growth of separatist organizations. In the last chapter, we examined one of the most destructive ethnosecessionist conflicts found in Asia, the Sinhalese–Tamil struggle. Within the developing world, however, Africa accounts for a large proportion of ethnic conflicts.

Studying cases from Africa is particularly important because the continent is demarcated by state boundaries that are arbitrary and were imposed from without, is where ethnic groups are numerous, and is where weak central governments are commonplace. Ian Lustick observed that "After more than thirty years of independence . . . the hegemonic status of the belief that African borders are immutable, and thereby excluded from calculations about how Africans can respond to the exigencies of their existence, appears to be breaking down." As a result, "Africa faces, among its other woes, the possibility of cascading patterns of fragmentation and attachment."[1]

Examining cases of fragmenting states can help us understand the role played by ethnicity in these processes, as well as the part played by international actors: As we have seen time and time again, international actors are reluctant to recognize the validity of ethnosecessionists' arguments and prefer status-quo arrangements. The statist bias of the international system makes no concessions, even when fragmenting states are peripheral to the global economy and state system and the movements assaulting them seem to have justififiable historical grievances, land claims, sense of oppression, and other moral claims. Not only borders, therefore, but central government itself comes under attack in many African states.

WEAK STATES

Weak or unsettled states may be charitable descriptions for what William Zartman has bluntly termed state collapse—a widespread phenomenon across Africa. "Current state collapse—in the Third World, but also in the former Soviet Union and in Eastern Europe—is not a matter of civilizational decay. . . . Nor is the process merely an organic characteristic of growth and decay, a life cycle in the rise and fall of nations."[2] For Zartman, state collapse entails the loss of a multiplicity of functions:

> As the decision-making center of government, the state is paralyzed and inoperative: laws are not made, order is not preserved, and societal cohesion is not enhanced. As a symbol of identity, it has lost its power of conferring a name on its people and a meaning to their social action. As a territory, it is no longer assured security and provisionment by a central sovereign organization. As the authoritative political institution, it has lost its legitimacy, which is therefore up for grabs, and so has lost its right to command and conduct public affairs. As a system of socioeconomic organization, its functional balance of inputs and outputs is destroyed; it no longer receives supports from nor exercises controls over its people, and it no longer is even the target of demands, because its people know that it is incapable of providing supplies.[3]

State collapse, like the related notion of unsettled states, may not simply be a byproduct of ethhnonationalism, then; it may represent a factor promoting a retreat into ethnic identities.

We begin this chapter by looking at examples of separatist movements organized shortly after the first African colonies were granted independence in the early 1960s. With the widely perceived illegitimacy of colonially demarcated borders, the power vacuum created by the withdrawal of European colonial powers, and the precarious existence of nascent independent states, this seemed to be a propitious time for breakaway movements to be successful. The most serious bids were made in the Congo and Nigeria.[4] Pivotal ethnic groups that were concentrated in Katanga and Biafra respectively sought to break away from states formed on the basis of the interests of colonial powers. Their failed efforts to achieve statehood owed much to the role played by international political actors, which contrived to keep intact dubious states lacking much legitimacy.

We then examine a more recent case of separatism, one that proved successful against all odds: Eritrea's declaration of independence and secession from Ethiopia in May 1993.[5] The role of outside parties, including the superpowers, was again critical in making this a rare example of successful secession in the developing world. What was different about the Eritrean case of secession was, ironically, that it had "enjoyed" colonial status in the past and therefore, like other colonies, demanded statehood.

We conclude this chapter by analyzing what many consider classic cases of ethnic violence: the mass killings in Rwanda and Burundi in the mid–1990s. While ethnic division is a necessary condition for such mass violence, by itself it is not sufficient for explaining why genocide should be perpetrated; background conditions also are important. Thus, in order to to prop up colonial governments in the past, efforts were made to politicize preexisting ethnic divisions, to favor one group over others, and to maintain centralized rule on the basis of divide-and-rule tactics. We refer to the conflicts in Central Africa as an example of the ethnicization of a struggle for power between political leaders of different ethnic groups.

The case studies of African states can also tell us whether external intervention is the norm for resolving ethnosecessionist disputes. We inquire whether outside intervention to manage conflicts between local peoples is likely in cases where not the integrity of existing states but only control of political power in them is under challenge.

SECESSIONISM IN THE CONGO

European exploration into the uncharted African continent was first undertaken in the fifteenth century by the Portugese, but it was only in the nineteenth century that the interior of the Congo basin was reached by renowned British explorers David Livingstone and H.M. Stanley. The latter's activity in the heart of Africa aroused the interest of Belgian King Leopold II. At the Berlin Conference between November 1884 and February 1885, land disputes between European countries over African possessions were adjudicated. Leopold was authorized to become sovereign of the Congo Free State and, in 1908, it was officially transferred to Belgium as a colony. In June 1960, under the auspices of the United Nations, the first group of colonies in Africa was given independence and the Congo was among them.

Less than two weeks after Congo's independence, the mineral-rich region of Katanga declared its secession.[6] The region's leader was Moise Tshombe, founder of the Conakat movement that rallied the indigenous Lunda and Bayeke peoples of Katanga against incoming settlers, above all the Baluba from the Kasai region, who now outnumbered the native Katagans. Katanga itself was divided, therefore, with ethnosecessionism strongest in the south where the Lunda and Bayeke lived. The secessionist movement was never able to mobilize peoples throughout Katanga.[7]

Even after decolonialization, Belgium continued to enjoy profitable investments in the region, especially through its *Union Minière du Haut-Katanga*. Belgium was prepared to lend support to the Katangan secessionists, substantiating the hypothesis that armed secessionist movements are usually launched if external support can be secured.[8] Tshombe disowned the virulent anticolonialism of Congo leader Patrice Lumumba, who was backed by the Soviet Union. As a result, Tshombe was able to obtain support from other European states with close ties to Belgium, such as France and Britain. European powers took opposite sides in the conflict, therefore, but a crucial international intervention was made in August 1960 by the Conference of

Independent African States. It condemned "any secession and all colonialist maneuvers aimed at dividing the territory of the Republic of the Congo."[9]

Partly as a result of this declaration and partly in order to avoid a precedent-setting case of ethnosecessionism in a postcolonial state, the UN Security Council passed a resolution shortly afterward calling on Belgium to withdraw its forces from Katanga. It also announced that a UN peacekeeping force (ONUC) would be dispatched to the breakaway region. Though supposedly neutral in the Congo's internal political struggles, the UN force played the role of kingmaker. In late 1960 Lumumba was ousted as Congo's prime minister by President Kasavubu and replaced by Congolese officer Mobutu, marking the beginning of what was to be a 35-year-long personal dictatorship in the renamed state of Zaire (changed back to Congo in 1997 when Mobutu was ousted by rebel forces). The removal of the pro–Soviet Lumumba cleared the last obstacle to Western support for the central government forces.

The UN operation was largely influenced and funded by the United States. It was able militarily to defeat the secessionist Katangan army in 1963 and thus preserve state unity. It should be noted, however, that during the course of the bitter struggle against the secessionists, some countries pulled their military contingents out, claiming ONUC intervention was proving to be a fiasco.

Lack of crosscutting support from ethnic groups within Katanga, Tshombe's discredited policy of collaborating with former colonial powers, and opposition to its secession by key international actors—the pan–African congress, the UN, and the United States—were the key factors behind Katanga's failed bid at statehood. The fact that it was a resource-rich region stimulated the independence effort but also produced the international coalition that conspired to end it. Katanga would not be permitted by the international system to set a precedent at an early stage of decolonization. An earlier, African version of matrioshka nationalism was cut short. But, as with the disintegration of the USSR, so the collapse of central authority in Zaire in 1997 provided a new opportunity structure for secessionists in Katanga.

SECESSIONISM IN NIGERIA

As with the Congo, so the lands that now make up the West African state of Nigeria were initially penetrated by the Portugese late in the fifteenth century and then, a century later, by the English. In 1861 the British established their first colony in these territories around the future capital, Lagos. Growth of a form of nationalism led to Nigerian independence in 1960.[10] It did not sever all ties with the colonial power but did become a member of the British Commonwealth. Due to its ethnic heterogeneity—the largest groups include the Hausa, Ibo, Yoruba, and Fulbe—Nigeria became a federation in 1963. But as Crawford Young has noted, Nigeria was a "constructed nation" from the outset. "Nigeria has little cultural logic; its peoples would never have chosen to live together."[11]

Tensions between the two most important groups, the Hausa and the Ibo, broke out in fighting in November 1966. The two peoples each possessed their own respective states as far back as in medieval times, providing a basis to competing historical and territorial grievance claims. Creating a federal structure with shaky, colonially demarcated borders exacerbated mutual recriminations and distrust. Moreover, two successive coups d'etat in the first half of 1966 led to the overthrow of the nascent democratic system and its replacement with military rule under the leadership of a senior northern officer, Lieutenant Colonel Yakubu Gowon. Political instability in Lagos spurred the growth of separatist feelings among peoples and regions distant from the capital.

The eastern region, largely inhabited by the enterprising Ibo people, refused to accept Gowon's leadership and tried to break away from the federation. He responded by exploiting the presence of non–Ibo minorities in the region and partitioning the eastern region into three states or provinces. The stimulus-response dynamic continued when, in May 1967, eastern region military governor Colonel Chukwuemeka Odumegwu Ojukwu proclaimed the region to be the independent state of Biafra.[12]

Between 1967 and 1970, a brutal war was fought between the Nigerian army and the Biafran rebel forces, leaving hundreds of thousands dead. As in the case of the Congo–Katanga dispute, international actors lined up on opposite sides. The Biafran cause aroused considerable sympathy in the West, partly as a result of the Biafran attempt to define the conflict in religious terms between themselves as Christians and the Nigerians as Muslims.[13] Among the former British colonizers, the Ibo had the image of being an industrious, individualistic, capitalistic-oriented people. Ibo leaders claimed that their economic development was held back by the more traditional, less vibrant cultures of the rest of Nigeria. More than members of other groups, many Ibo had emigrated to England when it was still easy to do so (before the passage of the 1968 Commonwealth Immigration Act). The Ibo diaspora secured favorable press coverage for Ojukwu's movement. Even where Western governments were hesitant to support the Biafran cause for fear of breaking up an existing state, their populations offered considerable support through church and nonprofit aid organizations.

Biafra also possessed oil resources that affected the interests of French, British, and U.S. oil companies. Both the British and American governments sought a return, therefore, to political stability in the west African country, and London also wanted to maintain the unity of the British Commonwealth. Both countries threw their support behind the Nigerian federal government. They were joined this time by the Soviet Union, which wanted to be on the side of the central government in a federal system struggling against ethnosecessionism. The USSR's policy on Nigeria was also aimed at its communist rival for influence in Africa, Mao Zedong's China, which had already begun to penetrate parts of east Africa. A majority of the new independent states of Africa—fearing the precedent of successful secession as well as being hypersensitive to any signs of neocolonial interference in the politics of the continent—also backed Gowon's government.

On the side of the Biafrans were China and France. China persuaded its allies in Africa—Tanzania and Zambia—to recognize Biafra and help Ojukwu's forces. In turn, France employed two francophone African states—Gabon and the Ivory Coast—that had recognized Biafra to serve as conduits for its support for the breakaway region. International nongovernmental organizations also provided vital support to the Biafran civilian population during the brutal war.

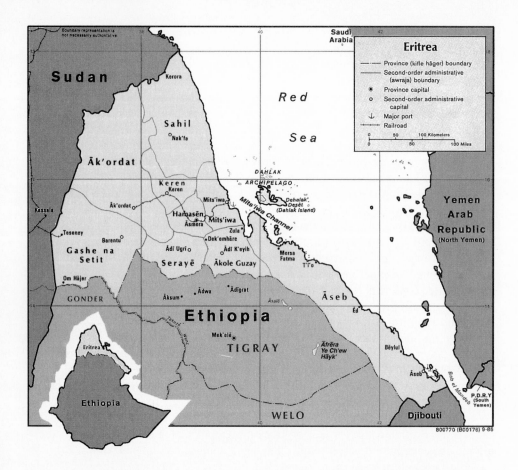

External support prolonged the conflict, but in 1970 the Nigerian army, possessing superior numbers and weapons, defeated the insurgency. War termination may have also been speeded up by the clandestine involvement of the British government. Leading British newspapers made allegations that Prime Minister Harold Wilson—foreseeing the imminent military rout of the rebel forces—paid off Ojukwu to abandon the war effort. Indeed the Biafran leader vanished days before the war officially ended.[14] In order to prevent a recurrence of conflicts based on ethnically defined regions, Nigeria has been progressively divided from the three regions in existence during British rule to four, then twelve, nineteen, twenty-one, and most recently thirty states. A quarter of a century after the Biafran war, political instability continues to affect Nigeria as a result of ethnic schisms, corrupt leadership, and democratic breakdown.[15]

From these two cases of failed secessionism in fragile African states, we see the importance of third parties to determining the final outcomes. In particular, former colonial powers continued to intervene in the internal affairs of their former possessions. Preserving fragile states, however arbitrary their borders, was their overriding objective. Even the USSR, perceived in the 1960s and 1970s as a champion of national liberation movements throughout the third world, came to the support of central governments in both cases against groups seeking self-determination. As we see next, the failure of the Soviet Union to prop up the central government of one of its client states in Africa led two decades later to an example of successful secession.

SECESSIONISM IN ETHIOPIA

Eritrea stretches along the Red Sea coast for 600 miles from Sudan to Djibouti, roughly across the Red Sea from Yemen and Saudi Arabia, in what is known as the Horn of Africa. It straddles the strategic choke point, the Bab el-Mandab Strait, that leads into the Gulf of Aden and through which much of the Western world's oil passes. Not surprisingly, then, both in colonial times and during the cold war, the major world powers regarded control over Eritrea's geopolitical position of strategic importance. For these powers, the calculus was whether such control could be better established by incorporating Eritrea into Ethiopia, a large country to the south with some overlapping ethnic affinities and with imperial ambitions, or whether control over the Red Sea choke point could be more easily exercised through an independent Eritrea.

Sources of Conflict: The Colonial Legacy

Eritrea has a relatively small population of approximately three million, but it is remarkably diverse. It consists of nine principal ethnic groups, split roughly half and half into Muslim and Christian communities; the latter includes Coptic Christians and Protestants. These groups speak seven languages, including a minority that uses Arabic dialects, a fact that has occasionally raised the issue (as we discuss later) whether Eritrea is part of Africa or part of the Arab world. As with Ethiopia, with which it was integrated for most of the postwar period, Eritrea is an ethnically very heterogenous society.

The first major European presence in Eritrea dates from 1869 when the Italian government purchased the port of Assab from the local sultan. Concerned about the growing French presence in Somalia, the British encouraged the Italians to encroach further into Eritrea. Not for the only time in their history, the Italians suffered a humiliating defeat in 1887 at the hands of the Ethiopian army. Three years later, however, the Italian forces had recouped enough to allow the king of Italy to issue a decree creating the Italian colony of Eritrea. Emboldened by their capture of this strategic part of the Ethiopian empire, the Italians sought to increase the territory under their control and briefly took control of the adjoining Tigre region that spills over into Ethiopia. But Ethiopian Emperor Menelik II's forces stopped the Italian advance and, at the battle of Adowa in 1896, decimated the Italian army. Menelik could have marched on Italian positions in Eritrea itself, but he was more concerned about consolidating Ethiopian territorial gains in the southwest part of the empire. As a result he was willing to sign the Addis Ababa peace treaty later that year that, curiously, expanded the Italians' territorial acquisitions in the area. Thereafter, as one historian put it, Italy forged an Eritrea "by an act of surgery: by severing its different peoples from those with whom their past had been linked and by grafting the amputated remnants to each other under the title of Eritrean."[16]

In the second half of the 1930s, the Italian military presence in the Horn of Africa increased. Mussolini's Pyrhhic victory over Ethiopia in 1936 led to the transfer of the northern Tigre province to Eritrea, thereby doubling its size. But in early 1941 the Italians were driven out of Eritrea for good when British forces marched in; they were attempting to stop the military advance of Italy's ally, Germany, whose forces were led by Field Marshal Erwin Rommel.

At the end of World War II, Italy's former colonies were to be "disposed of" jointly by Britain, France, the United States, and the Soviet Union. The Four Powers deliberated on the question of independence for Eritrea but could not come to an agreement. The United States, for example, proposed a collective trusteeship over Eritrea for ten years, with Ethiopia being guaranteed access to the Red Sea, after which an Eritrean state would come into being. The Soviet Union opposed this plan and, in the end, the Four Powers referred the issue to the United Nations for resolution. In late 1948, the United States began to lean toward the Ethiopian side following a verbal agreement between the two countries: the United States would support Ethiopian acquisition of Eritrea in return for American access to airfields and ports in the Asmara and Massawa area and control over a communications center (Kagnew Station) near the Eritrean capital.[17]

With the United States no longer supporting the idea of Eritrean statehood, in late 1950 the UN General Assembly passed resolution 390A (V) which asserted that Eritrea should "constitute an autonomous unit federated with Ethiopia under the sovereignty of the Ethiopian Crown."[18] Following promulgation of an Eritrean constitution, elections to parliament, and ratification of the Ethiopian Federal Act in 1952, Eritrea formally passed to the control of Ethiopia. One year later, the United States signed the Mutual Defense Assistance Pact with Ethiopia providing for military aid, and the Defense Installations Agreement ratifying United States' basing rights in Eritrea. As one critic of American policy on the Horn of Africa contended, "The Ethio-Eritrean federation was installed by the Western powers under the leadership of the United States purely for geopolitical considerations. This U.N.-sanctioned federation in essence became a denial of Eritrea's right to national self-determination."[19]

The Ethiopian government and its traditional ruling elite, the Amharas, rejected Eritreans' claim to constituting a separate group. They contended that such supposed separateness, and the political configuration based on it, was the illegitimate legacy of colonialism and could not serve as a criterion for postcolonial demarcation. But those were exactly the same grounds that Eritreans used to support statehood. Eritrea had already been defined when it was an Italian colony between 1890 and 1941. Moreover, Ethiopia had forfeited any claim on Eritrea by the Addis Ababa peace treaty of 1896. Eritrea's claim to a separate identity was based on its distinct history, then. Eritreans claim that domination for centuries by the Ottoman Empire and then later by Egyptians, Italians, and the British set them apart from the other peoples of Ethiopia.

One writer has captured the irony of the colonial legacy argument: Because Eritrea had been a self-contained European colony, it could "itself rely on the principle of the sanctity of colonial boundaries which is the holy writ in the Third World, above all in Africa."[20]

Pan-Africanism and Pan-Ethiopianism

Paradoxically, a movement ostensibly opposed to the ambitions of Western powers in Africa concurred with Ethiopia's annexation of Eritrea. Pan–Africanism, whose leading exponent in the 1930s had been Haile Selasse, provided an ideological rationale for coerced African unity. As Ruth Iyob explained, "That African unity was used to justify the violation of the basic rights of Africans by Africans has not eroded its appeal as a common political desideratum."[21] For the sake of pan–African unity, most African states ignored Eritrea's claims for statehood even though the main secessionist organization, the Eritrean People's Liberation Front (EPLF), mindful of the criticism that Eritrea contained Arabic peoples, constantly stressed its Africanness and denied any interest in establishing an Arab state.

The ideology of pan–Ethiopianism had been gaining strength for some time. In the 1940s many observers taken with Ethiopia's precocious anticolonialism viewed the country as a political or Black Zion. "The mythical allure of biblical Ethiopia and Menelik's victory against Italy at the battle of Adowa in 1896 served to underscore the symbolic image of an independent African state, and the expansionist nature of the empire was seldom questioned."[22] With the transfer of Eritrea to its control, an important stage of pan–Ethiopianism—absorbing neighboring territories having cultures similar to Ethiopia's—seemed to have been completed.

The 1952 federation of Eritrea and Ethiopia turned Eritrea into the northernmost region of the expanded state. But from the outset, Ethiopian Emperor Haile Selassie sought to subvert even this circumscribed Eritrean autonomy. His rule was authoritarian, largely at odds with the more democratic spirit reflected in the Eritrean constitution. In 1956 Selassie suspended the Eritrean elected assembly and gradually stripped the province of its remaining powers. The end for Eritrean political autonomy occurred in November 1962. In violation of the provision that only the UN could amend the Federal Act, the Emperor's government declared that the federation of Ethiopia and Eritrea was null and void. The latter was incorporated into a unitary Ethiopian state as its fourteenth province.

Selassie's regime was closely identified with personal autocracy, backwardness, and the country's Christian community. This served to mobilize both progressive forces and Muslim peoples in a common struggle to overthrow the emperor. An urban revolt led by students and unions rocked the country between January and June 1974. At the end of June, leaders of the armed forces and the police created a coordinating committee that became known as the Dergue ("committee"). By September it had declared itself a provisional military government and by December it was fully in control of the country.[23] Haile Selassie was too weak and senile—he died a year after the Dergue's seizure of power—to defend his regime.[24]

Military Repression

From February 1977 until the fall of the Dergue in 1991, Colonel Mengistu Haile Mariam, a young officer in the Ethiopian army, was the uncontested leader of Ethiopia. His military government held power for fourteen years by playing the ethnic card effectively. He obtained the support of the Amharic-speaking community, dominant in the capital and representing Ethiopia's traditional governing elite, that had backed Selassie against the hordes of "barbarians" and "bandits" living among "the barren stones of Tigre," as Mengistu described one group of rebels opposed to his regime. The military government's army was, therefore, dominated by Amhara officers. While to a degree disparaging about the Tigre population, Amharic-speakers welcomed their identification with Ethiopia. The Tigre region regarded itself as the birthplace of the 1500-year old Ethiopian Orthodox Church.

Like Emperor Selassie's regime, the Dergue was bent on eliminating Eritrean ethnosecessionism, which had spawned a number of different armed resistance movements. After an initial halfhearted effort to reach a political settlement with some of them, the Dergue returned to the use of military force to suppress Eritrean resistance. Both Selassie's government and the military Marxist one that followed adopted essentially the same counterinsurgency strategy against the separatist Eritrean rebels. The Ethiopian army employed a scorched-earth policy, saturation bombing, and destruction of Eritrea's infrastructure that left 60,000 guerrillas and 40,000 civilians dead by war's end. Two thirds of the population became dependent on some form of food aid. Amara, the capital, escaped with less-serious destruction than other areas.

When the Mengistu government resumed the military assault on the breakaway region, the EPLF and the Eritrean Liberation Front (ELF)—the two principal rebel forces at the time—began to coordinate their resistance struggle. For nearly two decades the Eritrean struggle for independence was crippled by inter–Eritrean military rivalry. From 1977 to 1980 attempts were made to integrate the two fronts more closely, but they ultimately proved unsuccessful. The rivalry was only resolved when, in 1981, EPLF forces crushed ELF units to become the only liberation front in the country.

The Marxist government's policy on Eritrea was similar to Selassie's, but in other areas it did reflect a more nuanced approach to ethnic challenges. For example, the seizure of power by communist forces in 1974 did not lead to the imposition of a monolithic form of Marxism on the country, as had happened in Soviet bloc states. The Ethiopian communist movement refracted ethnic diversity: it broke into more than twenty factions or sects, most of them based on ethnic or regional factors rather than ideological ones. Even the Tigrean and Eritrean rebel armies, which joined forces to defeat the communist regime in 1991, were for a long time self-styled Marxist liberation movements.

With its solid Marxist credentials, the Mengistu government soon received backing from the USSR, then at the height of its expansionist phase. Mengistu established close relations with both Leonid Brezhnev, the Kremlin leader, and Fidel Castro, Cuban ruler and champion of third-world revolution. The growing dependency of the Dergue on Soviet bloc help is described later in our analysis of the internationalization of the Ethiopian conflict.

Ethiopia's Collapse, Eritrea's Independence

The impending collapse of the Soviet Union was mirrored in the Horn of Africa with the disintegration in 1991 of the central government in Addis Ababa. The strength of regionally based national liberation fronts made Mengistu's position untenable, just as the central leadership of Gorbachev was being eroded by the rise of the republics, with Yeltsin serving as spearhead. Eritrea's successful secession would not have been possible without its ability to exercise coalition-building skills that secured the communist government's military defeat in May 1991. A weak Ethiopian state was about to fragment into pieces.

There were two key developments that brought down the Dergue: One was the loss of the USSR as a patron; the other was the deal struck between the EPLF and the Ethiopian People's Revolutionary Democratic Front (EPRDF)—an umbrella group of six armies that was controlled by the Tigre People's Liberation Front (TPLF)—to cooperate militarily and politically. As we have seen, political divisions in Ethiopia have traditionally been ethnic; Mengistu's fall reflected them. There was a division of labor between the EPLF and TPLF. The rebels who captured Addis Ababa in May 1991 were Tigreans. The EPLF would liberate remaining parts of Eritrea from Ethiopian army control. The Tigreans recognized Eritreans' right to self-determination when the war was over; in turn, the EPLF indicated that it would grant the rest of Ethiopia access to the port of Assab on the Red Sea.

In July 1991 the province of Eritrea formally won the right to seek independence from Ethiopia. A thirty-year war of independence that had begun in 1962 had finally produced victory for the battle-hardened Eritrean resistance forces, numbering some 100,000 troops. The capture of the Eritrean capital of Asmara from the Ethiopian army garrison of 120,000 in May 1991, together with the seizure of the two main ports of Assab and Massawa, allowed the rebel forces to satisfy a major criterion for obtaining diplomatic recognition—exercising control over the territory they laid claim to.

Two years after the rebel victory, independence was formalized by way of a referendum. About 1.2 million Eritreans registered to vote for the referendum held in April 1993. One quarter of these were in Sudanese refugee camps, in other parts of Ethiopia, or in the West, pointing to the enthusiasm exhibited by exiles for independence. Voters gave an overwhelming endorsement of independence in the referendum, (officially announced as 99.8 percent for) monitored by 350 outside observers, including a UN Observer Mission to Verify the Referendum in Eritrea (UNOVER). The following month, President Issaias Afeworki, who had been secretary general of the victorious Eritrean resistance forces, declared independence, and Eritrea was admitted into the OAU as its fifty-second member.

Afeworki pledged that building a democratic system was, alongside political stability, the priority of his government. He envisaged devolution of power to regions but also discouraged ethnopolitics. Thus he viewed a multiparty system as potentially destabilizing in that it could lead to the organization of political parties on religious, clan, and tribal bases. Even nomadic ethnic groups spread across Eritrea might be prone to seek a collective identity previously denied them and to politicize it; this would put them at odds with the "nationhood" that Eritrean leaders had proclaimed.

The four-year transitional government established in May 1993 was to step aside for elections in 1997, but President Afeworki left open the possibility that they would be canceled if they would destabilize the young state. He was thinking of the grim events taking place in neighboring Sudan, where a fundamentalist regime was locked in a protracted conflict between Muslims and Christians.

Afeworki disputed the precedent-setting nature and possible domino effect of Eritrean secession. He asserted that its special claim to independence rested on its nineteenth-century status as a distinct European colony. He also advanced the argument often used by secessionist movements, whether they are successful or not, that the achievement of independence by a breakaway state would actually promote closer cooperation among the various states in the region. Afeworki left open the possibility of a form of confederation with Ethiopia at a later time, but his actions seemed to contradict this "good neighbor" approach. Once Eritrea obtained independence, for example, providing a corridor to Ethiopia giving it access to the Red Sea became entangled in legal complexities. Ethiopia became a landlocked country in the Horn of Africa.

What was the fate of Ethiopia after 1991, a state further weakened with the defection of Eritrea? The construction of a coalition government following the overthrow of Mengistu and the secession of Eritrea was a delicate task. The main insurgent group, the EPRDF, headed by new Ethiopian President Meles Zenawi, was based in Tigre province in the north, whose population is primarily Christian. In order to form a national government, the EPRDF had to ally with the Oromo Liberation Front (OLF), centered on the largely Muslim Oromo people of the southern region. The Oromo are Ethiopia's largest ethnic group and speak a language different from the Tigreans. Shortly after the victory over the communists, tensions grew between the two groups as a result of the Tigrean army's (now proclaimed to be the national army) march south into Oromo, where an inevitable tide of reactive nationalism appeared. Skirmishes between the two former coalition partners resulted. Subsequently, in an effort to defuse a further round of ethnonationalism, the Tigrean-dominated EPRDF leadership sought to secure the support of the Oromo, Somali, and previously dominant Amhara through the creation of ethnically defined client parties.

Nevertheless by 1996 the Tigrean-based TPLF came to dominate the Transitional Government of Ethiopia (TGE): Because the Tigres had demonstrated their greater military strength, this balance of power was reflected in the TGE.[25] But the TPLF faced much criticism from a variety of sources. Because of its wartime cooperation with the EPLF and its acceptance of Eritrean independence, it was accused of being a puppet of the EPLF. Undoubtedly the EPLF had some influence over the TPLF; it thereby completed the process by which Eritrea, once a fiefdom of Ethiopia, had become an important player in the rest of Ethiopia's politics.[26]

The Ethiopian legislature created in July 1991 was designed to balance representation among ethnic groups. One third was drawn from the ranks of the EPRDF, one third were Oromo members, and one third were representatives of other groups. Among the twenty-eight Oromo members, twelve belonged to the more nationalist OLF faction, which for a time demanded independence for its region. Matrioshka nationalism seemed to be at work in the Horn of Africa.

The overriding issue casting doubt on the ability of Meles to govern was his recognition of Eritrean independence. It provided ammunition to the internal political opposition that held him responsible for partitioning the country. The Ethiopian president defended his policy, arguing that recognizing Eritrea was "the only sane option" after thirty years of war. Antigovernment feelings in Addis Ababa were not mollified; the loss of an important region was a devastating experience for Ethiopia.

In May 1995 national and local elections were held throughout Ethiopia, the final act in the four-year transition process. The EPRDF formalized its political position as the only national institution of any strength in the country. The new parliament reflected a single-party dominant type of political system.[27] Other regional parties boycotted the elections. Surprisingly, given (or perhaps because of) the experience of Eritrean secession *and* the threat of new ethnosecessionist demands, "The new Ethiopian constitution goes further than any other existing in the world today toward enshrining the principle of ethnic self-determination, up to and including the right of secession."[28]

International Reaction to Eritrean Independence

Shortly after the referendum on independence in May 1991, Eritrea was accepted as a full member of the international system. The TGE as well as the Organization of African Unity (OAU) were now committed to recognizing the 1993 referendum result. OAU Secretary General Salim A. Salim met with Afeworki in July 1991, signaling the first de facto recognition of Eritrea. The Arab Parliamentary Union had consistently supported the Eritrean cause and urged governments of Arab and Islamic states to recognize its independence. There was a danger, of course, that Islamic support could constitute a Trojan horse and allow fundamentalism to spread into the new state. But in sum all the important players in international politics espoused the legitimacy of Eritrean independence.

Eritrea's relations with Ethiopia were normalized: "The end of Cold War politics and superpower rivalry, which had favored Ethiopian interests over those of Eritrea, also equalized the balance of power between the two countries."[29] Following the referendum, the United States still expressed its preference publicly for some kind of loose confederation between Eritrea and Ethiopia. But as key regional actors had accepted Eritrean statehood, it too went along with recognizing Eritrea's independence.

International capital flowed into the state, reaching a total of $250 million in 1995. Prospects of offshore oil stimulated foreign investor interest in the country, and many major oil companies (Mobil, Shell, Total) opened branches in Asmara. A Red Sea vacation resort was also developed. What nearly all international actors were unwilling to do—recognize Eritrea—so long as a war dragged on in the country, they were prepared to accept once a weak state with weak central government imploded.

Internationalization

The Eritrean conflict was internationalized from the time the Four Powers could not agree on a common approach to the Horn of Africa in the late 1940s. Both sides to the conflict relied heavily on external support to carry on the struggle. From the figures we give below, we clearly see how the wars in Ethiopia became internationalized.

The military capacity of the Ethiopian army was heavily dependent on the United States until the fall of the emperor. Between 1953 and 1970 the United States provided about $150 million in military assistance to Ethiopia, representing one half of such aid to all African countries combined. In 1970 two thirds of American military aid to Africa went to Addis Ababa. By 1976, two years after the fall of the emperor, cumulative U.S. military aid to Ethiopia had risen to $280 million, and an additional $350 million had been given in economic assistance.[30]

If the degree of U.S. commitment comes as a surprise, an illuminating explanation has been provided by Andargachew Tiruneh: "Observers of Ethiopian politics often express surprise at the extent of U.S. support for Ethiopia. However, this overlooks one important fact: Ethiopia during that period was not so much in military competition with the African countries as with those of the Middle East."[31] Many Middle Eastern states, influenced by pan–Islamism, Pan–Arabism, or both, considered that the world Islamic community and the Arab fatherland stretched to the mountains and plains of Ethiopia. It was these forces that the United States set out to stop in giving extensive support to Ethiopia.

It was only in 1977 that U.S. President Jimmy Carter, concerned about human rights abuses in Ethiopia, and the U.S. Congress, upset by a $100 million arms deal between the Dergue and the Soviet Union, cut off all further American military aid. In May 1977 a secret pact with the USSR provided Addis Ababa with $500 million worth of arms, including MiG-21 jets and SA-7 surface-to-air missiles. Following a massive airlift of sophisticated military equipment in 1978, it was reported that Soviet aid had topped $1 billion. Later that year, the USSR signed a twenty-year treaty of friendship with Ethiopia which included a provision for military cooperation.

By 1979 other allies of the USSR contributed support to the Mengistu government. Cuba sent 18,000 troops to Ethiopia. Libya, which switched sides following Ethiopia's 1974 Marxist revolution, gave $100 million in 1977 alone. Other Warsaw Pact members, especially East Germany, along with South Yemen, also gave military assistance to the Dergue. To be sure, not all of this aid was earmarked for Ethiopia's struggle with Eritrean rebels. The 1977–1978 war that began when Somalia attacked the Ogaden region of Ethiopia, where many ethnic Somalis live, was another reason for such massive aid. Massive arms transfers and direct participation by the Cuban military allowed Ethiopia to prevail in the Ogaden. Somalia had itself been a Soviet client state between 1969 and 1977 when Brezhnev switched his support to Ethiopia; in addition to strategic factors, Ethiopia's population of 25 million compared to Somalia's 3 million prompted the change. Somalia tried, in turn, to find a new patron and turned to the United States for aid against the communist forces in the Ogaden. But President Carter turned the request down. It is debatable, then, whether "proxyization" of the conflict in the Horn of Africa came about. Rather than viewing conflicts in the Horn of Africa, including the Ethiopian–Eritrean struggle, in terms of proxy wars between the superpowers, a more accurate view is that of changing patron–client relationships.

After the United States, Israel was the next most important supporter of Selassie's government. Depicting Ethiopia as an island in a Muslim sea similar to itself, Israel was also concerned about keeping open its shipping lanes through the Red Sea that an Eritrea that controlled the Bab al-Mandeb Strait could cut off. As a result, Israeli military advisers helped train Selassie's Imperial Bodyguard and Ethiopian commandos in counterinsurgency techniques. Israel continued to give support to the Dergue until early 1978 when, like the United States, it pulled the plug once the Soviet–Ethiopia axis was forged.

For its part, the Eritrean resistance was unable initially to find any one large donor nation and had to make do with piecemeal support from a variety of sources, mostly in the Arab world. The ELF began to receive military and financial aid from the anti–Israeli Syrian regime from the mid–1960s and, later, from Iraq. It also had the backing of the government in neighboring Sudan, but that was ended temporarily in 1967 when a deal was struck between Addis Ababa and Khartoum under which each country would stop supporting rebel forces in the other country. But in 1969 three coups d'etat in the region—in Libya by Mu'ammar al-Gadhafi, in Somalia by Muhammad Siad Barre, and in the Sudan by General Gaafar Numeiri—resulted in increased support for the ELP. Another radical regime backing the ELF for a time was Southern Yemen. Eritrean forces also received limited economic aid from two conservative Arab states—Saudi Arabia and Kuwait. But as Iyob pointed out, "These links to the Arab world proved to be more a liability than an asset to the Eritrean cause because they were interpreted as a continuation of the 'Arab' and 'balkanization' threat to Ethiopia and Africa."[32] Repeated efforts to depict the Eritrean struggle as that of an African country colonized by another had limited impact.

Let us now examine the part played by international actors in the events leading to the breakup of Ethiopia. Until early 1991 U.S. policy had been to adhere to the concept of a unified Ethiopia, even if it was being governed by a Soviet-backed communist regime. The United States was concerned with creating a precedent for Africa if the independence of a breakaway state was recognized: Eritrean independence could set off a demonstration effect, giving encouragement to other movements in what was left of Ethiopia, in other countries in the Horn of Africa (such as northern Somalia), and across the continent. As we have stressed, African countries' colonially imposed borders made them particularly vulnerable to breakup.

Gorbachev's rise to power in the USSR in 1985 had begun to mollify American objections to the Soviet presence in Ethiopia. Gorbachev's "new thinking" included a reconsideration of Soviet policy in Africa. In 1988 Soviet Deputy Premier Anatoly Adanishin met with U.S. Assistant Secretary of State for African Affairs Chester Crocker in London to discuss reducing superpower competition in the Horn of Africa. Soviet propaganda attacks on Eritrea were subsequently scaled back. At the same time, in 1990 Crocker openly acknowledged that Haile Selassie's unilateral abrogation of the federation with Eritrea had been illegal. He stated that the United States recognized Eritrea's right to self-determination within the framework of Ethiopian territorial unity.

At the June 1990 summit between Gorbachev and President Bush, both leaders signaled their intent to cooperate on the Ethiopian problem. Both promised relief aid for Ethiopia, which was in the midst of a famine. The summit communique also asserted that "the U.S. and U.S.S.R. will support an international conference of governments under the auspices of the U.N. on settlement of conflict situations in the Horn of Africa."[33] As events turned out, by 1991 only the United States was in a position to offer mediation during the endgame phase of the conflict.

External Mediation

While Soviet efforts to prop up the Dergue in the 1970s and 1980s are well known, it is surprising to learn of the pivotal role played by the United States in engineering the downfall of Mengistu, his replacement by Meles, and the change in political status of Eritrea. In the last days of the war in May 1991, the United States announced for the first time that it would support Eritrea's right to self-determination. With the sudden collapse of Africa's largest army, the Ethiopian communist government forces, in April 1991—largely due to the withdrawal of political and military support for it by the Soviet Union—the United States entered into secret diplomacy with Mengistu.

To begin with, the United States masterminded the transfer of Ethiopia's 15,000-strong Jewish population to Israel for which Mengistu and his cohorts may have received a $35 million payment from Israel.[34] The United States simultaneously became involved as a mediator to create an orderly succession to Mengistu. Bush administration envoys signaled to the communists, now in an untenable position, that in exchange for letting the Ethiopian Jews leave, Washington was prepared to mediate peace talks between government and rebel forces, thereby assuring the "extrication" of the Dergue. In May 1991, U.S. Assistant Secretary of State for African Affairs Herman Cohen chaired a peace conference of contending Ethiopian forces in London. He sought to ensure an orderly transition process involving both the removal of Mengistu and the secession of Eritrea, consistent with the facts on the ground.

Once Mengistu had safely departed the country for exile in Zimbabwe, the United States next tried to create conditions for a peaceful takeover by the Tigre rebels. Efforts were made to reassure the Amharas in Addis Ababa that the Tigre forces entering the city on May 28 would do them no harm. An American statement was broadcast announcing that Tigre rebels would be entering Addis Ababa the next day with Washington's approval. In addition, U.S. envoys secretly asked Eritrean rebel leaders to hold back on their announcement of a referendum on the region's independence, in this way postponing the dramatic news that Ethiopia was to be partitioned.

Nevertheless, as Tigrean forces moved into the capital, the Amhara population learned that a referendum on Eritrean independence would indeed be held. Violent demonstrations broke out, and the U.S. embassy was attacked for its role in approving the partition of Ethiopia.[35] Incongruously, then, the Amhara population protested Eritrean secession by demonstrating against the incoming Tigre rebel forces and condemning the eleventh-hour support the United States had lent to the latter. Nevertheless, the military realities in Ethiopia that U.S. realism accepted were to determine the final outcome of the conflict.

One international actor that had a responsibility for helping mediate the conflict in Ethiopia was the OAU. For nearly three decades, however, the approach taken by the OAU toward Eritrean secession was to keep out of the conflict. Refusing to mediate was, of course, to side with whoever was winning on the battlefield. Formed in May 1963 in Addis Ababa, five months after Ethiopia's incorporation of Eritrea, the OAU Charter was biased toward preserving the integrity of existing states. Article III, paragraph 3 of its charter affirms "respect for the sovereignty and territorial integrity of each State and for its inalienable right to independent existence." OAU refusal, until the early 1990s when the military balance had changed, to address the issue of Eritrean independence was based, ironically, on its desire not to dispute colonial borders. Iyob explained OAU behavior in more searing terms: "By 1964 the OAU had become sufficiently dominated by Ethiopia to function as little more than a rubber stamp for the hegemon's claims. Ethiopia's role in the drafting of the OAU Charter and the emphasis on non-intervention and the safeguarding of existing boundaries legitimated its claims and delegitimated any claims which countered the prevailing consensus."[36]

The unique case of successful secession that we have examined shows the importance of external actors to the final outcome. In turn the United States and USSR sought to bolster a weak Ethiopian state. The determination of Eritrea's resistance forces to make good on its past status as colony and gain statehood was reinforced by assistance from largely Arab countries. In the last days of the war, the United States engaged in complex and often secret diplomacy to ensure an orderly collapse of a weak state. Finally, the one domino effect that was clear in the wake of Eritrea's proclamation of independence in 1991 was the diplomatic recognition extended by one external actor after another.

WEAK STATES, POLITICIZED IDENTITIES IN CENTRAL AFRICA

Perhaps nowhere else is the perception that ancient hatreds account for mass killings more accepted than to explain events in Rwanda and Burundi in the 1990s. Hutu and Tutsi identities and their hatred of each other are taken as given by many observers. Yet, even in Central Africa, we discover that ethnic identities are sometimes not so much acquisitions inherited at birth but ascriptions, engendered by the need to anchor artificial states in collective identities.

Here is an analysis of the bases of identity in a part of Africa that has seen the worst explosion of ethnic conflict in the 1990s: "A woman living in central Africa drew her identity from where she was born, from her lineage and in-laws, and from her wealth. Tribal or ethnic identity was rarely important in everyday life and could change as people moved over vast areas in pursuit of trade or new lands. Conflicts were more often within tribal categories than between them, as people fought over sources of water, farmland, or grazing rights."[37]

The reference by John Bowen, author of this passage, is to the conflict in Rwanda, site of a tragic genocide between April and July 1994. While accepting that in parts of the country ethnic identities have more salience (northern Rwanda) than in others (southern Rwanda), he nevertheless contended that "It was the colonial powers, and the independent states succeeding them, which declared that each and every person had an 'ethnic identity' that determined his or her place within the colony or the postcolonial system." The colonial powers had long ago recognized the importance of securing allies from among the native population. The prerequisite for fomenting ethnic schism and, therefore, divide-and-rule tactics was forging ethnic markers between groups. The early colonizers of the region were the Germans, followed by the French and Belgians. After World War II both Burundi and Rwanda became United Nations trust territories, and both obtained independence in 1962.

Colonial powers politicized ethnicity. Bowen writes how "In Rwanda and Burundi, German and Belgian colonizers admired the taller people called Tutsis, who formed a small minority in both colonies. The Belgians gave the Tutsis privileged access to education and jobs and even instituted a minimum height requirement for entrance to college." The irony was, of course, that "Hutus and Tutsis had intermarried to such an extent that they were not easily distinguished physically (nor are they today)."[38] The two groups share the same language and customs in Rwanda, just as they share another language and other customs in Burundi. Hutus are set off from each other by clan and regional affiliations, just as Tutsis are. They are not unified communities whose only dividing line is Hutu-Tutsi.

For René Lemarchand, then, "it is the interplay between ethnic realities and their subjective reconstruction (or manipulation) by political entrepreneurs that lies at the root of the Hutu-Tutsi conflict."[39] Thinking in ethnic categories and inflating and politicizing their significance serve as a smokescreen for conflict over the more fundamental matters of power and resources.

As in South Africa, Burundi and Rwanda faced political transitions in the early 1990s that might have led to greater democratization. Unlike South Africa, however, the two Central African states ended up with "aborted transitions" because of a lack of clarity in the transition bargain, a failure of leadership, an obstructionist attitude by opposition forces, and the lack of support for the transition by the military.[40] In Burundi, Melchior Ndadaye, the country's first popularly elected president and a moderate Hutu, was killed by Tutsi extremists in October 1993. Tutsi control over Burundi's security services had always made Ndadaye's power seem limited. Employing a stimulus-response model, this assassination was the catalyst for revenge by Hutu extremists carried out in neighboring Rwanda. Rwanda's President Juvénal Habyarimana was a Hutu who became a pawn in the hands of extremists from his own ethnic group. Well-supplied with military equipment by France, which wished to ensure that power in the ethnically divided country remained centralized, Habyarimana, who became ruler in 1973, had no reason to pursue a policy of reconciliation. France conveniently ignored the increasing human rights abuses taking place in Rwanda.

The genocide in Rwanda began when the president was killed in a mysterious plane crash in April 1994. Hutu-dominated militias were formed and incited to slaughter one-half million or more Tutsis, a minority that had formed the traditional ruling class in the region. "'The [Hutu] extremists' aim,' says Africa Rights, 'was for the entire Hutu populace to participate in the killing. That way, the blood of genocide would stain everybody.'"[41] The murderous Hutu "response" had the effect of producing ethnic polarization in Rwanda as well as in Burundi, where ethnic massacres had taken place in 1965, 1972, and 1988. It also was the "stimulus" Tutsis needed in the two countries to launch their own round of reprisals.

In mid–1994, the Tutsi-dominated Rwandan Patriotic Front (RPF), which had first launched an attack on the Habyarimana regime in 1990 but was beaten back with Belgian, French, and Zairian military assistance, inflicted a series of defeats on the Hutus and brought Tutsi leaders to power in the country. Despite their denials, these rulers presided over the revenge killings of more than 100,000 Hutus. Even more died of cholera, dysentry, and violence when two million Hutus had to flee to refugee camps in Tanzania and Zaire. In 1995 the ethnic conflict spread to neighboring Burundi where the similar fault lines prevail. The killings were contained on a lesser scale than in Rwanda, but Tutsis again consolidated their power base. In October 1996, taking advantage of the terminal illness of long-standing Zairean dictator Joseph Mobutu, the RPF attacked a Hutu refugee camp in Goma, located in Zaire and then joined forces with Zairean rebels to drive Mobutu from power in May 1997.

Ethnic conflict had been internationalized, to be sure, but it seemed to have been transformed into an empire-building project. Rwandan leaders were accused of seeking to establish a Tutsi empire that would replace the weak states of the region. A variation on this perspective is that only the creation of two new states in place of Rwanda and Burundi, defined ethnically (which would require ethnic resettlement) and called Uhutu and Tutsiland, offers a prospect for long-term peace in the region.

State collapse and the struggle for political power between two groups was primarily responsible for genocide in Rwanda. The existence of weak states in neighboring Burundi and Zaire contributed to the spread of ethnic conflict. International actors were powerless to do anything about the mass killings other than provide the most basic forms of humanitarian relief. Peacekeeping missions, whether by the UN or by European states with an interest in the region such as Belgium and France, never got off the ground. Taken together with seemingly intractable conflicts in Angola, Liberia, Somalia, and Sudan, the Rwanda massacre gave new urgency to the creation of African structures that could help manage civil strife.

Africa specialist Ali Mazrui, for example, recognized that the United Nations could serve as a peacekeeper in Africa but not as a peacemaker or peace enforcer. The UN could make a bigger difference in Africa, where the stakes in human lives is high, than elsewhere: "Even its 'failed' enterprise in Somalia probably saved more lives than its 'success story' in Cambodia."[42] But Mazrui echoed the position of many others, including that elaborated by U.S. Secretary of State Christopher during his visit to Africa in October 1996, that "Africans must establish an African peace enforced by Africans."[43] He recommended the establishment of an African Security Council that would be made up of key regional states. As an example he cited the probable regional power in Central Africa of the future, Zaire, which had the population and resources necessary to play an important role. "If Zaire can avoid collapsing into chaos in the near future, it will be one of the major actors in Africa in the twenty-first century, taking Burundi and Rwanda under its wing."[44] Paradoxically, Laurent Kabila, head of the rebel coalition that ousted Mobutu, was accused by detractors of surrendering Zaire to Rwandan Tutsi forces. The notion of a pan–African peacekeeping force to interpose itself in conflicts has gained adherents in the absence of other kinds of international intervention but its composition is highly problematic.

On the other hand, Barry Buzan and Gerald Segal among others have noted that there is fading support for a global humanitarian agenda. "Given the half-hearted response to the horrors of Rwanda, it is not too farfetched to think that humanitarian issues are becoming more theater than reality for most of the developed world."[45] In sum, third parties remain more prone to internationalize ethnic conflict when their national interests can be advanced. They demonstrate less commitment to the international mediation of such conflict.

DISCUSSION QUESTIONS

1. What are the characteristics of weak states? How do ethnonationalist groups exploit the weakness of central authorities to advance their own political autonomy? Are these dynamics limited to states in Africa?
2. Explain why armed ethnosecessionist movements in the Congo and Nigeria were defeated. What was the importance of external actors to these outcomes? Did international organizations play a pivotal role in either of the countries?
3. What historical grievances were advanced by Eritrean nationalists to justify independence from Ethiopia? Explain the part played by colonialism in differentiating Eritrea from Ethiopia.
4. Did international organizations serve as impartial mediators during the protracted military conflict between Eritrea and Ethiopia? What part did they play in formalizing Eritrean independence? What part did the United States have in making Eritrean independence possible?
5. Do politicized identities or ethnic ones explain the atrocities committed between Hutus and Tutsis in Rwanda and Burundi in the 1990s? Did any third parties seek to perform peacemaking roles? Did any seek to carry out humanitarian missions?

NOTES

1. Ian S. Lustick, *Unsettled States, Disputed Lands: Britain and Ireland, France and Algeria, Israel and the West Bank-Gaza.* (Ithaca, NY: Cornell University Press, 1993), p. 442.
2. I. William Zartman, "Introduction: Posing the Problem of State Collapse," in Zartman, ed., *Collapsed States: The Disintegration and Restoration of Legitimate Authority.* (Boulder, CO: Lynne Rienner, 1995), p. 1.
3. *Ibid.,* p. 5. We examine Kaplan's related analysis of African states in Chapter 9 concerned with the U.S. response to an ethnicized world order.
4. On the Congo, Nigeria, and other cases of "subnationalism," see Victor A. Olorunsola, ed., *The Politics of Cultural Sub-Nationalism in Africa: Africa and the Problem of "One State,*

Many Nationalisms." (Garden City, NY: Anchor Books, 1972). For a study before decolonialization, see Thomas Hodgkin, *Nationalism in Colonial Africa.* (New York: New York University Press, 1957). For one after indigenization, see Timothy K. Welliver, ed., *African Nationalism and Independence.* (Hamden, CT: Garland Publishing, 1993).

5. Dan Connell, *Against All Odds: A Chronicle of the Eritrean Revolution.* (Trenton, NJ: Red Sea Press, 1993). This book provides an eyewitness account of the last years of the war.

6. On Katanga, see Howard M. Epstein, ed., *Revolt in the Congo, 1960–64.* (New York: Facts on File, 1965); Jules Gerard-Libois, *Katanga Secession.* (Madison, WI: University of Wisconsin Press, 1966); Catherine Hoskyns, *The Congo Since Independence: January 1960–December 1961.* (Oxford: Oxford University Press, 1965); Ernest W. Lefever, *Crisis in the Congo: A United Nations Force in Action.* (Washington, DC: Brookings Institute, 1965); Ernest W. Lefever, *Uncertain Mandate: Politics of the U.N. Congo Operation.* (Baltimore, MD: Johns Hopkins University Press, 1967); Crawford Young and Thomas Turner, *The Rise and Decline of the Zairian State.* (Madison, WI: University of Wisconsin Press, 1985); Stephen R. Weissman, *American Foreign Policy in the Congo, 1960–1964.* (Ithaca, NY: Cornell University Press, 1974). We are grateful to Stephen M. Saideman for constructive criticism of and bibliographic references for this section.

7. Donald Horowitz, *Ethnic Groups in Conflict.* (Berkeley, CA: University of California Press, 1985), pp. 255–256.

8. Alexis Heraclides, "Secessionist Minorities and External Involvement." *International Organization.* 44, 1990, p. 343.

9. Thomas Hovet, Jr., *Africa in the United Nations.* (Chicago: Northwestern University Press, 1963), p. 46.

10. See James Coleman, *Nigeria: A Background to Nationalism.* (Berkeley, CA: Universtiy of California Press, 1958).

11. Crawford Young, "The Impossible Necessity of Nigeria: A Struggle for Nationhood." *Foreign Affairs,* 75, 6, November/December 1996, p. 143.

12. See Zdenek Cervenka, *A History of the Nigerian War, 1967–1970.* (Ibadan, Nigeria: Onibonoje Press, 1972); Suzanne Cronje, *The World and Nigeria: the Diplomatic History of the Biafran War 1967–1970.* (London: Sidgwick and Jackson, 1972); John de St. Jorre, *The Brothers' War: Biafra and Nigeria.* (Boston: Houghton Mifflin, 1972); A.H.M. Kirk-Greene, ed., *Crisis and Conflict in Nigeria: A Documentary Sourcebook, 1966–1970.* (Oxford: Oxford University Press, 1971); John J. Stremlau, *The International Politics of the Nigerian Civil War, 1967–1970.* (Princeton, NJ: Princeton University Press, 1977). We acknowledge the helpful comments and list of sources supplied by Stephen M. Saideman.

13. The Muslim–Christian divide still has political salience. See Obi Igwara, "Holy Nigerian Nationalisms and Apocalyptic Visions of the Nation." *Nations and Nationalism,* 1, 3, November 1995, pp. 327–355.

14. This information was discussed by one of the authors in the course of an interview with then deputy minister for Africa in the British Foreign Office, the Right Honorable Maurice Foley, M.P., in June 1970.

15. See Wole Soyinka, *The Open Sore of a Continent: A Personal Narrative of the Nigerian Crisis.* (New York: Oxford University Press, 1996).

16. G.K.N. Trevaskis, *Eritrea: A Colony in Transition.* (London: Oxford University Press, 1960), pp. 10–11.

17. Okbazghi Yohannes, *Eritrea: A Pawn in World Politics.* (Gainesville, FL: University of Florida Press, 1991), p. 91.

18. For the text, see Habtu Ghebre-Ab, *Ethiopia and Eritrea: A Documentary Study.* (Trenton, NJ: Red Sea Press, 1993), pp. 135–140.

19. Yohannes, *Eritrea,* p. 258.

20. Tom J. Farer, *War Clouds on the Horn of Africa.* (Washington, DC: Carnegie Endowment for International Peace, 1976), p. 137.
21. Ruth Iyob, *The Eritrean Struggle for Independence: Domination, Resistance, Nationalism, 1941–1993.* (Cambridge: Cambridge University Press, 1995), p. 51.
22. Ruth Iyob, "Regional Hegemony: Domination and Resistance in the Horn of Africa." *Journal of Modern African Studies,* 31, 2, June 1993, p. 270.
23. For a detailed study of the 1974 revolution, see Andargachew Tiruneh, *The Ethiopian Revolution 1974–1987: A Transformation From an Aristocratic to a Totalitarian Autocracy.* (Cambridge: Cambridge University Press, 1993).
24. See Ryszard Kapuscinski, *The Emperor: Downfall of an Autocrat.* (New York: Vintage Books, 1984).
25. Edmond J. Keller, "Remaking the Ethiopian State," in Zartman, ed., *Collapsed States,* pp. 133–135.
26. For a critique of this view, see John Young, "The Tigray and Eritrean Peoples Liberation Fronts: A History of Tensions and Pragmatism." *Journal of Modern African Studies,* 34, 1, March 1996, pp. 105–120.
27. Terence Lyons, "Closing the Transition: the May 1995 Elections in Ethiopia." *Journal of Modern African Studies,* 34, 1, March 1996, p. 142.
28. Crawford Young, "Africa: An Interim Balance Sheet." *Journal of Democracy,* 7, 3, July 1996, p. 64.
29. Iyob, *The Eritrean Struggle for Independence,* p. 138.
30. Cited by Richard Sherman, *Eritrea: The Unfinished Revolution.* (New York: Praeger, 1980), pp. 75, 83. For other details of U.S. involvement in Ethiopia, also see pp. 141–148.
31. Tiruneh, *The Ethiopian Revolution,* p. 20.
32. Iyob, *The Eritrean Struggle for Independence,* p. 127.
33. U.S.–USSR Joint Statement on Ethiopia, June 2, 1990. Reported in Yohannes, *Eritrea,* p. 278.
34. We should recall that during "Operation Moses" in 1984–1985, Israel airlifted more than 7000 Jews out of Ethiopia in a clandestine mission.
35. This account is taken from Jane Perlez, "New View of Ethiopia." *The New York Times.* May 31, 1991.
36. Iyob, *The Eritrean Struggle for Independence,* p. 27.
37. John R. Bowen, "The Myth of Global Ethnic Conflict." *Journal of Democracy,* 7, 4, October 1996, p. 6.
38. *Ibid.,* p. 6.
39. Rene Lemarchand, "Managing Transitional Anarchies: Rwanda, Burundi, and South Africa in Comparative Perspective." *Journal of Modern African Studies,* 32, 4, December 1994, p. 588.
40. *Ibid.*
41. Jack Snyder and Karen Ballentine, "Nationalism and the Marketplace of Ideas." *International Security,* 21, 2, Fall 1996, p. 32.
42. Ali A. Mazrui, "The New Dynamics of Security: The United Nations and Africa." *World Policy Journal,* 13, 2, Summer 1996, p. 38.
43. *Ibid.,* p. 40.
44. *Ibid.,* p. 39.
45. Barry Buzan and Gerald Segal, "The Rise of 'Lite' Powers: A Strategy for the Postmodern State." *World Policy Journal,* 13, 3, Fall 1996, p. 7.

chapter 9

The U.S. Response to Nationalism

STUDYING POST–BIPOLAR POLICY MAKING

The turn-of-the-millennium world is, as we have observed in this book, a world of spreading ethnonationalist unrest. Ethnic conflicts frequently become internationalized, but, conversely, it is not often that international organizations can effectively manage them. The postmodern world is one of fragmenting identities; there seems to be no force presently capable of forging a widely accepted, more universal identity. Moroccan writer Fatima Mernissi has trenchantly described the postmodern dilemma that we have encountered in this book: "Our fin-de-siècle era resembles the apocalypse. Boundaries and standards seem to be disappearing. Interior space is scarcely distinguishable from exterior."[1]

In such a kaleidoscopic world of changing identities, alliances, and affiliations, defining the role that a state should play in the international system requires fresh thinking. The usefulness of past experiences, precedents, analogies, and axioms to making foreign policy decisions is limited, for where the distinction between interior and exterior political space is fading and boundaries are increasingly permeable, it is hard to formulate a foreign policy that has fixed and constant perimeters.

No country carries as great a responsibility in the international system as the world's sole superpower, the United States.[2] Numerous factors affect a state's foreign policy, and in the case of a superpower, many international organizations, regions, and issue areas require a response from it. In this chapter, we analyse U.S. foreign policy as it relates to problems posed by ethnic conflicts. We also examine the factors that are influential in the evolution of such foreign policy. Often, domestic influences are as important as international exigencies, so we briefly examine policy toward ethnic and minority questions in the United States. But U.S. foreign policy responses to crises in Russia, Somalia, and Bosnia must, above all, be framed in terms of U.S. national interests, and moral arguments are likely to be of secondary importance. In this chapter, then, we identify the policy options on resolving ethnic conflict that serve U.S. interests. We also compare the moral and political consequences of an interventionist approach where the United States manages ethnic conflict, and an isolationist one where the United States believes it has no important stake in such conflicts. Finally, as a case study that gives evidence of both these approaches, we study the evolution of the Clinton administration's policy on Bosnia.

THE U.S. EXPERIENCE AS FOREIGN POLICY INFLUENCE

It is easy to exaggerate the importance of our own United States national experience as a factor that exerts influence on foreign policy, but it would be remiss to ignore this theme. In his first inaugural address, delivered in March 1861, Abraham Lincoln stated: "I hold that, in contemplation of universal law, and of the Constitution, the Union of these states is perpetual. Perpetuity is implied, if not expressed, in the fundamental law of all national governments. It is safe to assert that no government proper ever had a provision in its organic law for its own termination." Lincoln's argument against secession went further: "If the United States be not a government proper, but an association of states in the nature of contract merely, can it, as a contract, be peaceably unmade by less than all the parties who made it? One party to a contract may violate it—break it, so to speak; but does it not require all to lawfully rescind it?"[3] This reasoning against the fragmentation of an existing state, combined with the tragedy of the Civil War that followed, made the United States, more than most countries, wary of the phenomenon of secessionism.

The United States experience reinforces the bias of the international normative regime mitigating against the breakup of states. The antisecessionist bias of U.S. foreign policy was demonstrated in the September 1995 accord concluded in New York by the warring sides to the Bosnian conflict to preserve the territorial integrity of that precarious state. Russia stood with the United States in upholding this norm. In his meetings with Bosnian contact group members immediately after the New York accord, Foreign Minister Andrei Kozyrev admitted that for Russia to take any position other than support for the integrity of existing states would produce more Chechnyas within the Russian Federation itself. Russia also backed off supporting independence for breakaway groups like the Abkhaz in Georgia. With two great powers declaring opposition to the idea of secession, the international system provided scant opportunity for the creation of new states out of parts of old ones.

Cultural Diversity

The United States' experience lends some weight to the view that a plurality of cultures can coexist in one state. The first interpretation of American identity as cultural pluralism was presented by Horace Kallen in 1915.[4] The next year, a rare U.S. social-ist writer, Randolph Bourne, endorsed the path of cultural development taken by an otherwise individualistic, capitalist society:

> America is already the world federation in miniature, the continent where for the first time in history has been achieved that miracle of hope, the peaceful living side by side, with character substantially preserved, of the most heterogeneous peoples under the sun. Nowhere else has such contigu-ity been anything but the breeder of misery.[5]

In the 1960s, before it became fashionable to celebrate diversity, Louis Hartz wrote about "fragment cultures"—societies founded upon settlers coming from vari-ous parts of Europe, each representing a part of the total culture of Europe. He con-tended that in the United States the fragment ethic, crystallized early on in the Puritan consensus, was converted into a source of national identity and was preserved by the principle of federalism. In the nineteenth century, the fragment ethic had been chal-lenged by the institution of slavery. Hartz noted the peculiarity of attempting to resolve the contradiction between fragment culture and slavery: "The clash here took place, for all of the activity of the Negro, mainly within the European population; the violence of the slave relationship, because it could not be digested by the fragment morality, was transferred to a struggle among the masters themselves. That struggle ended with the emancipation of the African, the termination of legalized force against him, but it did not bring him fully into the Lockean community."[6] Only with the Civil Rights movement of the 1960s did the U.S. multicultural experience finally reach out and subsume the black minority, long left out of the U.S. fragment culture.

Whether U.S. exceptionalism has embraced diversity in an unqualified way has been subject to scrutiny by generations of scholars. The mythical character of the idea of "a nation of immigrants" has been repeatedly challenged: "Belief in that overarch-ing ideal is why America remains the most successful experiment in ethnic diver-sity—a cruel irony, considering that the country rests on a wholesale cleansing of its native people."[7]

The historical experience of African Americans also seriously questions the diversity myth. Black American nationalism has its own history and E.U. Essien-Udom, for example, described how the Nation of Islam movement sought to discover "a saving identity with which to transcend the social, psychological, and spiritual bar-riers of the 'invisible ghetto.'"[8] Discrimination and exploitation suffered by black Americans were mirrored, some black nationalists argued, in U.S. neocolonial atti-tudes to the developing world. This interpretation contrasted with Hartz's diversity desideratum from which it could be extrapolated that recognizing diversity at home was likely to lead to recognition of the benefits of diversity in the world.

More recently, sociologist Seymour Martin Lipset juxtaposed the experience of African Americans and Jews to contrast still-prevalent racism against blacks with "the United States at its best"—the Jewish success story in the United States.[9] In turn, histo-rian Michael Lind traced the evolution of the United States from its "First Republic"—"Anglo-America"—which reached its apogee in the mid–nineteenth century, through its Second—"Euro-America," which arrived at its zenith in the mid–twentieth century.

Whereas both were founded on white supremacy, the building in the 1960s of a Third Republic—"Multicultural America"—was a repudiation of the melting-pot conception of U.S. identity. In its place a "mosaic" conception was advanced: "five races or race-like communities—whites, blacks or African-Americans, Hispanics or Latinos, Asian and Pacific Islanders, and native Americans. . . . These races are not mere ingredients to be blended in a future unity, but permanently distinct communities." What is more, "Those who criticize the fivefold race-culture-political bloc scheme are, by definition, racists who wish to turn back the clock to the era of white supremacy."[10] But Lind noted that some thirty years after its founding, the Third Republic had still not received widespread legitimacy among the people of the United States. By pouring scorn on the contrived nature of "Multicultural America" and its failure to address the real problems of ethnicity, immigration, and racism, the author questioned whether diversity has been successfully realized in this country.

Even the "nation of immigrants" idea has come under fire in recent years. A growing number of U.S. residents react to the idea by saying "that was then; this is now." One immigration scholar, summarizing the evidence, concluded that "recent reports do not suggest that immigration's domestic economic effects are completely positive anymore." In fact, in the 1980s the effects of immigration, legal or not, may have become negative. As a result, "These changes certainly weaken the electorate's conviction that current immigration is in the national self-interest of the United States."[11] U.S. insularity was in evidence, then, in both domestic and some foreign policy areas.

Let us accept the reservations about the U.S.'s real commitment to diversity recorded by some scholars but also contend that the U.S. experience has, in comparative terms, been a positive one for a remarkably large number of groups. How can this fact influence the making of U.S. foreign policy? Writing in the 1990s, historian John Lewis Gaddis affirmed the linkage between diversity in U.S. life and tolerance of it in the international arena:

> It requires no great insight to note that the world is a diverse place. But it required a rather remarkable combination of both luck and skill to maintain a political system that was comfortable with diversity at home, and hence prepared, for the most part, to tolerate it in the world at large. The success with which Americans accomplished this task, the extent to which they were able to reconcile the appeal of spontaneity with the fact of power, may well have been, more than anything else, the key to the influence they were able to bring to bear over the rest of the world during the twentieth century.[12]

Bourne's reference to "the American mind in the world" that projects a multicultural vision of states still has resonance today. The advantage of such an understanding is that it offers a view of existing multinational states, which comprise the vast majority in the international system, as viable rather than doomed to breakup. Summarizing the U.S. position in contemporary international politics, Daniel Patrick Moynihan posited: "This may be harsh, and yet American policy seemed at times incapable of conceptualizing a world in which states break up."[13]

Moynihan criticized Woodrow Wilson's foreign policy during World War I. In his view, the United States defined itself in an arbitrary, unexpected way:

> While the American people knew themselves to be singularly various, American elites were offering up a mere three identities. We could be German, Anglo-Saxon, or American. Wilson *could* have kept us out of war, thereby hugely enhancing the notion of American isolation and exceptionalism. He *could* have sided with Germany in the emergent cause of anti-imperialism, espousing freedom for Ireland and India. The Germans, a decent, democratic folk, were actively supporting both these fine insurgencies. . . . But no. Wilson . . . took us *into* war to preserve the British Empire with its huddled masses on which never set the sun.[14]

Moynihan implied that "Woodrow Wilson, Scotch-Irish that he was, believed that Americans were of the 'Anglo-Saxon race' and need come to the rescue of their brethren in Britain."[15]

With his stress on self-determination of peoples in multinational European empires, Wilson seemed to part ways with the mainstream U.S. tradition of lending support to multinational states. To be sure, his intention was to dismantle antiquated empires, not multicultural states. Still, his concern with "natural" ethnically defined boundaries for Poland, Italy, and other countries was an endorsement of homogeneous communities. Taking into account the peculiar nature of ethnonational communities—"Ethnic conflict does not require great differences; small will do"[16]—the Wilsonian project was bound to fail. Indeed, it was invoked by Hitler to justify irredentism and expansionism, justifying his coming to the rescue of the German minority stranded in the Sudentenland and to secure the German identity of Austria by way of its annexation.

Wilsonian idealism was somewhat of an aberration, then, in U.S. foreign policy. But for those who support U.S. activism in international affairs, it remains an important guide map. Arguing the case for U.S. engagement in certain contemporary ethnic conflicts, political scientist Tony Smith asserted: "The genius of Wilsonianism has been that it has not tried to challenge so much as to channel this upsurge of nationalist sentiment."[17] We return to the contentious issue of interventionism below. Here we should note that from the Civil War onward, the United States—the first nation to assert the right of self-determination—was inconsistent and frequently sought to deny that right to others.

Cultural Features

There are other features of U.S. political life that help explain its conduct in the international arena. Let us look for a moment at U.S. culture. Political scientist Richard Payne has argued that cultural values espoused by ordinary U.S. citizens have an impact on how the United States reacts to foreign crises. In particular, he has sought to make the linkage between the culture of violence found in the United States with the country's readiness to adopt force to settle international problems, most recently in military action against Iraq.[18] From this argument, it is only a short step to claim that the troubled state of race relations may influence U.S. foreign policy makers' perceptions of ethnic conflict elsewhere. Accordingly, we should take note of David Hollinger's admonition that "it would be a mistake to conflate America's version of the battle between the ethnic and the civic nation with the versions of this battle now being fought in Kurdistan, Bosnia, and most of the other parts of the world that generate today's headlines about nationalism."[19] Racial problems in the United States share little with civil wars of an ethnic kind fought in other states.

Can we posit a connection between the culture of violence found among right-wing groups in the United States and coercive U.S. foreign policy abroad? It would be difficult to establish such linkage because fringe groups operate outside the political process in the United States and are unrepresentative of values held by most U.S. citizens. But the April 1995 bombing of a federal building in Oklahoma City that killed close to 200 people drew attention to a growing culture of violence within the self-styled "patriot movement."

This movement, made up of diverse groups, holds that the federal government has conspired to deprive citizens of their constitutional rights. The April 1993 assault by federal agents on the Waco compound of the Branch Davidians, leaving eighty dead, was a catalyst for U.S. citizens who harbor antigovernment sentiments. A year earlier, the FBI sought to apprehend a suspect, Randy Weaver, charged with stockpiling weapons. In the siege that followed at Ruby Ridge, federal agents killed his wife and fourteen-year old son. Right-wing groups viewed these as acts of state terrorism. By stressing U.S. citizens' constitutional right to bear arms, the National Rifle Association has provided white extremists with an excuse to go one step further and claim the right to use arms for self-defense against the government.

Armed extremism in the United States has diverse sources and agendas. It includes groups like the Ku Klux Klan, the Aryan nations, tax protesters, survivalists, and property rights radicals. One of the suspects in the Oklahoma bombing belonged to the Christian Identity movement, which believed that only whites of European stock constitute God's chosen people. Black left-wing extremist groups, like the Black Panthers, that organized in the 1960s and 1970s represented an exception to the general rule that, in the United States, white-supremacist right-wing groups have accounted for most political violence. By the mid–1990s, the secretive, heavily armed militias scattered throughout the country may have comprised as many as 100,000 members in 30 states. According to the Southern Poverty Law Center, about one quarter of these had ties to neo–Nazi or white-supremacist groups. Militias found particularly fertile ground in isolated white communities suffering economic decline, as in the Midwest and Northwest. But these groups skillfully exploited modern communications media—radio talk shows, videotapes, shortwave radio, computer bulletin board forums—to propagate their views.

The relevance of such groups to U.S. foreign policy is especially tenuous. Some extremist groups believe that the U.S. government is controlled by foreign governments or by the United Nations. As a result, they fear that the United States is about to be taken over by foreign interests. These fears are ludicrous, but some conservative politicians have taken advantage of the existence of such groups to advocate hard-line foreign policy that seeks to impose a *Pax Americana* on various parts of the world. Other conservative leaders opt for isolationism and demand that the United States stop propping up weaker countries or graft-ridden international organizations and should sever ties with them, and advocate that the United States should let bloody conflicts caused by "ancient hatreds" run their course without U.S. mediation or intervention.

We have considered how U.S. nation-building, culture, and extremist domestic groups may seem to be connected to U.S. foreign policy on ethnic conflict in the contemporary world. Although we cannot establish a causal relationship, it seems plausible that the multicultural, fragment, diversity model held to be the crux of the U.S. political tradition seems to reflect the U.S. foreign policy approach most of the time. In the next section, we want to examine a more specific issue: how do U.S. foreign specialists themselves perceive the relevance of ethnic conflict to U.S. interests?

TOWARD A U.S. GRAND STRATEGY ON ETHNIC CONFLICT

There can be no hard-and-fast rules indicating when the United States should become involved in ethnic conflict, what means—diplomatic or miltary—should be employed, whether the United States should act unilaterally or as part of a multilateral force, and which side the United States should support.[20] The rapid spread of what Conor Cruise O'Brien called holy nationalism—the interaction of religion and nationalism that produces, "in ascending order of arrogance and destructiveness, 'chosen people,' 'holy nation,' and finally 'deified nation,' the most manic malign and literal version of God Land."[21]—has made the task of foreign-policy making more daunting. As O'Brien concluded, "The management of holy nationalism is the greatest problem in peacekeeping. Ideally those responsible for international affairs ought to be able to understand and moderate the holy nationalism of their own country and to discern, even when disguised, the operations and limits of holy nationalism in rival countries as well as in third-party countries."[22] A vague injunction, it nonetheless identifies what the cornerstone of foreign policy today should be.

Stephen Van Evera, an international security specialist, advanced his own typology of nationalisms to determine those that were so disruptive that they required a foreign policy response. Criteria telling us whether nationalisms were dangerous included whether nationalisms exist with or without statehood, whether they seek to incorporate a diaspora via expansion, whether other nations' rights to independence are respected, and how internal minorities are treated within a nation. Van Evera's useful primer helped distinguish benign from malignant nationalisms and provided some indicators to policy makers on how they could assess the risks to peace and stability and, subsequently, craft appropriate foreign policy responses.[23]

In yet another approach to culturally defined conflict, political scientist Samuel Huntington wrote about the clash of civilizations. In his view the world has been moving from nation–state conflict to ideological conflict to cultural conflict: "First, differences among civilizations are not only real; they are basic;" second, "the interactions between peoples of different civilizations are increasing; these increasing interactions intensify civilization consciousness;" third, "the processes of economic modernization and social change throughout the world are separating people from longstanding local identities."[24]

In the future, Huntington predicted, interlocking conflicts would arise among Hindu, Muslim, Slavic Orthodox, Western, Japanese, Confucian, Ibero–American, and possibly African civilizations. On the other hand, "The central axis of world politics in the future is likely to be . . . the conflict between 'the West and the Rest.'"[25] In the short term, greater cooperation and unity within Western civilization is required, but in the longer term, understanding and accommodation of non–Western civilizations have to be a foreign policy priority. Huntington believed that by concentrating on civilizations' faultlines, foreign policy could meet the challenges posed by world disorder.

Historical precedents can also furnish a guidepost to understanding and responding to contemporary and future ethnonationalism. Canadian journalist Michael Ignatieff identified three great reorderings of the nation-state system of Europe in the twentieth century: at Versailles in 1918, at Yalta in 1945, and during 1989–1991 within the Soviet bloc. "What distinguishes the third of these is that it has occurred without any imperial settlement whatever. No treaty exists to regulate the conflict between the territorial integrity of nation–states in Eastern Europe and the right to self-determination of the peoples within them." Exaggerating somewhat, Ignatieff argued that "For every resolution of this conflict by civilized divorce, Czech-style, there have been a dozen armed conflicts. The basic reason is obvious enough: the imperial police have departed."[26]

The United States and the Third Reordering

In light of our case studies, let us reconsider the spontaneous nature of the third reordering. For a brief period and under specific circumstances, the United States and the West supported the breakup of existing states and offered quick recognition to the smaller successor states that emerged out of the Soviet bloc. This departure from the international normative regime represented the final act of the cold war. The victors organized no Versailles or Trianon conferences, no Yalta or Potsdam meetings, to institutionalize their plans for the defeated side. Invoking the principle of self-determination, the West came to the recognition that the way to dismantle the highly centralized Soviet bloc was to splinter it by promoting excessive polycentrism. A host of new, weak, collapsing, or unviable states was countenanced.

The international normative regime adapted itself to the post–bipolar reality and accepted separation under specific conditions. Separation was circumscribed in time and space. As noted in Chapter 2, if self-determination had been made available only to European nations immediately after World War I and only to European colonies in the two decades following World War II, self-determination was extended after the cold war only to those titular nations found within communist states. No referenda were necessary, no outside observers were asked to monitor the process of state creation in the former Soviet Union, Yugoslavia, or Czechoslovakia. The rules of state creation were more rigorous for an African communist state: the breakaway Ethiopian province of Eritrea was required to hold a plebiscite on independence with international observers on hand. Nevertheless, any communist state that was multiethnic was a candidate for what, had it been a military victory, would have been called partition. The ingenuity of the 1990s formula was that almost no one, other than the losing communist oligarchs, recognized partition as anything but the noble principle of self-determination at work.

What was the role of the United States in destroying the Soviet empire and replacing it with a proliferation of states? We can say that the United States did not lead the way in promoting the dismantling of federal communist states. The Bush administration was slow, even reluctant, to recognize the independence of the breakaway Baltic republics, of Croatia and Slovenia. In the Bush administration, Paul Goble, a State Department specialist on Soviet Union ethnic relations, cautioned that Soviet collapse could lead to the creation of twenty or more independent states by the end of the century. The Pandora's box metaphor was employed to signal the danger of a proliferation of unstable states in what had been an adversarial but stable federation. Although aware of a demonstration effect on ethnosecessionist movements elsewhere, U.S. leaders were still surprised by the quickness with which the domino theory went into operation in the communist world. There was little that the United States could do to curb the growth of ethnosecessionism, but by the end of the Bush presidency, the United States had come to discern the advantages of having a plethora of states seeking Western approval replace the USSR.

The unprecedented nature of the third reordering was distinguishable not only by a lack of a formal settlement but by the absence of an enforcer. Explaining the reticence of the United States to act as global gendarme, Ignatieff contended that "The Americans may be the last remaining superpower, but they are not an imperial power: their authority is exercised in the defense of exclusively national interests, not in the maintenance of an imperial system of global order."

U.S. disinterest in an imperial project allowed a political vacuum to emerge in the international system after Soviet collapse. For ethnonationalists, the vacuum was an opportunity structure. How can we explain U.S. disinterest in empire building after its one-sided victory over the USSR? According to John Armstrong, it could be related to the general Western tradition of pluralism. In his study of the emergence of nations within Islamic and Christian cultures, the author traced the separate paths of development each of them took. Islam created a civilization of unprecedented cultural unity while tolerating diverse ethnic identities. In eastern Christianity, both Byzantine and Russian empires confronted the task of ingathering dispersed peoples. This process led toward cultural homogenization. By contrast, in Western Europe, "imperial rulers could not reject the legitimacy of independent secular polities. Although for centuries the fluid, multiform nature of medieval polities ranging from local baronies to city–states obscured the presence of a legitimate multilateral international order, it was present in the West at least from the tenth century on."[27] For Armstrong, "a plural international order has perpetuated a diffusion of power that, except for brief intervals, has precluded a single imperial tyranny throughout the West."[28]

Part of the explanation for U.S. international disengagement after the cold war—apart from its revised calculus of national interests—lies in this cultural heritage. Today, when presented with an opportunity to assume leadership of a potential liberal-democratic imperium, the United States has opted to remain within the millennial Western tradition of a plural international order.

This same plural Western tradition can have a negative impact on developing, non–Western countries. A consequence of the new pluralism is that many states are no longer located in a great power's sphere of influence. Being left out of any such sphere has had the incidental effect of condemning much of the underdeveloped world to its own meager resources. Ignatieff concluded: "Huge sections of the world's population have won the 'right of self-determination' on the cruelest possible terms: they have been simply left to fend for themselves. Not surprisingly, their nation–states are collapsing."[29]

The United States and Internationalization of Conflicts

Does the disintegration of poor and distant states have any bearing on the world's only superpower? In theoretical terms, it can be argued that, where state boundaries dissolve and interior space merges with international space, the United States is indirectly affected. Failing to react to one case of genocide, ethnic cleansing, or outright conquest—wherever it has taken place in the world—creates a perilous precedent for the global system. To be sure, ethnic conflict on the North American continent—whether in Chiapas or Quebec—has more direct policy consequences for Washington than that occurring in Bosnia and Chechnya, let alone Kashmir and KwaZululand. But how matters are settled in the latter cases can influence events in the U.S. backyard.

A compelling case has been made by Robert Kaplan for linking conflicts and the way they are resolved in developing states to U.S. power. Generalizing on the experience of one case—the West African state of Sierra Leone—he described the process of "the withering away of central governments, the rise of tribal and regional domains, the unchecked spread of disease, and the growing pervasiveness of war. West Africa is reverting to the Africa of the Victorian atlas. It consists now of a series of coastal trading posts . . . and an interior that, owing to violence, volatility, and disease, is again becoming, as Graham Greene once observed, 'blank' and 'unexplored.'"[30] Citing African specialist Ali Mazrui, who regarded the continent as being on the verge of large-scale border upheaval,[31] Kaplan elaborated:

> Africa may be as relevant to the future character of world politics as the Balkans were a hundred years ago, prior to the two Balkan wars and the First World War. Then the threat was the collapse of empires and the birth of nations based solely on tribe. Now the threat is more elemental: nature unchecked. . . . The coming upheaval, in which foreign embassies are shut down, states collapse, and contact with the outside world takes place through dangerous, disease-ridden coastal trading posts, will loom large in the century we are entering. . . . Africa suggests what war, borders, and ethnic politics will be like a few decades hence.

Kaplan pointed to inconsistencies in U.S. foreign policy as constituting part of the problem: "America's fascination with the Israeli–Palestinian issue, coupled with its lack of interest in the Turkish–Kurdish one, is a function of its own domestic and ethnic obssesions, not of the cartographic reality that is about to transform the Middle East." He closed his analysis with the relevance of Africa to the United States: "Africa may be marginal in terms of conventional late-twentieth-century conceptions of strategy, but in an age of cultural and racial clash, when national defense is increasingly local, Africa's distress will exert a destabilizing influence on the United States," for "The spectacle of several West African nations collapsing at once could reinforce the worst racial stereotypes here at home."[32]

It would be facile to suggest either that a general formula can be devised to apply to all ethnic conflicts, or that each such conflict must be approached on its own terms. It is true that, as former Defense Secretary James Schlesinger put it, "With so many conflicting objectives and with an inability to focus those means appropriate for achieving a limited set of objectives, now foreign policy is likely to be shaped by a capricious flow of events—rather than defined guideposts and a careful plan."[33] But we can suggest that just as the Truman Doctrine offered a game plan for dealing with communism, so a strategy must be developed for responding to nationalist unrest. It should rest on an established hierarchy of U.S. national interests—what Schlesinger regarded as the longer-term interests of American society—that may be latent even in "capricious" and faraway ethnonationalist conflicts.

Other policy lessons can be drawn from the proliferation of ethnic conflicts. Journalist William Pfaff cited twentieth-century versions of internationalism that challenged the hegemony of nationalism, two of which produced pathologies of their own. "Nationalism's rival, internationalism, has had three important modern secular manifestations. The first was Marxism, given political existence in the three Socialist Internationals and the Communist system established after 1945. The second was Nazi racialism, which attempted to impose the rule of the Nordic peoples on allegedly lesser races, peoples, and their nations. The third is liberal internationalism."[34] For Pfaff, international law and global economic interdependence were the essential features of this last variant.

Although he did not explicitly make these connections, each of the three forms of internationalism has been associated with the leadership of a particular state—Russia, Germany, and the United States respectively. The institutionalization of liberal internationalism through the United Nations, the Bretton Woods economic system, GATT, and NATO were the results of U.S. policy initiatives. But liberal internationalism was also evidenced in the functionalist approach that spurred economic and political integration in Western Europe. The European Economic Community (EEC) of the 1960s was an institutional response to the "European civil wars"—the world wars—and attempted to transcend particularistic nationalisms through a building-block approach. The EEC was created by the will of its member states, but even here, U.S. approbation was instrumental in the transnational organization's success.

If today, as part of its foreign policy, the United States was to promote functionalist solutions in those parts of the world troubled by ethnic conflict, some of the causes of such conflict, for example, economic inequalities, could be removed. While functionalism is not an immediate solution to messy territorial and ethnic conflicts, it could serve the United States well as a grand strategy to control the risks of world disorder.

ETHNIC CONFLICT AND U.S. FOREIGN POLICY MAKERS

U.S. thinking about nationalism, ethnic conflict, and self-determination underwent a change in the 1990s as the international problems associated with these forces reverberated in various parts of the world. Hostage taking by the Bosnian Serb military and Kashmiri militants, terrorist attacks by Algerian and Egyptian fundamentalists on Western tourists, insurgency and counterinsurgency in Afghanistan, Guatemala, Sri Lanka, and Turkey—all with an ethnic dimension to them—have provided different tests for peace and stability in the international system. Not surprisingly, CIA Director R. James Woolsey went so far as to suggest that "This world that we are beginning to see looks more and more like a more lethal version of the old world that existed before 1914 when a range of nationalist sentiments produced the holocaust of World War I."[35]

The use of different tactics by often uncoordinated, ethnically defined organizations, together with the more intransigent political demands made by separatist groups worldwide, posed problems that could not be met head on, as in the case of rivalry between the superpowers. An adapted version of "flexible response," which was U.S. nuclear doctrine of the late 1960s, seemed the most pragmatic approach to meeting the challenge of global pandemonium and ethnonationalist apocalypse. But in order to craft an appropriate, calibrated response to ethnic conflict, a number of crucial analytic distinctions have to be made.

The first is that between humanitarian intervention and balance-of-power considerations; the second is that between peacekeeping and peacemaking; the third is that between protecting the helpless and punishing the aggressor. A case where these distinctions were blurred was the UN-sponsored military intervention in Somalia from May 1993 to March 1995. As part of the UN mission, the United States sought to bring humanitarian relief to a starving country. But this initially well-defined mission became blurred when a few Somali warlords turned against the U.S. presence. One of their "successes" was an ambush that killed eighteen U.S. servicemen. Realizing the interconnected nature of food distribution to the starving and the balance of power prevailing between rival warlords, the United States discovered that military power had to be used to achieve a laudable humanitarian goal. The equation proved too intricate, and the United States abandoned its mission. The so-called "Mogadishu line" that emerged from this debacle highlighted the subtle difference between humanitarian efforts enjoying broad consensual endorsement and zero-sum intervention in complex ethnic and clan rivalries where any type of aid to one side could be perceived as hostile activity by a rival party.[36]

In his Foreword to Daniel Moynihan's *Pandaemonium,* Adam Roberts inquired about the connection among ethnic conflict, U.S. foreign policy, and morality: "If international politics consists largely, not of a Manichean struggle of right versus wrong, but of impossibly competing ethnic identities and mutually incompatible dreams of national self-determination, might this not reinforce American disenchantment, not just with the supposed New World Order, but with all involvement in a hopelessly benighted world?"[37] Roberts was not merely asking a rhetorical question: The U.S. intervention against Iraq in 1991 had already revealed the nature of the dilemma. The United States supported Resolution 688 (1991) of the UN Security Council that condemned "the repression of the Iraqi civilian population in many parts of Iraq, including most recently in Kurdish populated areas." But other than carving out a "safe haven" for the Kurds by way of an air exclusion zone that Iraqi aircraft could not violate, no action was taken to promote self-determination in the region, nor were Kurds even protected from land-based incursions launched by Saddam's military, as occurred in September 1996.

The U.S. reluctance to back self-determination movements was in evidence in another part of the world in 1991. As mentioned earlier, the United States was conspicuously slow to recognize the independence of Baltic states, preferring to deal with the Soviet government headed by Mikhail Gorbachev. In early August 1991, just prior to the failed putsch in Moscow that sealed the fate of the USSR, President Bush went to the Ukraine capital to lecture on political concepts: "Freedom is not the same as independence," he told the more-and-more independence-minded parliament. "Americans will not support those who seek independence in order to replace a far-off tyranny with a local despotism. They will not aid those who promote a suicidal nationalism based upon ethnic hatred."[38] One U.S. pundit dubbed this Bush's "chicken Kiev" speech and indeed, by the end of the year, Ukraine had achieved independence and greater freedom despite Washington's general timidity.

Other high-level foreign policy makers have spoken out about the challenge of ethnic conflict. President Bush's last secretary of state, Lawrence Eagleburger, stressed how the different character of every ethnonationalist struggle would not permit any one formula to address every contingency. "There is no rule or strategy that can be applied across-the-board as a remedy to this kind of problem," he stated. "Each instance of trouble in a multiethnic nation, whether it's Yugoslavia or whatever, has its own historical, political, economic and cultural context and has to be approached on a case-by-case basis."[39]

A more activist role for the United States was envisaged by Anthony Lake, the Clinton administration's National Security Affairs presidential assistant. Explaining the principles of the Clinton administration's foreign policy, he admitted that "There is no longer a consensus among the American people around why, and even whether our nation should remain actively engaged in the world." To compound this lack of vision, Lake noted how "A major challenge to our thinking, our policies and our international institutions in this era is the fact that most conflicts are taking place within rather than among nations." Furthermore, "These conflicts are typically highly complex; at the same time, their brutality will tug at our consciences. We need a healthy wariness about our ability to shape solutions for such disputes; yet at times our interests or humanitarian concerns will impel our unilateral or multilateral engagement."[40] Madeleine Albright, U.S. Secretary of State, echoed this view: "Increasingly, threats to international order are not clear but rather devilishly complex."[41] In her view, the challenge lay not in edifying international law but in effective enforcement.

Lake sought to explain why the United States should remain engaged in world affairs. He reviewed its actions throughout this century: "As we fought aggressors and contained communism, our engagement abroad was animated both by calculations of power and by this belief: to the extent democracy and market economics hold sway in other nations, our own nation will be more secure, prosperous and influential, while the broader world will be more humane and peaceful." Lake's emphasis on economic interdependence was testimony to the soundness of the functionalist approach described earlier. It also recalled the stress Ernest Gellner had placed on the distinctive character of the post–1989 ethos when compared to the post–1918 one: "This second great post–imperial eruption of nationalism takes place in a different and new ideological climate, one in which the old link between territory and wealth has been broken, and the new political supremacy of growth-rates established."[42] In its role as the world's principal economic power, the United States could spur growth rates in troubled countries, promote their economic interdependence, and thereby mitigate centrifugal tendencies and ethnic unrest within them.

According to Lake, Woodrow Wilson had been the first to underscore how U.S. security was shaped by the character of foreign regimes. Subsequent presidents recognized that promoting democracy and capitalism abroad both protected U.S. interests and reflected values that were simultaneously American and universal. For the National Security Affairs assistant, promoting democracy and capitalism worldwide necessitated a change in security policy: "The successor to a doctrine of containment must be a strategy of enlargement—enlargement of the world's free community of market democracies."[43]

As a corollary, U.S. policy toward *backlash states*—those refusing to join the community of multiplying democracies and ruled by lawlessness, violence, racism, ethnic prejudice, religious persecution, xenophobia, and irredentism—should be to isolate them diplomatically, militarily, economically, and technologically. Other than employing the tactic of isolation against backlash states, "there will be relatively few intranational ethnic conflicts that justify our military intervention. Ultimately, on these and other humanitarian needs, we will have to pick and choose.

Another choice that Washington had to make was whether to act alone or in concert with allies. Lake asserted that "We should act multilaterally where doing so advances our interests, and we should act unilaterally when that will serve our purpose." But he did point to the advantage of inculcating "the habits of multilateralism [that] may one day enable the rule of law to play a far more civilizing role in the conduct of nations."[44]

Zbigniew Brzezinski, President Carter's National Security Affairs adviser, in a recent book, proposed a grand strategy of geopolitical pluralism. In it, Russia would be "encouraged to be a good neighbor to states with which it can cooperate in a common economic space but which it will not seek or be able, politically and militarily, to dominate."[45] By paying greater attention to the distinct interests of the non–Russian post–Soviet states, the United States would help inhibit any Russian temptation to reinvent its empire and would, by contrast, also help Russia define itself as a normal state rather than multinational empire. Under certain conditions, the United States could even play the role of peacekeeper in ethnic conflicts occurring in post–Soviet space. Clearly, this did not happen in the festering Chechnya conflict. Indeed, in the uncertainty following Yeltsin's reelection, Russia seemed bent on reasserting itself as the dominant power in Eurasia, prepared to act unilaterally to resolve ethnic conflicts.

FOREIGN POLICY ANALYSTS ON CONTEMPORARY ETHNIC CONFLICT

We have reviewed the approaches taken by leading figures in the U.S. foreign policy-making establishment on the subject of ethnic conflict. Their policy recommendations are nuanced, tentative, and based on a discrete, case-by-case approach. Academic writing has also addressed the same topic and its destructive potential in the post–bipolar world. We survey below perspectives that oppose and support U.S. activism in ethnic conflicts.

The Anti-Interventionists

A detailed critique of foreign policy activism in the aftermath of the cold war was advanced by two specialists, Christopher Layne and Benjamin Schwarz. Attacking many of the assumptions on which a policy of engagement was based, they disputed the view that held that the end of the cold war had not reduced the need for an interventionist U.S. foreign policy. They listed the principles invoked to justify continued interventionism: preserving the inviolability of borders, preventing instability, punishing aggression. This set of principles produced the punitive U.S. action against Iraq in January 1991.

But for these two authors, the next major foreign policy crisis, in former Yugoslavia, brought a different set of principles to the fore. "The Clinton administration and the foreign policy community generally have viewed the Balkan crisis as a crucial test of America's leadership in creating order in the post-Cold War world."[46] They cited Clinton's remark that the Balkans would set "the standard for addressing other ethnic conflicts and the effectiveness of vital international institutions, including the European Community, the Atlantic Alliance, and the United Nations itself." Clinton painted the choice as "between unstable, highly nationalistic states with centralized and potentially oppressive governments, on the one hand, and democratic states . . . on the other."[47] Layne and Schwarz imputed to the interventionist group in the administration and the foreign policy establishment an espousal of such ephemeral notions as contest of wills, tests of leadership, and moral crusades.

In the interventionists' view, the greatest post–cold war danger stemmed from imperial understretch—a shrinking of U.S. global commitments—rather than imperial overstretch. Relying on military preponderance could reduce escalating regional tensions by making it unnecessary for other states to provide for their own security. Layne and Schwarz phrased the interventionists' logic this way: "Because the United States discourages others from assuming greater international responsibilities, it often finds itself taking the lead in security interventions—despite the rhetorical mantra that it is not the 'world's policeman.'"[48]

But the two authors pointed to the superiority of the reverse logic: "Removing the umbrella of U.S. protection would force other states to 'renationalize' their foreign and security policies."[49] To be sure, many allies found such a generous interpretation of the U.S. security umbrella convenient. They could accept a secondary role in security matters as a tradeoff for the sizeable cuts that could be made in their defense budgets. But bankrolling others' security could be counterproductive for the United States: "Today, America's insecurity is the self-inflicted consequence of a foreign policy that equates national interests with the maintenance of world order."[50]

These two authors further attacked the interventionist position on the grounds that it made a series of inaccurate assumptions. They quoted Bush administration Defense Secretary Dick Cheney that "The worldwide market that we're part of cannot thrive where regional violence, instability, and aggression put it at peril."[51] William Perry, President Clinton's defense secretary, shared Cheney's assessment, but Layne and Schwartz criticized the logic underlying the "world order mindset" that assumed that "America's prosperity depends upon international economic interdependence and that the precondition for economic interdependence is the geopolitical stability and reassurance that flow from America's security commitments."[52] For the modified version of the domino theory, imputing chain reactions to political events, was flawed: "In the world of statecraft, crises are usually discrete happenings—not tightly linked events. The outcome of events in potential hotspots like Nagorno–Karabakh, Moldova, the Baltics, Ukraine, Transylvania, and Slovakia will be decided by local conditions, not by what the United States does or does not do in the Balkans."[53]

Other scholars have made the case against interventionism in ethnic conflicts. The dean of U.S. foreign policy analysis, George Kennan, invoked John Quincy Adams's speech of July 4, 1823—a time when the United States was tempted to become involved in the conflict between Spain and its colonies in Latin America—to argue against interventionism in a new period of collapsing empires: "America . . . well knows that by once enlisting under other banners than her own, were they even the banners of foreign independence, she would involve herself beyond the power of extrication, in all the wars of interest and intrigue, of individual avarice, envy, and ambition, which assumed the colors and usurped the standards of freedom."[54] Kennan, like Adams, contended that the United States could best lead by force of example.

Journalist Jonathan Clarke framed the contemporary policy-maker's dilemma in different terms: "It is bad analysis to equate minor, regionally containable problems with threats to world peace. That sort of bloated language may be tolerable in U.N. resolutions, but it should find no place in American thinking." He pointed to the counterproductive nature of intervention in certain conditions as, for instance, in Islamic fundamentalist resurgence in Egypt or the Hindu backlash against Muslims in India: "Overt U.S. interference in such internal conflicts most probably would make difficult situations much worse by allowing the disadvantaged side to appeal to antiforeign nationalism."[55]

Qualified Interventionists

A number of leading academics has taken the view that the power balance in the 1990s is conducive to U.S. intervention in the international arena. What becomes important is to identify when an ethnic or regional conflict qualifies for U.S. intervention. Richard Betts, a specialist on security policy, contended that intervention was undesirable in the post–cold war period *except* if carried out with consequence. He proposed the intriguing notion of "imperial impartiality" to depict selective but committed involvement in ethnic and other conflicts in the international system:

> If outsiders such as the United States or the United Nations are faced with demands for peace in wars where passions have not burned out, they can avoid the costs and risks that go with entanglement by refusing the mandate—staying aloof and letting the locals fight it out. Or they can jump in and help one of the contenders defeat the other. But can they bring peace sooner than exhaustion from prolonged carnage would, if they remain impartial? Not with a gentle, restrained impartiality but with an active, harsh impartiality that overpowers both sides: an imperial impartiality.[56]

Betts's approach was implemented in Bosnia when the United States, acting under UN auspices, began simultaneously to target Serb military assets and to increase diplomatic pressure on the Bosnian government to accept a form of partition.

Henry Bienen, another international relations expert, agreed that cold war domino theory continued to shape U.S foreign policy. This policy anticipated "demonstration and contagion effects: if the aggressor can get away in Bosnia with rape, murder, genocide, the forcible change of territorial boundaries, and the effective destruction of an independent state, what is to stop others in Eastern Europe, Russia, and perhaps in Western Europe from playing the nationalism card and creating instability in the very heart of Europe?"[57] Contagion theory suggests that "If we do not stop ethnic cleansing and the ugly nationalisms in the former Yugoslavia, we will see extreme nationalist behavior emulated elsewhere in Europe."[58]

But where others were drawn to the disengagement option, Bienen recommended that "We should encourage the viability and strength of multiethnic states by working with our NATO allies and with others to provide carrots—access to markets, assistance, and association and eventual entrance into the European Community—to states that obey norms of tolerance and maintain the rights of minorities."[59] Again we see the argument in favor of a functionalist solution. It was seconded by Charles Kupchan: "The international community can, through multilateral institutions and nongovernmental organizations, also help the new democracies create institutions and pass legislation to protect minorities."[60] Kupchan added that, in particular, "Collective security institutions would help states define their national interests in ways that contribute to international stability."[61]

Bienen was sanguine about the threat posed by intolerant states: "While ethnically based nationalisms run against the grain of many things we wish and hope for, and while they often violate our values and sometimes harm our interests, they are not likely to be profoundly destabilizing or harmful to *vital* interests."[62] More dangerous to U.S. interests would be large-scale conflicts *between* states of the former Soviet bloc.

The author distinguished between *globalists* and *regionalists* in the foreign policy community. The former were concerned with global security issues and less bothered by regional and ethnic conflict. They exerted most influence over U.S. foreign policy making: "National Security Advisors, Directors of the CIA, Secretaries of Defense, usually Secretaries of State, and, broadly speaking, members of the national security establishment can be labeled 'globalists.'"[63] The less influential regionalists were more sensitive to, and often advocated intervention in, ethnic conflicts in various parts of the world. Bienen sided with the regionalists and recommended that they be given greater input into foreign policy making.

Other foreign policy experts believe that, while tragic, ethnic conflicts no longer have the powder-keg potential to break into world wars as occurred in 1914. Pfaff argued, for example, that the principal dangers posed by ethnonationalism were primarily in the moral and political spheres rather than in the security one.[64] As a result, it was not necessary to force incompatible ethnic groups to stay bound to each other for the sake of international stability. Foreign relations specialist Michael Mandelbaum elaborated this view: "The prevailing attitude for a long time was that tampering with national boundaries was like opening a Pandora's box—that even unjust boundaries were better than unstable ones."[65]

In their study of the real world order of the 1990s, two other academics, Max Singer and Aaron Wildavsky, singled out the formative experience of democratic countries in the "zones of peace"—areas characterized by "the freedom from military dangers to national survival and the political impossibility of wars with other democracies."[66] In the past, threats to internal peace in the democracies included "religious wars, factional or family wars (such as the Wars of the Roses), ideological wars, wars about slavery or secession, wars between ethnic groups, and conflict between people simply fighting for personal power."[67] The authors described how difficult it was to achieve domestic peace but added: "Against great obstacles eventually we were able to do it, so maybe others can too."[68] Intervention by democracies so as to reduce hostilities in the "zones of turmoil" had, therefore, to be framed by the way their own domestic peace was achieved.

Still, many integral principles of democratic systems may not easily transplant well to another cultural context. Singer and Wildavsky remarked how "In Yugoslavia, none of the following principles gave us a clear answer about what to do: preventing ethnic conflict, self-determination, preservation of national borders and stability of government, support for democracy, encouragement of negotiated solutions for conflict, prevention or punishment of aggression, neutrality, or preserving or restoring peace." In fact, many of these principles were in conflict with each other. But "even if we had picked one goal over all the others, supporting that goal would have required that we change policy during the course of the crisis."[69] This indeed happened in September 1995 when the United States shifted from neutrality in the Bosnian war to punishing the Bosnian Serbs, viewed as the aggressor in the war. This was recognition that the path to domestic peace was indeed different in Yugoslavia than in the United States.

Despite acknowledging the uniqueness of each ethnic conflict, many foreign policy analysts are inevitably drawn to the explanation that nationalist unrest was the result of the end of the cold war. For decades the United States and the USSR had their respective client states, cultivated local elites, and supplied them with money and arms. In turn these oligarchies, juntas, and dictatorships had the means to quash all attempts at separation within their own borders. When the Soviet Union disappeared and the United States slashed overseas economic and military aid, the old elites found themselves defenseless against the upsurge of separatism that they had been able to repress hitherto.

A more pointed argument has been that the nature of bipolarity created the illusion that nationalism had disappeared as a destabilizing force. As historian John Lewis Gaddis put it, "The very existence of two rival superpowers—which is really to say, two *supranational* powers—created this impression [that nationalism was on the wane]. We rarely thought of the Cold War as a conflict between competing Soviet and American nationalism; we saw it, rather, as a contest between two great international ideologies, or between two antagonistic military blocs, or between two geographical regions imprecisely labeled 'East' and 'West.'"[70]

Gaddis put forward the ingenious proposition that for the post–cold war world, "The search for freedom . . . tends toward fragmentation in the political realm, while the search for prosperity tends toward integration in the economic realm." Indeed "The Cold War itself, it now appears, was a departure from that pattern, in that it fostered integration in politics as well as economics" through the system of military pacts and economic blocs. The evidence we have provided in this book corroborates Gaddis's thesis: "All of this suggests, then, that the problems we will confront in the post–Cold War world are more likely to arise from competing processes—integrationist versus fragmentationist—than from the kinds of competing ideological visions that dominated the Cold War."[71]

For Gaddis, the U.S. role in postwar Europe had been to promote integrative forces over those of fragmentation. In the 1990s, the challenge was to adapt these integrative structures to subsume former adversaries in Eastern Europe. Optimists about the post–bipolar future had considerable faith in the power of functionalist integration. Pessimists stressed the ineluctable strength of fragmentation. Gaddis acknowledged that integration was not a panacea under all circumstances, but it represented an effective way of neutralizing the forces of fragmentation.

CLINTON AND THE PRINCIPLE OF SELF-DETERMINATION

In the first years of the Clinton administration, criticism was leveled at the low priority it assigned to foreign policy issues. This criticism may have been justified, but so were President Clinton's priorities. George Bush had lost the 1992 election partly because he was too preoccupied with international politics. Rightly or wrongly, the Bush administration took credit for the wave of democratization that swept the world in the early 1990s, from Chile to Nepal and from Ethiopia to Mongolia, but economic recession at home proved to be of greatest concern to U.S. voters.

Even though he broke a twelve-year Republican lock on the White House, Clinton came to power with no pressure on him to change foreign policy. Because he did not make any significant changes, his foreign policy team was criticized for being "stuck in its own passivity, contempt for American power and 'therapeutic' attitude toward America's role in the world." The United States, it was charged, was becoming "self-neutralized."[72] Although ethnic conflicts occurred in many parts of the world, Clinton stuck with his domestic agenda, making an exception for democracy in Haiti in 1994 and peace in Bosnia in 1995. The series of Israeli–PLO accords between 1993 and 1995, signed with Clinton's prompting, and the effort to revive them in October 1996, were another example of the administration's activism in the international arena.

As with Bush, so Clinton was presented with a historic opportunity on coming to power. If Bush had lent support to the global wave of democratization, Clinton could spur the realization of a principle closely related to democracy—self-determination. As we discussed in Chapter 2, political theory has often viewed the two principles as intricately tied to each other, but the Clinton foreign policy team—like its predecessors—made efforts to delink the two ideas.

Self-determination was stigmatized in the post–cold war era. It had been used as an excuse to justify ethnic cleansing, ethnic rape, genocide, and ethnocracy. Movements for self-determination did not automatically lead to the establishment of liberal democratic societies but could produce just the reverse. Under Clinton, foreign policy makers rediscovered that most modern nation–states were not only multiethnic, but they also rarely embodied a national community at all. They also learned that shoring up the precarious unity of ethnically plural states seemed the only practical alternative to countenancing a cycle of secessionism and ethnic violence.

The Clinton administration rejected the Wilsonian temptation and concluded that self-determination could not be endorsed as a universal principle of equivalent importance to liberal democracy. On the other hand, it seemed to engage in an experiment involving "sovereignty à la carte."[73] The solutions brokered by the United States giving far-reaching political autonomy to Palestinians on the West Bank and Serbs in Bosnia indicated that self-determination did not have to be understood dichotomously as being either present in the form of statehood or absent in the form of subordination.

Moreover, a rival principle to self-determination was conveniently available. The idea of noninterference in the internal affairs of countries had been enshrined in the UN charter. According to David Rieff, a critic of the UN, the ethos of the organization that rationalized noninterference was that "interstate aggression was something it could respond to effectively, whereas intrastate aggression or outbursts of intercommunal violence was something that it was largely powerless to prevent."[74]

In the bipolar world the principle of noninterference had never stopped the USSR or the United States from becoming involved in countries where their respective interests were at stake. But in the 1990s, paradoxically, it was handy for the United States to shelter behind the noninterference principle whenever unmanageable conflicts flared. The principle of noninterference allowed the United States to get off the hook when ethnic conflicts in Chechnya, Kurdistan, or Rwanda tore at an existing state.

The Clinton administration had another reason for treading carefully in ethnic conflicts. U.S. power to do much about such conflicts was limited anyway. As Bienen put it, "We should not entertain the idea that we can micromanage ethnic conflicts." For "the creation of constitutional and political formulas for managing ethnic disputes and allocating power based on the ways that communities differentiate themselves" was complicated.[75] Furthermore, the structure of the U.S. military, its training and weapons inventory, and general military doctrine were largely inappropriate for use in ethnic conflicts, often fought with unconventional methods. U.S. military doctrine endorsed intervention only under conditions of overwhelming advantage or near-invulnerability, as in the 1991 Gulf War. Consequently, becoming bogged down in a complex conflict as in Bosnia was a fear shared by interventionists and isolationists alike.[76]

The NATO alliance itself was not structured to respond to local wars involving irregular armies and militias using hit-and-run guerrilla tactics or scorched-earth policies. Just how different armed conflict could be in the future was described by a military historian: Martin van Creveld sketched a "pre–Westphalian" scenario of worldwide low-intensity conflict in the future. War-making entities would not be restricted to a specific territory, while tribalistic identity and control would mean more. Further, "Once the legal monopoly of armed force, long claimed by the state, is wrested out of its hands, existing distinctions between war and crime will break down." If crime and war became indistinguishable, national defense would increasingly resemble a local concept, too. Future wars would be those of communal survival.[77] The lesson for the UN and for Western powers was clear. Before effective intervention could be carried out in localized wars, cold war armies had to be transformed into "New Age" ones characterized by multifaceted, flexible-response capabilities.[78]

Kupchan proposed that "the international community should focus its attention on improving its ability to deploy forces in preventive ways. Creating buffers between hostile parties, protecting pockets of minority populations, enforcing ceasefires while negotiations proceed—these are the new military missions for which multilateral institutions and national militaries should prepare."[79] Charles William Maynes also exhorted the UN to enhance its "ability to practice preventive diplomacy so ethnic or religious tensions can be addressed before they erupt into violence."[80]

From these considerations about the nature of future conflict and peacemaking, it is evident that much restructuring of military forces must be undertaken. UN Secretary-General Boutros Boutros-Ghali recognized the need for a new approach to resolving conflicts when he proposed setting up a permanent UN peacekeeping force that would include U.S. units under UN mandate.[81] This proposal contained problems of its own, such as U.S. domestic opposition to having U.S. forces serve under multilateral command structures.[82] The fact that killing or capturing U.S. armed service members would always remain the main prize for adversaries was another disincentive to implementing this otherwise needed reorganization of UN peacekeeping.

Given these problems, it was surprising that in late summer 1995, under U.S. and French pressure, the UN did indeed redefine its mission in Bosnia. It not merely provided peacekeepers or peace enforcers but now also combatants. Only in rare circumstances, such as Korea in the early 1950s and the Congo in the early 1960s, had the UN assumed such a role. While NATO forces launched air strikes on Bosnian Serb targets, the UN rapid reaction force stationed in the Sarajevo region fired artillery at Serb guns. The role of UN representative to the region, Yasushi Akashi, changed from

Newly Independent Balkan States

725140 (B01344) 5-92

defending the humanitarian mission in Bosnia to asserting how air strikes had forced the Serbs to the negotiating table. The redefined UN mission was in large part the product of a change of policy on Bosnia by the Clinton administration. Let us use Bosnia as an example of U.S. foreign policy activism in an ethnic conflict.

BOSNIA AS CASE STUDY OF U.S. INTERVENTION

The United States adopted an interventionist role in the Bosnian conflict in late summer 1995 not simply as a result of continuing Serb atrocities. The impasse within the Clinton administration and among the Western allies about how to respond to Serb aggression was broken by a bill sponsored by Bob Dole, then Senate majority leader and Republican presidential hopeful and a long-serving legislative leader with great influence over U.S. foreign policy. In July 1995, Dole steered his bill—calling for a lifting of the arms embargo on the Bosnian government—through both houses of Congress with apparently veto-proof majorities. The rationale for lifting the embargo was simple: to even the balance of military power between Muslims and Serbs.

Clinton was also prodded into taking action by the election in 1995 of more-activist French President Jacques Chirac. The new leader had threatened to withdraw his country's 4000 peacekeepers in Bosnia—the largest national contingent in the 23,000-strong UN mission—if the West refused to use military force to stop Serb aggression. Reversing the humiliations suffered by French and UN peacekeepers became a matter of national honor for the conservative French leader. He supported reinforcement of UN safe havens and was instrumental in creating a 10,000-member rapid reaction force. Its first major emplacement was on Mount Igman, a strategic site south of the Bosnian capital of Sarajevo, overlooking a road used to bring in supply convoys.

Cautious U.S. behavior in Yugoslavia was acknowledgment of the complex history of the Balkans. Whether Yugoslavia had ever been little more than an idea, an artificial creation, an imagined community, or a natural, primordial community bringing together Southern Slav peoples into a common political structure has sparked considerable debate. Serbs, Croatians, and Bosnian Muslims speak the same language—Serbo-Croatian—though to write the same word, Serbs use the Cyrillic alphabet and Croats the Latin one. Slovenes speak a closely related language of the same linguistic group. Ethnic markers are no less distinct among these peoples than language. However, they have experienced very different histories and profess different religions, thus forming the basis for differentiation.

The first successful union of the South Slav peoples only came in the twentieth century in the aftermath of World War I. In the vacuum created by the collapse of the Habsburg and Ottoman empires, a Kingdom of Serbs, Croats, and Slovenes was established, changing its name in 1929 to the Kingdom of Yugoslavia. In 1945 a Federative People's Republic of Yugoslavia was created by communist insurgents. This Yugoslav state disintegrated during 1991–1992 into six successor states based on the former constituent republics. Although the name *Yugoslavia* was retained to describe the Serb republic's union with Montenegro, its symbolism lay in the Serb claim to be the core South Slav nation.

The fault line separating Western, Eastern Orthodox, and Muslim civilizations was established centuries ago in the Balkans, but it was the scars left after World War II that largely propelled ethnic violence in the 1990s. When Hitler invaded Yugoslavia in April 1941, the anti–Serb Croatian Ustasa ("insurgent") movement gained his approval for setting up a puppet fascist Croatian state. The German Reich also agreed to incorporate the ethnically heterogeneous region of Bosnia–Hercegovina into the new Croatian state. The Ustase committed numerous acts of barbarism against Serbs and Jews that even Hitler found extraordinary. It also recruited Muslims to carry out massacres against Serbs in Bosnia and, indeed, some Bosnian Muslim fighters wanted to set up their own SS detachments. In many parts of this republic, four times more Serbs were killed than Muslims, a fact helping explain Serb vengeance fifty years later.

Fear of a brutal Serb settling of accounts with the defeated allies of Hitler led to the construction of an intricate ethnic checks-and-balances system in Yugoslavia, presided over by socialist leader Josip Broz Tito. Nationalism was to be neutralized through the establishment of a federal structure made up of five constituent nations. Only Bosnia, because of its ethnic heterogeneity, was not immediately given the status of a "titular" nation living in a "home" republic. But in 1964 the Muslim population was finally recognized as Yugoslavia's sixth nation, and Bosnia–Hercegovina was unofficially regarded as a homeland for the Muslims of Yugoslavia, 80 percent of whom lived here. However the population of the republic was only 41 percent Muslim, with 31 percent Serb and 18 percent Croat, so all were treated as "constitutive peoples" rather than minorities.

As democratic revolutions broke out across Eastern Europe in 1989, in Yugoslavia it took the form of nationalist competition between the six republics over power. As William Pfaff contended, "The troubles caused throughout the Balkans and Southeastern Europe at the beginning of the 1990s . . . have not resulted from external threats but from the anxieties caused by the existence of national or ethnic minorities in countries where other communities are dominant. In each of these countries, the minority is perceived as a threat to the integrity of the host nation, producing a hostility which reinforces the insecurity of the minority."[83] The group that formed a majority in one Yugoslav republic but the most important minority in most of the other republics was the Serbs.

In December 1990 Slovenia held a referendum on independence that was overwhelmingly approved. Quickly, Croatia announced that it would follow suit and also declare independence from the Yugoslav federation. The leader of Bosnia, Alija Izetbegovic, realized that his republic was likely to become the main victim of the spiraling tide of nationalism among the peoples of Yugoslavia. As a multiethnic state with a large Serb minority, it would in particular be the obvious target of Serb nationalist leader Slobodan Milosevic's greater Serbia policy. U.S. Ambassador to Yugoslavia Warren Zimmerman captured the ongoing dynamics: "The breakup of Yugoslavia is a classic example of nationalism from the top down—a manipulated nationalism in a region where peace has historically prevailed more than war and in which a quarter of the population were in mixed marriages. The manipulators condoned and even provoked local ethnic violence in order to engender animosities that could then be magnified by the press, leading to further violence."[84]

Having control of the former Yugoslav People's Army (JNA) was of critical importance to Milosevic's greater Serbia project. This army was the fifth-largest in Europe and was supplied by both a large domestic arms industry and by the Soviet defense juggernaut. When Slovenian and Croatian leaders urged conscripts from their republics not to join the JNA, the Yugoslav army was, within a short time, transformed into a Serbian one. In June 1991 U.S. Secretary of State James Baker sought to mediate the brewing conflict but failed to persuade Milosevic to agree on new constitutional arrangements. Zimmerman wrote of the Baker visit: "Never was a green light given or implied to Milosevic or the army to invade the seceding republics. . . .

But was there a red light? Not as such because the United States had given no consideration to using force to stop a Serbian/JNA attack on Slovenia or Croatia."[85] It was just a few days after Baker's failed mission that Slovenia and Croatia declared their independence.

Discreetly encouraged by Milosevic, leaders of Serb minorities in other republics seemed bent on annexing as much of the territory of the fledgling new states as possible. But when it came to Bosnian territory, Serbs and Croats found common ground. Early in their war on the Bosnian Muslims, they seemed ready to partition the republic between themselves, and the West could do little about it. Diplomatic measures were uncoordinated and halfhearted. To be sure, in summer 1991 the European Community (EC) and the United Nations combined their efforts to put an end to fighting in Croatia, thanks in part to the work of two special envoys, Cyrus Vance (a former U.S. Secretary of State) and Lord Peter Carrington (former British foreign minister). The latter stressed that the West would not recognize the independence of any Yugoslav republic until they had defined their relationships with each other. But under German prodding, the EC decided to extend formal recognition to the breakaway Yugoslav republics in December 1991 if certain conditions concerning human and minority rights and territorial claims against other republics were met.

The decision to offer automatic recognition of statehood to the constituent parts of the Yugoslav federal system—depending on their resolving border disputes and pledging to observe human rights—was made in the last month of the existence of the Soviet Union. The contingent recognition of Yugoslav republics as states was part of a grander design, therefore, for dealing with the breakup of the communist bloc. To the West the policy of diplomatic recognition represented the line of least resistance and the only orderly way to handle an expected proliferation of claims for sovereignty. But it was also at odds with the prevailing international normative regime that discriminated against secessionism.

Of the four candidates applying in December 1991 for recognition, the EC recognized only Croatia and Slovenia; Bosnia–Hercegovina and Macedonia were asked to wait. Bosnian leader Izetbegovic now calculated that proclaiming his republic's independence was the most effective way to ensure protection of its territorial integrity from Serb designs. In a referendum on independence held in March 1992, 64 percent of Muslims and Croats voted in favor, while the vast majority of the 1.3 million Serbs in Bosnia did not vote. Just days after the referendum and even before Izetbegovic proclaimed Bosnian independence, Bosnian Serb leader Radovan Karadzic declared a Serbian republic that laid claim to more than 70 percent of Bosnia's territory. A Bosnian Serb army, supplied by and partially under the command of the JNA, was created, and a Bosnian Serb parliament and government, located in the outskirts of Sarajevo in Pale, were established. The belated Western recognition of the Muslim government was the pretext Milosevic needed to give full support to Karadzic and the Bosnian Serbs wishing to set up their own state and, in time, to join a greater Serbia. Bosnian Serb nationalists, quickly joined by their Croatian counterparts, sought dismemberment of this state.

Beginning in April 1992, a frenzy of Serb ultranationalism led to a level of atrocities committed against Muslims that Europe had not experienced since World War II.

Murder, torture, rape, expulsion, and wanton destruction became instruments of ethnic cleansing that turned the Serbs from being viewed as World War II's victims to being seen as the perpetrators of genocide in the 1990s. The barbarism was consciously selected to destroy the value systems of others. As Pfaff wrote, "This was the rationale for the systematic rape of Moslem women: doing so desecrated and 'ruined' them."[86] Another preferred strategy of the Serb forces in Bosnia was to blockade Muslim–held towns, set up heavy artillery positions on hills overlooking them, and shell the trapped population randomly. As one writer put it, "This method—the Vukovar Technique— bespeaks an oafish, slovenly army without brains on top, discipline below, or morale anywhere. Apart from its barbarity, the method doesn't even work."[87] Sarajevo, Tuzla, Bihac, and Mostar did not fall to the Serbs who used this strategy. This was also largely due to their being designated by the UN as safe havens. But Srebrenica, another safe haven, was finally overrun by the Serbs in July 1995 and mass executions of its civilian population followed. By this stage, 200,000 people, mainly Muslims, had been killed in the war.

For a long time, most NATO members shied away from the use of punitive air strikes against Serb positions, fearing it would lead to Serb reprisals (as it did in the case of Srebrenica) and even the spread of terrorism to Western Europe. The contact group on Bosnia, consisting of the United States, England, France, Germany, and Russia, was split on the issue of prolonging economic sanctions against Serbia. The British, French, Dutch, and Canadians sent in peacekeepers, while the United States refused to deploy ground forces. Peacekeepers regularly were held hostage by the Serbs whenever action was contemplated against them. As a result, in 1995 a rapid deployment force was organized, partly to carry out rescue and evacuation missions of UNPROFOR, partly to deliver food supplies to starving, besieged Muslim enclaves.

In contrast to the Bush administration, President Clinton pledged greater support for a unified Bosnia after 1992. Serbs had already regarded the United States as the architect of UN economic sanctions: "They believe that the demonization of the Serbs was designed in Germany and manufactured in the United States."[88] Still, Clinton's vascillation about taking action caused one high-level mediator in the Balkan war to tell the U.S. administration "to piss or get off the pot."[89]

Aside from these factors, another consideration hardening the U.S. policy response to the Bosnian conflict was the calculation that—in contrast to Somalia— simply abandoning the UN peacekeeping mission in former Yugoslavia would be costly and dangerous. Under NATO operations plan 40104 published in July 1995, evacuating UN personnel and equipment (5000 light tanks and other vehicles alone) would require 22 weeks to complete and would necessitate additional ground forces in Bosnia—estimated at 60,000, including 25,000 U.S. troops. It therefore seemed no riskier an option to engage UN-approved NATO air power—the "dual key" system that required formal UN approval of NATO-recommended military action—directly against the Serbs.

In addition to salvaging the UN mission, propping up the Western-recognized state of Bosnia, and bringing a halt to atrocities, a fourth factor that entered into U.S. calculations about why it should now intervene was, paradoxically, that the war had officially become "internationalized" (as if it had not up to then) when Serbs from the Croatian province of Krajina joined Serbs from Bosnia in attacking the northern Bosnian town of Bihac in July 1995. The international border between Bosnia and Croatia in this region had in practice been nonexistent because Serbs in Bosnia and Krajina controlled most of these territories. Another border—between Serb–held lands in eastern Bosnia and Serbia itself (part of the new Yugoslav federation)—had been permeable for several years, too, but had not elicited strong Western reaction. Even though Yugoslav leader Slobodan Milosevic had promised the West in 1994 that he would stop resupplying Bosnian Serbs so that the economic sanctions leveled against his regime could be eased, this international border was never sealed. The pretext of the internationalization of the conflict with the Bihac attack, however, allowed the United States and UN to drop their adherence to the principle of noninterference in a state's internal affairs.

What made Krajina Serbs crossing into Bosnia to fight different was that it offered final proof of the ambition to forge a greater Serbia out of three internationally recognized states—Bosnia, Croatia, and the new Yugoslavia. In order to make this distinction clearer, let us invoke a somewhat imperfect historical analogy. Western allies reluctantly accepted the *Anschluss* (annexation) of Austria in 1938 into the Third Reich, and they grudgingly recognized German claims to the Sudetenland in Czechoslovakia through the Munich agreement of that same year. But the allies declared war on Hitler when he attacked a non–German state, Poland, in September 1939. Analogously, in the Balkans in the 1990s the West conceded to Serbia certain historic rights (over Serb minorities living in Bosnia and Croatia), but it did not recognize the claim that one of these minorities, the Krajina Serbs, made on Bosnia as legitimate.

The Clinton administration decided that the principle of respecting even nonfunctioning international borders should be invoked to justify intervention when such borders were transgressed. After more than three years of war, the United States concluded in 1995 that ethnic conflict in Bosnia had officially become internationalized when ethnic kin from one country came to the support of their brethen in another. The United States and its allies responded by, first, giving the green light to Croatia to retake occupied territory using military force and, second, undertaking pinpoint targeting of Bosnian Serb military assets through NATO air strikes.

Following Bosnian Serb acceptance of NATO conditions for an end to the bombing missions and, above all, removal of heavy artillery pieces from strategic positions, a cease-fire was put into effect in October 1995. Pressing its initiative, the United States insisted on immediate negotiations among representatives of the Muslim, Croatian, and Serbian groups in Bosnia. These talks took place outside of Dayton, Ohio, in November. The draft of an agreement, signed in Paris the following month, granted 51 percent of Bosnian territory to a Muslim–Croat federation; the remaining 49 percent (roughly corresponding to the balance of power on the ground) was to go to a Serb substate. The OSCE was to monitor compliance with the agreement, including holding elections in 1996 and arresting war criminals. Neither of these provisions was enforced in a strict way: the September 1996 state and national elections included large-scale voter disenfranchisement based on ethnicity and election fraud, while leading indicted war criminals moved about freely in their respective ethnic zones. But this lack of enforcement itself helped keep the peace.

A special force was set up for peacemaking duties in Bosnia. In December 1995, a 60,000-strong NATO Implementation Force (IFOR), one third of whom were U.S. soldiers, began to move into Bosnia. The U.S. command made clear that it would reject any "mission creep," that is, in any way expanding its peacekeeping role in the Balkans. With the president entering an election year, this low-risk, narrowly defined U.S. mission promoted the Clinton administration's interests well.

So far we have not dwelt on the moral case for intervention—one that was strongly supported by many observers of the conflict, such as former British Prime Minister Margaret Thatcher. It is clear that U.S. military intervention in the Bosnian war was justified by moral, humanitarian considerations. The ostensible direct cause for beginning aerial bombardment was a Serb mortar attack on a Sarajevo marketplace in August 1995 that killed nearly forty civilians. Coupled with irrefutable evidence made known about the same time of the Serb massacre of more than 5000 Muslim prisoners-of-war taken from Srebrenica in July, as well as with the formal indictment that summer by the War Crimes Tribunal in The Hague of a dozen Serbian leaders considered responsible for ethnic cleansing, killings, and rape, the moral grounds for intervention were unassailable. The resignation in August of highly respected UN human rights envoy Tadeusz Mazowiecki—the first noncommunist prime minister of a former Soviet bloc country—on the grounds that nothing was being done to prevent large-scale human rights abuses, added to the ethical case for intervention. To be sure, the moral case had been made for three years—including by presidential candidate Clinton in 1992—but had been ignored, causing tens of thousands to die in the interim. Only in conjunction with other considerations did morality trigger military intervention in this ethnic conflict.

By contrast, neither before nor during military intervention was U.S. foreign policy toward Bosnia linked to vital national interests. Public opinion surveys consistently showed that a majority of U.S. citizens regarded the Bosnian conflict as not a U.S. problem. Neither Clinton nor Dole identified key U.S. interests in the Balkans that could justify intervention. Inevitably the generic "prosperity argument" identified above—that any war causes disruption of international trade and possible loss of jobs at home—was advanced. In addition, in explaining why U.S. troops were sent to Bosnia as peacekeepers Clinton conjured up the specter of an escalating conflict that would eventually require U.S. involvement, as in the century's two world wars.

National Security Affairs Advisor Lake summarized the reasons for U.S. engagement: "The conflict in Bosnia deserves American engagement: it is a vast humanitarian tragedy; it is driven by ethnic barbarism; it stemmed from aggression against an independent state; it lies alongside the established and emerging market democracies of Europe and can all too easily explode into a wider Balkan conflict."[90] There was no explicit reference to U.S. national interests.

We have examined the U.S. decision to manage conflict in Bosnia to determine whether it can be regarded as a precedent presaging greater American interventionism in the world's ethnic conflicts. From the nature of the military mission itself—to destroy Serb military assets so as to level the playing field and make clear that no side had a chance to win the war—it is clear that this operation could not be replicated in the vast majority of conflicts. As a rule, then, where no national interests are at stake the arguments against intervention reviewed in this chapter outweigh those for activism. Only where a special case can be made, such as the danger of genocide occurring in Europe, will interventionism become a serious option.

CONCLUSION

In this book we have stressed how ethnic conflicts are not all the same. Fittingly, then, the U.S. response to such conflicts has been differentiated. This is as it must be because the phenomenon of ethnonationalism is elusive, sometimes illusory, and oftentimes transient. For foreign policy decision makers, applying established principles to govern international relations is as important as acting on full information about a particular conflict. In the case of the United States, remaining consistent with its own cultural experience is a serious consideration. Our intervention in other countries is more credible when we do it for principles we cherish and uphold at home, such as liberty, democracy, and ethnic harmony. With or without intervention, the United States cannot always determine who the victors and who the victims of an ethnic conflict will be. But it does ultimately have the power to decide who will be recognized as a victor in the international order.

DISCUSSION QUESTIONS

1. Is the experience of "making the American nation" a factor influencing U.S. perceptions of nationalist conflicts in the world today? In particular, examine the relevance of U.S. cultural diversity and the United States as a nation of immigrants. Is the United States more sensitive to ethnic conflicts because of these factors?
2. The collapse of the communist world produced pandemonium, a world marked by ethnic conflicts. Could the United States have planned a new world order for the 1990s that would have reduced the salience of ethnic identities? Contrast traditional and contemporary understandings of the principle of self-determination.
3. What are the chief arguments made by policy makers and scholars opposing a policy of U.S. interventionism? Is U.S. participation through larger international peacekeeping organizations part of the solution to managing ethnic conflicts, or is it part of the problem?
4. Can the collapse of weak and remote states as a result of ethnosecessionism have an impact on the world's one superpower? Apart from moral arguments, does the United States have a political stake in resolving ethnic disputes abroad? Make the case for a policy of U.S. interventionism.
5. What was it about the twentieth-century history of the Balkans that made the United States wary to intervene when the wars of the Yugoslav succession broke

out in 1992? Explain the timing of U.S. military intervention when it came in 1995. Do the U.S.-brokered Dayton accords show how effective the United States can be in resolving an intractable ethnic conflict, or was it a one-time success?

NOTES

1. Fatima Mernissi, *Islam and Democracy: Fear of the Modern World.* (New York: Addison-Wesley, 1992), p. 8.
2. For the argument that other great powers will emerge to balance unchecked American power, see Christopher Layne, "The Unipolar Illusion: Why New Great Powers Will Rise." *International Security,* 17, 4, Spring 1993, pp. 5–51.
3. Abraham Lincoln, "First Inaugural Address, March 1861," in Omar Dahbour and Micheline R. Ishay, eds., *The Nationalism Reader.* (Atlantic Highlands, NJ: Humanities Press, 1995), p. 286.
4. Kallen's article was titled "Democracy Versus the Melting Pot: A Study of American Nationality," published in *The Nation* in February 1915. For a discussion, see Philip Gleason, "American Identity and Americanization," in William Petersen, Michael Novak, and Gleason, eds., *Concepts of Ethnicity.* (Cambridge, MA: Belknap Press, 1982), pp. 96–103.
5. Randolph Bourne, "Trans-National America," in Dahbour and Ishay, *The Nationalism Reader,* p. 298. It was first published in 1916 in the *Atlantic Monthly.*
6. Louis Hartz, "A Comparative Study of Fragment Cultures," in J. Rogers Hollingsworth, ed., *Nation and State Building in America: Comparative Historical Perspectives.* (Boston: Little, Brown, 1971), p. 24.
7. "Ethnic Cleansing," *The Economist,* 336, 7933, September 23, 1995, p. 18.
8. E.U. Essien-Udom, *Black Nationalism: A Search for an Identity in America.* (Chicago: University of Chicago Press, 1962 and 1971), p. 325.
9. Seymour Martin Lipset, *American Exceptionalism: A Double-Edged Sword.* (New York: W.W. Norton, 1996), p. 175.
10. Michael Lind, *The Next American Nation: The New Nationalism and the Fourth American Revolution* (New York: Free Press, 1995), p. 98.
11. Ivan Light, "Nationalism and Anti-Immigrant Movements in Europe and North America." University of California, Center for German and European Studies Working Paper 4.3 (August 1995), p. 15.
12. John Lewis Gaddis, *The United States and the End of the Cold War: Implications, Reconsiderations, Provocations.* (New York: Oxford University Press, 1992), p. 16.
13. Daniel Patrick Moynihan, *Pandaemonium: Ethnicity in International Politics.* (New York: Oxford University Press, 1994), p. 165.
14. *Ibid.,* pp. 13–14.
15. *Ibid.,* p. 14.
16. *Ibid.,* p. 15.
17. Tony Smith, "In Defense of Intervention." *Foreign Affairs,* 73, 6, November/December 1994, p. 45. For a discussion of internationalism, see "The Crisis of Internationalism." *World Policy Journal,* 12, 2, Summer 1995, pp. 49–70.
18. Richard J. Payne, *The Clash with Distant Cultures: Values, Interests, and Force in American Foreign Policy.* (Albany, New York: SUNY Press, 1995). A similar argument applying to Central America has been made in Roland H. Ebel, Raymond C. Taras, and

James D. Cochrane, *Political Culture and Foreign Policy in Latin America: Case Studies from the Circum-Caribbean.* (Albany, New York: SUNY Press, 1991).

19. David A. Hollinger, *Postethnic America: Beyond Multiculturalism.* (New York: Basic Books, 1995), p. 137.
20. For a similar view by one organization, see the Atlantic Council of the United States, "Ethnic Conflicts: Old Challenges, New Dimensions." July 1995.
21. Conor Cruise O'Brien, *God Land: Reflections on Religion and Nationalism.* (Cambridge, MA: Harvard University Press, 1988), p. 41.
22. *Ibid.,* p. 80.
23. Stephen Van Evera, "Hypotheses on Nationalism and War." *International Security,* 18, 4, Spring 1994, pp. 5–39.
24. Samuel P. Huntington, "The Clash of Civilizations?" *Foreign Affairs,* 72, 3, Summer 1993, pp. 25–26.
25. *Ibid.,* p. 41.
26. Michael Ignatieff, *Blood and Belonging: Journeys into the New Nationalism.* (New York: Farrar, Straus and Giroux, 1993), p. 12.
27. John A. Armstrong, *Nations Before Nationalism.* (Chapel Hill, NC: University of North Carolina Press, 1982), p. 298.
28. *Ibid.,* p. 299.
29. Ignatieff, *Blood and Belonging,* pp. 12–13.
30. Robert D. Kaplan, "The Coming Anarchy: How Scarcity, Crime, Overpopulation, Tribalism, and Disease are Rapidly Destroying the Social Fabric of Our Planet." *The Atlantic,* 273, 2, February 1994, p. 44ff.
31. Ali A. Mazrui, "The Blood of Experience: The Failed State and Political Collapse in Africa." *World Policy Journal,* 12, 1, Spring 1995, pp. 28–34.
32. Kaplan, "The Coming Anarchy." See also Zartman's analysis described in Chapter 8.
33. James Schlesinger, "Quest for a Post–Cold War Foreign Policy." *Foreign Affairs,* 72, 1, 1992/93, p. 18.
34. William Pfaff, *The Wrath of Nations: Civilization and the Furies of Nationalism.* (New York: Touchstone Books, 1993), pp. 201–202.
35. Cited in Jonathan G. Clarke, "American Foreign Policy Must Evaluate New Priorities." *USA Today Magazine,* July 1994, p. 13.
36. For a more positive appraisal of intervention in Somalia, see Chester A. Crocker, "The Lessons of Somalia: Not Everything Went Wrong." *Foreign Affairs,* 74, 3, May/June 1995, pp. 2–8.
37. Adam Roberts, "Foreword," in Moynihan, *Pandaemonium,* p. x.
38. Quoted in Moynihan, *Pandaemonium,* p. 166.
39. Cited in John Goshko, "Ethnic Strife Replaces Cold War Rivalries." *The Washington Post,* July 14, 1991.
40. Anthony Lake, "From Containment to Enlargement: Current Foreign Policy Debates in Perspective." *Vital Speeches,* 60, 1, October 15, 1993, pp. 13ff. Transcript of speech delivered on September 21, 1993.
41. Madeleine K. Albright, "International Law in U.S. Foreign Policy." *The Brown Journal of World Affairs,* 2, 2, Summer 1995, p. 42.
42. Ernest Gellner, *Encounters with Nationalism.* (Oxford: Blackwell, 1994), p. xi.
43. Lake, "From Containment to Enlargement," p. 18.
44. *Ibid.*
45. Zbigniew Brzezinski, "The Premature Partnership: America and Russia." *Current,* June 1994, p. 21.

46. Christopher Layne and Benjamin Schwarz, "American Hegemony—Without an Enemy." *Foreign Policy,* 92, Fall 1993, p. 6.
47. Cited in *Ibid.,* pp. 6–7.
48. *Ibid.,* pp. 19–20.
49. *Ibid.,* p. 9.
50. *Ibid.,* p. 22.
51. Cited in *Ibid.,* p. 11.
52. *Ibid.,* pp. 10–11.
53. *Ibid.,* p. 16.
54. Cited by George F. Kennan, "On American Principles." *Foreign Affairs,* 74, 2, March/April 1995, p. 118.
55. Clarke, "American Foreign Policy Must Evaluate New Priorities," p. 13.
56. Richard K. Betts, "The Delusion of Impartial Intervention." *Foreign Affairs,* 73, 6, November/December 1994, pp. 28–29.
57. Henry Bienen, "Ethnic Nationalisms and Implications for U.S. Foreign Policy," in Charles A. Kupchan, ed., *Nationalism and Nationalities in the New Europe.* (Ithaca, NY: Cornell University Press, 1995), p. 159.
58. *Ibid.,* p. 162.
59. *Ibid.,* p. 160.
60. Charles A. Kupchan, "Conclusion," in Kupchan, ed., *Nationalism and Nationalities in the New Europe,* p. 187.
61. Charles A. Kupchan and Clifford A. Kupchan, "The Promise of Collective Security." *International Security,* 20, 1, Summer 1995, p. 58.
62. Bienen, "Ethnic Nationalisms and Implications for U.S. Foreign Policy," p. 160.
63. *Ibid.,* p. 176.
64. William Pfaff, "Invitation to War." *Foreign Affairs,* 72, Summer 1993, p. 107.
65. *Ibid.*
66. Max Singer and Aaron Wildavsky, *The Real World Order: Zones of Peace/Zones of Turmoil.* (Chatham, NJ: Chatham House Publishers, 1993), p. 23.
67. *Ibid.,* p. 161.
68. *Ibid.*
69. *Ibid.,* p. 163.
70. Gaddis, *The United States and the End of the Cold War,* p. 199.
71. *Ibid.,* p. 201.
72. Georgie Anne Geyer, "U.S. Military Muscle Weakens." *Chicago Tribune.* March 3, 1995.
73. This term was coined by William Safran, University of Colorado. We are grateful for his comments on chapters of this book.
74. David Rieff, "The Illusions of Peacekeeping." *World Policy Journal,* 11, 3, Fall 1994, p. 7.
75. Bienen, "Ethnic Nationalisms and Implications for U.S. Foreign Policy," p. 167.
76. For a proposal to restructure the U.S. military, see Colin L. Powell, "U.S. Forces: Challenges Ahead." *Foreign Affairs,* 71, 5, Winter 1992/93, pp. 32–45.
77. Martin L. van Creveld, *The Transformation of War.* (New York: Free Press, 1991).
78. Robert L. Pfaltzgraff, Jr., and Richard H. Shultz, Jr., *Ethnic Conflict and Regional Instability: Implications for U.S. Policy and Army Roles and Missions.* (Carlisle, PA: U.S. Army War College, 1994). For another account of change in future warfare, see Edward N. Luttwak, "Toward Post–Heroic Warfare." *Foreign Affairs,* 74, 3, May/June 1995, pp. 109–122.
79. Kupchan, "Conclusion," pp. 189–190.
80. Charles William Maynes, "Containing Ethnic Conflict." *Foreign Policy,* 90, Spring 1993, p. 15.

81. See Boutros Boutros-Ghali, "Empowering the United Nations." *Foreign Affairs,* 71, 5, Winter 1992/93, pp. 89–102.
82. On public attitudes toward military intervention, see Kurt Taylor Gaubatz, "Intervention and Intransitivity: Public Opinion, Social Choice, and the Use of Military Force Abroad." *World Politics,* 47, 4, July 1995, pp. 534–554.
83. Pfaff, *The Wrath of Nations*, pp. 199–200.
84. Warren Zimmerman, "The Last Ambassador: A Memoir of the Collapse of Yugoslavia." *Foreign Affairs,* 74, 2, March/April 1995, p. 12.
85. Ibid., pp. 11–12.
86. Pfaff, *The Wrath of Nations,* p. 229.
87. Mark Thompson, *A Paper House: The Ending of Yugoslavia.* (New York: Vintage Books, 1992), p. 329.
88. Misha Glenny, "Heading Off War in the Southern Balkans." *Foreign Affairs,* 74, 3, May/June 1995, p. 100.
89. Glenny, "Heading Off War in the Southern Balkans," p. 100.
90. Lake, "From Containment to Enlargement."

Selected Bibliography

Alexander, Yonah, and Robert A. Friedlander (eds.), *Self-Determination: National, Regional, and Global Dimensions*. Boulder, CO: Westview Press, 1980.

Almond, Gabriel A., and James S. Coleman (eds.), *The Politics of Developing Areas*. Princeton, NJ: Princeton University Press, 1960.

Almond, Gabriel A., and G. Bingham Powell, *Comparative Politics: A Developmental Approach*. Boston, MA: Little Brown, 1966.

Alter, Peter, *Nationalism*. London: Edward Arnold, 1989.

Amalrik, Andrei, *Will the Soviet Union Survive Until 1984?* New York: Harper and Row, 1970.

Anderson, Benedict, *Imagined Communities: Reflections on the Origin and Spread of Nationalism*. New York: Verso, 1993.

Armstrong, John A., *Nations Before Nationalism*. Chapel Hill, NC: University of North Carolina Press, 1982.

Azar, Edward E., and John W. Burton (eds.), *International Conflict Resolution*. Boulder, CO: Lynne Rienner, 1986.

Bahadur, Kalim (ed.), *South Asia in Transition: Conflicts and Tensions*. New Delhi: Patriot Publishers, 1986.

Bailey, Sydney D., *How Wars End: the United Nations and the Termination of Armed Conflict, 1946–1964*. Oxford: Clarendon Press, 1982.

Banac, Ivo, *The National Question in Yugoslavia: Origins, History, Politics*. Ithaca, NY: Cornell University Press, 1993.

Barker, Ernest, *National Character and the Factors in its Formation*. London: 1927.

Barth, Frederick, *Ethnic Groups and Boundaries: the Social Organization of Cultural Differences*. London: Allen and Unwin, 1970.

Bertelsen, Judy S. (ed.), *Nonstate Nations in International Politics: Comparative System Analyses*. New York: Praeger, 1977.

Birch, Anthony H., *Nationalism and National Integration*. London: Unwin Hyman, 1989.

Brass, Paul R., *Ethnicity and Nationalism: Theory and Comparison*. Newbury Park, CA: Sage Publications, 1991.

Bremmer, Ian, and Ray Taras (eds.), *New States, New Politics: Building the Post–Soviet Nations*. New York: Cambridge University Press, 1997.

Breuilly, John, *Nationalism and the State*. Chicago: University of Chicago Press, 1994.

Brown, Michael E. (ed.), *Ethnic Conflict and International Security*. Princeton, NJ: Princeton University Press, 1993.

Brubaker, Rogers, *Nationalism Reframed: Nationhood and the National Question in the New Europe*. Cambridge: Cambridge University Press, 1996.

Buchanan, Allen, *Secession: The Morality of Political Divorce from Fort Sumter to Lithuania and Quebec*. Boulder, CO: Westview Press, 1991.

Buchheit, Lee C., *Secession: The Legitimacy of Self-Determination*. New Haven, CT: Yale University Press, 1978.

Bugajski, *Nations in Turmoil: Conflict and Cooperation in Eastern Europe*. Boulder, CO: Westview Press, 1993.

Caplan, Richard, and John Feffer (eds.), *Europe's New Nationalism: States and Minorities in Conflict*. New York: Oxford University Press, 1996.

Carens, Joseph H. (ed.), *Is Quebec Nationalism Just? Perspectives from Anglophone Canada*. Montreal: McGill-Queen's University Press, 1995.

Carment, David, and Patrick James, *The International Politics of Ethnic Conflict*. Pittsburgh: University of Pittsburgh Press, 1996.

Carr, Edward Hallett, *Nationalism and After*. London: Macmillan, 1945.

Carrere d'Encausse, Helene, *The End of the Soviet Empire: The Triumph of the Nations*. New York: Basic Books, 1993.

Chazan, Naomi (ed.), *Irredentism and International Politics*. Boulder, CO: Lynne Rienner, 1991.

Clift, Dominique, *Quebec Nationalism in Crisis*. Montreal: McGill-Queen's University Press, 1982.

Cobban, Alfred, *The Nation State and National Self-Determination*. London: Collins, 1969.

Colton, Timothy, and Robert Legvold, *After the Soviet Union: From Empire to Nations*. New York: W.W. Norton, 1992.

Connor, Walker, *Ethnonationalism: The Quest For Understanding*. Princeton, NJ: Princeton University Press, 1994.

Conquest, Robert (ed.), *The Last Empire: Nationality and the Soviet Future*. Stanford, CA: Hoover Institution Press, 1986.

Dahbour, Omar, and Micheline R. Ishay (eds.), *The Nationalism Reader*. Atlantic Highlands, NJ: Humanities Press, 1995.

Dawson, Jane I., *Eco-Nationalism: Anti-Nuclear Activism and National Identity in Russia, Lithuania, and Ukraine*. Durham, NC: Duke University Press, 1996.

de Silva, K.M., and S.W.R. de A. Samarasinghe (ed.), *Peace Accords and Ethnic Conflict*. New York: Pinter, 1993.

Deutsch, Karl W., *Nationalism and Social Communication*. Cambridge, MA: MIT Press, 1953.

Deutsch, Karl W., and William Foltz (eds.), *Nation-Building*. New York: Atherton Press, 1963.

Dewitt, David, David Haglund, and John Kirton (eds.), *Building a New Global Order: Emerging Trends in International Security*. Toronto: Oxford University Press, 1993.

Doyle, Michael W. *Empires*. Ithaca, NY: Cornell University Press, 1986.

Dunlop, John, *The Rise of Russia and the Fall of the Soviet Empire*. Princeton, NJ: Princeton University Press, 1993.

Earle, Robert L., and John D. Wirth, *Identities in North America: The Search For Community*. Stanford, CA: Stanford University Press, 1995.

Eckstein, Harry (ed.), *Internal War: Problems and Approaches*. New York: Free Press, 1964.

Enloe, Cynthia H., *Ethnic Conflict and Political Development*. Boston, MA: Little Brown, 1973.

Esman, Milton J., *Ethnic Politics*. Ithaca, NY: Cornell University Press, 1994.

Esman, Milton J., and Shibley Telhami (eds.), *International Organizations and Ethnic Conflict*. Ithaca, NY: Cornell University Press, 1995.

Esposito, John L., *The Islamic Threat: Myth or Reality?* New York: Oxford University Press, 1993.

Falk, Richard A. (ed.), *The International Law of Civil War*. Baltimore, MD: Johns Hopkins University Press, 1971.

Franck, Thomas M., *The Power of Legitimacy Among Nations*. Oxford: Clarendon Press, 1990.

Geertz, Clifford, *Old Societies and New States: The Quest for Modernity in Asia and Africa*. Glencoe, IL: Free Press, 1963.

Gellner, Ernest, *Conditions of Liberty: Civil Society and its Rivals*. London: Penguin, 1994.

Gellner, Ernest, *Encounters with Nationalism*. Oxford: Blackwell, 1994.

Gellner, Ernest, *Nations and Nationalism*. Ithaca, NY: Cornell University Press, 1983.

Gellner, Ernest, *Thought and Change*. Chicago: University of Chicago Press, 1978.

Gibbon, Edward, *The History of the Decline and Fall of the Roman Empire.* Vols. I–III. New York: Allen Lane, 1994.

Glazer, Nathan, and Daniel P. Moynihan, *Beyond the Melting Pot: The Negroes, Puerto Ricans, Jews, Italians, and Irish of New York.* Cambridge, MA: MIT Press, 1963.

Glazer, Nathan, and Daniel P. Moynihan (eds.), *Ethnicity: Theory and Experience.* Cambridge, MA: Harvard University Press, 1975.

Gleason, Gregory, *Federalism and Nationalism: The Struggle for Republican Rights in the USSR.* Boulder, CO: Westview Press, 1990.

Glenny, Misha, *The Fall of Yugoslavia: The Third Balkan War.* New York: Penguin Books, 1993.

Gottlieb, Gidon, *Nation Against State: A New Approach to Ethnic Conflicts and the Decline of Sovereignty.* New York: Council on Foreign Relations Press, 1993.

Grand, Ronald M., and E. Spenser Wellhofer (eds.), *Ethno-Nationalism, Multinational Corporations, and the Modern State.* Denver, CO: University of Denver Graduate School of International Studies, 1979.

Greenfeld, Liah, *Nationalism: Five Roads to Modernity.* Cambridge, MA: Harvard University Press, 1992.

Griffiths, Stephen I., *Nationalism and Ethnic Conflict: Threats to European Security.* New York: Oxford University Press, 1993.

Gurr, Ted Robert, *Minorities at Risk: A Global View of Ethnopolitical Conflicts.* Washington, DC: United States Institute of Peace Press, 1993.

Gurr, Ted Robert, and Barbara Harff, *Ethnic Conflict in World Politics.* Boulder, CO: Westview Press, 1994.

Gwyn, Richard, *Nationalism Without Walls.* Toronto: McLelland and Stewart, 1996.

Hardgrave, Robert L., *India Under Pressure: Prospects For Political Stability.* Boulder, CO: Westview, 1984.

Hayes, Carlton J.H., *Essays on Nationalism.* New York: Macmillan, 1926.

Hayes, Carlton J.H., *The Historical Evolution of Modern Nationalism.* New York: R.R. Smith, 1931.

Hayes, Carlton, *Nationalism: A Religion.* New York: Macmillan, 1960.

Heraclides, Alexis, *The Self-determination of Minorities in International Politics.* London: Frank Cass, 1991.

Hertz, Frederick, *Nationality in History and Politics: A Study of the Psychology and Sociology of National Sentiment and Character.* New York: Oxford University Press, 1944.

Hobsbawm, E.J., *Nations and Nationalism Since 1780: Programme, Myth, Reality.* New York: Cambridge University Press, 1993.

Hobson, John A., *Imperialism: A Study.* Ann Arbor, MI: University of Michigan Press, 1965.

Hockenos, Paul, *Free to Hate: The Rise of the Right in Post–Communist Eastern Europe.* New York: Routledge, 1993.

Hollinger, David. A., *Postethnic America: Beyond Multiculturalism.* New York: Basic Books, 1995.

Horowitz, Donald L., *Ethnic Groups in Conflict.* Berkeley, CA: University of California Press, 1985.

Howard, Michael, *The Lessons of History.* New York: Oxford University Press, 1991.

Hunter, Shireen T., *The Transcaucasus in Transition: Nation-Building and Conflict.* Washington, DC: Center for Strategic and International Studies, 1994.

Huntington, Samuel P., *The Third Wave: Democratization in the Late Twentieth Century.* Norman, OK: University of Oklahoma Press, 1991.

Hutchinson, John, and Anthony D. Smith (eds.), *Nationalism.* New York: Oxford University Press, 1994.

Ignatieff, Michael, *Blood and Belonging: Journeys into the New Nationalism*. New York: Farrar, Straus, and Giroux, 1993.

Jackson, Peter and Jan Penrose (eds.), *Constructions of Race, Place and Nation*. London: UCL Press, 1993.

Jackson, Robert H., *Quasi-States: Sovereignty, International Relations, and the Third World*. Cambridge: Cambridge University Press, 1990.

Juergensmeyer, Mark, *The New Cold War? Religious Nationalism Confronts the Secular State*. Berkeley, CA: University of California Press, 1993.

Kadian, Rajesh, *India's Sri Lanka Fiasco: Peacekeepers at War*. New Delhi: Vision Books, 1990.

Kamenka, Eugene (ed.), *Nationalism: the Nature and Evolution of an Idea*. London: Edward Arnold, 1976.

Kann, Robert A., *The Multinational Empire: Nationalism and National Reform in the Habsburg Monarchy 1848–1918,* 2 Vols. New York: Columbia University Press, 1950.

Kaplan, Robert D., *Balkan Ghosts: A Journey Through History*. New York: Vintage Books, 1994.

Karklins, Rasma, *Ethnopolitics and Transition to Democracy: The Collapse of the USSR and Latvia*. Washington, DC: Woodrow Wilson Center Press, 1994.

Kearney, Robert, *Communalism and Language in the Politics of Ceylon*. Durham, NC: Duke University Press, 1967.

Kedourie, Elie, *Nationalism*. London: Hutchison, 1960.

Kellas, James G., *The Politics of Nationalism and Ethnicity*. London: Macmillan, 1991.

Kennedy, Paul, *The Rise and Fall of the Great Powers: Economic Change and Military Conflict From 1500 to 2000*. New York: Random House, 1987.

Keyes, Charles F. (ed.), *Ethnic Change*. Seattle, WA: University of Washington Press, 1981.

Kodikara, Shelton U. (ed.), *South Asian Strategic Issues: Sri Lankan Perspectives*. New Delhi: Sage, 1990.

Kohn, Hans, *The Idea of Nationalism: A Study in its Origins and Background*. New York: Collier Books, 1969.

Kohn, Hans, *Nationalism and Realism: 1852–1879*. Princeton, NJ: Van Nostrand, 1968.

Kohn, Hans, *Prophets and Peoples: Studies in Nineteenth Century Nationalisms*. London: Collier Books, 1969.

Kupchan, Charles A. (ed.), *Nationalism and Nationalities in the New Europe*. Ithaca, NY: Cornell University Press, 1995.

Kymlicka, Will, *Multicultural Citizenship*. Oxford: Clarendon Press, 1996.

Laqueur, Walter, *Black Hundred: The Rise of the Extreme Right in Russia*. New York: Harper Perrenial, 1994.

Lemco, Jonathan, *Turmoil in the Peaceable Kingdom: The Quebec Sovereignty Movement and Its Implications for Canada and the United States*. Toronto: University of Toronto Press, 1994.

Leone, Bruno (ed.), *Nationalism*. St. Paul, MN: Greenhaven Press, 1986.

Lind, Michael, *The Next American Nation: The New Nationalism and the Fourth American Revolution*. New York: Free Press, 1995.

Lipset, Seymour Martin, *American Exceptionalism: A Double-Edged Sword*. New York: W.W. Norton, 1996.

Little, Richard, *Intervention: External Involvement in Civil Wars*. London: Martin Robertson, 1975.

Lustick, Ian S., *Unsettled States, Disputed Lands: Britain and Ireland, France and Algeria, Israel and the West Bank-Gaza*. Ithaca, NY: Cornell University Press, 1993.

Manogaran, Chelvadurai, *Ethnic Conflict and Reconciliation in Sri Lanka*. Honolulu: University of Hawaii Press, 1987.

Mayall, James, *Nationalism and International Society*. New York: Cambridge University Press, 1990.

McRoberts, Kenneth (ed.), *Beyond Quebec: Taking Stock of Canada.* Montreal: McGill-Queen's University Press, 1995.

Miall, Hugh (ed.), *Minority Rights in Europe: Prospects for a Transitional Regime.* New York: Council on Foreign Relations Press, 1995.

Midlarsky, Manus I. (ed.), *The Internationalization of Communal Strife.* London: Routledge, 1992.

Miller, David, *On Nationality.* Oxford: Clarendon Press, 1995.

Montville, J. (ed.), *Conflict and Peacemaking in Multiethnic Societies.* Toronto: Lexington, 1990.

Motyl, Alexander J. (ed.), *The Post-Soviet Nations: Perspectives on the Demise of the USSR.* New York: Columbia University Press, 1992.

Moynihan, Daniel Patrick, *Pandaemonium: Ethnicity in International Politics.* New York: Oxford University Press, 1994.

National Executive Council of the Parti Québécois, *Quebec in a New World: The PQ's Plan for Sovereignty.* Toronto: Lorimer, 1994.

Neuberger, Benjamin, *National Self-Determination in Postcolonial Africa.* Boulder, CO: Lynne Rienner, 1986.

Niebuhr, Reinhold, *The Structure of Nations and Empires.* New York: Charles Scribner's Sons, 1959.

Nimni, Ephraim, *Marxism and Nationalism: Theoretical Origins of a Political Crisis.* Boulder, CO: Pluto Press, 1991.

Nincic, Djura, *The Problem of Sovereignty in the Charter and in the Practice of the United Nations.* The Hague, Netherlands: Martinus Nijhoff, 1970.

O'Brien, Conor Cruise, *God Land: Relections on Religion and Nationalism.* Cambridge, MA: Harvard University Press, 1988.

Pfaff, William, *The Wrath of Nations: Civilization and the Furies of Nationalism.* New York: Touchstone Books, 1993.

Phadnis, Urmila, *Ethnicity and Nation-Building in South Asia.* Newbury Park, CA: Sage Publications, 1990.

Ponnampalam, S., *Sri Lanka: The National Question and the Tamil Liberation Struggle.* London: Zed Books, 1983.

Prasad, Bimal (ed.), *India's Foreign Policy: Studies in Continuity and Change.* New Delhi: Vikas, 1979.

Premdas, Ralph R., S.W.R. de A. Samarasinghe, and Alan B. Anderson (eds.), *Secessionist Movements in Comparative Perspective.* New York: St. Martin's, 1990.

Ramet, Sabrina P., *Nationalism and Federalism in Yugoslavia, 1962–1991.* 2nd ed. Bloomington, IN: University of Indiana Press, 1992.

Rezun, Miron (ed.), *Nationalism and the Breakup of an Empire: Russia and Its Periphery.* Westport, CT: Praeger, 1992.

Roberts, Michael (ed.), *Collective Identities, Nationalism, and Protest in Modern Sri Lanka.* Colombo: Marga Institute, 1979.

Rosenau, James N. (ed.), *International Aspects of Civil Strife.* Princeton, NJ: Princeton University Press, 1964.

Rosenau, James N. (ed.), *Linkage Politics: Essays on the Convergence of National and International Systems.* New York: Free Press, 1969.

Rothschild, Joseph, *Ethnopolitics: A Conceptual Framework.* New York: Columbia University Press, 1981.

Rubinstein, Alvin Z., and Donald E. Smith, *Anti–Americanism in the Third World.* New York: Praeger, 1985.

Rudolph, Richard L., and David F. Good (eds.), *Nationalism and Empire: The Habsburg Monarchy and the Soviet Union.* New York: St. Martin's, 1992.

Ryan, Stephen, *Ethnic Conflict and International Relations.* Aldershot: Dartmouth, 1990.

Said, Abdul A., and Luiz R. Simmons (eds.), *Ethnicity in an International Context.* New Brunswick, NJ: Transaction Books, 1976.

Schermerhorn, R.A., *Comparative Ethnic Relations.* New York: Random House, 1970.

Seers, Dudley, *The Political Economy of Nationalism.* New York: Oxford University Press, 1983.

Seton-Watson, Hugh, *Nations and States: An Enquiry into the Origins of Nations and the Politics of Nationalism.* Boulder, CO: Westview Press, 1977.

Seton-Watson, Hugh, *The New Imperialism.* Totowa, NJ: Rowman and Littlefield, 1971.

Shafer, Boyd C., *Faces of Nationalism.* New York: Harcourt, Brace, Jovanovich, 1972.

Shafer, Boyd C., *Nationalism: Myth and Reality.* New York: Harcourt, Brace and World, 1955.

Shiels, Frederick L. (ed.), *Ethnic Separatism and World Politics.* Lanham, MD: University Press of America, 1984.

Shoup, Paul, *Communism and the Yugoslav National Question.* New York: Columbia University Press, 1968.

Sisk, Timothy D., *Power Sharing and International Mediation in Ethnic Conflicts.* Washington, DC: U.S. Institute of Peace, 1996.

Smal-Stocki, Roman, *The Nationality Problem of the Soviet Union and Russian Communist Imperialism.* Milwaukee, WI: Bruce Publishing Company, 1952.

Smith, Anthony D., *The Ethnic Revival.* Cambridge: Cambridge University Press, 1981.

Smith, Anthony D., *The Ethnic Origins of Nations.* Oxford: Basil Blackwell, 1986.

Smith, Anthony D., *National Identity.* Reno, NV: University of Nevada Press, 1991.

Smith, Anthony D., *Nationalism in the Twentieth Century.* New York: New York University Press, 1979.

Smith, Anthony D., *Theories of Nationalism.* New York: Holmes and Meier, 1983.

Smith, Graham (ed.), *The Nationalities Question in the Post-Soviet States.* London: Longman, 1996.

Smith, Graham (ed.), *The Nationalities Question in the Soviet Union.* London: Longman, 1991.

Snyder, Jack, *Myths of Empire: Domestic Politics and International Ambition.* Ithaca, NY: Cornell University Press, 1991.

Snyder, Louis L., *Encyclopedia of Nationalism.* New York: Paragon House, 1990.

Snyder, Louis L., *Macro–Nationalisms: A History of the Pan-Movements.* Westport, CT: Greenwood Press, 1984.

Snyder, Louis L., *The Meaning of Nationalism.* New Brunswick, NJ: Rutgers University Press, 1954.

Stack, John F. Jr. (ed.), *Ethnic Identities in a Transnational World.* Westport, CT: Greenwood Press, 1981.

Strachey, John, *The End of Empire.* New York: Frederick Praeger, 1966.

Study Group of Members of the Royal Institute of International Affairs, *Nationalism.* London: Oxford University Press, 1939.

Suhrke, Astri, and Lela Garner Noble (eds.), *Ethnic Conflict and International Relations.* New York: Praeger, 1977.

Sureda, A. Rigo, *The Evolution of the Right of Self-Determination: A Study of United Nations Practice.* Leiden, The Netherlands: A.W. Sijthoff, 1973.

Szporluk, Roman, *Communism and Nationalism.* New York: Oxford University Press, 1988.

Szporluk, Roman (ed.), *National Identity and Ethnicity in Russia and the New States of Eurasia.* Armonk, NY: M.E. Sharpe, 1994.

Tamir, Yael, *Liberal Nationalism.* Princeton, NJ: Princeton University Press, 1993.

Taras, Ray (ed.), *National Identities and Ethnic Minorities in Eastern Europe.* London: Macmillan, 1997.

Taylor, Charles, *Reconciling the Solitudes: Essays on Canadian Federalism and Nationalism.* Montreal: McGill-Queen's University Press, 1993.

Taylor, Edmond, *The Fossil Monarchies: The Collapse of the Old Order 1905–1922.* Harmondsworth, Middlesex: Penguin Books, 1967.

Teich, Mikulas, and Roy Porter, *The National Question in Europe in Historical Context.* New York: Cambridge University Press, 1993.

Thompson, D.L. and D. Ronen (eds.), *Ethnicity, Politics, and Development.* Boulder, CO: Lynne Rienner, 1986.

Thompson, Mark, *A Paper House: The Ending of Yugoslavia.* New York: Vintage Books, 1992.

Touval, S., and I. William Zartman (eds.), *International Mediation in Theory and Practice.* Washington, DC: SAIS, 1985.

Weaver, R. Kent (ed.), *The Collapse of Canada?* Washington, DC: Brookings Institution, 1992.

Weinbaum, Marvin G., and Chetan Kumar (ed.), *South Asia Approaches the Millennium: Reexamining National Security.* Boulder, CO: Westview, 1995.

Welliver, Timothy K. (ed.), *African Nationalism and Independence.* Hamden, CT: Garland Publishing, 1993.

Wiener, Myron, *The Global Migration Crisis: Challenge to States and to Human Rights.* New York: HarperCollins, 1995.

Young, M. Crawford, *The Politics of Cultural Pluralism.* Madison, WI: University of Wisconsin Press, 1976.

Young, M. Crawford, *The Rising Tide of Cultural Pluralism: The Nation–State at Bay?* Madison, WI: University of Wisconsin Press, 1993.

Young, Oran, *The Intermediaries: Third Parties in International Crises.* Princeton, NJ: Princeton University Press, 1976.

Young, Robert A., *The Secession of Quebec and the Future of Canada.* Montreal: McGill-Queen's University Press, 1995.

Zartman, I. William (ed.), *Collapsed States: The Disintegration and Restoration of Legitimate Authority.* Boulder, CO: Lynne Rienner, 1995.

Znaniecki, Florian, *Modern Nationalities: A Sociological Study.* Westport, CT: Greenwood Press, 1973.

Zwick, Peter, *National Communism.* Boulder, CO: Westview Press, 1983.

Index

A

Abkhazians, ethnic conflict involving, 5

Action Démocratique du Québec, and Quebec constitution, 172–173

Adams, John Quincy, 262

Adanishin, Anatoly, 239

Addis Ababa peace treaty (1896), 231, 232

Aden, Gulf of, 231

Adowa, battle of, 231

Advanced groups, 27

Advantaged minorities, 24

Afeworki, Issaias, 235–236

Affective motives
vs. instrumental motives, 78
for third party intervention, 75, 77

Affirmative action, in Russia, 138

Afghanistan
de facto partitioning of, 89
and drug trade, 91
ethnic conflict in, 6, 87
Iranian influence in, 89
peace settlement in, 110
Soviet withdrawal from, 108
and U.S. weapons, 90

Africa. *See also specific countries*
African Security Council, proposed, 243
and American fears, 239–240
British colonialism in, 228
chaos in, 256–257
and U.S. foreign policy, 257
Chinese influence in, 229
Christians in, 229, 236
colonialism in, 227, 242
decolonization of, 227–228
France in, 229
Muslims in, 229, 233, 236
Pan-Africanism, 233
secessionism in, 225–246
Soviet Union in, 229–230
state hegemony in, 18
states, collapse of, 86, 225–246
sub-Saharan, tribal groups in, 24
United Nations in, 243

African Americans
as communal group, 24
historical experience of, 249
in post-bipolar world, 5

After the Soviet Union (Colton), 136

AIADMK. *See* All India Anna Dravida Munnetra Kazhagam

Akashi, Yasushi, 267–268

Albania, hostilities in, 119

Albright, Madeleine, 259–260

Alesina, Alberto, 28

al-Gadhafi, Mu'ammar, 239

Algeria
democratic elections in, 4
and Muslim militants, 89
war of 1950s, 121

All India Anna Dravida Munnetra Kazhagam (AIADMK), 202

Allaire, Jean, 171

Allaire report, 171

Alliance building, in post-bipolar world, 6

All-Party Conference (APC), 203–204

Almaty accords (1991), 135

Alsatians, nationality of, 10

Amalrik, Andrei, 152

Amnesty International, and ethnonationalist lobbying, 74

Amrithalingam, A., 204

Ancestry, common, as basis of ethnic identity, 7

Anderson, Benedict, 11

Andreyeva, Nina, 142

Anglo-Irish agreement (1985), 180

Angola, civil war in, 3, 119

Anti-interventionists, 261–265

Anti-secession bias
of international community, 32
of Russia, 248
of United Nations, 102–103, 108
of United States, 248

Anti-Tamil riots (1983), 199, 202

APC. *See* All-Party Conference

Arab League

and ethnonationalist lobbying, 72, 73
intervention in Lebanon, 118

Arab Parliamentary Union, and Eritrean independence, 237

Arab-Israeli War (1973), political impact of, 73

Arafat, Yasir, 73

Arbitration, definition of, 99

Armenia, ethnic conflict in, 5

Arms trade
and ethnic conflict, 90–91
and LTTE, 215

Armstrong, John, 20, 255

Aryan nations, 252

ASEAN. *See* Association of South East Asian Nations

Asia. *See also specific countries*
central, and end of Cold War, 89
ecological stress in, 25

Assamese rebel group, 91

Assimilation, and national integration, 14

Association of South East Asian Nations (ASEAN), 119

Austin, Dennis, 4

Australia, independence of, 48

Australian aboriginals, as communal group, 24

Austria, annexation by Germany (1938), 273

Awami League, 185, 187–188

Azerbaijan, ethnic conflict in, 5, 155

B

Backlash states, U.S. policy towards, 260

Backward groups, 27

Bahini, Mukti, 187

Baker, James, 150, 270

Balakumar, V., 198

Balance of power
and material resources, 131

Baltic states
incorporation into USSR, 61
independence of, 45

Baluch nationalist movement, 21
Bandaranaike, Sirimavo, 210
Bandyopadhyaya, Jayantanuja, 116
Bangladesh
  Chittagong Hill Tracts region,
    rebels in, 91
  ethnic conflict in, 6
  recognition of, 188
  and right of secession, 52
  secession of, 79, 102, 185–188
Bargaining, and dispute resolution, 97
Barkashov, Alexander, 143
Barre, Muhammad Siad, 239
Barth, Frederick, 8
Bashkir minority, 144
Basques
  and minority separatism, 26
  in post-bipolar world, 5
  and secession, 60, 64
Becker, Gary, 29
Beissinger, Mark, 137
Belgium, stability of, 17
Belligerency status, criteria for, 46
Bengalis
  nationalist struggle, 21, 184–188
    internationalization of, 186–187
  repression of, 116
  secession of, 76
  secessionists, in Pakistan, 81
Bercovitch, Jacob, 154
Berezovsky, Boris, 149
Berlin Conference (1884–1885), 227
Bertelsen, Judy S., 69, 81–82
Betts, Richard, 98
Biafra
  and right of secession, 52
  secession of, 64, 229
  war in, 102
Bienen, Henry, 263–264, 266
Bilingualism parity, 133
Bipolar superpower rivalry, end of,
  and ethnic conflict, 88–90
Birch, Anthony, 27
Black, Conrad, 180
Black Panthers, 252
Bloc Québécois (BQ), 171–172
  and Quebec constitution, 172
BNA Act. *See* British North America
  Act
Bodos tribal movement, 21
Bosnia
  ethnic conflict in, 69
  origin of, 270
  peace-enforcement in, 115–116

role of IGOs in, 76
third party intervention in, 75
United Nations Implementation
  Force in, 107, 274
United Nations peacekeeping in,
  105, 109
U.S. policy in, 261–264, 268–275
Bosnian Serb army, creation of, 271
Bouchard, Lucien, 171, 173, 178
Boundaries, artificial, 5
Bourassa, Robert, 170–171
Bourne, Randolph, 249
Boutros-Ghali, Boutros, 113
  and United Nations peacekeeping
    force, 267
Bowen, John, 242
BQ. *See Bloc Québécois*
Branch Davidians, attack on,
  252
Brass, Paul, 22
Brazil, and ethnic unrest, 22
Bretons, in post-bipolar world, 5
Bretton Woods economic system,
  113
  and liberal internationalism, 257
Brezhnev, Leonid, 234
  and support of Ethiopia, 238
Brierly, J. L., 43, 45
British colonialism
  in Africa, 228
  in Canada, 161–163
British North America Act (1867),
  164, 166–167
Brussels Treaty (1948), 120
Brzezinski, Zbigniew, 260
Buchanan, Allen, 52, 57–58, 60–61
Buchanan, Patrick, 130
Buchheit, Lee C., 51, 54–55, 61
Buddhism, in Sri Lanka, 191–193
Buddhist Revivalist Movement, 196
Bulgaria, hostilities in, 119
Burlatsky, Fyodor, 135
Burma, and right of secession, 52
Burundi
  aborted transition to democracy,
    242
  proposed partitioning of, 243
  violence in, 241–244
Bush, George, 4, 177
  and 1992 election, 265
  and collapse of Soviet Union, 255
  and recognition of Baltic states, 259
  summit with Gorbachev, 240
Buzan, Barry, 244

C
Cambodia
  and drug trade, 91
  peace settlement in, 110
  political settlement in, 109
  United Nations Transitional
    Authority in (UNTAC), 105
Canada
  confederation of, 163–164
  conflict in, and external parties,
    161, 180–181
  conscription crises in, 165–166
  control of foreign policy, 165–166
  disputed borders in, 166–167
  Federal Task Force on Canadian
    Unity, 169
  French-speaking, *See also* Quebec
    autonomy of, 166
    economic stagnation of,
      164–165
    rights of, 165
  independence of, 48
  nationalism, emergence of, 163
  Quebec, exclusion from Canadian
    constitution, 169–171
  Quebec Act (1774), 163
  Quebec Liberal Party (QLP), 167
  stability of, 17
Capitalism, U.S. policy promoting,
  260
Capitalist empires, 130
Carment, David, 69
Carrington, Peter, 271
Carter, Jimmy, 71, 238, 260
Cartier, Jacques, 161
Castilians, and minority separatism,
  26
Castro, Fidel, 57, 167, 234
Casualties, civilian, of ethnic con-
  flict, 69
Catalans
  and European market, 29
  in post-bipolar world, 5
Celts, political mobilization of, 21
Central America, peace settlements
  in, 3
Central Committee plenum on
  nationalities policy (1989), 135
Ceylon Citizenship Act (1948), 196
Ceylon National Congress (CNC),
  196
CFE Treaty. *See* Conventional
  Forces in Europe Treaty
Chad, conflict in, 118

Champlain, Samuel de, 161
Charlottetown Accord, 171
Charter of the French Language (Bill 101), 168
Chechnya
  contested borders of, 151
  ethnosecessionism in, 147–149
  internationalization of conflict in, 151–154
  minorities in, 143–144
  OCSE in, 155–156
  recognition of, 45
  revolt in, 143–144
  and Russia, 144–147
  secession of, 58, 130
  third party intervention in, 153–156
Cheney, Dick, 262
Chernomyrdin, Viktor, 149
China
  and Africa, 229
  and Bangladesh secession, 187
  People's Republic, recognition of, 44
  and Sri Lankan ethnic war, 200–201
  U.S., friction with, 4
  as weapons supplier, 90
Chirac, Jacques, 178, 269
Chittagong Hill Tracts (CHT) region, rebels in, 91
Chola kingdom, 190
Chrétien, Jean, 171, 173
Christian Identity movement, 252
Christians, in Africa, 229, 236
Christopher, Warren, 178, 243
Chuvash minority, 143
CIS. See Commonwealth of Independent States
Civic nation, definition of, 10
Civic nationalism, definition of, 11
Civil Rights movement, U.S., 249
Civil War, and secessionism, 248
Civilian casualties, of ethnic conflict, 69
Clarke, Jonathan, 262
Clinton, Bill
  and Balkan policy, 261–262, 269–275
  and nuclear test ban treaty, 41
  and self-determination, 265–268
  visit to Canada (1995), 177
CNN factor, 81
Cohen, Herman, 240

Cohesion
  negative theories of, 15–18
  problems with theories of, 18
Cold War
  end of, and ethnic conflict, 88–90
  as stabilizing influence, 265
  termination of, 3–4
  United Nations' peacekeeping during, 104
Collapsed states, 87
Collective action phenomenon, 69
Collective security, principle of, 103
Colombian drug lords, and Tamils, 84
Colonial powers, and third party intervention, 72
Colonialism, 12
  in Africa, 227–228, 242
  Berlin Conference (1884–1885), 227
  in Canada, 161–163
  Declaration on the Granting of Independence to Colonial Countries and Peoples(1960), 51, 54
  legacy of, 5, 231
  and national self-determination, 49
  in Sri Lanka, 193–195
Colonialism approach, 21–22
Colton, Timothy, 136
Comité Catholique, 167
Commonwealth Immigration Act (1968), 229
Commonwealth of Independent States (CIS), creation of, 135
Communal groups, in twentieth century, 24
Communalist approach, 22–23
Communism, 131. *See also* Lenin, Vladimir; Marxism; Soviet Union
  vs. Nationalism, 257
  and Russia, 137
Conakat movement, 227
Conduct, international, red lines of, 109
Conference of Independent African States, intervention in Congo, 227–228
Confidence-building, as peace building, 111
Conflict. *See also* Ethnic conflict(s); International conflict
  limiting of, 102
  vs. problem, 100

Conflict Regulation in Divided Societies (Nordlinger), 17
Congo
  as Belgian colony, 227
  ethnic war in, 5–6, 104, 118
  independence of, 227
  intervention in, by CIAS, 227–228
  secessionism in, 227–228
Congress of Vienna (1815), 54
Connor, Walker, 20
Conscription crises, in French Canada, 165–166
Consent of the governed, 58
Consociationalism, 15–17
Constitutional Act (1791), 163
Constitution-based dispute, internationalization of, 178–180
Constitutive theory of recognition, 44
Constructivist school, 6–9
Contagion theory, 263
Conventional Forces in Europe (CFE) Treaty, 146
Corsicans, in post-bipolar world, 5
Cossack movement, 141
Council of Europe, and Russia, 154
Country, optimum size for, 28–29
Creveld, Martin van, 267
Crimean Tartars, ethnic conflict involving, 5
Croatia, recognition of, 271
Croatian Ustasa movement, 269
Croats, conflict with Serbs, 5, 80, 87
Crocker, Chester, 116, 239
Cuba, military aid to Ethiopia, 238
Cuban Missile Crisis, 115
Cultural claims to independence, 30
Cultural diversity, and U.S. policy, 248–251
Cultural imperialism, Russia and, 131–132
Culture(s)
  fragment, 249
  preservation of, and secession, 60–61
  shared, as basis of ethnic identity, 7
  and sovereignty, 60
Cyprus
  civil war in, 104
  conflict in, 112, 118
  ethnic conflict in, 17

Czechoslovakia
  collapse of, 32, 58, 175
  economic growth in, 29
  ethnic trouble in, 5
  recognition of, 45

D
Dayton Accords, 273
DDC. *See* District Development
  Committee
de Cuéllar, Javier Pérez, 108
de Gaulle, Charles, and Quebec
  independence, 178
de Silva, K. M., 189–191
de Soto, Alvaro, 113–114
December 19 proposals, 205
*Declaration of the Rights and Duties
  of States* (1949), 47
*Declaration on the Granting of
  Independence to Colonial
  Countries and Peoples* (1960), 51,
  54
*Declaration on the Rights of the
  Peoples of Russia* (Lenin), 49
Declaratory acts of recognition, 45
*Decline and Fall of the Roman
  Empire* (Gibbon), 130
Decolonization, of Africa, 227–228
Defense Installations Agreement,
  (U.S.- Ethiopia), 232
Definitions of terms, 9–12
del Castillo, Graciana, 113–114
Democracy
  consociational, 16–17
  formation of, 264
  as goal, 12
  industrial, and demographic stress,
    25
  and multiethnicity in Russia,
    136–137
  and national self-determination, 57
  promoting, and U.S. policy, 260
  renewed emphasis on, 3
Democracy in Plural Societies, 16
Democratic world order, obstacles
  to, 4
Demographic stress, and industrial
  democracies, 25
Demonstration effect, and shrinking
  world, 83
Dergue, 233–234
  fall of, 235
Derzhava, 143
Descent

genetic, 8
social, 8
Deutsch, Karl W., 14, 79
Developing world
  classification of states, 116
  national integration in, 14
  and nationalism, 12–13
  third party intervention in, 79
Diaspora
  immigrant, definition of, 9
  Russian, 150
Diefenbaker, John, 167
Differential incorporation, definition
  of, 16
Diffusion and encouragement policy,
  74–75
Dipavamsa, 189
Diplomatic activity, international
  motives for, 69–71
  preventive, 104, 107–108
  targets of, 71–74
Disadvantaged communal con-
  tenders, 24
Discrimination
  economic, 25
  vs. intergroup differentials,
    24–25
  systematic, and secession, 63
Disintegration, indirect theories of,
  18–19
Disputes, resolving, methods of, 97
District Development Committee
  (DDC), 199
Diversity
  commitment to, U.S., 250
  promotion of, 59
Dixon, Simon, 133
Doctors Without Frontiers, and eth-
  nonationalist lobbying, 74
Dole, Bob, and U.S. Bosnia policy,
  268
Domino theory, 57, 262–263
Donoughmore Commission, 196
Donskoi, Dimitri, 132
Doyle, Michael W., 130, 131
Dravidians, settlement in Sri Lanka,
  189–191
Drug trafficking, and ethnic conflict,
  90–91
Duchacek, Ivo, 28
Dudayev, Dzhokhar, 144–145, 147,
  154
  assassination of, 148
  and OSCE, 156

Dumbarton Oaks Proposals, 50,
  112
Dunlop, John, 134, 139
Durham, John G. L., 163
Durham report, 163

E
Eagleburger, Lawrence, 259
East India Company, 130
East Timor, atrocities in, 102
Eastern Europe, 102. *See also spe-
  cific country*
  collapse of Communism in, 3
  ethnic conflict in, 22
  transformation of, 5
EC. *See* European Community
Ecological stress, 25
  in Asia, 25
  in Latin America, 25
Economic and Social Council
  (ECOSOC), 111–112
Economic development
  as peace building, 111
  and political change, 4
Economic Development Council,
  Canadian, 167
Economic discrimination, 25
Economics, and secession, 28
ECOSOC. *See* Economic and Social
  Council
Edinstvo party, 142
Education, as peace building, 111
EEC. *See* European Economic
  Community
Eelam National Liberation Front
  (ENLF), 204
Eelam People's Revolutionary
  Liberation Front (EPRLF), 198
  and Thimpu talks, 204
Eelam Revolutionary Organization
  of Students (EROS), 198, 201
  and Thimpu talks, 204
Egypt, and Muslim militants, 89
El Salvador
  civil war, ending of, 108
  National Civil Police, creation of,
    114
  peace settlement in, 110
  postconflict peacebuilding in, 113
ELF. *See* Eritrean Liberation Front
Elite predominance, 17
Empire(s). *See also Imperialism*
  breakdown of, 129–131
  and ethnic conflict, 86–88

formation of, 130
mercantile, 130
England, immigrant communities in, in post-bipolar world, 5
Enloe, Cynthia, 20
EPLF. *See* Eritrean People's Liberation Front
EPRDF. *See* Ethiopian People's Revolutionary Democratic Front
EPRLF. *See* Eelam People's Revolutionary Liberation Front
Equivalent incorporation of citizens, definition of, 16
Eritrea
  autonomy, end of, 233
  conflict in, internationalization of, 237–240
  creation of, 231–232
  ethnic groups in, 231
  grounds for statehood, 232
  secession of, 57, 231, 235–237
    international reaction to, 237
Eritrean Liberation Front (ELF), 234
  aid to, 239
Eritrean People's Liberation Front (EPLF), 233–234
Erlanger, Stephen, 89
EROS. *See* Eelam Revolutionary Organization of Students
Esman, Milton J., 6, 12, 175
Essien-Udom, E. U., 249
Ethiopia
  collapse of, 235–237
  external mediation in, 240–241
  Jews released from, 240
  legislature, creation of, 236
  migration in, 25
  military repression in, 234
  and Ogaden region, 76
  partition of, 240–241
  secessionism in, 231–241
  separatist conflicts in, 116
  Tigre region, 234
  transitional government of, 236–237
Ethiopian Federal Act (1952), 232
Ethiopian Orthodox Church, 234
Ethiopian People's Revolutionary Democratic Front (EPRDF), 235–237
Ethnic affinity, and third party intervention, 76
Ethnic chosenness, 7
Ethnic community, definition of, 9

Ethnic conflict(s)
  and arms trade, 90–91
  civilian casualties of, 69
  and collapse of empire, 129–131
  and drug trafficking, 90–91
  finding solutions to, 33
  globalization of, 83–84
  importance of resolving, 96
  interdependence of, 83–84
  internationalization of, 68–82
  partisan intervention in, 74–81
  in post-bipolar world, 3–6, 88–90
  potential for expansion, 264
  prevention of, 267
  questions raised by, 32
  and refugee flow, 82, 201–202
  resolution of
    techniques for, 102*t*
    by third parties, 97–101
    by United Nations, 101–114
  theories of, 13*t*
  and U.S. policy, 253–261
Ethnic diasporas
  and ethnonationalist lobbying, 71–72
  Russian, 150
Ethnic group(s)
  autonomy arrangements for, 56
  definition of, 9
  loyalty to, 11
  political mobilization of, 12–13
  transition to a nation, 10
Ethnic identity
  definition of, 6
  formation of, 6–9
  vs. secular ideology, 21
  six foundations of, 7
  as social construction, 7–8
  and sociopolitical action, 8
Ethnic insecurity, and ethnic politics, 88
Ethnic kin, protection of, 117
Ethnic minorities, and national self-determination, 49
Ethnic nation, definition of, 10
Ethnic nationalism
  definition of, 11
  persistence of, 12
Ethnic pluralism, causes of, 12
Ethnic political mobilization, 23–30
Ethnic political movement, definition of, 11–12
Ethnic politics
  and ethnic insecurity, 88

vs. nationalist politics, 23
  terms associated with, 9–12
The Ethnic Revival (Smith), 20–21
Ethnic solidarity, definition of, 12
Ethnic war, protracted, 184–185
Ethnicity
  multiple, and democracy, in Russia, 136–137
  politicized, 8
Ethnicization of international politics, 68, 83–91
Ethnoclasses, in twentieth century, 24
Ethnonationalism, 25–26
  interactive, 147
  international norms affecting, 42
Ethnonationalist groups, 6
  definition of, 23
Ethnopolitical identities, of Soviet citizens, 136
Ethnosecessionism, 42, 48–53
  Chechen, 147–149
Etzioni, Amitai, 56–57, 60
EU. *See* European Unity
Europe. *See also* Eastern Europe; *specific country*
  western, recession in, 4
European Community (EC), and Croatia, 271
European Economic Community (EEC)
  and ethnonationalist lobbying, 73
  and liberal internationalism, 257
European Union (EU)
  and regional crisis management, 119
  and ethnonationalist lobbying, 72
Evera, Stephen Van, 253
Expectations, rising, and frustration, 14, 19
Exploitation, concept of, 21
Exploited groups, and secession, 59
External support, factors for gaining, 70

F
Facilitation, as peacemaking, 100
Falk, Richard A., 48, 105
Falkland/Malvinas islands, Argentina's attack on, 85
FAO. *See* Food and Agricultural Organization
Fast unto death, 209
Federal Task Force on Canadian Unity, 169

Fitzwater, Marlin, 150
Flemish culture, and secession, 5, 60
Food and Agricultural Organization (FAO), 111
Force
    nonuse of, 47–48
    in peacekeeping, 998
Fourteen Points (1918), 41
Fragment cultures, 249
France
    in Africa, 229, 242
    immigrant communities in, in post-bipolar world, 5
    in Rwanda, 242
Franck, Thomas, 54
Freedom Force, 186
French speakers, in Canada, rights of, 165
Front de Libération du Québec (FLQ), 168
Frustration, from rising expectations, 14, 19
Furnivall, J. S., 8, 15

G
Gaddis, John Lewis, 250, 265
Gandhi, Indira, 187–188, 202, 203
    assassination of, 204–205
Gandhi, Rajiv
    assassination of, 82, 214
    and Indo-Sri Lankan Accord, 207
    and Thimpu talks, 204–205
GATT
    and liberal internationalism, 257
    and nation size, 28
Geertz, Clifford, 8, 14
Gellner, Ernest, 11, 60, 260
General Agreement on Trades and Tariffs. *See* GATT
Genetic descent, 8
Georgia, ethnic conflict in, 5, 153
Gere, Richard, as spokesperson, 71
Germany
    immigrant communities in, 5
    reunification of, 4
Gibbon, Edward, 130
Glastnost, 133, 134
Glazer, Nathan, 8, 20
Gleason, Gregory, 133
Globalists vs. regionalists, in U.S. foreign policy, 263–264
Globalization of ethnic conflicts, 83–84
Golden Crescent, 91

Golden Triangle, 91
Gorbachev, Mikhail, 58, 133
    and American fears, in Africa, 239–240
    liberalization policies of, 134
Gorbachev, Raisa, 133
Gottlieb, Gidon, 55
Government
    performance evaluations of, 138
    responsive, 56–57
Gowon, Yakubu, 229
Grachev, Pavel, 146
Gramsci, Antonio, 21
Greater Serbia movement, 270–271
Greene, Graham, 256
Grotius, Hugo, 54
Groulx, Abbé Lionel-Adolphe, 166
Group. *See* Ethnic group(s)
Grozny, fighting over, 148–149
Gurr, Ted Robert, 6, 18, 23–26, 77

H
Haas, Ernst, 11
Habyarimana, Juvénal, death of, 242
Haiti, U.S. role in, 106
Halfway house states, 87
Hamas
    and Muslim Brotherhood, 84
    third party support for, 77
Hammarskjöld, Dag, 104
    and preventive diplomacy, 104
Habsburg empire, 132
    collapse of, 269
Harff, Barbara, 6, 24, 77
Harm principle, and defense of liberty, 58
Hartz, Louis, 249
Hausa group, 228–229
Hechter, Michael, 21–22
Hegemonic exchange theory, 15–18
Hennayake, Shantha, 147
Heraclides, Alexis
    on creation of states, 43, 51–52, 57, 61–62, 78
    on ethnic identity, 26–27, 54
    on recognition of states, 45
Hero, Alfred, 179
Historical grievances, over territory, 61, 63t
Historical memories, as basis of ethnic identity, 7
Hitler, Adolph
    and invasion of Yugoslavia, 269

irredentism of, 251
    and national self-determination, 53
Hizbollah
    and Iranian Revolutionary Guards, 84
    third party support for, 77
Hobbes, Thomas, 54
Hobson, John, 130
Holland, stability of, 17
Hollinger, David, 252
Homeland societies, definition of, 9
Hong Kong, economic success of, 29
Horowitz, Donald, 20, 27
Hostage-taking, 82
Human rights, and national self-determination, 50
Humanitarian agenda, fading support for, 244
Humanitarian considerations, and third party intervention, 76
Humanitarian crises, exacerbation of, 80
Hungary
    claims on Transylvania, 118
    crisis of 1956, 121
    ethnic trouble in, 5, 119
Huntington, Samuel, 14, 253–254
Hurting stalemate, and negotiations, 100
Hussein, Saddam, 86
Hutus
    slaughter of, 243
    and Tutsis
        distinction between, 242
        violence between, 241–244

I
Ibo group, 228–229
IBRD. *See* International Bank for Reconstruction and Development
Ichkeria, 147
Ideal states, 87
Identity. *See* Ethnic identity
Ideological criteria, for state recognition, 44
Ideological ties, and third party intervention, 76–77
IFOR. *See* NATO Implementation Force
Ignatieff, Michael, 254, 255
IGOs. *See* Intergovernmental organizations
ILO. *See* International Labor Organization

IMF. *See* International Monetary
  Fund
Immigrant diasporas, definition of, 9
Immigrants, to Canada, 166–167
Imperialism, cultural, by Russia,
  131–132
*Imperialism: the Highest Stage of
  Capitalism* (Lenin), 130
Imperialism (Hobson), 130
Incompatibility theory, 15–16
Independence
  economic cost of, 29
  forcible seizure of, and interna-
    tional normative regime, 43
India
  cooperation with U.S., post-bipo-
    lar, 214
  ethnic conflict in, 6, 22
  intervention in Pakistan, 81
  and Sri Lankan ethnic conflict,
    199–213
    withdrawal from, 213–215
  tribal movements in, 21
Indian and Pakistani Residents
  (Citizenship) Act (1949), 196
Indian Doctrine of Regional Security
  (1983), 202–203
Indian Peacekeeping Force (IPKF),
  and Indo-Sri Lankan Accord,
  208–211
India-Pakistan War, 186
Indonesia, and repression of
  Bengalis, 116
Indo-Soviet Treaty of Peace and
  Friendship (1971), 187
Indo-Sri Lankan Accord, 205–208
  collapse of, 209–213
  implementation of, 208–211
INGOs. *See* International
  Nongovernmental Organizations
Injustices, rectification of, and seces-
  sion, 61
Instrumental motives, for interven-
  tion, 75
Instrumentalist school, 6–9
Insurgency status, criteria for, 46
Integration, 12–13
  negative theories of, 14–15
Interactive ethnonationalism, 147
Interdependence of ethnic conflicts,
  83–84
Interfront, 142
Intergovernmental organizations
  (IGOs)

international, and ethnonationalist
    lobbying, 72–73
  regional, and national self-determi-
    nation, 51
  as third party mediator, 73–74
Intergroup differentials, vs. discrimi-
  nation, 24–25
Internal colonialism approach,
  21–22
International Bank for
  Reconstruction and Development
  (IBRD), 111
International Committee of Red
  Cross, 120–121
International community, pro-state
  stand of, 32
International conduct, red lines of,
  109
International conflict, ethnic fallout
  of, 84–86
International Court of Justice, and
  national self-determination, 50
International diplomatic activity. *See*
  Diplomatic activity, international
International Justice, Permanent
  Court of, 44
International Labor Organization
  (ILO), 111
International law
  and acquisition of sovereignty,
    43–44
  enforcement of, 106–107
  national self-determination and,
    51–52
International Monetary Fund (IMF),
  111
  and Russia, 154
International nongovernmental organizations (INGOs)
  effectiveness of, 120–121
  and ethnonationalist lobbying, 74
  third party intervention by,
    120–122
International normative regime, 41
  and ethnonationalism, 42
International order, new, 3–4
  and ethnic conflicts, 4–5
International politics, ethnicization
  of, 83–91
International relations, and ethnic
  conflict, 31–33
International relations scholars,
  focus of, 31–32
International system

current, 42
  vs. international normative regime,
    41
Internationalization of ethnic con-
  flict, 82
Intervention. *See* Partisan interven-
  tion; Third party intervention
IPKF, withdrawal of, 213–215
Iran
  ceasefire with Iraq, 104
  and drug trade, 91
  influence in Afghanistan, 89
  Iraq war, ending of, 108
  Revolutionary Guards, and
    Hizbollah militia, 84
Iraq
  ceasefire with Iran, 104
  ethnic conflict in, 69, 87
  and Kurds, 116
  and Kuwait, 104–105
  United Nations' peacekeeping in,
    105
  United Nations war against, 110
  U.S. intervention in, 251–252, 259,
    261
Ireland. *See* Northern Ireland
Irish, in post-bipolar world, 5
Irish Free State, recognition of, 49
IRMO, and Ustasha, 84
Irredentist conflicts, and intrastate
  repercussions, 84–86
Irredentist movements in 1990s,
  62–63
Islam. *See also* Muslims
  development of, 255
  fundamentalism, 4
    and U.S. Policy, 262
  Nation of Islam, 249
Isolation and suppression policy, 75
Israel
  Arab-Israeli War (1973), political
    impact of, 73
  and Sri Lankan ethnic war,
    200–201
  and support of Ethiopia, 239
  terrorism and, 82
  violence in, 4
Ivan the Terrible, 132
Ivory Coast, ethnic balance in, 18
Iyob, Ruth, 233, 241
Izetbegovic, Alija, 270–271

J

Jaffna kingdom, 190

James, Alan, 42
Janatha Vimukthi Peramuna (JVP),
   reign of terror of, 210–211
Japanese Red Army
   and PLO, 84
   Tel Aviv airport massacre (1972),
   77
Jayawardhana, Walter, 90
Jayewardene, J. R., 90, 198–199,
   203, 205–206, 212
Jewish homeland, United Nations
   blueprints for, 56
Jewish state, moral grounds for, 61
Jews, experience in U.S., 249
Judicial Committee of the British
   Privy Council, 166
JVP. See Janatha Vimukthi
   Peramuna

K
Kabila, Laurent, 244
Kachin rebels, 91
Kadian, Rajesh, 209
Kallen, Horace, 249
Kandyan Kingdom, 190
Kaplan, Robert, 256
Karen rebels, 27, 91
Karklins, Rasma, 136–137
Karpinsky, Len, 135
Karunanidhi, M., 202
Kashmir
   dispute over, 102
   Pakistan policy toward, 76
Kashmiri secessionists, and hostage-
   taking, 82
Katanga, secession of, 227
Kazakhstan, and ethnic unrest, 22
Kedourie, Elie, 11
Keenan, George, 262
Keeny Meeny Services, 200
Kellas, James G., 23
Kennedy, Edward, 187
Kennedy, Paul, 130
Kenya, ethnic balance in, 18
Keyes, Charles, 8
Keylor, William, 3
Khan, Yahya, 185, 188
Khasavyurt accords, 151
Khasbulatov, Ruslan, 147
Kissinger, Henry, 44, 186
Klare, Michael, 90
Kodikara, Shelton U., 204, 210
Kohn, Hans, 11
Kosovo

civil war in, 63
   hostilities in, 119
Kotte kingdom, 190
Kozyrev, Andrei, 248
Krajina Serbs, and Croatia, 80
Ku Klux Klan, 252
Kukis rebel group, 91
Kumarappa, suicide of, 209
Kumaratunga administration (Sri
   Lanka), 214–215
Kupchan, Charles A., 263, 267
Kuper, Leo, 8
Kurds
   in Iraq, 116
   Iranian support for, 79, 81
   lobbying of, 73
   as non-state nations, 10
   oil deposits beneath, 77
   and Turkey, 76, 116
Kuwait
   and Iraq, 104–105
   and support of Ethiopia, 239

L
La Francophonie, 179
Labrador, annexation of, 166
Lake, Anthony, 259–260, 274
Language
   Charter of the French Language
      (Bill 101), 168
   Official Language Act (Sri Lanka,
      1956), 197
   Official Languages Act (Canada,
      1969), 167
   Russian, use of, by ethnic minori-
      ties, 140
   Sinhalese disputes regarding,
      193–194
   Sri Lankan official, 193–195
   of Tamils, disputes regarding,
      193–194
Lapidoth, Ruth, 55
Laqueur, Walter, 137, 140–143
Latin America. See also specific
   country
   ecological stress in, 25
   national liberation movements in,
      48
Latvia, independence of, 136
Laurentian state, autonomous, 166
Law, international. See International
   law
The Law of Nations (Brierly), 43
Layne, Christopher, 261–262

LDCs. See Less-developed countries
League of Nations, covenant of, and
   national self-determination, 50
League of Nations system, 44
Lebanon
   ethnic conflict in, 6, 17, 104
   hostages in, 108–109
Lebed, Alexander, 143, 144, 149
Legal Status of Eastern Greenland
   case, 44
Legends, symbolic, and ethnic iden-
   tity, 8
Legislative Council, in Sri Lanka,
   communal representation in,
   195–196
Lemarchand, René, 242
Lemco, Jonathan, 171, 177–178
Lenin, Vladimir, 21, 130–132
   Declaration on the Rights of the
      Peoples of Russia, 49
   Imperialism: the Highest Stage of
      Capitalism, 130
   seizure of power, and Russian
      identity crisis, 137
   on self-determination, 49
Leopold II, 227
Lerner, Daniel, 14
Lesage, Jean, 167
Less-developed countries (LDCs)
   national integration in, 14
   and nationalism, 12–13
   third party intervention in, 79
Levesque, René, 168, 169
Liberal democracy, as policy goal,
   266
Liberal Democratic Party (Russia),
   142
Liberal internationalism, 257
Liberal values, and national self-
   determination, 50
Liberation Tigers of Tamil Eelam
   (LTTE), 90, 198, 201
   assassination of Rajiv Gandhi, 213
   and December 19 Proposals, 205
   and Indo-Sri Lankan Accord, 206
   rejection of, 208–209
   intractability of, 212
   and IPKF, 209–210
   tarnished image of, 214–215
   and Thimpu talks, 204
Liberty, defense of, and harm principle, 58
Libya, military aid to Ethiopia, 238
Lijphart, Arend, 16–17

Likhachev, D. S., 133
Lincoln, Abraham, arguments against secession, 248
Lind, Michael, 249
Lipset, Seymour Martin, 249
Lisée, Jean-François, 179
Lithuania, secession of, 58
Lithuanian Communist Party, secession of from Soviet Union, 135
Livingstone, David, 227
Locke, John, 54
Lod international airport massacre (1972), 77
Loyalties, group, 11
LTTE. See Liberation Tigers of Tamil Eelam (LTTE)
Lumumba, Patrice, 227–228
Lustick, Ian, 225

M

Maastricht option, 56
Macedonia, hostilities in, 119
Mahavamsa, 189
Maheswaran, Uma, 198
Major powers, and third party intervention, 72
Malays, as communal group, 24
Malaysia
 ethnic conflict in, 102
 and Sri Lankan ethnic war, 200–201
 stability of, 17
Mandelbaum, Michael, 105–106, 264
Manipuris rebel group, 91
Manning, Preston, 175
Mari minority, 143
Mariam, Mengistu Haile, 234
Marxism. See also Communism; Lenin, Vladimir; Soviet Union
 and collapse of Soviet Union, 6
 vs. Nationalism, 257
 neo-Marxist theories, 31
 preoccupations of, 12
Maskhadov, Aslan, 149
Material resources, and balance of power, 131
Matrioshka nationalism, 130
Matthews, Bruce, 191, 211
Mauritius
 economic success of, 29
 ethnic balance in, 18
Mayall, James, 43, 50, 56
Maynes, Charles William, 267
Mazowiecki, Tadeusz, resignation of, 274

Mazrui, Ali, 243, 256
Mediation. See Third party mediators
Meech Lake Accord (1987), 170–171
Menelik II, 231
Mengistu, downfall, and U.S. involvement, 240
Mercantile empires, 130
Mernissi, Fatima, 247
Metrocentric collapse of empire, 130–131
Middle East peace process, 3
Migrations
 causes of, 25
 characteristics of, 9
 and ethnically plural states, 12
Militias, in U.S., 252
Mill, John Stuart, 15
Milosevic, Slobodan, 80, 270–271, 273
Minorities
 advantaged, 24
 ethnic, and national self-determination, 49
 political demands of, 25–26
 rights for, 141
 in Soviet Union, 133
 status of, United Nations norms, 52
Minorities at Risk, 19
Minority groups, status of, 24–25
Missile Technology Control Regime (MTCR), 90
Mizos tribal movement, 21, 91
MNCs. See Multinational companies
Mobilization, and national integration, 14
Mobutu, Joseph, 228
 fall of, 243
Modelski, George, 69, 116
Modernization, 12–13, 22–23
 effects of, 20
Mogadishu line, 258
Moldova
 ethnic conflict in, 5
 OSCE presence in, 155
Monaco, economic success of, 29
Monarchists, Russian, 141
Montcalm, General, 162
Montenegro, hostilities in, 119
Mordovian minority, 144
Morganthau, Hans, 130

Moros, as backward group, 27
Motives, affective vs. instrumental, 75–78
Moynihan, Daniel, 8, 20, 250, 258–259
Mozambique
 civil wars in, 3
 hostilities in, 119
MTCR. See Missile Technology Control Regime
Mujahideen, third party intervention of, 77
Mukti Bahini, 186
Mulroney, Brian, 170–171, 179
Multicultural America, 249–251
Multi-ethnic state, creation of, 15–17
Multinational companies, and ethno-nationalist lobbying, 74
Multinational-states, definition of, 10
Munich Agreement (1938), 273
Muslim Brotherhood, and Hamas, 84
Muslims. See also Islam
 in Africa, 229, 233, 236
 in Ethiopia, 238
 and ethnic conflict, 5
 militant, 30
 and Afghan war, 89
 in Russian federation, 152
 in Sri Lanka, 211
 and violence against Serbians, in WW II, 269–270
Mutual Defense Assistance Pact, U.S. and Ethiopia, 232
Mutual tolerance, 57
Myanmar
 and drug trade, 91
 ethnic conflict in, 6, 102
Myths, symbolic, and ethnic identity, 8

N

NAFTA. See North American Free Trade Agreement
Nagas tribal movement, 21, 27, 91
Nagorno-Karabakh
 Armenia's link with, 87
 ethnic conflict in, 5, 63, 119
 peacekeeping forces in, 155
Nahaylo, Bohdan, 136
Name, as basis of ethnic identity, 7
Namibia
 independence of, 108–109
 and national self-determination, 50
Narcotics trade, and LTTE, 215

Nation(s)
civic, definition of, 10
ethnic, definition of, 10
ethnic group's transition to, 10
League of Nations system, 44
non-state, definition of, 10
size of, and GATT, 28
small, economic advantages of, 29–30
Nation of Immigrants idea, 250
Nation of Islam, 249
National Bolsheviks, 139
National home regimes, vs. sovereign states, 55
National liberation movements, in Latin America, 48
National Rifle Association, and right to bear arms, 252
National self-determination, 20, 41, 42, 48–53
and Clinton policy, 265–268
and colonialism, 49–50
and covenant of League of Nations, 50
definition of, 10
in international law, 51–52
as discredited principle, 53
ethnic minorities, 49
excessive, 57
and NATO, 267
origin of, 48
in post-Cold War era, 266
and United Nations, 50–53
and World War I, 49
Nationalism
alternatives to, 257
civic, definition of, 11
definition of, 10–11
and developing world, 12–13
ethnic, definition of, 11
momentum of, 176
vs. nationalist sentiment, 11
nineteenth-century, 42–43
and nuclear weapons, 87
persistence of, 12
rise of, in 18th century, 48
Russian, 4, 21, 131–149
core ideas of, 139–140
and non-Russian groups, 132, 136–137
resurgence of, 140–143
and secession, 59
and war, 12

Nationalism and Social Communication (Deutsch), 14
Nationalist sentiment, vs. nationalist movements, 11
Nation-state system, reorderings of, 254–256
Nation-states, definition of, 10
Native Americans, as communal group, 24
NATO. *See* North Atlantic Treaty Organization
Natural resources, and likelihood of third party intervention, 77
Nazi racialism, vs. Nationalism, 257
Ndadaye, Melchior, murder of, 242
Negative image of ethnic other, changing, 101
Negotiation, and dispute resolution, 97
Nehru, Jawaharlal, 74
Neuberger, Benjamin, 48
Nevsky, Alexander, 132
New France, founding of, 161–163
New World Order (NWO), 4, 259
obsolescence of United Nations in, 106
Newman, Saul, 21
Nicosia Master Plan, 112
Nigeria
ethnic balance in, 18
ethnic conflict in, 6, 22
secessionism in, 228–231
Nixon, Richard, 186, 188
Nongovernmental organizations, international. *See* International nongovernmental organizations
Noninterference, in U.S. policy, 266
Nonintervention, 47–48
definition of, 47
Non-state communal groups, definition of, 24
Non-state nations, definition of, 10
Nonviolent protest, as communal action, 30
Nordlinger, Eric, 17
Normative regime, international, 41
North American Air Defense Command (NORAD), incorporation of Quebec, 178
North American Free Trade Agreement (NAFTA), and Quebec, 29, 179
North Atlantic Treaty Organization (NATO), 118–119

alternatives to, 120
and Balkan war, 272
Implementation Force (IFOR), in Bosnia, 107, 274
and liberal internationalism, 257
and Quebec, 179
and self-determination, 267
and third party intervention, 75–76
as United Nations military arm, 119
North Korea, as weapons supplier, 90
Northern Ireland, violence in, 102, 175
Northern League, and European market, 29
Nuclear weapons, and nationalism, 87
Numeiri, Gaafar, 239

O

OAS. *See* Organization of American States
OAU. *See* Organization of African Unity
Objective cultural markers, 6–7
Occupation of territory, definition of, 43–44
October Revolution (Russia), 49
Offe, Claus, 136
Office of High Commissioner on National Minorities, 155
Official Language Act (Sri Lanka, 1956), 197
Official Languages Act (Canada, 1969), 167
Ojukwu, Chukwuemeka Odumegwu, 229
Onuf, Nicholas, 42
Operation Liberation Two, 206
Organization of African Unity (OAU), 119
and Eritrean independence, 237, 241
and ethnonationalist lobbying, 72, 73
interventions by, 118
Organization of American States (OAS)
interventions by, 118
and Quebec, 179
Organization on Security and Cooperation in Europe (OSCE), 119, 154–155

Original inhabitancy dispute, in Sri Lanka, 189–191
Orphan conflicts, 110
OSCE. *See* Organization on Security and Cooperation in Europe
Ossetian minority, 144
Ottoman empire, 132, 269

P
Padmanabha, K., 198
Pakistan
  Baluch insurgency in (1973), 76
  Bengalis in, 81, 116
  and drug trade, 91
  ethnic conflict in, 6
  and India, war with, 186
  Kashmir, policy toward, 76
  nationalist movements in, 21
  Pashtun Mujahideen, support for, 89
  and Sri Lankan ethnic war, 200–201
Palestine Liberation Organization (PLO), 108
  dependence on Syria, 81
  lobbying of, 73
  and Sri Lankan conflict, 201
  state status of, 32
  third party support of, 77
Palestinian state, drive for, 61
Palestinian terrorism, 82
Pali Chronicles, 189
Pallava kingdom, 190
Pamyat, 141
Pan-Africanism, 233
Pandaemonium (Moynihan), 258–259
Pandyan kingdom, 190
Pan-Ethiopianism, 233
Pan-Islamism, fears of, 238
Parity bilingualism, 133
Parizeau, Jacques, 172–173, 178
Parliamentary Elections (Amendment) Act (1949), 196
Parochialism, and instability, 14
Parochialist secession model, 55
Parthasarathy, G., 203
Parthasarathy Formula, 203–204
Parti Québécois (PQ), 167
  creation of, 167
  defeat of, 170
  election to power, 168
  and Quebec constitution, 172
Partisan intervention, 74–81. *See also* Third party intervention

characteristics of, 78–79
consequences of, 80–81
constraints of, 79–80
reliability of, 78–79
Pashtun Mujahideen, 89
Patriot movement, in United States, 252
Payne, Richard, 251
Peace
  building, 101, 102
    postconflict, 113
    by United Nations, 110–114
  enforcement of, 98, 102
  keeping, 102
    concept of, 104
    and politics, 105
    requirements for success of, 97–98
    by third party, 97–98
  making, 98–102
    by United Nations, 107–110
Peace of Westphalia (1648), 42
People's Liberation Army of Tamil Eelam (PLOTE), 198, 201
People's Republic of China, recognition of, 44
People's Revolutionary Front, reign of terror of, 210–211
People's War Group, 215
Pepin-Robarts commission, 169
Perestroika, 134
Pericentric collapse of empire, 130–131
Permanent Court of International Justice, 44
Perry, William, 262
Pfaff, William, 257
Picco, Giandomenico, 109
Pierre, Andrew J., 83
Plains of Abraham, battle of (1759), 161–162
PLO. *See* Palestine Liberation Organization
PLOTE. *See* People's Liberation Organization of Tamil Eelam
Plural society approach, 15–16
Poland
  partitioning of, 54
  recognition of, 45
Political change, economic development and, 4
Political mobilization
  ethnic groups and, 12–13

indirect theories of, 14–19
theories of, 13*t*
Political unions, obsolete, 59
Politico-diplomatic support, 75
Politics, and peacekeeping, 105
Ponnampalam, S., 190, 196
Posen, Barry, 86, 149
Post-bipolar world
  intensification of ethnic identity in, 5–6
  resurgence of ethnic conflict in, 3–6
Postconflict peace building, 113
Poverty, as restraint on political reforms, 4
Power, balance of, and material resources, 131
The Power of Legitimacy Among Nations (Franck), 54
PQ. *See Parti Québécois*
Prabhakaran, Velupillai, 198, 205, 206, 208
Premadasa, Ranasinghe, 207, 213
Premdas, Ralph R., 27, 206
Prevention of Terrorism Act, 207
Preventive diplomacy, 104, 107–108
Primordial causes of secession, definition of, 27
Primordialist school, 6–9, 19–21
Problem, vs. conflict, 100
Progressive Conservative Party, 170
Pulendran, suicide of, 209
Pulikovsky, General, 148–149
Puri, Hardeep, 206

Q
Qualified interventionism, in U.S. policy, 262–265
Quebec
  constitution for, 172–173
  diplomatic missions abroad, 167
  and economic success, 29
  exclusion from Canadian constitution, 169–171
  and foreign investment, 178
  independence movement, growth of, 171–174
  and NAFTA, 29, 179
  referendum on sovereignty, 160–183
    international reaction, 176–178
  secession, 60, 64
    impact of, 174, 179–180
  U.S. involvement in, 181

Quebec Act (1774), 163
Quebec Liberal Party (QLP), 167
"Qu'est-ce qu'une nation?" (Renan),
    10
Quiet Revolution (1960), 167

R
Rabat Conference, 73
Ramachandran, M. G., 202, 205
Rao, Narasimha, 202
Rapid Deployment Force (U.S.), and
    Sri Lankan conflict, 201
Rasanayagam, C., 190
Reactive ethnicity, theory of, 138
Realpolitik, 44, 75
Recognition
    constitutive theory of, 44
    as declaratory act, 45
    problems with, 44–46
Reconstruction, of newly recognized
    states, 105
Red Cross
    and ethnonationalist lobbying, 74
    International Committee of,
        120–121
Refugees, and internationalization of
    conflict, 82, 201–202
Regional conflicts, settlement of, in
    1990s, 3
Regional organizations, as third
    party mediators, 118–120
Regional powers, as third party
    mediators, 116–118
Regionalism, and instability, 14
Rehman, Mujibur, 185
Relative deprivation, definition of,
    18–19
Remedial secession model, 54–55
Renan, Ernest, 10
Report of the Royal Commission on
    Bilingualism and Biculturalism
    (1965), 167
"Report on the Affairs of British
    North America," 163
Research and Analysis Wing (RAW),
    201
Resolving disputes, methods of, 97
Rest of Canada (ROC), 174
La revanche des berceaux (Revenge
    of the cradles), 164
Rex, John, 7
Rhodes, Cecil, 165
Ribbentrop-Molotov pact (1939), 61
Rieff, David, 266

Riel, Louis, 165
Riggs, F. W., 116
Right of secession, recognition of, 52
Roberts, Adam, 258–259
Rokkan, Stein, 14–15
Romania
    claims on Transylvania, 118
    ethnic conflict in, 5, 119
    northern, incorporation into USSR,
        61
Rome, fall of, 130
Rommel, Erwin, 232
Rosenau, James, 138
Rothchild, Donald, 16, 18
Ruby Ridge, siege at, 252
Russia. *See also* Soviet Union
    affirmative action in, 138
    anti-secessionist bias of, 248
    and Chechnya, 5, 144–147
    communism and, 137
    and cultural imperialism, 131–132
    democracy and multiethnicity in,
        134–137
    identity crisis of, 137
    and International Monetary Fund,
        154
    Liberal Democratic Party, 142
    and minority separatism, 26
    monarchists in, 141
    and Muslims, 152
    nationalism, 4, 21, 131–149
        core ideas of, 139–140
        emergence of, 134
        and non-Russian groups, 132,
            136–137
        resurgence of, 140–143
        ultranationalism, 133
    new minorities in, 143–144
    October Revolution, 49
    as peacekeeper, 106
    political future of, 261
    relationship with non-Russians,
        132, 136–137
    street violence in, 143
    as weapons supplier, 90
Russian diaspora, 150
Russian Federation, ethnic conflict
    in, 5
Russian language, use of, by ethnic
    minorities, 140
Rutskoi, Alexander, 143, 144
Rwanda
    ethnic conflict in, 69
    French policy in, 106

genocide in, 242–243
proposed partitioning of, 243
and role of IGOs, 76
violence in, 241–244
Rwandan Patriotic Front (RPF), 243
Ryan, Stephen, 5, 31, 117, 151
Rybkin, Ivan, 149

S
Sabaratnam, Sri, 198
Safran, William, 42
Sahara. *See* Western Sahara
Said, Abdul A., 82, 90
Saideman, Stephen, 87–88
Salim, Salim A., 237
Samarasinghe, S.W.R. de A., 206
San Francisco Conference (United
    Nations), 50, 112
Saudi Arabia
    support of Ethiopia, 239
    support of Pashtun Mujahideen, 89
Schlesinger, James, 257
Schroeder, Paul, 106
Schwarz, Benjamin, 261–262
Scots
    and European market, 29
    in post-bipolar world, 5
Secession(ism), 6
    in Africa, 225–246
    anti-secession bias
        of international community, 32
        of Russia, 248
        of United Nations, 102–103, 108
        of United States, 248
    in Congo, 227–228
    and economics, 28
    and exploited groups, 59
    general case for, 52, 53–57
    Lincoln's opinion on, 248
    moral grounds for, 53–54, 57–64
    and nationalism, 59
    peaceful, rarity of, 174–176
    in 1990s, 62–63
    secondary factors of, definition, 27
*Secession: The Legitimacy of Self-
    determination* (Buchheit), 54–55
Secular ideologies, vs. ethnic identi-
    ties, 21
Security dilemma, 86
Seers, Dudley, 11
Segal, Gerald, 244
Selassie, Haile
    abrogation of federation with
        Eritrea, 239

fall of, 233–234
Self-defense, and secession, 61
Self-determination. *See* National
    self-determination
Senanayake, D. S., 196
Senewiratne, Brian, 197
Serbs
    atrocities against Muslims,
        271–272
    and ethnic conflict, 5, 87, 119
    Greater Serbia movement,
        270–271
    indictments for war crimes, 274
    and third party intervention, 75
    violence against, in WW II,
        269–270
Seton-Watson, Hugh, 132
Sèvres, Treaty of (1920), 54
Shan rebels, 91
Shariat courts, in Chechnya, 153
Shevardnadze, Eduard, 153
Shiels, Frederick L., 76
Sierra Leone, collapse of, 256–257
Sikhs
    political mobilization of, 19
    and secession, 64
Simmons, Luiz R., 82, 90
Singapore
    economic success of, 29
    and Sri Lankan ethnic war,
        200–201
Singer, Max, 264
Singh, Vishwanath Pratap, 213
Sinhalese
    culture of, 191–193
    intractability of, 212
    language disputes, 193–194
    settlement in Sri Lanka, 189–191
    Tamil relations
        historical, 188–189
        and original inhabitancy dispute,
            189–191
SLFP. *See* Sri Lanka Freedom Party
Sliyanie, policy of, 131
SLMC. *See* Sri Lanka Muslim
    Congress
Slovakia, and Czech republic, 29
Slovenia
    independence of, 270
    recognition of, 271
Small nations, economic advantages
    of, 29–30
Smal-Stocki, Roman, 132–133
Smith, Anthony D., 7, 20–21

Smith, M. G., 15–16
Smith, Tony, 251
Snyder, Jack, 139
Social descent, cultural construction
    of, 8
Sociopolitical action, and ethnic
    identity, 8
Solidarity
    as basis of ethnic identity, 7
    ethnic, definition of, 12
Solzhenitsyn, Aleksandr, 139–140
Somalia
    ethnic conflict in, 69, 119
    peace-enforcement in, 115–116
    and right of secession, 52
    and role of IGOs, 76
    United Nations intervention in,
        109, 258
    resistance to, 106
Soulbury Commission, 196
South Africa
    ethnic mobilization in, 175
    and Sri Lankan ethnic war,
        200–201
South Yemen, and support of
    Ethiopia, 239
Sovereign states, vs. national home
    regimes, 55
Sovereignty
    claims to, 96
    definition of, 42
    and partisan intervention, 79–80
    popular, 48
    recognition of, and international
        law, 43–46
    of states, 42–48
Sovereignty movement, growth in
    Quebec, 171–174
Sovetskaya Rossiya, 142
Soviet Disunion (Nahaylo and
    Swoboda), 136
Soviet Union. *See also* Russia
    in Africa, 229–230
    breakup of authority in, 5
    citizens, ethnopolitical identities
        of, 136
    collapse of, 3, 6, 32, 52, 129–159
    and Afghanistan, 89
    and authoritarian past, 135
    effect on Russian psyche, 137
    and ethnic conflict, 86
    international reaction, 149–151
    and minorities, 143
    U.S. role in, 255

and world order, 254–255
and Eritrea, creation of, 231–232
Ethiopia
    support of, 234–235
    treaty of friendship with, 238
ethnic conflict in, 22, 102
expansion of power, 132
imperialism, 131–149
Indo-Soviet Treaty of Peace and
    Friendship (1971), 187
intervention in Eastern Europe,
    115
Lithuanian secession from, 135
military aid to Ethiopia, 238
minorities in, 133
nationalist movements in, 21
OSCE activity in, 119
political system of, 131–132
regional conflicts in, 4
and right of secession, 52
and self-determination, 49
and Sri Lankan ethnic war,
    200–201
withdrawal from Afghanistan, 108
Soyuz, 141
Spolaore, Enrico, 28
Srebrenica, Serbian capture of, 272
Sri Lanka
    anti-Tamil riots (1983), 199
    British rule, effects of, 193–195
    constitution of (1972), 197–198
    constitution of (1978), 198
    cultural issues, 191–193
    division of, 190–191
    economic issues in, 195
    ethnic conflict in, 17, 63, 69, 102,
        112
        causes of, 188–199
        escalation of, 199
        international reaction to,
            199–200
    Indian peacekeeping mission in,
        117
    legislative council, communal rep-
        resentation in, 195–196
    official language of
        disputes regarding, 193–195
        Official Language Act (1956),
            197
    political battles in, 195–197
    standardization policy in, 197
    Tamil-Sinhalese dispute, 76,
        184–224
    third party action in, 202–213

Sri Lanka Freedom Party (SLFP), 203, 210
Sri Lanka Muslim Congress (SLMC), 211
Sri Lankan Tamils, terrorism and, 82
Stack, John F., Jr., 73, 84
Standardization policy, in Sri Lanka, 197
Stanley, H. M., 227
State(s)
  collapse of
    in Africa, 225–246
    ethnic conflict as result of, 86–88
  definition of, 10
  disintegration of, and U.S. policy, 256
  formation of, 43–44
  obsolescence of, 53–57
  role of, defining, 247
  sovereignty of, 42–48
  as third-parties in ethnic conflict, 114–118
Statist bias, of international system, 225–226
Strachey, John, 130
Strain theory, failure of, 19
Sub-Saharan Africa, tribal groups in, 24
Sudan
  ethnic conflict in, 6
  migration in, 25
Sufism, 152
Sully, Duke of, 15
Sunderji, K., 215
Sunnis, as communal group, 24
Superpower rivalry, end of, and ethnic conflict, 88–90
Support, external, factors for gaining, 70
Survivance strategy, 164
Swabhasha movement, 193
Switzerland, stability of, 17
Swoboda, Victor, 136
Syria, and support of Ethiopia, 239
Systemic collapse of empire, 130–131
Szporluk, Roman, 137

T
Tajikistan
  ethnic conflict in, 87
  Islamic upsurge in, 89
Tajik-Uzbek crisis, potential for, 89

Taliban takeover in Afghanistan, 89
Tamil(s)
  disenfranchisement of, 196–197
  intractability of, 212
  language disputes, 193–194
  militancy, rise of, 197–199
  origin of, 191
  political mobilization of, 19
  secessionists, 76
  separatist groups, 90
    and drugs, 84, 90
  settlement in Sri Lanka, 189–191
Tamil Eelam Army, 198
Tamil Eelam Liberation Army, 198
Tamil United Liberation Front (TULF), 199
Tamil Eelam Liberation Organization (TELO), 198
  military training of, 201
  and Thimpu talks, 204
Tamil Nadu, government, dismissal of, 213
Tamil New Tigers, 198
Tamil-Sinhalese conflict, 184–224
Tangible support, 75
Taylor, Charles, 165, 168, 176
Tel Aviv airport massacre (1972), 77
TELO. See Tamil Eelam Liberation Organization
Terms, definitions of, 9–12
Territorial representation, in Sri Lankan legislature, 196
Territory
  attachment of, as basis of ethnic identity, 7
  sovereignty over, and international law, 43–44
  and state formation, 43–44
Terrorism, 81–82
TGE. See Transitional Government of Ethiopia
Thailand, and drug trade, 91
Thatcher, Margaret, and Bosnian intervention, 273
Thileepan, fast unto death, 209
Thimpu talks, 204–205
Third party intervention, 97–101.
  See also Partisan intervention
  affective motives for, 75, 77
  and Bosnia, 75
  and Chechnya, 153
  colonial powers and, 72
  ethnic affinity and, 76

and Hamas, 77
and Hizbollah, 77
humanitarian considerations and, 76
ideological ties and, 76–77
by intergovernmental organizations (IGOs), 73–74
by international nongovernment organizations, 120–122
justifying, 47
and less-developed countries, 79
and major powers, 72, 114–116
and Mujahideen, 77
and natural resources, 77
and North Atlantic Treaty Organization, 75–76
opposition to, 261–265
and Palestine Liberation Organization, 77
and peacekeeping, 97–98
regional organizations and, 118–120
and regional powers, 116, 117
and Serbs, 75
in Sri Lanka, 202–213
by states, 114–118
United Nations and, 75–76
and U.S. policy, 261–265
Third party mediators
  credibility of, 99–100
  dangers faced by, 180
  in Ethiopia, 240–241
  intergovernmental organizations as, 73–74
  international third parties as, 99
  knowledge required of, 101
  leverage of, 99
  regional organizations as, 118–120
  regional powers as, 116–118
Third reordering, of nation-state system, 254–256
Third world. See Developing world
Thirty Years' War, 42
Tibet, and Chinese occupation, 71
Tigre People's Liberation Front (TPLF), 235–236
Tiruneh, Andargachew, 238
Tito, Josip Broz, 270
Togo, ethnic balance in, 18
Tolerance, mutual, 57
Touval, Saadia, 100, 110
TPLF. See Tigre People's Liberation Front
Trade disputes, 4

Traditional homeland issue, in Sri Lanka, 189–191
Trans-Dniester Russians, ethnic conflict involving, 5
Transitional Government of Ethiopia (TGE), 236–237
Transitional states, 116
Transnational regimes, 56
Transylvania
 ethnic trouble in, 5
 Hungarian and Romanian claims on, 118
Treaty of Sèvres (1920), 54
Treaty of Trianon (1920), 54
Treaty of Versailles (1919), 54
Treaty of Yalta (1945), 254
Trudeau, Pierre Elliot, 167, 169
Truman Doctrine, 257
Tshombe, Moise, 227
TULF. See Tamil United Liberation Front
Turkey
 and conflict with Kurds, 116
 ethnic conflict in, 69
 and suppression of Kurdish minority, 76
Turkish Cypriots, 108
 lobbying of, 72–73
Turks, as communal group, 24
Tutsis
 Belgian privileging of, 242
 as communal group, 24
 and Hutus
  distinction between, 242
  violence between, 241–244
 slaughter of, 242–243

U

Ukraine, ethnic conflict in, 5, 22, 119
Ukrainians, and minority separatism, 26
ul Haq, Zia, 201
Ultranationalism, Russian, 133
UNDP. See United Nations Development Program
UNESCO. See United Nations Educational, Scientific and Cultural Organization
UNHCR. See United Nations High Commissioner for Refugees
Uniform incorporation of citizens, definition of, 16
Union Minière du Haut-Katanga, 227

United National Party (UNP), 196, 198, 199
United Nations
 and Africa, 227, 243
 agencies of, 111
 and Balkan war, 272
 and Bangladesh, 187
 charter
  allowable responses to ethnic violence, 103
  and intervention, 47
  on peacebuilding, 111
  on peacemaking, 107
  on settling of local disputes, 155
 and colonial independence in Africa, 227
 Covenants on Human Rights (1966), 50
 and Croatia, 271
 Declaration on the Granting of Independence to Colonial Countries and Peoples(1960), 51, 54
 Declaration on the Rights of Persons belonging to National or Ethnic, Religious and Linguistic Minorities, 52
 disappointing record of, 105–106
 enforcement capability, lack of, 108
 and Eritrea, creation of, 231–232
 and ethnonationalist lobbying, 72–73
 fact-finding activity, 108
 Friendly Relations Declaration (1970), 50, 51, 54
 Implementation Force (IFOR), in Bosnia, 107
 Liaison Committee, 113
 and liberal internationalism, 257
 limited funding of, 103
 and military action, 109, 267–268
 and minorities' status, 52
 and national self-determination, 50–53
 as peacebuilder, 110–114
 as peacekeeper, 103–107
  during Cold War, 104
  conditions of, 105
  duties, expanded, 104–105
  future of, 107
  in post bi-polar world, 112–114
 as peacemaker, 107–110
 and permanent military force, 119

pro-state stand of, 102–103, 108
 Resolution 47/135, 52
 Resolution 1514, 51
 Resolution 390A (V), 232
 Secretary General of, 109
 Security Council
  obsolescence of, 105–106
  and peacekeeping troops, 155
  veto power of, 103
 and third party intervention, 75–76
United Nations Development Program (UNDP), 112
United Nations Educational, Scientific and Cultural Organization (UNESCO), 111, 112
United Nations High Commissioner for Refugees (UNHCR), 112
United Nations International Law Commission, 47
United Nations Observer Mission to Verify the Referendum in Eritrea (UNOVER), 235
United Nations peacekeeping force, origin of, 267
United Nations Transitional Authority in Cambodia (UNTAC), 105
United States (U.S.)
 anti-secession bias of, 248, 259
 and Baltic states, recognition of, 259
 and Bangladesh, 186–188
 Bosnia policy, 264
 China, friction with, 4
 and Congo, intervention in, 228
 and cultural diversity, 248–251
 cultural features of, 251–253
 and Eritrea, creation of, 231–232
 and Ethiopia, military aid to, 238
 ethnic conflict, policy regarding, 253–261
 foreign policy
  and chaos in Africa, 256–257
  globalists vs. regionalists, 263–264
 immigrant communities in, 5
 and India, post-bipolar cooperation with, 214
 international conduct, 251–253
 intervention in Latin America, 115
 isolationism of, 253
 militias in, 252
 noninterference policy, 266
 patriot movement, 252

United States (U.S.) (*cont.*)
  and qualified interventionism,
    262–265
  racial problems in, 252
  responsibilities of, 247–248
  and Sri Lankan ethnic war, 200–201
  as weapons supplier, 90
UNOVER. *See* United Nations
  Observer Mission to Verify the
  Referendum in Eritrea
UNP. *See* United National Party
UNTAC. *See* United Nations
  Transitional Authority in Cambodia
Uruguay Round, 28
U.S.. *See* United States
Ustasha, and IRMO, 84
Utrecht, Treaty of (1713), 161
Uzbekistan, Islamic upsurge in, 89

V

Vance, Cyrus, 271
Veddhas, settlement in Sri Lanka,
  189–191
Versailles, Treaty of (1919), 54, 254
Vienna, Congress of (1815), 44
Vilnius, secessionist movement in, 58
Violence
  escalation in Sri Lanka, 199
  factors leading to, 160–161
  nationalist, in Quebec, 168
von Vattel, Emmerich, 54
Vukovar Technique, 272

W

Waco, debacle in, 252
Walloons, in post-bipolar world, 5
Waltz, Kenneth, 6
Wangchuk, Jigme, 204
War, and nationalism, 12
War of 1812, 163
Warsaw Pact members, military aid
  to Ethiopia, 238
Warsaw Treaty Organization (WTO),
  118

Weak states, and ethnic conflict,
  225–227
Weaver, Randy, 252
Weber, Max, 7–8
Weiner, Myron, 31, 56, 82, 84, 85
Weiss, Thomas, 107
Welsh, in post-bipolar world, 5
Western European Union (WEU),
  120
Western Sahara
  conflict in, 118
  and national self-determination,
    50
Western Union (WU), 120
Westminister majoritarian model,
  16–17
Westphalian system, 42–53
WEU. *See* Western European
  Union
What is a Nation? (Renan), 10
White man's burden, 50
White supremacist groups, 252
WHO. *See* World Health
  Organization
Why Men Rebel (Gurr), 18
Wijesekera, N. D., 190
Wildavsky, Aaron, 264
*Will the Soviet Union Survive until
  1984?* (Amalrik), 152
Wilson, Harold, 229
Wilson, Woodrow, 4, 49, 260
  foreign policy of, 251
  Fourteen Points of, 41
Wolfe, General, 162
Woolsey, R. James, 258
World, shrinkage of, and demonstra-
  tion effect, 83
World Health Organization (WHO),
  111
World order, for 21st century, 3
World Trade Organization (WTO),
  28
World War I, and national self-deter-
  mination, 49

WTO. *See* Warsaw Treaty
  Organization; World Trade
  Organization
WU. *See* Western Union

Y

Yakut minority, 144
Yalta, Treaty of (1945), 254
Yandarbiev, Zelimkahan, 153
Yeltsin, Boris, 58, 134–137
  and Chechnya, 144–146
  nationalist position of, 142–143
Yemen, and Muslim militants, 89
Yemen, South, and support of
  Ethiopia, 239
Young, Crawford, 228
Young, Oran, 121
Young, Robert, 174
Yugoslavia
  collapse of, 32, 86, 160
  Nazi invasion of, 269
  peace in, 3
  resistance to United Nations in,
    106
  and right of sucession, 52
  status of, 269

Z

Zaire
  founding of, 228
  as future African power, 243
Zambia, ethnic balance in, 18
Zapatista National Liberation Army,
  and humanitarian crisis, 80–81
Zartman, I. William, 86, 226
Zavidia, Andrei, 142
Zedillo, Ernesto, 81
Zedong, Mao, 44
Zemshchina, 141
Zenawi, Meles, 236–237
Zhirinovsky, Vladimir, 139, 142
Zimbabwe, ethnic balance in, 18
Zimmerman, Warren, 270